THE GREENWOOD ENCYCLOPEDIA OF
LGBT Issues
WORLDWIDE

THE GREENWOOD ENCYCLOPEDIA OF
LGBT Issues
WORLDWIDE

VOLUME 3

Edited by
Chuck Stewart

GREENWOOD PRESS
An Imprint of ABC-CLIO, LLC

A B C  C L I O

Santa Barbara, California • Denver, Colorado • Oxford, England

Library of Congress Cataloging-in-Publication Data

The Greenwood encyclopedia of LGBT issues worldwide /
edited by Chuck Stewart.
        p. cm.
    Includes bibliographical references and index.
    ISBN 978-0-313-34231-8 (set hard copy : alk. paper) — ISBN 978-0-313-34233-2
(vol 1 hard copy : alk. paper) — ISBN 978-0-313-34235-6 (vol 2 hard copy : alk. paper) —
ISBN 978-0-313-34237-0 (vol 3 hard copy : alk. paper) — ISBN 978-0-313-34232-5
(set ebook) — ISBN 978-0-313-34234-9 (vol 1 ebook) — ISBN 978-0-313-34236-3
(vol 2 ebook) — ISBN 978-0-313-34238-7 (vol 3 ebook)
1. Homosexuality—History—Encyclopedias.   2. Gays—History—Encyclopedias.
3. Bisexuals—History—Encyclopedias.   4. Transgender people—History—
Encyclopedias.   I. Stewart, Chuck, 1951–   II. Title: Greenwood encyclopedia of
lesbian, gay, bisexual, and transgender issues.
    HQ76.G724   2010
    306.76'609—dc22   2009027698

ISBN: 978-0-313-34231-8
EISBN: 978-0-313-34232-5

14   13   12   11   10   1   2   3   4   5

This book is also available on the World Wide Web as an eBook.
Visit www.abc-clio.com for details.

Greenwood Press
An Imprint of ABC-CLIO, LLC

ABC-CLIO, LLC
130 Cremona Drive, P.O. Box 1911
Santa Barbara, California 93116-1911

This book is printed on acid-free paper ⃝∞

Manufactured in the United States of America

Cartography by Bookcomp, Inc.

CONTENTS

Asia and Oceania

VOLUME 2
Europe

VOLUME 3

Africa and the Middle East

AFRICA

SET PREFACE

The Greenwood Encyclopedia of LGBT Issues Worldwide is a multivolume set presenting comprehensive, authoritative, and current data related to the cultural, social, personal, and political experiences of lesbian, gay, bisexual, and transgendered (LGBT) people. The set encompasses more than 80 countries with each volume covering major populated world regions: Africa and the Middle East, Asia and Oceania, the Americas and the Caribbean, and Europe. Volumes are organized regionally and then alphabetically by country (including Hong Kong and the European Union, the latter because of its importance to European laws) with chapters that reflect LGBT geopolitical and historical context and follow a broad outline of topics—Overview of the country, Overview of LGBT Issues, Education, Employment and Economics, Social/Government Programs, Sexuality/Sexual Practices, Family, Community, Health, Politics and Law, Religion and Spirituality, Violence, and Outlook for the 21st Century. Under these topics, contributors explore a range of contemporary issues including sodomy, antidiscrimination legislation (in employment, child adoption, housing, immigration), marriage and domestic partnerships, speech and association, transsexualism, intersexualism, AIDS, safe-sex educational efforts, and more. As such, the set provides an unparalleled global perspective on LGBT issues and helps facilitate cross-national comparisons.

The term *LGBT* was chosen for this encyclopedia as a shorthand, yet inclusive, notation for the class of people who experience marginalization and discrimination perpetrated by heterosexual norms. In the late 19th century, the word *heterosexual* was invented to denote abnormal sexual behaviors between persons of the opposite sex. Ten years later, the word *homosexual* was invented for the same purpose of medicalizing same-sex behaviors and psychology. Many people found it offensive to categorize their lifestyle as pathology. They also thought that the emphasis on sex restrictive in describing their experiences and, instead, created and used the term *homophile* or *Uranian*. By the mid-20th century, the word *gay* came into common usage. As the gay political movement took roots in the 1950s and 1960s, it became apparent that, in the eyes of the public, gay women were invisible. In response to that phenomenon, many gay organizations changed their names to include women, as in—"lesbian and gay" or "gay and lesbian." Still, bisexuals, the transgendered (which includes transsexuals, transvestites, and intersexed people), and those questioning their sexual orientation believed that "lesbian and gay" was not inclusive enough to describe their experiences and challenged the status quo.

By the 1980s and 1990s, more gay organizations modified their names to include their moniker. However, a backlash occurred with many groups because the names became un-wielding. At the same time, radical street organizations, such as Queer Nation and ACT UP, appropriated the epithet *queer* and embraced its shocking value. This is a common practice by people who are marginalized and discriminated against to defuse the power of hateful words. Further, academia appropriated the word *queer* since it was a concise term denoting all persons outside heteronormative power structures. Still, many community organizations resisted the attempts to include *queer* in their names but rather stuck to some version of lesbian, gay, bisexual, and transgendered (LGBT). In the chapters, readers will encounter many variations of *LGBT*. Sometimes this will be written as "gay community," "lesbian and gay," LGBT, queer, or other terminology. The word usage reveals much about the community's level of understanding concerning LGBT issues.

Contributors were chosen based on their expertise in LGBT issues and knowledge of their country. Every effort was made to find contributors who live, or have lived, in the country in question. This was important, as gay people are often a hidden minority not easily quantified. Some contributors are from countries where gay people are routinely rounded up and killed. Contributors from these countries have taken great personal risk to participate in this encyclopedia and we commend their courage. Each contributor provides an authoritative resource guide that strives to include helpful suggested readings, Web sites, organizations, and film/video sources. The chapters and resources are designed for students, academics, and engaged citizens to study contemporary LGBT issues in depth for specific countries and from a global perspective.

CHUCK STEWART

ACKNOWLEDGMENTS

This ambitious project has been made possible through the work of many scholars. I wish to thank the advisory board—Robert Aldrich of the University of Sydney, David Foster of Arizona State University, John Goss of the Utopia Asian Gay and Lesbian Resources, Jan Lofstrom of the University of Helsinki, Ruth Morgan of the Gay and Lesbian Archives of South Africa, David Paternotte of the University of Brussels, Gerard Sullivan of the University of Sydney, and Walter Williams of the University of Southern California—for their dedicated work and leads to so many wonderful contributors. I want to thank the Institute for the Study of Human Resources (ISHR), D/B/A One for their generous financial support toward completion of this encyclopedia. With so many essays to review, this project could not have been possible without the help of first-level editing by Jessica Chesnutt, Jennafer Collins, Benjamin de Lee, William "B. J." Fleming, Winston Gieseke, Aimee Greenfield, Nicholas Grider, Alice Julier, and Bonnie Stewart. A heartfelt thanks goes to Astrid Cook, Gabriel Molina, Matt Moreno, and Rachel Wexelbaum for their editorial review of many of the essays. A special thanks goes to Wendi Schnaufer of Greenwood Press for her editorial assistance over the entire project.

This project took more than two years to complete. Locating experts on LGBT issues, especially for the smaller countries or in countries where it is dangerous to be gay, was a monumental task. In working with the contributors, I was struck by their dedication to making the world safe for all people. They are much more than just writers; they are people interested in changing the world to make it a better place. They understood that the first step toward reducing heterosexism and homophobia is to educate the public on LGBT culture and issues. To that end, they were eager to participate—even if they faced language difficulties or possible persecution from their governments. I commend each writer for the courage to be part of the solution toward overcoming sexual orientation bias. I hope this encyclopedia will further their vision.

ADVISORY BOARD

EDITOR AND CONTRIBUTORS

EDITOR

Chuck Stewart
Institute for the Study of Human
Resources
Los Angeles, California

CONTRIBUTORS

Tom Ochieng Abongo
Nyanza, Kenya

Brandon L. H. Aultman
Baruch College, City University of
New York

Unoma N. Azuah
International Resource Network for
Sexuality Studies in Africa
Ibadan, Nigeria

Hongwei Bao
The University of Sydney
Australia

Natalie D. A. Bennett
DePaul University
Chicago, Illinois

Martin Blais
Université du Québec à Montréal
Canada

Marianne Blidon
Université Paris 1-Panthéon Sorbonne
Paris, France

Matteo Bonini Baraldi
European Study Centre on
Discrimination
Bologna, Italy

Viachaslau Bortnik
Amnesty International
Gomel, Belarus

Jen Westmoreland Bouchard
Lucidité Writing
Minneapolis, Minnesota

Christopher Burke
University of Otago
Dunedin, Otago, New Zealand

Sinziana Carstocea
Université Libre de Bruxelles
Brussels, Belgium

Line Chamberland
Université du Québec à Montréal
Canada

Beng Chang
University of Minnesota
Minneapolis

Dau-Chuan Chung
University of Sydney
Australia

Donn Colby
Harvard Medical School
Cambridge, Massachusetts

Cristina Corleto
University of Sydney
New South Wales, Australia

Patrice Corriveau
University of Ottawa
Ontario, Canada

Julien Danero Iglesias
Cevipol—Université libre de
   Bruxelles
Brussels, Belgium

Zowie Davy
University of Leeds
United Kingdom

Benjamin de Lee
University of California
Los Angeles

Carmen De Michele
Ludwig-Maximilians University
Munich, Germany

Alexis Dewaele
University of Antwerp, Policy Research
   Centre on Equal Opportunities
Belgium

Marco Díaz-Muñoz
Michigan State University
East Lansing

James Dochterman
University of Southern California

Héctor Domínguez-Ruvalcaba
The University of Texas at Austin

Jesse Field
University of Minnesota
Minneapolis

José Ignacio Pichardo Galán
Universidad Complutense de Madrid
Spain

Jaime Galgani
Universidad Católica de Chile
Santiago

Natalia Gerodetti
Leeds Metropolitan University
United Kingdom

Keith Goddard
GALZ
Milton Park, Harare, Zimbabwe

Kristijan Grđan
Iskorak
Zagreb, Croatia

Michele Grigolo
Italy

Charles Gueboguo
University of Yaounde
Cameroon

Gert Hekma
University of Amsterdam
The Netherlands

Tone Hellesund
Stein Rokkan Center for Social Studies,
   University of Bergen
Norway

Adnan Hossain
University of Hull
Hull, England

Leo Igwe
International Resource Network for
   Sexuality Studies in Africa
Jackson, Tennessee

Hitoshi Ishida
International Christian University
Mitaka-shi, Tokyo, Japan

Frédéric Jörgens
Berlin, Germany

Sanja Juras
KONTRA
Zagreb, Croatia

Krister Karttunen
Helsinki University
Finland

Mark E. King
University of Hong Kong
Hong Kong, China

Anna Kirey
Labrys
Bishkek, Kyrgyzstan

Kurt Krickler
Vienna, Austria

Roman Kuhar
Peace Institute and University
    of Ljubljana
Slovenia

Ann Kristin Lassen
University of Copenhagen
Denmark

Laurence Wai-Teng Leong
Department of Sociology, National
    University of Singapore

Joseph Josy Lévy
Université du Québec à Montréal
Canada

Ed Madden
University of South Carolina
Columbia

Derek Matyszak
GALZ
Milton Park, Harare, Zimbabwe

Eduardo Alfonso Caro Meléndez
Arizona State University
Phoenix

Sukhragchaa Mijidsuren
We Are Family-Mongolia
Ulaanbaatar, Mongolia

Joanna Mizielinska
Warsaw School of Social Psychology
Poland

Nadine Moawad
Rmeyl, Beirut, Lebanon

Maria Federica Moscati
School of Oriental and African Studies
University of London
United Kingdom

Kateřina Nedbálková
Masaryk University
Brno, Czech Republic

Nancy Nteere
Nairobi, Kenya

Caleb Orozco
University of Belize

Emrecan Özen
Lambdaistanbul
Istanbul, Turkey

Evelyne Paradis
IGLA-Europe (Policy Director)
Brussels, Belgium

David Paternotte
Université libre de Bruxelles
Brussels, Belgium

Joseph M. Pierce
The University of Texas at Austin

Monika Pisankaneva
Bilitis Resource Center
Sofia, Bulgaria

Eva Polášková
Masaryk University
Brno, Czech Republic

Álvaro Queiruga
Montevideo, Uruguay

Régis Revenin
Université Paris 1-Panthéon
    Sorbonne / Université Lille
    3-Charles-de-Gaulle
Paris, France

Gabrielle Richard
Université du Québec à Montréal
Canada

Bill Ryan
McGill University
Montreal, Quebec, Canada

Paata Sabelashvili
Inclusive Foundation
Tbilisi, Georgia

Fabiola Fernández Salek
CUNY Department of Humanities
Jamaica, New York

Joel Samper Marbà
Pompeu Fabra University
Andorra la Vella, Andorra

Alexandra Sandels
Menassat
Beirut, Lebanon

Ana Cristina Santos
Birkbeck Institute for Social Research,
   University of London
United Kingdom

Diego Sempol
Universidad Nacional General
Sarmiento-IDES
Montevideo, Uruguay

Fernando Serrano
Bogotá, Colombia

Shivali Shah
Washington, D.C.

Johan H. B. Smuts
AnthroCon RSA Ethnographic
   Research
Port Elizabeth, South Africa

Katsuhiko Suganuma
University of Melbourne
Parkville, Victoria, Australia

Ikuko Sugiura
Chuo University
Hachioji-shi, Tokyo, Japan

Gerard Sullivan
University of Sydney
New South Wales, Australia

Judit Takács
Institute of Sociology of the
   Hungarian Academy of Sciences
Budapest, Hungary

Ferdiansyah Thajib
KUNCI Cultural Studies Center
Yogyakarta, Indonesia

Larry Villegas-Perez
Washington, D.C.

James Daniel Wilets
Nova Southeastern University
Ft. Lauderdale, Florida

Walter L. Williams
University of Southern California
Los Angeles

James A. Wilson Jr.
University of Texas at Austin

Sam Winter
University of Hong Kong
Hong Kong, China

INTRODUCTION

AFRICA AND THE MIDDLE EAST

Most African and Middle Eastern countries are extremely dangerous for lesbian, gay, bisexual, and transgendered people. On a daily basis, LGBT people face discrimination and violence because of their sexual orientation. South Africa is the shining exception to this state of affairs. South Africa is the only nation in the world where equality based on sexual orientation is written into its constitution. Still, long-standing antigay cultural norms affect the personal experiences of LGBT people in South Africa through subtle discrimination at home, work, and in the community at large.

Africa and the Middle East have endured invasions for thousands of years by different cultural, ethnic, and religious groups. Along the Mediterranean Sea, the earliest societies including the Sumerians, Babylonians, and Egyptians continually fought one another before being conquered by the Greeks, Romans, the Ottoman Empire, Christian Crusaders, and European colonialists. Each wave of conquerors brought their own set of beliefs and attitudes. Often times, the cultural beliefs of the indigenous people were obliterated, Balkanized, or mingled with the cultural beliefs of conquering armies. Thus, attitudes toward homosexual behavior or homosexual relationships in a particular geographical area changed with time and due to outside influences.

This process of changing cultural norms is still ongoing. A particular country may be somewhat gay friendly, and then change with the next election or war. Namibia is a modern example where, in just two generations, the country went from generally accepting homosexuality to banning homosexual behaviors with stiff jail sentences and fathers engaging in honor killings of their homosexual sons.

Lebanon is a prime example of a country with a complex history in regard to accepting diversity in sexual orientation. While under the 400-year control of the Ottoman Empire, Lebanon was not particularly antihomosexual. Yet once the Anglo-French forces took control in 1918, their legal system made homosexuality illegal. Civil war shook Lebanon to its foundation in the 1930s and the following period saw an influx of Palestinian and Iraqi refugees that in turn made governing ever more difficult. The small Jewish community also vanished after the Lebanese-Israeli War of 1978. The 1990s brought relative peace to Lebanon and changes in attitudes toward homosexuality. The Internet provided a forum for lesbian and gay people to organize with the first Yahoo Group for gay Arabs founded in Lebanon in the late 1990s. By 2006, *Out Travel* magazine rated Lebanon the "Arab world's most gay-friendly city." However, this does not mean that Lebanon became a paradise for the LGBT community. Rather, gay rights have never been brought up by Lebanese politicians or political parties, same-sex couples have no political rights, sex toys are considered pornographic and illegal, interfaith marriages are prohibited, passports and other legal identification papers must list religious affiliation, and all religious groups in Lebanon view homosexuality as an abomination and encourage LGBT people to seek medical treatment. Therefore, a discussion of a country's attitudes toward LGBT people must be considered through its long history of cultural clashes and forces.

In the context of LGBT issues, it is impossible to present one common view of Africa as a whole, or of the Middle East. The countries bordering the Mediterranean Sea have experienced vastly different histories and cultural impacts than central or southern Africa. Morocco, Algeria, Tunisia, Libya, Egypt, Israel, Lebanon, Syria, Iraq, and Jordan were exposed to thousands of years of European militaries and the impacts of international commerce. Conquest and the flow of goods and ideas have marked the Mediterranean experience. Religious ideas swept from one country to the next, only to be replaced by different religions originating from far away places. Most of the Arab states eventually became Islamic. Israel was founded as a Jewish state. Christianity has also had an influence in the region through the projection of force by the United States and European countries. The proximity of three competing religious systems has created great political tension in the region.

For central and southern Africa, belief systems changed very slowly until the European colonization period of the 15th and 16th centuries. Although Christianity and later Islam migrated into Africa along the commerce routes of the Red Sea, it was the Europeans who brought Christianity to most of Africa through enforced indoctrination and the enslavement of indigenous people. Today, many of the countries in central and southern Africa have a mixture of indigenous, Christian, and Islamic religions. Typically the indigenous religions were not antihomosexual. It was the colonization by European Christians and the imposition of their legal systems that codified antihomosexual statutes.

The question as to whether indigenous African cultures were heterosexist and homophobic, or if they were accepting of gay people, has become an important issue for many burgeoning LGBT organizations in Africa. A number of African presidents have publicly stated their negative opinions about homosexuality. For example, President Robert Mugabe of Zimbabwe claimed that homosexuality was unnatural and a phenomenon alien to Africa; that it was imported from the imperialist West, that homosexuals were lower than dogs and pigs, and encouraged arresting and imprisoning them. However, history shows that antigay beliefs are, themselves, an import and that indigenous Africans were mostly indifferent to homosexuality. President Mugabe and other African leaders often claim to be redefining Africa for Africans in response to centuries of colonialization. Yet, they are imposing beliefs—mostly Christian and Islamic—that are themselves imported from conquering forces.

SEXUAL AND RELATIONSHIP ARRANGEMENTS

The terms *gay, lesbian, bisexual, transgender,* and *homosexual* are 20th-century Western concepts. They do not apply to most of the cultures in Africa and the

Middle East. The best way to describe the difference is that *sexuality* is something that is done in Arab and African cultures, whereas *sexuality* has become an identity in Western cultures.

In Africa and the Middle East, cultural forces structure the traditional family as a marriage between a man and a woman who will then produce children. It is not uncommon for multiple generations of the same family to live together in the same household. When a son marries, he often brings his bride to live with him and his parents. The traditional family structure is reinforced through religious teachings and political forces. Within this structure, it is accepted that the man has outside sexual relationships. The wife is restricted to the home, and must remain faithful to the husband and act as a caregiver to the children.

For LGBT persons, there are few avenues for personal fulfillment. Most LGBT persons will marry and produce children, keeping outside same-sex relationships secret. Of course, being in the closet takes its toll psychologically and strains the family. Being open about same-sex attraction in African or Arab countries is dangerous. Iran and Egypt have reported an increase in cases of fathers killing their homosexual sons as a form of honor killings. Similarly, lesbians face a difficult task when coming out. As sex roles relegate women to the household, few have the skills appropriate for outside employment. Sex roles have given men higher-paying jobs than what are available to women. Further, if a woman is discovered to be a lesbian, she will face overt job discrimination and experience constant sexual advances from male strangers and male co-workers. If a woman comes out as a lesbian to her family, she may be forced to marry, raped to try and change her sexual orientation, and/or forced to leave the family. With job prospects slim, she often has to resort to prostitution to support herself. Prostitution is dangerous in Islamic countries since it is punishable by death through stoning.

Humans have always engaged in same-sex sexual behaviors. Only recently have these behaviors become a source of identity. Gender and sexual politics of 20th century Western countries have evolved to include homosexual identities including gay, lesbian, bisexual, and transgendered identities. For most Arabs, and people living in Africa and the Middle East, these identities do not exist. For example, many men have sex with other men, but as long as this occurs occasionally, is not a primary relationship, and the man performs in the active position, the man does not identify as homosexual. This is so prevalent that sex researchers have created a category of men-who-have-sex-with-men (MSM). Engaging in the *active* (also known as *top*) position keeps the man in his proscribed sexual role, that being as the dominant sexual figure over the woman, who is expected to be passive (also known as *bottom*). Men in these cultures are confused by other men who take on the passive role. In their mind, why would any man give up the privileges afforded being a man to take on the woman's role? Sexual roles involve significant power differentials with men expected to remain dominant over women.

Sex roles are so ingrained from early childhood training and cultural forces that when LGBT persons try to form same-sex relationships, there is often significant miscommunication. Not only are same-sex couples faced with ostracism and overt discrimination in African countries and the Middle East, they are also not prepared to communicate effectively with their partners. Sex-roles distort how people communicate. Most men from these cultures do not know how to be involved with other men in romantic sexual relationships. Women face the same forces and often times have difficulty forming same-sex relationships.

OVERVIEW OF LGBT ISSUES

Sodomy

Sodomy is defined differently within different legal systems. Typically, antisodomy statutes vaguely define sodomy as sex that is "unnatural," "perverted," or "against God." Since these terms are not defined, they are interpreted through cultural norms. For Christian- and Islamic-dominated countries, these terms have typically been applied to mean homosexual. In other legal systems, specific sexual behaviors between specific categories of people may be used to define sodomy. For example, it may state that anal sex between persons of the same sex is classified as sodomy. Sometimes it also includes the age and consent of the persons involved.

Sodomy statutes are important to LGBT rights because they deem homosexual behavior illegal and, by extension, homosexuality illegal. As seen in many of the African and Middle East countries, sodomy statutes make it virtually impossible for LGBT persons to organize, educate, or promote civil rights. Organizing is an important first step toward obtaining safety. Further, because of sodomy statutes, countries such as Iran, Botswana, Cameroon, Ghana, Ethiopia, Namibia, Nigeria, and Zimbabwe are extremely dangerous for LGBT people. In these countries, the simple act of asking for equal rights is forbidden. Many LGBT people are arrested each year and some are executed.

Most of the countries in Africa and the Middle East have sodomy statutes in place, but other cultural forces mitigate the severity of enforcement. Countries such as Egypt, Kenya, Tanzania, Uganda, and Morocco have sodomy statutes but they are rarely enforced. Diversity in religion and histories of tolerance have reduced the impact of their sodomy statutes such that they are rarely enforced and, if enforced, they are primarily used to make a political statement. For example, Egypt has been very tolerant of same-sex sexual behaviors for centuries. Sodomy statutes were not implemented until occupation by the British. Even still, they were rarely enforced. However, in 2001, 52 men were arrested at The Queen Boat Disco and charged with debauchery (since homosexuality is technically not illegal in Egypt). Twenty-three of the men were sentenced to between one and five years in prison. This has begun a period of harassing and arresting of gay men in Egypt. Some political analysts believe this change was prompted by attempts by the government to divert attention away from economic scandals.

Antidiscrimination Statutes and Violence

No countries in Africa or the Middle East have enacted antidiscrimination statutes based on sexual orientation, with the exception of South Africa. This is understandable since the first step in organizing for equal rights in regard to the LGBT community is to overturn sodomy statutes—which most countries have not achieved.

South Africa is the exception. It was controlled by a white minority descended from European colonists until 1994. A system of apartheid was used to segregate blacks from whites, giving whites control over the economy, law, and politics. It was a brutal system that segregated and killed untold numbers of black citizens in defense of white privilege. After decades of international sanctions and internal civil disobedience, apartheid and the controlling white government were overthrown. A new constitution was written that gave constitutional protection for many classes of citizens. Years of oppression made the populace sensitive to the need to take a strong stance against all forms of discrimination. As such, the constitution included sexual orientation as a protected class.

As sexual orientation was included in South Africa's constitution, there would appear to be no need for additional legislation to ensure the rights of LGBT people. The reality has proven to be very different. Cultural norms among the mostly Christian population have not been very accepting of LGBT rights. LGBT groups have organized and been responsible for bringing forth issues of inequality in housing, employment, and marriage to the attention of the media, government, and the general population. Slowly, LGBT people are securing equal rights in South Africa.

Marriage and Child Adoption

There are no countries in Africa or the Middle East that sanction same-sex marriages. South Africa has a civil union statute, but that is being challenged by LGBT organizations. They claim that a civil union is not the same as marriage and the constitution requires equality based on sexual orientation. Although Israel does not conduct same-sex marriages, it does recognize same-sex marriages performed in other countries. The city of Tel Aviv recognizes unmarried couples, including same-sex couples for purposes of family law. Similarly, only South Africa and Israel allow homosexuals or same-sex couples to adopt children.

Education

With the exception of South Africa, no country in Africa or the Middle East provides education on LGBT issues. Not only are most of the countries in Africa and the Middle East antigay, but they are classified as third-world economies. The lack of money directly affects the educational opportunities available to children and young adults. Most school systems are struggling and there is no thought of allocating precious resources to sexual issues; particularly to ones that are considered immoral and illegal.

South African LGBT organizations have been successful at implementing educational programs on LGBT issues. Although the constitution includes sexual orientation as a protected class, centuries of antigay religious teachings must be overcome. The Bill of Rights requires South African schools to not discriminate against LGBT students and staff. For larger school systems, this policy has been well implemented. For poorer school systems, this has not been the case and there continues to be reports of harassment and violence toward LGBT students. Colleges and universities have been, and continue to be, at the forefront of liberalism and advocates for full equality for LGBT students, faculty, and staff.

AIDS

AIDS has ravaged much of Africa. Tens of millions have died and tens of millions are currently infected. Entire towns and villages have been decimated and there is a crisis in the swelling number of orphans of parents who have died from AIDS. Considering that many of the countries in Africa are classified as third-world economies, there is a lack of health resources to combat the epidemic. AIDS medications are out of reach for many Africans due to cost factors. Likewise, condoms are too expensive for people who live on less than $100 a year.

The two major ways AIDS is transmitted is through the sharing of hypodermic needles between infected drug users, and through the exchange of bodily fluids during sex. Educating the public about the causes of AIDS is problematic throughout much of Africa and the Middle East. Users of illegal drugs are stigmatized and marginalized in these countries. Allocating resources for needle-exchange or educational programs is the lowest priority for most health agencies, and the general public tends to dismiss the health needs of drug users. Further, discussion of sex and sexually related issues are restricted in religious fundamentalist societies. Creating safer-sex educational programs is virtually impossible in Islamic countries. A few Islamic countries, like Egypt, have created AIDS educational programs but refuse to include information about same-sex sexual behaviors or the use of condoms.

Prisons are one location where AIDS spreads rapidly. Although it is recognized that the use of condoms would reduce the spread of AIDS, most African countries refuse to provide condoms to prisoners. As the Chief Prison Officer for Zimbabwe clarified, homosexuality is considered to be an offence and providing condoms would be tantamount to legalizing homosexual acts in prison. Instead, he suggested the money be used to find ways to stop inmates from engaging in those illicit behaviors.

Religion

There are four major religious influences on Africa and the Middle East. These include indigenous religions, Christianity, Islam, and Judaism. Indigenous religions have absorbed many of the beliefs of Islam, Christianity, and Judaism, but still reflect a purer form of original local religions.

Currently, a great chasm has formed in the Anglican Church over the issue of homosexuality. Bishops from the Anglican Church in Nigeria and Kenya have spearheaded an attempt to split the more conservative African churches from the main church. They complain that homosexuality is *un-African* and that the Bible does not condone the ordination of gay priests. This came to a head when the American branch of the Anglican Church ordained openly gay bishop, Gene Robinson, in 2003. Splitting the African churches away from the main body of the Anglican Church is problematic since the African churches receive almost three-quarters of their funding from the United States and Europe.

Transgender

Being transgendered is dangerous in Islamic Africa and the Middle East. For women who live as or become men, being discovered almost always leads to violence and perhaps death. Women are relegated to second-class status under the dominion of men. In many Islamic countries, women are not allowed outside the household without being accompanied by a male relative; they are also not allowed to work or drive cars. For a woman to dress and act as a man is considered a violation of religious codes and an act of usurping male power. A transgendered woman trying to pass as a man is inconceivable in the minds of most Africans and may result in violent subjugation.

For men who live as or become women, they too face violence and perhaps death if they are discovered. A man dressed as a woman would be considered to have defiled his manhood and violated religious codes. In any Islamic country, a man discovered in this condition would face immediate imprisonment and perhaps death.

Surprisingly, Iran, which is a fundamentalist Islamic country, views transgenderism differently. Instead of seeing it as a violation of religious codes, they consider transgenderism as a mental disorder that can be corrected through medical surgery and intervention. The state provides thousands of dollars to those desiring transsexual medical procedures. Tens of thousands of Iranians have had gender reassignment surgery and Iran ranks second to Thailand with respect to the number of gender reassignment surgeries conducted. This push to correct transgenderism has encouraged many homosexuals to obtain gender reassignment surgery. They view this option as the only outlet for their homosexuality, which would otherwise be condemned.

Even in those few African and Middle Eastern countries that are not as violent against transgendered people, daily discrimination in employment and housing make it difficult to live. Many male-to-female transgendered women have no choice but to engage in prostitution, an occupation that, in itself, is very dangerous.

Intersexed

None of the countries of Africa or the Middle East even acknowledge the existence of intersexed people.

OUTLOOK FOR THE 21ST CENTURY

The outlook for gay rights in Africa and the Middle East for the 21st century is complex. Israel has made great progress in recognizing same-sex couples, fully integrating gays in the military, allowing adoption rights for homosexuals, and hosting an annual gay pride parade and festival. Still, there is terrible religious backlash to these advances. It is expected that gay marriage will eventually be approved alongside the sodomy statutes being removed.

South Africa will likely continue building and enforcing the constitutional guarantee of equal rights for LGBT people. Greater educational programs will help modify and mediate antigay religious sentiments. There should be a general improvement in the acceptance of LGBT people in South African society at all levels.

North African countries are continually exposed to commerce from Europe and elsewhere. The flow of materials and ideas should lead to greater acceptance of sexual diversity. However, much of this process will be influenced by the continued struggle in the Middle East between Arab states and both Israel and the United States. If political tensions increase, then the Northern African states may become more conservative and less accepting of sexual diversity.

There are many factors that will influence the acceptance of LGBT people in Central Africa and southern Africa. Political turmoil, wars, commerce, and religious conflicts impact these countries with conflicting beliefs and goals concerning homosexuality and gay rights. The Anglican Church may even split over the issue of homosexuality. AIDS is also having a major impact on the acceptance of the LGBT community. It is changing the dynamics of the cultures and forcing educational systems to speak about sexual issues, including homosexual conduct and homosexual identity. As seen in Zimbabwe and Uganda, a country can change from being accepting or indifferent about homosexuality at one time, to becoming extremely antigay due to a coupe or change in government.

The Internet is also playing a major role in the acceptance of homosexuality and the organizing of gay-rights groups. The Internet facilitates the dissemination of information and allows gay-rights groups to organize in even the most repressive country. Although poverty in Africa and the Middle East prevents many people from having access to the Internet, the Internet is still playing an important role in liberalizing these societies. This process is expected to continue and grow.

As of 2009, world economies have entered into a recessionary period. This is creating tremendous strain on many governments and local economies. It has been observed by anthropologists that when a culture comes under stressors such as economic depression, war, famine, and disease, they typically become more politically conservative and human rights generally suffer as a result. The impact of this recession on Africa and the Middle East could be severe for LGBT people. Some believe civil war may break out in some of the oil-producing states. In these conditions, LGBT people may be treated as scapegoats and persecuted mercilessly. Gender and sexual roles will be harshly enforced, thereby marginalizing LGBT people.

AFRICA

BOTSWANA

Nancy Nteere

OVERVIEW

Botswana is located in the southern part of Africa; it shares borders with Namibia to both the north and west, South Africa to the east and south, Zimbabwe to the northeast, and Zambia to the north. Botswana is landlocked. The various regions of Botswana experience different weather patterns depending on their proximity to the Kalahari Desert. The desert dominates the western and southern parts of Botswana, and the southwest is greatly affected by desert-like weather conditions. The Kalahari Desert occupies 77 percent of Botswana's landmass, leaving the country with limited natural resources such as agricultural land, fresh water, and rain.[1] Rain is scarce in Botswana, and sometimes there is none for close to one year; this may have influenced the naming of the country's currency, the *Pula,* which means "rain" in Setswana, the national language. The Kalahari is mainly inhabited by the San-bushmen and wildlife.

The eastern areas of Botswana have enough rainfall and suitable weather conditions to sustain farming. Due to the fertile land and suitable weather conditions, an estimated 75 percent of Botswana's population lives in the eastern areas of the country, and 25 percent live in small settlements in the western part of the country. Of the total population, 20 percent live in the four urban areas of Gaborone, Francistown, Lobatse, and Selebi-Phikwe.[2]

Botswana occupies an area of 224,607 square miles (581,730 sq km), with a population of 1.8 million.[3] The life expectancy for women is 40 years, and 39 years for men. The fertility rate is 3.6 children per woman.[4] Two languages are predominantly spoken in Botswana. English is the official language, and Setswana is the national language. The country has never carried out an ethnic census, but the ethnic distribution is estimated as follows: Tswana comprise 79 percent of the population, Kalanga 11 percent, Basarwa 3 percent, and the remaining 7 percent consist of other groups, including Kgalagadi and the white minority.[5] The population is dominated by the Tswana; however, the earliest inhabitants were the San, followed by the Tswana. Each ethnic group has its own language, some have different dialects, and some have different customs and traditions. *Botswana* means the "place of Tswana," and the citizens are referred to as *Batswana,* or "the Tswana people."

A British protectorate was established in Botswana in 1885 by the financier and statesman Cecil Rhodes. The British had intended to establish their protectorate in South Africa but lost it to the British South Africa Company. Three Tswana kings influenced the transition as they opted to be ruled by the British instead of British South Africa, and as a result the British administration awarded more powers to the Tswana kings, hence the evident dominance of Tswana laws and customs in the 20th century. Known earlier as British Bechuanaland, Botswana followed South Africa's political, economic, and military methods. However, the new protectorate in South Africa had little infrastructure to support the new office, so they opted for the country to be governed from Mafeking, an area adjacent to the Bechuanaland Crown Colony. This colony was later integrated by South Africa in 1910. Botswana gained independence in 1966 after South Africa ended its practice of fully incorporating the colony due to the commencing of apartheid in 1948.[6]

Since independence, Botswana has been a multi-party democracy; it is Africa's oldest democratic nation. The Botswana Democratic Party (BDP) has managed to win freely and fairly all of the eight presidential elections since gaining independence. This has been influenced by the division and ultimate weakness of the opposition party. On March 31, 2008, President Festus Mogae stepped down before his second term was over, allowing Vice President Seretse Ian Khama to run as an incumbent in the 2009 general elections.

OVERVIEW OF LGBT ISSUES

Homosexuality is illegal in Botswana and is punishable as a criminal offense with up to seven years in prison. Although it is criminalized, prosecution rarely occurs. Similar to most African countries, gay and lesbians are ostracized and deemed to be deviants in society. This has been evident in press conferences and dialogs that have attempted to address LGBT issues, but end up condemning the acts. Although the larger population votes for inclusion of the population in all social programs, it has become impossible for gay organizations to be included in programs, as it would be impossible for them to have an office and therefore benefit fully from the government programs which are in place.

There is a high rate of HIV/AIDS infection in the country; by the end of 2005, 270,000 adults and children were living with HIV, with a recorded 18,000 AIDS deaths in the same year.[7]

In comparison with other past and present presidents in Africa, former president Festus Mogae, through the *Botswana Human Development Report 2000,* urged

Batswana to be considerate of people who were infected with HIV, whether they were prisoners or homosexuals; he did not make derogatory statements against homosexuality.

President Seretse Khama Ian Khama has made derogatory remarks in regard to the LGBT community in Botswana and the human rights organizations who support them.

Human rights organizations, especially the Botswana Network on Ethics, Law, and HIV/AIDS (BONELA) have been at the forefront of securing rights for the LGBT community. LEGABIBO, which stands for the lesbians, gays, and bisexuals of Botswana, is the only organization that fronts for LGBT rights in Botswana, in funding and organizing conferences, preparing reports to change government policy, and representing court cases which deal with LGBT concerns since 2004.

EDUCATION

Education is paramount to society in Botswana. Among the male youth between the ages of 15 and 24, the literacy level is 92 percent, and for females it is 96 percent. Overall, Botswana has an estimated 94 percent literacy rate (2006). Although there is a high enrollment rate during the first nine years of schooling, there has been a noticeable drop in the number of female students in higher education institutions. More male students graduate from universities and other tertiary institutions. The government of Botswana is keen on the education system, and this is evident in the high turnout in primary school enrollment. The formal education system caters to preschool, part of the primary schools which is estimated to have an enrollment of above 90 percent.[8]

The government does not have a policy for sex education in the school curricula; however, in one of the chapters of *Reproductive Health in the National Population Policy*, the authors write freely on sexuality. In the schools, students learn about sexuality from guidance and counseling teachers, and in subjects such as family life education or science. The curriculum is designed in a way to offer more detailed information to the students in higher classes, such as in secondary as opposed to primary levels. Therefore, in order for young adults to get access to information on LGBT issues, they would have to find it in the mass media or through locally available print media.

EMPLOYMENT AND ECONOMICS

Botswana depends chiefly on the European Union for trade, and also on the Southern Africa Customs Union (SACU), of which Botswana is a member. (The other member countries are South Africa, Namibia, Swaziland, and Lesotho.) The gross domestic product of Botswana is estimated to be $11.2 billion (2006 estimate), the GDP growth is estimated at 4.7 percent (2006 estimate), while the inflation rate in 2006 stood at 11.5 percent.[9]

Botswana is rich in metals and animal rearing. Their major industries are copper, nickel, tourism, and diamonds. Apart from beef, which they export to other countries, they rely heavily on imports of basic consumer goods and food, mainly from South Africa. Botswana is the largest producer of diamonds in the world; diamonds provide close to between 70-80 percent of the country's export income,[10] and total 30 percent of the county's GDP.[11]

In the 1970s and 1980s, the three largest diamond mines in the world were opened in Botswana. Consequently, in the last three decades Botswana's economy has risen steadily. Despite facing a budget deficit in 1999 due to a decline in the international diamond market, the economy has risen steadily, and this may be attributed to the fact that, among other African countries, Botswana is ranked as the least corrupt. In 2006, according to Transparency International, Botswana was ranked 25th among the least corrupt countries in the world.

The unemployment rate in Botswana was estimated to be 40 percent in 2001.[12] The employment acts in Botswana dictate that it is illegal for women to be employed as underground miners or soldiers in the army.

Unemployment cuts across both the rural and urban centers, and the LGBT community is no exception. There have not been any reported cases of discrimination at the workplaces due to sexual orientation, but this can be associated with the fact that most are still in the closet.

SOCIAL/GOVERNMENT PROGRAMS

Various programs have been initiated by the government in regard to human rights; however, women still remain marginalized by society and are not able to participate fully in arenas of development. Nongovernmental organizations (NGOs) have recently begun working alongside the government to implement environmental, job skills, and agricultural projects.

However, with limited funding, they are not able to reach all the minorities and women they target. The NGOs have set up policies and acted as umbrella bodies for the LGBT organizations in order to address their issues and concerns in front of the government.

The *Batswana* believe in community-based programs. They frequently join associations which assist them economically and financially, such as associations which offer rotating credit. The members operate as a team, and on a specified month they fundraise for one member, give the member the finances they have raised, and the routine is repeated until all the members obtain credit.

In recent years, due to the high rate of HIV/AIDS infections, international donors have distributed both financial and in-kind resources to curb the spread of HIV. However, funding to LEGABIBO has been stifled, despite their having programs which would assist in fighting the epidemic.

LEGABIBO is not registered as an NGO and is regarded as an illegal organization by the government. Due to the lack of legal documents, the government officials who are homophobic ensure that LEGABIBO does not participate in any government programs or events. However, they work under the umbrella of BONELA, and although they have programs for youth empowerment, they are restricted to work only in areas which deal with HIV/AIDS in order to merge their programs with BONELA's.

SEXUALITY/SEXUAL PRACTICES

As in most African countries, children rarely discuss sexuality with their parents. They opt to talk about sex with their peers or the older generations. This can be attributed to the fact that there is limited information concerning sexuality, or to the view that sexuality is a secretive topic and upholds a level of morality and should not be talked about between children and parents.

Homosexuality is taboo in Botswana. As in all African countries there have been statements describing homosexuality as un-African and a Western phenomenon that is not welcome in the community. LEGABIBO has fought a losing battle by trying to register their organization in order to benefit from those government programs which would help its members, but they have often been met with resistance. The stigma and discrimination is evident in meetings that normally are organized to address homosexuals' concerns. The openly gay community is still in its early stages and has faced several setbacks, including marginalization and homophobic statements made by presidents and influential leaders in the neighboring countries of Zimbabwe and Namibia.[13]

The main obstacles for the LGBT movement are the lack of committed activists who would volunteer for lobbying at a higher level, such as in the government or in churches. Also, the LGBT community consists of mainly young people who are not firmly committed to the cause and still comprise only a small community.

A smaller community consists of transgender people and transvestites. Apart from the few rumors that there are groups of transvestites who meet in bars in the towns, there has been no evidence of any transgender person outing himself.

LEGABIBO occasionally holds meetings in the capital city of Gaborone, but with much precaution, as the members who attend the meeting fear being seen in the conference or meeting rooms by family members or friends, which could result in ostracism or physical violence. While they cannot be arrested for holding meetings, as the law does not prohibit that, they are very careful about talking to others about their sexual orientation. They also pay a local newspaper to run a weekly column that addresses issues on sexuality.

Apart from the high rate of HIV/AIDS, there is a notably high rate of teenage pregnancies in Botswana. One in every three girls drop out of school due to unwanted pregnancies; this indicates a high number of teens who have sex without protection, which also puts them at risk of contracting HIV/AIDS. In most African countries, sex is chiefly dominated by men, whereby the men dictate the position, safety, and frequency of sexual intercourse. Women have little input on the various aspects of sex. In fact, research has shown that women relate sex to procreation rather than enjoyment or pleasure.

There are also few recreation facilities in Botswana, which has been held accountable for the rapid spread of HIV, as the unemployment rate is quite high and the laws which restrict the sale of alcohol to minors is lenient. Young people are liable to engage in risky sexual behavior as a result of overindulgence in alcohol and a lack of resources to direct their energy.

Although the government is fighting to minimize the prevalence of HIV, there has been slow progress in changing behaviors, especially prostitution and the growing number of young women who engage in risky sexual relationships with older men for economic benefits. There has also been an increase in the number of prostitutes who target long-distance drivers. The government has, however, begun distributing HIV information and conducting HIV spot checks in hospitals, a process which is more effective than the widely known voluntary counseling and testing conducted on all the citizens in the country.[14]

FAMILY

Family structures are very important in both rural and urban Botswana. There are laws that have been set for families to maintain high morality and standards. There is no law to protect a woman against domestic violence or spousal rape. However, a rapist is stipulated by the law to receive 10 years imprisonment, depending on his HIV status, 15 years with corporal punishment if the offender has infected his victim, and 20 years with corporal punishment if he knew earlier about his HIV status.

The size of the family of an urban *Batswana* homestead varies from two to four children, while in the rural settings it ranges from four to seven children. The *Batswana* have a traditional way of life and are strict with moral ethics; they are very friendly and welcoming to visitors as well. Almost half of the households in Botswana are headed by women, as there has been a steady increase in single motherhood and cohabitation homesteads.

The most preferred family planning method in Botswana among the rural women is postpartum abstinence and breastfeeding, but their urban counterparts choose various modern methods such as condoms, pills, intrauterine devices, or female sterilization. Condom use and sexual knowledge among urban adolescents and teenagers has been reported to be 100 percent, but there are a few obstacles to purchasing condoms due to embarrassment and stigma associated with sexuality. Abortion is illegal in Botswana, but some women who are wealthy go to South Africa to undergo the procedure. There have been cases reported of illegal abortions with dire consequences.

Rural-to-urban migration has led to erosion in family values, as young people leave their rural homes and are exposed to a more cosmopolitan way of life. There has been a steady rise in the visibility of gays and lesbians in the existing population as a result. Yet this increase is not only attributed to the migration to urban areas, but also to campaign strategies which have been enacted by LEGABIBO.

Each culture in Botswana has gender-specific initiation rites to prepare adolescents for marriage. The initiation rites may include circumcision, seclusion, teachings on tribal laws and customs, and counseling. These rites are prerequisites for entering into marriage. In order for a marriage to be regarded as legitimate, there must be an exchange of dowry from the man to the woman he intends to marry. Marriages are negotiated by family members, who set the bride-price to be paid. This is an age-old tradition and bears significance in both the urban and rural settings. The marriage ceremonies vary from civil ceremonies, customary marriage, or church weddings.

Due to the exchange of money, valuables, or cattle during the dowry negotiations, the woman ultimately loses her power of negotiation in the marriage, and therefore some of her rights are undermined, such as consensual sex in marriage. There have been reported cases of abuse in marriages as the man regards his wife as his property, as though he bought her.

Through the government and the Botswana police force, women who are abused by their husbands are sent to shelters that are funded by the government. In the shelters, the women are counseled and go through the laws that can protect them and their children.

It is illegal in Botswana to divorce for any reason before two years are over, and therefore most couples are forced to stay in abusive marriages.

COMMUNITY

African countries depend significantly on the closeness of a community to its people in the equal distribution of resources and opportunities. The *Batswana* maintain a close-knit family unit irrespective of where they work. They move from rural to urban areas frequently to maintain their ties. Some men opt to support two women; they might have a wife in the rural home and live with a girlfriend in the urban area, a common practice in most sub-Saharan African countries, which aggravates the spread of HIV. In Botswana, women hold insignificant roles in leadership, and the men hold key ministerial positions. Women are regarded as the homemakers, and men as the decision-makers in the community. This is evident in the fact that there are very few women in parliament or government ministries. Due to the closeness of family it is regarded as an abomination for a family member to declare he does not want to start a family, and therefore the gay community operates in secrecy, away from close family members who might react strongly to their choice of partner.

Cattle hold a very high significance in a *Batswana* homestead. Cattle play a big role culturally, socially, and economically. Bride price constitutes a number of cattle in the rural settings, but due to urbanization, as in most African customs, the bride price tradition is slowly fading away as more women choose to stay single. The number of cattle owned by a man can determine his prestige in a community. Despite rural-to-urban migration, most men prefer to maintain a village house in their community of origin and expect to be buried in their home villages.

Chiefs and headmen hold a lot of authority in certain tribes. If there is strife between two people in the tribe, the case is brought before the traditional court and a ruling is passed by the chief with the assistance of his advisors, councils, and hierarchical leaders. The cases that are handled by the chiefs are mainly minor cases such as theft, indecent exposure, or use of insulting language in the community. Most of the punishments passed are mainly applicable to male adolescents and adults.

The successor of the chief is always his first son. Marriage laws changed from being monogamous to polygamous. A man was allowed to substitute his wife for her sister in case his wife was barren or deceased, and a widow was inherited by her husband's brother. Due to the shift of the marriage structures, inheritance of the chiefship became a political battle.

Another hurdle came during the mid-20th century with the emergence of Christianity. The powers of the chiefs are slowly being dissolved, as most tribes have stopped believing in rituals and supernatural powers and instead seek religious interventions. The powers of the chiefs were further diluted when the first president, Sir Seretse Khama, in the pursuit to creating a unified nation, included the chiefs in democratic institutions in order to reduce the *Batswana's* identity as tribal and instead portray a more national allegiance.

However, some chiefs still have powers in certain tribes and oversee intertribal, civil, and domestic cases. They also serve in the National House of Chiefs, which acts as a consultation body to the parliament.

HEALTH

Government and NGOs have sidelined sustainable projects in order to help curb the spread of HIV/AIDS. Although still disputed, in 2006 it was estimated that over 30 percent of the population was infected with HIV. As of 2006,

70 to 85 percent of HIV-infected *Batswana* were on antiretroviral therapy. An estimated 256,000 of HIV-infected *Batswana* are between the ages of 15 and 19 years old.[15]

Currently, Botswana has one of the highest HIV rates in the world, but it is one of the only countries in Africa which has progressive programs, information, and knowledge of dealing with the disease. The government has been at the frontline of trying to fight the spread of HIV and sponsors close to 80 percent of HIV/AIDS-related programs.[16]

HIV/AIDS was declared a national emergency by the Ministry of Health in Botswana. The HIV rate has risen subsequently due to cultural practices and poverty.

Due to the fact that homosexuality is illegal in Botswana, the homosexual community has no access to safe-sex education and condoms. Consequently, prison inmates are not given condoms, as they are supposedly not allowed to have relationships or intercourse with one another. However, cases of homosexuality in prison have been reported. An HIV-positive prisoner is granted access to antiretroviral drugs as long as he is a citizen.

POLITICS AND LAW

Botswana has incorporated two legal systems that work simultaneously: the cultural laws which originated from the customs and traditions of different ethnic communities, and the general law that was set during the colonial period by the Romans and the Dutch. Botswana is one of the few countries that still upholds the death penalty. Since independence, 38 people have been executed.

The general law in Botswana clearly stipulates that homosexuality is a criminal offense. According to Chapter 8.01, Sections 164 to 167 of the legal code, homosexuality is an "unnatural tendency" and is punishable with up to seven years imprisonment.[17] In 1998, the penal code went a step further by including lesbian relations as a criminal offense punishable with seven years in prison. The criminalization of sexual acts between women was regarded as a way of gender-mainstreaming and minimizing gender-discriminatory terms from Botswana's legislation.

The inclusion of the clause regarding sex between women came about after a case was brought forward in 1995 in which two men were suspected of being involved in a gay relationship. Their case was heard in 2003 before the high court, and the judgment was issued at the court of appeal. The judgment stipulated that the penal code they had been charged under had not in any way violated the constitution. The court case, however, brought new views on the inclusion of women in the legal code.

As a result of the legal code, there is no recognition of same-sex couples. Consequently, reliable organizations have formed which can offer protection to an individual or a couple. In 2004, a task force was appointed by the government of Botswana, aimed at urging citizens to enjoy safety, security, freedom of expression, and tolerance. The result of these efforts was Vision 2016, a national manifesto for the country. However, due to the stigma and discrimination faced by the LGBT community in terms of registration, gay-friendly organizations cannot openly defend their rights using the manifesto.

In December 1994, two men were arrested on the grounds of engaging in "unnatural acts" and "indecent practices." Through the intervention of DITSH-WANELO, The Botswana Centre for Human Rights, the case received fair representation in court. The two men, one a Botswana citizen and the other a Briton, were both sentenced in the high court, with the Briton being deported back to his country and the *Batswana* facing the high court with the charges.

According to a local newspaper, in 1997, a customary court in Mahalapye ruled in a case between two prison inmates. According to the case, the two were married while in prison and one of the partners was unfaithful, so the other partner attacked him. The Mahalapye customary court chose to ignore the issue of spousal abuse and instead considered the legalities of engaging in homosexual acts. One of the prisoners received four lashes and an additional four months on his custodial term, and the other received an additional one and a half years on his term.[18]

RELIGION AND SPIRITUALITY

Religion is paramount in *Batswana* culture; Christianity and indigenous religions have a vast following. Indigenous churches have integrated Christianity and traditional beliefs and have coined their own Christian dogma. Some of the indigenous churches practice certain traditions that are deemed illegal by law, such as polygamy. The indigenous churches are popular in rural Botswana. Eighty-five percent of the population follows indigenous religions, while Christians are a minority at 15 percent.

The Evangelical Fellowship of Botswana, a coalition of evangelical churches, launched a petition among its congregation to reject any pleas from the LGBT community for support. The fellowship clearly stated that homosexuality was a foreign ideology that was slowly causing a moral decay in their society, and therefore should not be condoned.

There has, however, been a recent change brought about by the Anglican leader Walter Makhulu, Archbishop of Central and Southern Africa. When asked about his views on gays and lesbians, he retorted by citing that the *Batswana* appreciated development and community enhancement from groups of people without questioning their sexual orientation, so it should not be a concern that the LGBT community will bring more harm than good. In reference to the Bible and its stand against homosexuality, he urged people to realize that the Bible was contextual, written in a different era.

In another exchange of words between the Bishop of Harare, Nolbert Kunonga, and Bishop Trevor Mwamba of the Church of the Province of Central Africa, Kunonga accused Bishop Mwamba of being pro-gay and a homosexual. These sentiments evoked mixed reactions between the two bishops, as the main tussle was between rifts that had been created by the dioceses. Church leaders in Botswana who are seen as pro-gay may be excommunicated from church activities according to the church laws.

The Anglican Church of Botswana joined their counterparts in 2004 in denouncing the consecration of Reverend Gene Robinson as a bishop. In that same year, Bishop Robinson went on to become the first openly gay bishop in the diocese of New Hampshire in the United States.

VIOLENCE

There is no law in Botswana's legal system that condemns sexual harassment. Rather, institutions have taken it upon themselves to come up with clauses that address these issues. One such institution is the University of Botswana.

Domestic violence-related death is one of the concerns of the Botswana legal system. Defilement, rape, and incest are ranked highest in reported crimes; this can be attributed to the fact that women are still regarded as inferior to men, and some customs and cultures still inspire detrimental practices in relationships. There have been reported cases of passion killings in which men kill their wives or girlfriends out of jealousy.

Certain influential leaders have made statements to the public condemning homosexuality and insisting that the LGBT community has ignored their culture and religion, and should seek counseling to help them lead normal lives. Although the LGBT community is gaining visibility in both rural and urban areas, the LGBT community faces threats of physical violence, blackmail, verbal abuse, and denial of health care due to discrimination and stigmatization, mainly from friends, family, or society.

There have been reported cases of verbal attacks and discrimination based on gender identity. Although the cases sometimes go unmentioned in the media, the offenders are rarely prosecuted as there is no law which recognizes discrimination based on sexual orientation or gender identity. If an incident receives media coverage, the story is usually biased and condemns the act of homosexuality, focusing less on the individual or perpetrator of the crime and more on the deviance of homosexuality.

OUTLOOK FOR THE 21ST CENTURY

There have been debates on whether to legalize homosexuality in Botswana. One of the debates led to the inclusion of same-sex relations between women in the penal code. The Botswana government has been at the forefront in trying to fight the prevalence of HIV, and in the process has supported programs and initiatives started by the government and NGOs. One such program was designed for the distribution of antiretroviral drugs in prisons and to promote distributing condoms in the same institutions. There have been reports of inmates who are jailed while HIV negative and released HIV positive. The government has been alerted of these increasing cases and is working with the prison authorities on improving the health concerns of prisoners.[19]

During press conferences conducted by human rights organizations, there has been minimal participation from the religious community and government authorities. In the coming years, many in the LGBT community hope that their voices will be heard and that they will be publically supported in their quest for rights, respect, and human dignity.

RESOURCE GUIDE

Suggested Reading

William Beinart, *Twentieth Century South Africa* (Oxford: Oxford University Press, 2001).

Botswana Police Service, *Report of a Study on Rape in Botswana* (Gaborone: Government Printer, 1999).

Martha Cornog, Robert T. Francoeur, and Raymond J. Noonan, *The Continuum Complete International Encyclopedia of Sexuality* (New York: CCIES, 2004).

M. Guether, *The Nharo Bushmen of Botswana: Tradition and Change* (Hamburg: Helmut Buske Verlag, 1986).

Alan Cary Johnson, *Off the Map: How HIV/AIDS Programming is Failing Same-Sex Practicing People in Africa* (New York: International Gay and Lesbian Human Rights Commission, 2007).

Scott Long, A. Widney Brown, and Gail Cooper, *More Than a Name: State-Sponsored Homophobia and its Consequences in Southern Africa* (New York: Human Rights Watch, 2003).

Robert Morrell, *Changing Men in Southern Africa* (London: University of Natal Press and Zed Books Limited, 2001).

M. Schoofs, "AIDS: The Agony of Africa," *The Village Voice*, January 2000, http://www.villagevoice.com/specials/africa/.

Women and Law in Southern Africa Trust, ed., *Botswana Families and Women's Rights in a Changing Environment* (Gaborone: Lightbooks Publishers, 1997).

Web Sites

Behind The Mask, www.mask.org.za.
> Behind the Mask is an organization that reports on issues affecting the LGBT community in Africa by featuring an interactive website, magazine, and online debates on pertinent issues surrounding homosexuality.

Botswana Council of Non-Governmental Organisations, www.bocongo.org.bw.
> Nationally recognized umbrella organization for all non-governmental organizations in Botswana.

Coalition of African Lesbians, www.cal.org.za.
> CAL is an organization formed by members from different countries in Africa. Their mission is to promote equality for African lesbians and ensure organizational and personal growth to its members.

International Gay and Lesbian Human Rights Commission, www.iglhrc.org.
> IGLHRC works on human rights concerns among the LGBT community worldwide. They research and fight for the recognition of LGBT persons, irrespective of their HIV status, gender identity or sexual orientation.

Pride Network, http://www.pridenet.com.
> The Pride Network is an advertising website that hosts information in regard to LGBT organizations and events in different countries.

United Nations in Botswana, www.unbotswana.org.bw.
> The UN in Botswana is an umbrella body for all the United Nations programs such as UNDP, UNICEF, UNHCR, WHO, UNAIDS, UNFPA, FAO, and UNV.

Organizations

Botswana Centre for Human Rights (DITSHWANELO). www.ditshwanelo.org.bw/.
> DITSHWANELO fights for basic human rights and has been in the front line of fighting for LGBT rights in Botswana. They lobby for the decriminalization of same sex relations by providing literature to law makers, students, and members of the public, and by holding conferences with the media.

Botswana Network on Ethics, Law and HIV/AIDS (BONELA). www.bonela.org.
> BONELA aims at ensuring that ethics, the law, and human rights are granted to people who are infected and affected by HIV/AIDS. Their objectives are met by fighting HIV-related stigma and discrimination.

Childline Botswana, http://www.childline.org.bw/.
> Childline Botswana is a non-profit, non-governmental organisation that focuses on children's rights. It primarily addresses issues dealing with child abuse.

Lesbian Gay and Bisexuals of Botswana (LEGABIBO), www.legabibo.org.bw.
> LEGABIBO is the only LGBT organization in Botswana and is housed by BONELA due to the legalities of registering as a non-governmental organization.
> P O Box 402958, Gaborone, Botswana
> Tel: +267 393 2516
> Fax: +267 393 2517

Youth Health Organization of Botswana (YOHO). www.yoho.or.bw.
> YOHO is an organization whose objective is to offer sexual health information to the youth of Botswana, primarily between the ages of 14–29. Their main concern is minimizing the prevalence of HIV/AIDS and STDs.

NOTES

1. "The Environment in Botswana," OneWorld Batswana, http://uk.oneworld.net/guides/botswana/development (accessed April 10, 2008).
2. "Attractions of Botswana," Botswana Tourism, http://www.botswanatourism.co.bw/attractions/selebi_phikwe.html (accessed April 5, 2008).
3. "2006 Estimates—Country Profile: Botswana," British Foreign and Commonwealth Office, http://www.fco.gov.uk (accessed April 7, 2008).
4. "Country Information: Botswana," UNICEF, http://www.unicef.org/infobycountry/botswana_statistics.html (accessed April 10, 2008).
5. "Partnership to Fight HIV/AIDS in Botswana," the United State's President's Emergency Plan for AIDS Relief, http://www.pepfar.gov (accessed April 10, 2008).
6. Godisang Mookodi, Oleosi Ntshebe, and Ian Taylor, "Botswana," CCIES, http://www.kinseyinstitute.org/ccies/bw.php (accessed April 14, 2008).
7. "Sub-Saharan Africa–Botswana," British Foreign and Commonwealth Office, http://www.fco.gov.uk (accessed April 7, 2008).
8. "Country Information-Botswana-Statistics," UNICEF, http://www.unicef.org/infobycountry/botswana_statistics.html (accessed April 10, 2008).
9. "Sub Saharan Africa—Botswana—Economy," British Foreign and Commonwealth Office, http://www.fco.gov.uk/ (accessed April 7, 2008).
10. "Politics and Civil Society in Botswana," OneWorld UK, http://uk.oneworld.net/guides/botswana/development (accessed April 8, 2008).
11. "Sub-Saharn Africa—Botswana—Economy," Foreign and Commonwealth Office, http://www.fco.gov.uk/ (accessed April 7, 2008).
12. Godisang Mookodi, Oleosi Ntshebe, and Ian Taylor, "Botswana," CCIES, http://www.kinseyinstitute.org/ccies/bw.php (accessed April 14, 2008).
13. "More Than a Name: State-Sponsored Homophobia and Its Consequences in Southern Africa," Human Rights Watch, http://www.hrw.org/reports/2003/safrica/ (accessed June 8, 2008).
14. "Some Positive Results," *Aidsmap: Information on HIV & AIDS,* http://www.aidsmap.com (accessed April 12, 2008).
15. "Sub-Saharan Africa—Botswana—Development," Foreign and Commonwealth Office, http://www.fco.gov.uk/ (accessed April 7, 2008).
16. "Some Positive Results."
17. "The HIV Epidemic in Botswana," *Aidsmap: Information on HIV & AIDS,* http://www.aidsmap.com (accessed April 12, 2008).
18. Godisang Mookodi, Oleosi Ntshebe, and Ian Taylor, "Botswana," CCIES, http://www.kinseyinstitute.org/ccies/bw.php (accessed April 14, 2008).
19. "Botswana Guide: Human Rights in Botswana," OneWorld UK, http://uk.oneworld.net/guides/botswana/development (accessed April 9, 2008).

CAMEROON

Charles Gueboguo

OVERVIEW

Cameroon is a central African country with approximately 17 million inhabitants. It contains 183,568 square miles of land bordered by the Central African Republic to the east, Nigeria to the west, Chad to the northeast, and a small coastline along the Atlantic Ocean. Cameroon's natural features include mountains, beaches, savannas, deserts, and rainforests.

Cameroon was subjected to German, British, and French colonization before gaining independence from the French on January 1, 1960 and from the British on October 1, 1961. On May 20, 1962 both Cameroons (the Francophone and the Anglophone Cameroon) were united. This latter date was chosen to be the country's national holiday. It is this peculiar context that makes Cameroon a bilingual country—in which the official languages are French and English, with French being the dominant language of the two. The political capital is Yaoundé, still known under the name of the "City of Seven Hills," whereas the economic capital is Douala. These two cities alone represent a mosaic of populations from different parts of Cameroon as well as from the surrounding countries.

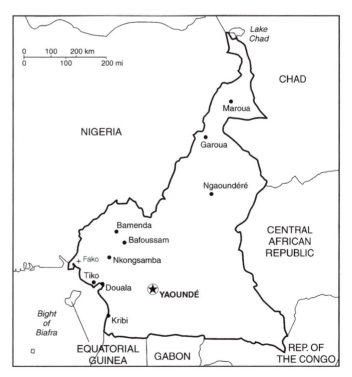

OVERVIEW OF LGBT ISSUES

Since 2006, there has been a sharp rise of antihomosexual feelings in Cameroon. The rise of homophobic feelings in Cameroon is linked to myth- and fear-based representations of homosexuality. Many people believe homosexuality is associated with pedophilia on the one hand, and with an opportunistic means of acceding to higher classes in society on the other. This imbroglio of how people commonly view the essence of what homosexuality means, along with the recent rise of homophobia, were accentuated further by the words of Catholic Archbishop of Yaoundé on December 25, 2005. His two hours of antigay rhetoric were followed by the Imam of Douala and finally taken up by the local press, who published a list of the top 50 homosexuals within the country's elite.

EDUCATION

The level of education among Cameroon's citizens is rising, primarily due to compulsory schooling at the primary school level. Generally, LGBT people in Cameroon have an average level of education:[1] 65 percent have stopped going to school at the secondary level, 30 percent are at university and among them, 60 percent have at least a GCE A level plus two years of university, and 29 percent are still attending school. Among those who have stopped going to school, 80 percent have at least a high-school level education, while only six percent stopped at the primary level.

Women constitute the least educated population among LGBT persons. Eighty-eight percent of them have only a secondary school level of education. Among them, 89 percent no longer attend school.

EMPLOYMENT AND ECONOMICS

Unemployment is very high in Cameroon, exceeding 20 percent, especially in the two major cities of Douala and Yaoundé. LGBT people in Cameroon generally fall into the categories of students (29%), employees (24%), and traders (13%). Given the low education level of women, the number of jobless individuals is the highest among lesbian women (16%).

SOCIAL/GOVERNMENT PROGRAMS

The Cameroonian government does not provide social programs or support for LGBT issues. Addressing the needs of the LGBT community, primarily in terms of health care services or in the context of AIDS, is not a priority for the government. However, there are local associations in the cities of Douala and Yaoundé that try to address the needs of the LGBT community, specifically in regard to AIDS and STDs.

SEXUALITY/SEXUAL PRACTICES

Homosexuality in Cameroon, as in many African societies, is placed under the umbrella of bisexuality because of the negative social context placed on homosexuality and on LGBT people. Many consider themselves bisexual because they also have partners of the opposite sex in order to remain accepted in their social environment.

No data are available on sexual practices, but current research is being conducted to better understand the practices and the needs of the LGBT community in Cameroon.

FAMILY

The idea of family in Cameroon is considered to include a large nuclear family as well as extended family, or relatives. LGBT people are not considered to be part of the family. Marriage between persons of the same sex or gender is not recognized by law. However, the percentage of LGBT couples is not negligible (22%). Compared to women, men more often engage in a coupled life (22%). Women mostly live without their partners (55%). This is justified by the fact that they are declared to be parents living with their children.

COMMUNITY

Since 2005, there has been a significant rise of homophobic sentiment in Cameroon, approved by the state authorities and by the rigid societal structures. In Cameroon, being gay or speaking about homosexuality is a big problem with a huge stigma is attached to it. Yet, there is also a growing portion of society engaging in clandestine associations in response to the social prejudice they face.

Most human rights organizations in Cameroon are not actively addressing the devastating situation facing homosexuals in Cameroon. The pretext to this is that homosexuality is not recognized as an African phenomenon. As such, social norms dictate that those who lend themselves to homosexual acts and are persecuted are receiving a fair punishment.

In the face of this injustice, a young association has been created called, *Alternatives-Cameroun*. The association is active at all levels, national and international, to denounce arrests and all the false judgments that are pronounced in Cameroon relating to homosexuality. It also provides homosexuals in Cameroon with legal, medical, and financial help when they are rejected by their families or imprisoned in Yaoundé. The association is one of the very few that helps educate the public about homosexuality and strives to be heard beyond the homophobic backlash. *Alternatives-Cameroun* represents a positive note for change that could still occur in the years to come.

HEALTH

The priorities of the LGBT community include free access to health services. Certain local associations try to address this need of the LGBT community in Cameroon. Health care workers in Cameroon need to be well-trained on the issues of stigmatization and discrimination of health access on the basis of sexual orientation. While there are no official data on the prevalence of AIDS among LGBT persons, a locally based LGBT association in Douala has reported an average of 18 percent of HIV prevalence among the community. The national average of HIV prevalence is 5.4 percent.

POLITICS AND LAW

In Cameroon, homosexual acts are prohibited by law. According to Article 347 of the Penal Code, any person who engages in sexual activity with a person of the same sex is liable to face imprisonment of two months to five years, as well as a fine ranging from 20,000 FCFA (about US$50) to 200,000 FCFA (about US$500). The immediate consequence of this is that homosexuality in Cameroon has the peculiar trait of being bi-sexualized meaning that bisexuality is more common than exclusive homosexuality. This is due to a rigid societal context as well as to the ambiguous legal context that prohibits homosexual practices. The law prohibiting homosexual acts is the result of Decree 72/16 signed September 28, 1972. The decree is a piece of executive law-making, rather than a statute voted on by Parliament. However, paragraph four of Law 96–06 of January 18, 1996, which modifies the Constitution of Cameroon dating from June 2, 1972 and relates to the relationship between the executive and the legislative powers, requires that the law be voted on by Parliament. Thus, Article 347b of the Penal Code of Cameroon violates both the Constitution of Cameroon and primary legislation.

RELIGION AND SPIRITUALITY

Christianity is the primary religion in Cameroon. A small percentage of people define themselves as Animist or Muslim. Many gays and lesbians in Cameroon are Catholics. For those lesbians or gays who claim to have a religion, it has minor influence on their sexual expression.

VIOLENCE

Violence against LGBT people in Cameroon is rampant. In the course of 2007, a great number of violations of persons' integrity on the basis sexual orientation were registered, as shown in the report of the first half of 2007 conducted by the Association Camerounaise de Défense des Droits de l'Homme Alternatives-Cameroun.[2] This is the only organization in the country that looks into the issues facing the LGBT community in Cameroon. Their report reveals several cases of aggressions and unlawful arrests of LGBT people.

1. The case of the "three"
   P. Y., N. N. and A. D. were detained, without judgment in the case of the latter, and convicted to one year in prison. They were finally released at the end of April 2007. P. Y. affirmed that he was subjected to verbal abuse during his prison sentence. When he got out of prison, he was rejected by his family who demanded that he either get married or that he should commit suicide—which he refused to do.

2. The case of F. A.
   F. A. was one of 11 prisoners arbitrarily detained for alleged homosexuality and was finally released in June 2006. In January 2007 he was again held in interrogatory detention in the 10th Arrondissement of Yaoundé, having been accused of pedophilia by his former employer who claimed he had sexually abused his mentally handicapped 10-year-old son. After investigation, the inspector recognized that the accusations were inconsistent and F. A. was released after six days in detention. According to F. A.'s account, his employer promptly reemployed him after the release, thereby avoiding paying seven months of salary that had been in arrears. The case shows the confusion between homosexuality and child abuse.

3. The arrest of M. M., A. K. and two employees of the bar/restaurant Fusion Plus
   On June 10, 2007 at 12:45 a.m. M. M., a 26-year-old living in Yaoundé, was just about to join friends at another bar in the city when he was arrested by the police close to the bar/restaurant Fusion Plus. The two men who conducted the arrest were in civilian clothing, even though they claimed to be police. M. M. was then forcefully taken to the police station of the 10th Arrondissment of Yaoundé together with A. K., co-owner of Fusion Plus, along with two employees who had come for help. The reason they were given for the arrests was that they were owners of a "bar for homosexuals" and that they should negotiate a payment for their

immediate release. Following their refusal to do so, their valuables and money were confiscated before being thrown into a cell. The employees were subjected to physical abuse with the aim that they should admit unlawful actions—which, however, they did not. At the police station, all four were undressed, mistreated, beaten, and insulted. They were not allowed to make a telephone call. Thanks to the intervention of one of the men's family, they were all released a few days later.

4. The attack on G. K.
    G. K. was attacked on July 20, 2007 at about 9 p.m. by someone who had asked him for help. This person pretended to have been thrown out of his home after his family had found out about his homosexual orientation. Intending to help the man, G. K. left his house at 8.30 p.m. to go to another neighborhood in Douala, after having asked his brother to lend him 10,000 FCSA (about US$25). When he arrived at the meeting place, G. K. noticed that he had fallen into a trap. Two other men dressed in military clothing stopped him, gagged him and dragged him into a dark corner, where they robbed him of all his belongings (money, mobile phone, and shoes), threatening to take him to the closest police station and report his homosexuality. Considering their loot insufficient, they forced him to call someone who could bring more money. G. K. escaped while the aggressors were arguing with one another and grabbed a motorcycle. G. K. recovered from the beatings he received during the attack.

5. The aggressions and thefts at the Celebrity Night Club
    The Celebrity Club is the only night club in Douala that is catalogued as a gay club. It is frequented by lesbian women and gay men who come from Yaoundé and other cities. Aggression and thefts are often reported by patrons of this club. The modus operandi is the clients are picked up by a motorbike taxi driver, who changes the itinerary of the agreed-upon journey and, instead, takes the client to a trap. The client is subsequently robbed of all his money and valuables. The victim is often threatened, insulted with homophobic remarks, and is sometimes physically attacked by these drivers.

Before this report, in June 2005, a group of 11 young men was arrested in a neighborhood of Yaoundé, all being accused of homosexuality. One of those men, a 25-year-old gay man, clarified that they were simply drinking and there was no touching or kissing. Apparently these young men offended the public just through the way they looked. On the legal level, Cameroon's Penal Code, in article 347b, ordinance 72/16, does not actually prohibit homosexuality, but instead condemns "any person who has sexual intercourse with a person of the same sex." In other words, it is homosexual practices, wrongly confounded with homosexuality, which are being repressed. Homosexuality, instead, is not generally understood and defined in terms of sexual acts, but instead in terms of a sexual identity. Homosexual identity indeed represents the self-recognition of an individual concerning his or her specificity as a man or woman who has a preference for persons of the same sex.

In 2008 another 11 detentions for reasons of male homosexuality in Douala and Yaoundé were reported. Often, arrests occur without proof. This leads to the suspicion that in Cameroon, on the simple presumption of homosexuality, one risks illegal detention at any time. Alleged homosexuality is used as a pretext to strip individuals of their basic rights as a person, both by the police and society. The homosexual or allegedly homosexual person is immediately convicted without judgment by a court. This procedure seems to be based on a social consensus, so even if the case is brought to court, the judges are often swayed by homophobia rather than the law. This situation led Alice Nkom, an internationally renowned Cameroon lawyer, to say in an internationally broadcasted radio show that Cameroon's justice minister was an "avowed homophobe." Often judges decide to convict those accused of homosexuality despite lack of proof. Also, those who suffer from homophobic aggressions do not have a chance to resort to legal remedies. Mostly, the aggressors threaten their victims to reveal their homosexuality once the police arrive. The silence that accompanies those aggressions seems to be the rule. Concerning extortion and blackmail of LGBT people in Cameroon, a study commandeered by IGLHRC was completed in 2008.

OUTLOOK FOR THE 21ST CENTURY

Currently it is important in Cameroon to remain silent about one's sexual orientation. There is no foreseeable change in that situation. LGBT people fear having their sexual orientation disclosed in public. To do so results in losing one's freedom. Worse, many LGBT people are forced into marrying or having a partner of the opposite sex. Thus, homosexuality in Cameroon is bi-sexualized. It is a presumed bisexuality, lived under constraint, which, subsequently, can lead to psychological strains for the individuals involved.

RESOURCE GUIDE

Suggested Reading

Charles Gueboguo, *La Question Homosexuelle en Afrique, le cas du Cameroun* (Paris: l'Harmattan, 2006).

Charles Gueboguo, "La problématique de l'homosexualité en Afrique: L'expérience Camerounaise," *L'Arbre à Palabre. Culture et Développment* 19 (2006): 18–59.

Charles Gueboguo, "L'homosexualité en Afrique: variations et sens d'hier à nos jours," *Socio-Logos* 1 (2006): http://sociologos.revues.org/document37.html.

Charles Gueboguo, "Pour une lecture revue et corrigée de l'homosexualité dans la pensée doxique africaine: Impacts, dérapages et risques," *L'arbre à Palabre. Culture et Développement* 20 (2007): 14–51.

Terroirs, *Revue Africaine de Sciences Sociales et de Philosophie.* Dossier: *L'homosexualité est bonne à penser.* n° 1/2, Academia Africana.

Organizations

Alternatives-Cameroun
Association Camerounaise pour la Défense des Droits de l'Homme
BP: 12 767 Douala, Cameroun
alternatives.cameroun@gmail.com

NOTES

1. All the data come from a preliminary report of a forthcoming survey among the LGBT community in Cameroon, funded by IGLHRC (C. Gueboguo, 2008, "La problématique de l'extorsion et du chantage sur la base de l'orientation sexuelle au Cameroun: sociologie de l'expérience des bisexual/les, gays, lesbiennes et transgenres"). Quantitative inquiry was conducted from February to May 2008 in the two mains cities of Cameroon, Douala and Yaoundé. The convenience sample used (depending on unities encountered during the survey) was made up of 214 respondents: 113 for the city of Douala and 101 for Yaoundé, among which 171 were men, and 43 were women. Disparity among women was great, as they were more heavily represented in Douala (25) than in Yaoundé (18).

2. "Rapport à mi-parcours Juin 2007," *Alternatives-Cameroun,* 2007.

EGYPT

Jen Westmoreland Bouchard

OVERVIEW

Egypt is located on the northeast corner of Africa on the Mediterranean Sea. Libya is located to the west, the Sudan to the south, and the Red Sea and Israel to the east. The northward-flowing Nile River begins 100 miles south of the Mediterranean and continues to the ocean at a port between the cities of Alexandria and Port Said. The Nile divides Egypt into two distinct regions.[1]

The Arab Republic of Egypt is governed by President Hosni Mubarak. Egypt's population is estimated at 80,264,543 (2007) with a birthrate of 22.6/1000, and an infant mortality rate of 30/1000. The average life expectancy is 72 years. Egypt's capital and largest city is Cairo, with a population of 7,629,866. Other large cities in Egypt are Alexandria (population 3,891,000), Giza (population 2,597,600), Shubra el Khema (population 1,018,000), and El Mahalla el Kubra (population 462, 300). The official currency is the Egyptian pound. The official language of Egypt is Arabic, but both English and French are used by the educated classes. Ninety percent of the Egyptian population is Muslim (mostly Sunni), nine percent are Coptic, one percent is Christian, and six percent subscribe to other belief systems.[2]

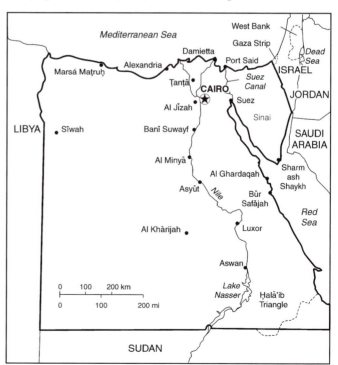

OVERVIEW OF LGBT ISSUES

Though Islam vehemently disapproves of sexual relations between members of the same sex, Muslim societies have historically been quite tolerant. This is especially true if and when such relationships are conducted behind closed doors. Many of the celebrated Egyptian poets of classical Arabic literature indulged in homoerotic activities, yet they were viewed as no less great than their heterosexual counterparts. The relatively liberal attitudes concerning homosexuality in Egypt (and other parts of the Arab world) both offended and fascinated protestant European travelers of the 18th and 19th centuries.

In fact, the first law against homosexuality was created in Egypt during the British colonial period. Over the last few decades, these ideological positions on homosexuality have been reversed.[3] During the past 20 years, Europe and North America have become more liberal toward homosexuality. Conversely, many Arab countries have become increasingly conservative.[4] For example, in 2001, 52 Egyptian gays were arrested in a gay nightclub, The Queen Boat Disco, an event that signified the regression into extreme Egyptian conservatism (sexual and other). After the "Queen Boat Affair," many Egyptian newspapers and magazines discussed homosexuality as a Western perversion that had invaded Egypt. However, many historians view the phenomenon of homosexuality in the Middle East much differently. Egypt turned a blind eye to homosexuals until European scholars began accusing Egyptians of oppressing women, yet allowing immoral sexual acts between men. According to certain scholars, Egyptians retaliated by oppressing homosexual men to rebuild their moral image in the West. Today, homosexual women are often doubly oppressed within social and religious systems that simultaneously protect and inhibit them from living openly homosexual lives.

Terminology, or the ways in which gays identify themselves (or are identified by others) linguistically, plays an important role in community formation. In Arab societies, the use of the word "gay" is loaded with certain Western connotations. The term "homosexual" carries with it images of a certain lifestyle that only Western gays assume (and that Arab gays may try to simulate). The Arabic language has no accepted equivalent to the word "gay." The term for homosexuality is *al-mithliyya al-jinsiyya* meaning literally "sexual sameness." This term is used mostly in academic and literary circles. The shortened version of the term, *mithli* is beginning to be used as a more commonplace word for gays. Both of these terms are relatively neutral and many Arab gays accept them. Religious conservatives and popular media publications often use the term *shaadh* (which translates as "queer," "pervert," or "deviant"), a heavily loaded and pejorative term. The conventional term for lesbian is *suhaaqiyya*. There are many lesbians who argue this term has inaccurate connotations; therefore, they prefer *mithliyya* (the feminine version of *mithli*).[5]

There exist no positively connoted terms in Arabic that express the complex interactions of sentimental and physical relations between two people of the same sex. The term *shouzouz jinsi* means "abnormal" sexuality and *loowat* is a negative way of expressing a homosexual act among men. This term refers to the Biblical fable of Lot, or Lut, in the Koran. The word *sihaq* expresses a homosexual act among women. The term bisexuality has no positive translation in Arabic. The lesbian publication, *Bint el Nas* uses the expression *mozdawijat el moyool el jinsiya* to express female bisexuality and *mozdawij el moyool el jinsiya* to express male bisexuality. The working term for hermaphrodite or intersexed, or a person who has both male and female reproductive organs, is *izdiwaji el jins*.

In regard to transsexual or transgender individuals, Arabic provides two terms. The negative term is *khanis*. A more positive option is *moghayir el jins*. An individual who is born with male reproductive organs but identifies as female is termed a *moghayirat el jins* (male-to-female transgender). This term helps when referring to a person with feminine adjectives out of respect for the way in which she identifies herself, whether she has undergone a gender transformative surgical procedure or not. An individual who is born with female reproductive organs but identifies as a male is called *moghayir el jins* (female-to-male transgender).[6]

EDUCATION

The Egyptian education system does not recognize at any level of schooling the problems and discrimination faced by LGBT students based on their sexual orientation. There are no programs that explicitly address LGBT issues. There are no antibullying policies and the very existence of LGBT students is denied. Attempts to develop generalized sex-education curriculum have been severely attacked by Muslim scholars. In 2005 Sheik Mohammed Sayed Tantawi, head of Al-Azhar[7] (one of the oldest and most prominent scholarly Muslim institutions), rejected the attempts to bring sex education to Egyptian schools, let alone "safe-sex" messages. According to Tantawi, Islam recognizes only one form of family and that is marriage between a man and a woman. This precludes issues of contraception, premarital sex, abortion, and sexual deviancy (e.g., masturbation, bestiality, and homosexuality).

It is dangerous for LGBT students to try and meet through the Internet. In 2004 a 17-year-old student at a private university posted a personal profile on a gay Arab dating site. The student was discovered, arrested outside the American University in Midan Al Tahrir (Liberation Plaza) in Cairo, accused of "offences" to the honor of society, and sentenced by the Jahah court to 17 years in prison with two years of hard labor.[8] Similarly, two male college students (ages 19 and 22) were arrested in 2002 for making a date via a college chat room; they were sentenced to multiyear suspended sentences.[9]

EMPLOYMENT AND ECONOMICS

There are no antidiscrimination statutes to protect LGBT employees from discrimination based on sexual orientation or HIV status. Although AIDS is primarily a disease found in heterosexuals in Egypt (estimated by UNICEF[10] to be about 90% of those infected by HIV), there is a public association between AIDS and homosexuality. Persons found to be infected are summarily dismissed from their jobs. Anonymous testing is not available so most people either don't know their status or have used a home test to determine their results.

SOCIAL/GOVERNMENT PROGRAMS

Since the 2001 Queen Boat Affair, Egypt has turned decidedly antigay. For example, after the abuses at the Abu Ghraib prison in Iraq by American military personnel were reported in 2004, demonstrators took to the streets of Cairo to protest the mistreatment of Arab prisoners by "homosexual American executioners."[11] The use of these labels blurred the distinction between homosexuality and torture, thus serving a broader antigay political agenda. Not only are there no social or governmental programs focused on LGBT issues, but there are informal cultural and religious attitudes that make Egypt extremely dangerous for nonheterosexuals.

SEXUALITY/SEXUAL PRACTICES

Generally, women are much more constrained than men in their expressions of sexuality. Even in moderate cities like Cairo, where women are allowed to wear Western attire there still exist powerful social and ethical demands that women remain chaste, modest, and honorable. A strict set of rules governs ethical actions for women. The strongest of these rules is that women marry under the age of 25 in order to maintain familial honor. Therefore, lesbian urges are often stifled and deeply buried. Cruising for sex, even in the most discreet of fashions, is unthinkable.

Lesbians have a particularly difficult time in Egypt. In a patriarchal society built on heterosexual relationships, lesbians are often ignored or invisible. However, lesbianism is more common than one might expect in Arab countries, Egypt included. Some married women engage in homosexual activities as a way of combating boredom in their marriages. Others, who were well aware of their homosexual preferences and chose to get married anyway (to conform to social or family expectations), keep one or several female lovers on the side. Many Egyptian husbands are paranoid that their wives are unfaithful to them (with men) yet they suspect nothing when their wives spend the evening with other women. These husbands are often relieved to hear that their wives prefer the company of women rather than men.

As a result of their virtual invisibility in Egyptian society, many lesbians face serious mental health challenges. With invisibility comes isolation and disconnection. It is difficult to find ways to meet and speak with other lesbians since there are no lesbian support or resource organizations in Egypt. Some gay Egyptian men have a girlfriend or get married to protect themselves from the shame and isolation of being homosexual. They keep boyfriends and secret private apartments on the side. As a result of extreme social pressure to live heterosexual lives, very few individuals feel comfortable enough to identify themselves publicly as being homosexual.

To understand how sexuality is viewed and constructed in Arab countries, one must bear in mind that sexuality was a Western concept that came to fruition in the late 19th century and takes as its core the notion that sexual behavior determines a person's identity and therefore defines (to a certain extent) his or her lifestyle.[12] Therefore, a person who defines him partly or entirely by his sexuality is considered to be under the influence of Western gay culture. Thus, he is considered an outsider on many levels.

FAMILY

In traditional Muslim families, homosexuality is denied, ignored, or at worst treated with psychological and physical violence. In Morocco, Egypt, and other Arab societies, there are many testimonials of homosexual sons being attacked by their fathers and brothers, or forced to leave home. Others are subjected to countless therapy sessions or forced to undergo electroshock treatment.

In many well-educated and affluent households, homosexuality is treated as an illness and considered to be curable with the right and appropriate length of treatment. Parents in this situation often believe that their child has been seduced or forced into homosexual behavior. To avoid these various forms of family induced trauma, many gay men take on faux girlfriends or even arrange marriages for themselves with lesbians who are similarly seeking safety.[13]

Marriage is obligatory in most Arab households. Most marriages are still arranged by parents. In cases where a gay or lesbian marries an arranged partner, many pursue homosexual relations outside the marriage.[14] While many never come out as openly homosexual, some wait to do so until after one or both parents have died. Others simply live in secrecy or move to another country in which they can live out their lives honestly and relatively safely.

Violent reactions from family members are especially common in traditional parts of Egypt. In these regions, the notion of family honor is of the utmost importance. Any type of sexual deviance, homosexuality included, brings shame upon the household and also shames past generations. Such emotional reactions often result in fathers killing their homosexual sons to preserve the family's honor.

Since homosexuality is highly stigmatized, it is hard for parents and siblings to find support and advice from friends and extended family members. The social taboo of bringing up intimate or sexual topics in the public domain prohibits families from obtaining the proper types of information and scientific data regarding homosexuality. A lack of information (or a proliferation of misinformation) motivates a vicious cycle of violence and intolerance.[15]

COMMUNITY

Since homosexuality and various forms of *queerness* are generally not accepted in Muslim societies, it is nearly impossible to meet in gay support groups, much less attempt to celebrate one's sexuality in the form of a gay pride festival. In interviews, numerous Egyptian gays have reported feeling extremely lonely, isolated, and pressured to conform to a traditional, heterosexual lifestyle.[16]

In major Egyptian cities with larger numbers of gay people per capita (such as Cairo and Alexandria), a gay man or woman can more easily move away from the constraints placed on them by family and friends and engage in a more open gay lifestyle. However, these individuals are few and far between. They have to be both brave enough to risk being seen with other gays in public (and face the social consequences) or have enough revenue to fund a private apartment for their affairs. A gay community exists online, but again, money and access are necessary to engage in this type of virtual socialization.

The Queen Boat Affair and the events that followed have prohibited gays from freely associating in public spaces. Even virtual affairs and online chats have become dangerous. Individuals seeking solace in gay chat rooms are often the prey of undercover police officers masquerading as fellow gay chatters. The Human Rights Watch (HRW) has called this situation an "increasingly harsh campaign of entrapment and arrest of men solely on the basis of alleged consensual homosexual conduct."[17] As a result of these political atrocities, many Egyptian homosexuals are forced to live in secrecy.

A unified gay community in Egypt does not currently exist, though there are resources within the global gay community that are available to Arab gays. In the aftermath of the 2001 Queen Boat Affair and the events that followed, organizations such as Al-Fatiha have become increasingly important. The Al-Fatiha Foundation is based in the United States. It is a nonprofit and nongovernmental organization. Their mission involves supporting Muslim individuals who are lesbian, gay, bisexual, transgender, intersex, or questioning (LGBTIQ). In lieu of recent challenges facing homosexual populations in Arab countries, they have started a fund to disseminate money to asylum seekers from Egypt.

The Al-Fatiha Foundation also works with organizations such as the Lesbian and Gay Immigration Rights Task Force (LGIRTF) and The International Gay and Lesbian Human Rights Commission (IGLHRC). Both of these organizations provide documentation on international human rights abuses towards homosexual communities.

Since 1963, a small group of Egyptian lesbians has been meeting secretly in group members' homes. The name of the organization, called *Hamd* ("to praise"), was started by a lesbian named Farduz Hussein. Through joining this group, many gay Arab women feel for the first time that they belong and that they are safe.[18]

The arrival of the Internet in Egypt marked a distinct change in how information about homosexuality was disseminated. Various gay Web sites and discussion groups allowed Egyptian homosexuals, who had previously been isolated and uninformed, to finally connect to a larger gay community. The Internet also connected them to international gay organizations and other gay people worldwide.

The majority of these Web sites are in French or English, thus literacy in these languages (and access to a computer) is required. Egypt's literacy rate is 71.4 percent. Many young Arab gays find general safety or sexual information that may be useful; however, most of the psychological references are geared toward a Western audience and do not offer advice on how to live as a homosexual in an Arab country.[19]

After the Queen Boat Affair, police started surfing the web and pretending to be men in search of homosexual relationships. As soon as they had gotten to know an individual online, they would ask to meet the unsuspecting gentleman in a public location for a date. When they arrived, the police would arrest the person waiting to meet them. As a result, nearly all of Egypt's main gay Web sites were shut down. Many of the webmasters were either arrested or went into hiding for fear of being caught.

HEALTH

As far as HIV/AIDS is concerned, Egypt appears to be a high-risk country. Rates of condom use are low, even when compared with other North African countries. In a 2005 study, only 24 percent of men said they had ever used a condom. In addition, HIV testing rates are low among all demographics. One statistic reveals that 99 percent of drug uses reported that they had never had a HIV test.[20]

Most individuals who test HIV positive in Egypt are men. In fact, recorded cases of HIV are four times more common among men than among women. Part of the reasoning behind this is that few women are tested. Only six percent of women have full knowledge of HIV, according to a 2005 Egyptian Demographic Health Survey. Educational outreach efforts to high-risk populations of women (sex workers, impoverished women, etc.) are extremely limited.[21]

There are approximately 5,300 people in Egypt living with HIV/AIDS.[22] For those who are living with HIV, antiretroviral drugs can cost up to $1,000 per month because the government, which for the most part refuses to acknowledge its country's AIDS epidemic, has not authorized legal imports on drugs.[23] There is a powerful stigma attached to those living with HIV/AIDS that can lead to isolation and depression. This discrimination is the result of myriad forms of misinformation (or simply lack of information) regarding HIV, even among the scientific and medical fields. Patients are frequently misdiagnosed several times before discovering that their symptoms are indeed those of HIV.[24]

There is no social or governmental push to encourage safe sex through the use of condoms. Doctors claim that AIDS in Egypt is the "foreigner's disease," and that moral Arabs are immune. The underlying message is that Egyptians never have sex outside of marriage as a result of their religious beliefs. Therefore, those who follow these religious and social codes are immune to the disease. When condoms are used, which is rare, it is strictly for contraception.[25]

Thus, the Egyptian government finds itself in a difficult place. By promoting safe sex, they may be viewed as condoning or even encouraging promiscuity among Egyptians.

UNAIDS and other international organizations are working together with the Egyptian government to promote change in the ways Egypt deals with HIV education and prevention.[26]

POLITICS AND LAW

Historically, Egyptian society has been relatively accepting of many types of erotic activity (homosexuality included). However, The Queen Boat Affair was an event that exemplified a return to extreme Egyptian conservatism regarding sexuality. Of the men who were arrested, 23 of them were sentenced to between one and five years in prison for debauchery (since homosexuality itself is not technically illegal). The arrested were described as shameful to the nation for committing sexually deviant acts.

The context for this event is the ongoing political struggle between the government and followers of Sunni conservatism. Even though Egypt professes to be a secular state, policies are often informed by the views of the Sunni religious leadership.[27] Thus, the unprecedented arrest was, in essence, a way of regaining conservative control of the nation. Egypt is one of the only Muslim states without explicitly antihomosexual statutes written into their laws. In other Muslim countries, homosexual acts may be punished by a number of severe sentences, including up to 10 years imprisonment.[28]

The importance of the Queen Boat Affair lies in the fact that, while not explicitly referred to in the country's laws, certain regulations regarding prostitution and public morality are used to persecute gay men. Morality is, of course, determined by Muslim law.

Since the Queen Boat Affair, the Egyptian government has unlawfully arrested and tortured men suspected of homosexual or *lewd* acts. Some of the detainees were forced to stand on their tiptoes for extended periods of time, others received electric shocks to the penis and tongue, and the rest were beaten on the soles of their feet with a *felaqa* (a rod) until they lost consciousness. These men were tortured until they relented and agreed to work as spies and report other homosexuals to authorities.

Events such as this have caught the attention of international gay and human rights associations. Though significant strides have been made on the governmental level toward the elimination of violence against homosexuals, a general homophobic trend persists and known gay establishments, such as the Queen, remain frequent targets.

RELIGION AND SPIRITUALITY

Islam is the dominant religion in Egypt and the Koran strictly prohibits homosexuality: "And as for the two of you who are guilty thereof, punish them both. If they repent and mend their ways, let them be. God is forgiving and merciful." (4:16). Another important Muslim source is the *Shari'ah* ("path"). The *Shari'ah* is, in essence, a divinely created code of conduct (expressing God's will) that all Muslims must follow.[29] According to the *Shari'ah*, homosexual behavior is strongly prohibited.

The *Shari'ah* contains information on both sex and the regulation of it. The basic premise is that sex is natural and condoned. In fact, most Muslim sects believe that sex in paradise leads to the fulfillment of the spiritual and bodily self.[30] However, because of human imperfection, sex on earth has become corrupt and must be regulated. Sex within marriage is encouraged. However, a partner of the same sex is considered to be an illicit partner because he or she could never be a spouse and because a homosexual act threatens the natural order. In more conservative sects, homosexual activities are considered a revolt against Allah.[31]

Therefore, according to Muslim law, these thoughts must be repressed and never acted upon. If a Muslim admits to having homosexual thoughts, religious leaders encourage him to ask Allah to rid them of these feelings, never to get physically involved with a person other than his own heterosexual spouse, to seek medical advice and treatment, and to seek religious support from a local imam.[32]

An important distinction between Islam and Christianity is that Islam addresses homosexual acts, but does not address homosexuality as an identity or lifestyle. Christianity tends to view homosexuality (the lifestyle, acts, and identity) as a sin, and preaches that this lifestyle is indeed a choice. The reasons for this distinction are clear if one bears in mind that homosexuality is perceived as a Western construction, a concept that came to fruition in the late 19th century and takes as its core the notion that sexual behavior determines a person's identity and therefore defines (to a certain extent) one's lifestyle.[33]

In a more general sense, homosexuality also refers to the public transgression of moral codes and behaviors. In Islam, homosexuality often becomes representative of unnatural, disorderly conduct that will eventually lead to chaos and societal decay. Likewise, homosexuals themselves are seen as subversive elements and a direct threat to social order. Therefore, the category of homosexuality can become extended to incorporate anyone who disturbs the mores of Islam (criminals, political opponents, outsiders, or foreigners).[34]

Traditional Muslim law prescribes harsh punishments for homosexual behavior. As mentioned, homosexual behavior is considered to be a form of adultery, thus the same guidelines hold true for heterosexual adulterers. The penalties consist of physical violence: stoning to death for married peoples, and 100 lashes for unmarried people. These extreme punishments, meant to deter homosexual activity, are often performed in public.

However, Islam recognizes that humankind is intrinsically fallible. Therefore, practice is gentler than theory. For corporal punishment to be carried out there must be an eyewitness to the homosexual event or a direct confession. If the accused seeks to repent and reform, punishment may be delayed or never carried out.

In 2003, Egypt's religious leader, Pope Shenouda III of the Coptic Orthodox Church heightened intolerance by calling for a campaign to fight the plague of gays in Egypt. He called for leaders of various faiths to join his crusade. In addition, he commends all those who are against gay marriage and the appointment of gay clergy, which defies "the teachings of the holy book and threaten the stability of marriage, the family, and social morality."[35]

VIOLENCE

To understand the increasing violence against homosexuals in Egypt, one must first be aware of the perception of homosexuality in general. Homosexuality is viewed as a foreign illness, one that must be eradicated in order to maintain stasis in Egyptian life and values. Much of this violence is also politically driven.

One of the men arrested on the Queen was 32-year-old Sherif Farahat, an Israeli and a regular visitor to Egyptian gay hotspots. His particular case was heard in the state security court, one designed to address the political action of suspected terrorists on Egyptian soil. During his trial, the following headline was used in a Cairo newspaper: "Perverts declare war on Egypt."[36]

OUTLOOK FOR THE 21ST CENTURY

Given the numerous antihomosexual acts of the past decade in Egypt, it is likely that this conservative trend will continue. Arab societies used to be much more tolerant of homosexual activity if it was kept private. Now, public displays of homosexuality are viewed as a Western illness that must be cured through various techniques including psychotherapy, social exclusion, and violence.

Many Egyptian homosexuals do not envision changes in Egyptian political or social priorities in the immediate future. Others believe that it is the responsibility of all Egyptians to fight for freedom of intimacy for both heterosexuals and homosexuals (premarital sex is currently not allowed). Some homosexuals do not feel any more victimized than any other marginalized group in the country, such as women. These individuals call for a banding together of all of the marginalized identities to create a powerful social force. In the days following the Queen Boat Affair up until the present day, being gay in Egypt has been viewed as a political rebellion that is dangerous to its participants.

As a result of the complex and layered antigay and anti-Western ideologies that exist in Egyptian culture, it will be a long time before homosexuals will feel safe living openly gay lives on Egyptian soil. Over the past 10 years, much scholarly work has been done on identity and community formation among gay Arabs. This is a positive phenomenon in that it informs a Western audience of the challenges faced by the gay Arab population. Hopefully, as result of education and bringing hidden acts of violence into the light, academics and human rights organizations can help to eventually create a safe environment and sense of community for Arab homosexuals.

RESOURCE GUIDE

Suggested Reading

Abdul Aziz Al-Fawzan, "The Evil Sin of Homosexuality," *Front Page Magazine* (2004), http://www.islamweb.net/english/family/sociaffair/socaff-84.html.

Abdelwahab Bouhdiba, *Sexuality in Islam*, trans. A. Sheridan (London: Routledge and Keagan, 1985).

Bruce Dunne, "Power and Sexuality in the Middle East," *Middle East Report* (Spring 1998).

Egypt Country Information 2007, http://www.infoplease.com/ipa/A0107484.html.

Madelaine Farah, *Marriage and Sexuality in Islam: A Translation of al Ghazzali's Book on the Etiquette of Marriage* (Salt Lake City: University of Utah Press, 1984).

Afdhere Jama, "A Few Good Women," *Huriyah Magazine,* September, 2003, http://www.huriyahmag.com.

Valentine M. Moghadam, *Modernizing Women: Gender and Social Change in the Middle East* (Boulder: Lynne Rienner, 2003).

Tom Musbach, "Egypt Uses Web to Snare Suspected Gays," March 27, 2003, Gay.com, http://channels.gay.com/news/article.html?2003/03/27/1.

Vincenzo Patané, "Homosexuality in the Middle East and North Africa," in *Gay Life and Culture: A World History,* ed. Robert Aldrich (New York: Universe Publishing, 2006).

Geoff Puterbaugh, "North Africa," in *The Encyclopedia of Homosexuality,* vol. 11, ed. Wayne Dynes (New York: Garland Publishing, 1990).

Maarten Schlid, "Islam," in *The Encyclopedia of Homosexuality,* vol. 1, ed. Wayne Dynes (New York: Garland Publishing, 1990).

UNAIDS, "Egypt Country Report 2007," UNAIDS, www.unaids.org.

Brian Whitaker, *Unspeakable Love: Gay and Lesbian Life in the Middle East* (Los Angeles: University of California Press, 2006).

Brian Whitaker, "Behind the Veil: Lesbian Lives in the Middle East," *Diva Magazine,* July 2006, http://www.divamag.co.uk/diva/features.asp?AID=1677.

Brian Whitaker, "Homosexuality on Trial in Egypt," *The Guardian,* November 19, 2001.

Web Sites

Bint el Nas Association for Arab Lesbians, www.bintelnas.org.
Bint el Nas is an international Arab lesbian association that maintains an informational Web site and published a biannual literary journal.

The Gay and Lesbian Arabic Society, www.glas.org.
Established in the United States in 1988, GLAS is an international organization that aims to promote positive images of gays and lesbians living in both Arab and non-Arab communities. Another goal is to provide a network and educational resources for members of homosexual Arab communities.

Gay Middle East, www.gaymiddleeast.com.
A comprehensive and diverse news source for those interested in homosexual issues in the Middle East. Provides links to articles from a variety of Middle Eastern, American, and British news sources. Gay tourism information is also available.

Video/Films

Alexandria Again and Forever (*Iskanderija, kaman oue kaman,* 1990).
Alexandria...Why? (*Iskanderija...Lih?,* 1979).
Alley of the Pestle (*Zuqaaq al-Midaqq,* 1963).
An Egyptian Story (*Hudduta Misrija,* 1982).
Daughter of Pasha in Charge (*Bint el-bash el-mudir,* 1938).
Miss Hanafi (*Al Anissa Hanafi,* 1954).
The Malatily Bath (*Hammam al-Malathily,* 1973).

NOTES

1. "Egypt Country Information 2007," http://www.infoplease.com/ipa/A0107484.html.
2. Ibid.
3. Geoff Puterbaugh, "North Africa," in *The Encyclopedia of Homosexuality,* vol. 1, ed. Wayne Dynes (New York: Garland Publishing, 1990), 22.
4. Brian Whitaker, "Homosexuality on Trial in Egypt," *The Guardian,* November 19, 2001.

5. Brian Whitaker, *Unspeakable Love: Gay and Lesbian Life in the Middle East* (Los Angeles: University of California Press, 2006), 14.

6. Bint el Nas is a Web site dedicated to serving the needs of lesbian, bisexual, and transgender women: www.bintelnas.org

7. U.S. Center for Disease Control and Prevention, "Religious Figures in Egypt Argue over Virtue of Sex Education," April, 8, 2005, CDC HIV/Hepatitis/STD/TB Prevention News Update. http://www.thebody.com/content/art25758.html (accessed September 23, 2009).

8. GayMiddleEast.Com, "Egyptian Teenager Sentenced for Gay Internet Posting," December 2, 2004, El Akhbar in Cairo. http://www.gaymiddleeast.com/news/article31.htm (accessed September 23, 2009).

9. Behind the Mask, "The Rights of Lesbian and Gay Teachers and Education Personnel: 2001–2004 Triennal Report." http://74.125.155.132/search?q=cache:98_Qe7T3X4J:download.ei-ie.org/docs/IRISDocuments/Human%2520and%2520Trade%2520Union%2520Rights/Gays%2520and%2520Lesbians/Trienniel%2520Survey%2520on%2520LGBT%25202006/2008-00125-01-E.doc+egypt+gay+discrimination+schools&cd=10&hl=en&ct=clnk&gl=us&client=safari (accessed September 23, 2009).

10. UNICEF, "HIV/AIDS-Egypt." http://www.unicef.org/egypt/hiv_aids.html (accessed September 23, 2009).

11. Patrick Letellier, "Egyptians Decry 'gay' U.S. Abusers in Iraq," *PlanetOut,* May 17, 2004. Yale Global Online. http://yaleglobal.yale.edu/content/egyptians-decry-gay-us-abusers-iraq (accessed September 23, 2009).

12. Maarten Schlid, "Islam," in *The Encyclopedia of Homosexuality,* vol. 1, ed. Wayne Dynes (New York: Garland Publishing, 1990), 618.

13. Whitaker, *Unspeakable Love,* 18–21.

14. Ibid., 25.

15. Ibid.

16. Ibid., 26.

17. Human Right's Watch, www.hrw.org.

18. Afdhere Ama, "A Few Good Women," *Huriyah Magazine,* September 2003, http://www.huriyahmag.com.

19. Whitaker, *Unspeakable Love,* 22.

20. UNAIDS, Egypt Country Report 2007, www.unaids.org.

21. Ibid.

22. Ibid.

23. Ibid.

24. Ibid.

25. Ibid.

26. Ibid.

27. Vincenzo Patané, "Homosexuality in the Middle East and North Africa," in *Gay Life and Culture: A World History,* ed. Robert Aldrich (New York: Universe Publishing, 2006), 284.

28. Ibid., 285.

29. Schlid, "Islam," 615.

30. Ibid., 616.

31. Ibid.

32. Whitaker *Unspeakable Love,* 145.

33. Schlid, "Islam," 618.

34. Ibid., 619.

35. Abdul Aziz Al-Fawzan, "The Evil Sin of Homosexuality," IslamWeb, 2004, http://www.islamweb.net/english/family/sociaffair/socaff-84.html.

36. Whitaker, "Homosexuality on Trial in Egypt."

ETHIOPIA

Maria Federica Moscati

OVERVIEW

The Democratic Federal Republic of Ethiopia is situated in the Horn of Africa. It borders on Eritrea in the north, Djibouti and Somalia in the east, Somalia and Kenya in the south, and Sudan in the west. The Federal Democratic Republic of Ethiopia is divided into nine regions on the basis of ethnic federalism, plus two autonomous cities: the capital Addis Ababa (meaning "new flower") and Dire Dawa.

Ethiopia is one of the oldest countries in the world with a history that can be traced back to the beginning of the Axumite Empire in the first century B.C., if not earlier. The country converted to Christianity in the third century A.D., and was ruled thereafter by a series of imperial dynasties, the most famous of which was the

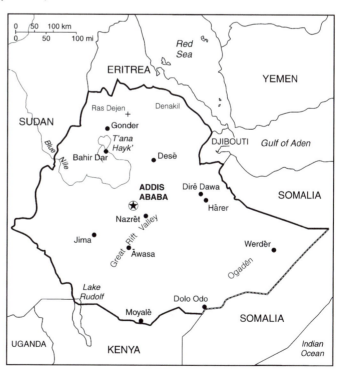

Solomonic Dynasty, which claimed to be descended from King Solomon and the Queen of Sheba. Emperor Haile Selassie I was the last of the Solomonic emperors to rule Ethiopia. Under Haile Selassie's reign, Ethiopia was invaded and occupied (1935–1941) by fascist Italy. In 1974, Haile Selassie was deposed and murdered in a *coup d'etat* led by the Soviet-backed Marxist-Leninist military *junta*, the *Derg*, headed by Mengistu Haile Mariam. Mengistu, later to be found guilty of genocide, established a one-party communist state; tens of thousands of Ethiopians were killed in his program, known as the Ethiopian Red Terror. Those who were not murdered were subjected to starvation, drought, and several wars including the Ogaden War with Somalia (1977–1978), and in the conflict with Eritrea (1962–1991). Mengistu's regime was eventually defeated in May 1991 by a coalition of rebel forces named the Ethiopian People's Revolutionary Democratic Front (EPRDF) and a transitional government was formed in July 1991 under Meles Zenawi. The Constitution of the Federal Democratic Republic of Ethiopia was adopted in December 1994, and Ethiopia's first multiparty elections were held in May and June of 1994, though these were boycotted by most of the opposition parties. The EPRDF has twice been re-elected under Zenawi's premiership (in 2000 and 2005), although the May 2005 elections were marred by violence and political detentions. Eritrea seceded from Ethiopia in May 1993.

OVERVIEW OF LGBT ISSUES

LGBT people in Ethiopia cannot express their identities, as homosexuality is a criminal offence and it is not socially accepted. LGBT people are not protected by law against discrimination or homophobia. As explained here, the Revised Criminal Code refers to homosexuality as sexual deviation.

Consequently, LGBT people live in fear and do not expose themselves to possible homophobic acts. LGBT are invisible or hidden. It is even suggested on Web sites to use false names to avoid arrest.

It is difficult to collect data regarding the LGBT community in Ethiopia due to several issues: namely, LGBT people are generally considered not to be part of the Ethiopian culture, thus few will acknowledge their presence. Additionally, Ethiopia is facing dramatic social and economic problems that do not permit a focus on LGBT issues by the government.

EDUCATION

Until the mid-20th century, education in Ethiopia was primarily exclusive to the province of the Ethiopian Orthodox Church, although several schools were also established by European missionaries. Since the formation of the Democratic Federal Republic, education has been regulated by state law and is compulsory for six years. Literacy currently stands at 42 percent of the population over 15 years of age.

EMPLOYMENT AND ECONOMICS

Ethiopia is one of the poorest countries in the world. Ethiopia's economy is primarily agricultural, with agriculture accounting for almost half of the GDP, as well as for 80 percent of total employment and 60 percent of exports (mainly coffee, oilseeds, sugar, and flowers). Conflict with Eritrea and civil conflict in other parts of the country, such as the Ogaden, together with recurrent drought have contributed to Ethiopia's economic problems. An estimated five million people were dependent on emergency food aid in 2007.

There are no records concerning discrimination in the work place based on sexual orientation.

SOCIAL/GOVERNMENT PROGRAMS

There are no specific state programs for the LGBT community. However, there are several projects to assist with the prevention of HIV/AIDS. Indeed,

NGOs and international organizations have developed programs with the Government of Ethiopia to reduce the transmission of HIV among children, youth, and women.[1]

SEXUALITY/SEXUAL PRACTICES

Ethiopian sexual mores are strongly influenced by religion, which views homosexuality as a sin. This vision contributes to the stigma against people who contract HIV/AIDS. Sexual liberty and chastity are protected by the Revised Criminal Code, Article 620 to 628. Generally speaking, men, women, and children are protected from rape and abuses.

It is very difficult for LGBT people to "come out" and meet. However, even though there are no data revealing how homosexual LGBT Ethiopians are trying to meet, it has been pointed out how the return of the Ethiopian Diaspora and the introduction of the Internet offer more opportunities for the LGBT community to meet.[2] Indeed, associations that work for the support of the rights of LGBT people are creating connections and are trying to work together.[3]

FAMILY

The Revised Family Code Proclamation No.213/2000, which came into force on July 4, 2000, is designed to bring existing Ethiopian family law up to date with the country's socioeconomic panorama. This proclamation states that the family is conceptualized as the natural basis of society and the state. Marriage—namely a union between a man and a woman—is based on the free consent of the spouses and their equality. Ethiopian law provides for civil marriage, while at the same time recognizing religious and other customary marriages. Article 13 rules that the habitual performance of sexual acts by one spouse with a person of the same sex is viewed as a fundamental error in consent and can be used to invalidate the marriage. The last section of Article 13 provides that the spouse who concludes marriage due to this error in consent can apply to the court to order its dissolution.

COMMUNITY

As a result of the criminalization of homosexuality in Ethiopia, together with the social stigma attached to being homosexual, Ethiopia's gay community is by necessity virtually invisible.

Homosexuality is widely seen as a sin or disease in Ethiopia. The coming-out process, therefore, tends to be hidden, making it difficult both to estimate the number of LGBT people in Ethiopia and to find out about their activities. Several testimonies published on the Internet[4] refer to episodes of intolerance and homophobia. Moreover, even though historical research shows that homosexuality was known in ancient Africa,[5] homosexuality is nonetheless commonly understood as part of Western culture, and is used to underline the independence of African states from their former colonial rulers.

Despite this situation, several initiatives for the rights of LGBT Ethiopians have been undertaken in both the country and abroad. The aim of these initiatives is to support homosexuals at every stage of their lives, from coming out onwards. Collaborating with similar organizations in other parts of Africa, Ethiopian LGBT associations on the Internet are working hard to create a network that will give a voice to homosexuals in Ethiopia.

HEALTH

HIV/AIDS affects 4.4 percent of Ethiopia's population, amounting to about 1.5 million people. There are no well-documented records about the effect of HIV/AIDS on gay men, lesbian women, transsexuals, and transgender individuals.[6]

In February 2004, Ethiopia signed "The Johannesburg Statement on Sexual Orientation, Gender Identity, and Human Rights." The statement, signed by several African states, asked the African member governments, and the United Nations, to support actions for the protection of rights of LGBT people. The statement highlights how LGBT people are denied access to health care and omitted from HIV prevention programs.[7]

POLITICS AND LAW

LGBT issues are not part of the political agenda in Ethiopia, and so LGBT people are beneficiaries of only ad hoc projects to promote and protect their rights. The lack of inclusion of LGBT's in the political agenda is due to the criminal law, which identifies homosexuality as a crime.

The Constitution of the Federal Democratic Republic of Ethiopia, adopted on December 8, 1994, provides the principle of equality in Article 25. The article states that sex and gender cannot be used as elements to discriminate. Sexual orientation is not included in this protection, which in turn opens the door to discrimination again homosexuals

Homosexuality in Ethiopia is a crime. The Criminal Code of the Federal Republic of Ethiopia, which came into effect on May 9, 2005, dedicates Title IV to the "Crimes against Morals and the Family." Section II of Chapter I focuses on "Sexual Deviations," which includes (Article 629) "Homosexual and other Indecent Acts."

Women and men who perform a sexual or any indecent act with a person of the same sex are liable for punishment by imprisonment. The basic penalty can be extended when the general aggravation listed in Article 630 occurs. Thus, the penalty of one year's imprisonment can be extended to a maximum of ten years when the accused is found guilty of having taken unfair advantage of the material or mental distress of the person with whom the sexual act was performed; or of having taken advantage of the authority exercised over that person by virtue of the office or capacity of the accused as guardian, tutor, protector, teacher, master, or employer in order to cause that person to perform or submit to the sexual act; or if the accused is found to be making a profession of such activities.

Furthermore, as the last section of Article 630 rules, homosexual acts can be punished by rigorous imprisonment of between three and 15 years, where the sexual acts are found to have been compelled by violence, intimidation or coercion, by trickery or fraud; or when the accused is found to have taken unfair advantage of the victim's inability to resist or to defend himself, or of their feeble-mindedness or unconsciousness; or when the accused has subjected his victim to acts of cruelty or sadism, or has knowingly transmitted to them a venereal disease; or when the [victim] has been driven to suicide by distress, shame or despair as a result of the sexual act or acts.

The legal framework on the criminalization of homosexuality also includes the crime of "Homosexual and other Indecent acts performed on minors" in Article 631 of the Criminal Code. This article provides a general punishment of imprisonment for between three and 15 years for anyone who performs a homosexual act on a minor, where the child is between 13 and 18 years of age; and between 15 and 25 years where the minor is below 13 years of age.

Article 631 states that a woman found to have performed a homosexual act on a female minor should be punished with rigorous imprisonment for a maximum of 10 years, whatever the age of the minor. The special treatment of female homosexuality in Ethiopian criminal law has not been fully explained either in the law or in jurisprudence.

The final part of Article 631 emphasizes that imprisonment is also the punishment for the performance of "other indecent acts" on a minor, although such acts are not defined. This lack of adequate definition increases the probability of discrimination and the prosecution of cases that are denied a proper possibility of defense.

RELIGION AND SPIRITUALITY

Culturally, the most influential religion in Ethiopia is the Ethiopian Orthodox Church. However, a high percentage of Ethiopia's population is Muslim. Ethiopia also contains many Christians of other denominations, together with people belonging to many different animist and other traditional religions. Among all of these religions there is a general hostility to sodomy.

Indeed, in December 2008 the Orthodox Church, the Roman Catholic Church, and the Protestant Churches adopted a resolution stating that homosexuality, defined as the "pinnacle of immorality," is the cause of pedophilia and sexual abuse. The principal aim of the resolution was to ask to the Parliament to constitutionally ban homosexuality.[8]

VIOLENCE

Web sites report violence against gay men. Furthermore, letters are being sent to blogs and other sites denouncing violence based on sexual orientation. However, according to the U.S. Department refers there are no official reported cases or instances of violence enacted upon LGBT people in Ethiopia.[9]

OUTLOOK FOR THE 21ST CENTURY

The criminalization of homosexual acts means that life for gay men, lesbian women, transgender, and transsexuals in Ethiopia is not easy. Several other factors, including religion, culture, and politics contribute to the difficulties they face. Moreover, Ethiopia's severe economic problems mean that attention is often focused more on basic needs than on issues related to sexual orientation.

Even with the support of the initiatives previously mentioned, significant progress towards full recognition of LGBT rights will be possible only with an accurate analysis of the social and cultural climate facing gays in Ethiopia in the 21st century.

RESOURCE GUIDE

Selected Reading

Daniel Iddo Balcha, *Homosexuality in Ethiopia,* Master's thesis, Lund University, Faculty of Social Science, Spring 2009, http://www.essays.se/essay/62c941a340/.

Minasse Haile, "Comparing Human Rights in Two Ethiopian Constitutions: The Emperor's and the Republic's. Cucullus Non Facit Monachum," *Cardozo Journal of International Law and Comparative Law* 13, no. 1 (2005).

Helen Pankhurst, *Gender, Development and Identity: An Ethiopian Study* (London: Zed Books, 1992).

Richard Pankhurst, *The Ethiopians: A History* (Oxford: Blackwell, 1998).

Will Roscoe and Stephen Murray, eds., *Boy-Wives and Female-Husbands: Studies of African Homosexualities* (New York: Palgrave, 1998).

Bahru Zewde, *A History of Modern Ethiopia 1855–1991* (Athens: Ohio University Press, 2001).

Web Sites

Behind the Mask, www.mask.org.za.
  Pan-African Web site with information about LGBT people in Africa.
Global Gayz, www.globalgayz.com.
  A charitable Web site on travel and culture. The site offers stories, pictures, and reports on the lives of LGBT people in 190 countries.
Meskel Square, www.meskelsquare.com.
  A Web log by Andrew Heavens on Africa. The blog features stories about LGBT people in Africa.

Organizations

Behind the Mask, www.mask.org.za.
  Nonprofit media organization publishing news regarding LGBT rights in Africa.
Human Rights Watch, www.hrw.org.
  Based in the United States. Human Rights Watch provides a detailed section of their Web site dedicated to LGBT rights worldwide and has a country section on Ethiopia.

NOTES

1. USAID, "Ethiopia," http://www.usaid.gov/our_work/global_health/aids/Countries/africa/ethiopia.html; Save the Children, http://www.savethechildren.net/ethiopia/key_wprk/hiv.html; UNICEF, http://www.unicef.org/ethiopia/activities.html.

2. Daniel Iddo Balcha, *Homosexuality in Ethiopia,* Master's thesis, Lund University, 2009, www.essay.se/essay/62c941a340.

3. Behind the Mask, http://www.mask.org.za/article.php?cat=ethiopia&id=2091.

4. Behind the Mask, http://www.mask.org.za/article.php?cat=62.

5. Will Roscoe and Stephen Murray, eds., *Boy-Wives and Female-Husbands: Studies in African Homosexualities* (New York: Palgrave, 1998).

6. USAID, "Ethiopia."

7. Human Rights Watch, http://hrw.org/en/node/19222.

8. Behind the Mask, http://www.mask.org.za/article.php?cat=ethiopia&id=2131

9. U.S. Department of State, http://www.state.gov/g/drl/rls/hrrpt/2008/af/119001.htm.

GHANA

Benjamin de Lee

OVERVIEW

A little smaller than Oregon, Ghana is a West African country on the Bight of Benin, a large gulf bordered by several West African countries. Ghana's southern coastal lands are tropical and humid, with some jungle remaining, while the rest of the country stretches northward to arid dry savannahs.

In 1957, Ghana was the first sub-Saharan African country to receive independence. A former British colony, it was economically prosperous but a series of disastrous coups and dictatorial mismanagement mired the country in continuous economic woe. However, since the 1980s and the approval of a new constitution and multiparty elections, Ghana has become one of Africa's most stable and vibrant democracies, with a truly free press and open criticism of government officials. The current president, John Kufuor, is barred from seeking a third term.

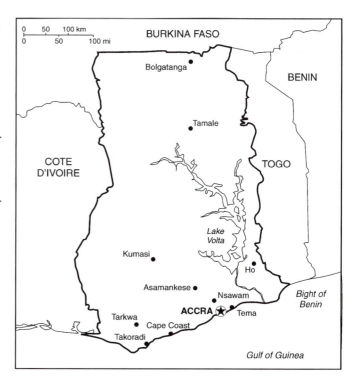

Ghana's transition to a liberal democracy has not been smooth. Postindependence was marked by a series of dictatorships that denied basic civil liberties. None of these regimes, however, were cruel or brutal, like dictatorships elsewhere in Africa. Most of them failed on account of economic mismanagement. The 1992 constitution guarantees basic civil liberties and an independent judiciary. The press in Ghana is free, and Ghanaians take pride in their civil liberties and actively engage in political debate, protest, and discussion. Still, corruption is a problem, and police have been known to engage in intimidation and bribery.

Ghana is one of the wealthier countries in sub-Saharan Africa. Recent high prices for gold and cocoa have sustained high rates of economic growth. Regardless, almost one-third of the population lives in poverty, and Ghana was still a recipient of debt relief in 2002. Recent discoveries of large petroleum reserves off the coast promise future economic development. The country has worked hard to develop a tourist infrastructure, but a tourism boom has yet to begin.

Ghana has a navy, army, and an air force, but its armed services are quite small. Service is voluntary, and the military consumes 0.8 percent of the country's gross domestic product.[1]

OVERVIEW OF LGBT ISSUES

Ghanaian homosexuals, as those in many African nations, are invisible. Ghanaians will frequently deny that homosexuality exists in their country, although attitudes toward it may vary. In traditional animism, same-sex unions were recognized and homosexual practices were tolerated.[2] In fact, individual Ghanaians may express relatively liberal attitudes toward homosexual acts while expressing disapproval or disgust toward homosexuality or gay individuals. Many Ghanaian men claim that homosexual experiences are quite common.[3] Ghanaians think nothing of men holding hands in public or affectionately embracing one another, signs of affection that are not any indication of a sexual relationship. Ghanaian men think nothing of living together or even sharing a bed. Thus, it is easy for homosexual acts to take place and for homosexual relationships to remain invisible. At the same time, many gay Ghanaian men claim that people are very suspicious of homosexuality, and young men that do not have girlfriends or get married are assumed to be gay, and thus face discrimination.[4]

However, things are changing in Ghana. More and more gay Ghanaian men and lesbians are demanding an end to the silence and invisibility. There are increased hostilities toward gay men in particular. Religious leaders and politicians have made a point of explicitly condemning homosexuality and claiming that it is contrary to Ghanaian culture and values and is illegal. Gay men in particular have begun organizing, and in 2006 Prince MacDonald, president of the Gay and Lesbian Association of Ghana, attempted to host an international conference in Ghana. The government, however, forbade the conference and even launched an investigation to criminally prosecute its organizers.[5] The Ghanaian media has begun to discuss homosexuality, with a lively debate that is far from over and is reminiscent of the debate on homosexuality in more conservative parts of the United States. At the same time, the media does not necessarily report evenly on injustices or rights violations that gays and lesbians sometimes face. While many gays and lesbians in Ghana claim oppression, others still insist that Ghana is a relatively tolerant society where homosexuality remains a tolerated but barely acknowledged phenomenon.

EDUCATION

Ghana has a basic primary and secondary education system, with technical schools and several universities. Instruction is primarily in English. HIV/AIDS awareness has become a focus in the school system, although abstinence is sometimes emphasized over safe-sex practices, and homosexual practices are rarely addressed.

EMPLOYMENT AND ECONOMICS

Ghana has an unemployment rate of 11 percent. However, over 28 percent are still below the poverty line, and many Ghanaians are subsistence farmers, craftsmen, and other laborers who do not have a steady income.

Gay men claim that they are particularly economically vulnerable. Many claim that they would lose their jobs if their sexual orientation were known. Many gay men who move to the cities and lack education or employment become sex workers.[6]

SOCIAL/GOVERNMENT PROGRAMS

There are no social or government programs for gays and lesbians in Ghana. In fact, HIV/AIDS programs only mention heterosexual contact as a means of transmission of the virus. LGBT organizations in Ghana are demanding recognition and support from the government. The two biggest challenges are government support and education in the area of HIV/AIDS, and equal protection under the law.

SEXUALITY/SEXUAL PRACTICES

While Ghanaians may be uncomfortable discussing sex and sexuality, most feel that sex is a basic human need. Ghanaian men claim that same-sex contacts are relatively common, but few consider themselves gay. Men who take the penetrative role (top) in particular do not usually consider themselves to be gay. Many men have both men and women as sexual partners. *Gay* is a designation usually reserved for those who take the passive role. Safe-sex awareness is a problem in Ghana, as sex education programs do not address or mention homosexual acts.

FAMILY

The family in West Africa can take many forms. Polygamy, even by Christians who supposedly disavow it, is common, although the wives may not all live in the same household. Single mothers are not unusual, and large extended families are not uncommon. Cousins and other relatives may all live in the same house, for work or economic reasons, or because of tradition. It can be difficult for an outsider to untangle the family relationships in a typical Ghanaian household. Someone may describe another male or female as a brother or sister, but upon further inquiry, the stated sibling may be a cousin.

For the most part, gays and lesbians report having a very difficult time coming out to family members.[7] However, the reasons for ostracism of a gay family member are complex. Ghana, like much of West Africa, is a shame-based society. Certain things connected to sexuality, like homosexuality or AIDS, whether contracted from homosexual or heterosexual contact, symbolize moral deviation and degeneracy, while an unplanned pregnancy or adultery does not. Many Ghanaians are devout Christians or Muslims and feel that their religion disapproves of homosexuality. Others feel that it is the duty of a child to have more children, to carry on the family name and customs. Yet, some report that Ghanaian families are generally tolerant, especially if the family member does not admit to being gay.[8] Ghanaians actually have quite liberal attitudes toward sex and sexuality. The rhetoric of clergy and political leaders may emphasize traditional heterosexual monogamy, but premarital sex is common. Adultery is relatively common, and few parents will ostracize a daughter for getting pregnant out of wedlock. At the same time, Ghanaians are not comfortable discussing sex and are largely silent on the subject. Parents and children almost never discuss sex. Thus, the silence about homosexuality applies to all aspects of sexuality.

COMMUNITY

Efforts by gays and lesbians to organize have been met with considerable opposition in Ghana. The Internet has played an increasingly important role in helping gays and lesbians to meet and organize. It is reported that there are gay bars in Accra, and gay and lesbian organizations operate clandestinely to educate and help gay and lesbian Ghanaians. Other human rights groups, otherwise well-organized and vigilant in Ghana, admit that they do not want to tackle civil rights violations against gays and lesbians because of the public disapproval it would bring.[9]

HEALTH

HIV/AIDS is a major issue in Ghana as in most of Africa. Ghana, however, like many other West African nations, has had a lower rate of HIV infection, perhaps because of the prevalence of male circumcision, common even among non-Muslims.[10] Thus, HIV/AIDS is not just a gay issue in Ghana, but also a societal and developmental issue. However, it is not necessarily the most pressing concern in spite of the attention and funding it has received from the West. Most Ghanaians still lack access to sufficiently clean drinking water. Malaria continues to be a pressing concern. Issues of malnutrition are still present, especially for the poor, both urban and rural. Other tropical illnesses, like schistosomiasis and guinea worm, are still problems in rural areas. Most of the population does not have access to adequate health care for any of these pressing health concerns, including HIV/AIDS. In addition, the stigma attached to HIV/AIDS leads many Ghanaians to avoid seeking treatment or even getting tested when they have symptoms. Many Ghanaians feel a great stigma attached to sexually transmitted diseases (STDs) and will not get treatment, even for easily curable STDs.

Gays and lesbians still face unique problems in receiving adequate health care. It is reported that hospitals require a person to report or bring his or her sexual partner for treatment if he is diagnosed with an STD. Thus, many gay men in particular would rather not get treatment. Also, ignorance is a huge problem. HIV/AIDS education programs often do not address homosexual sex practices, and many men, both homosexual and bisexual, believe that HIV/AIDS can only be contracted from sex with a woman.[11] Indeed, some men claim to prefer gay sex specifically to avoid contracting HIV.[12]

POLITICS AND LAW

Article 105 of the Penal Code (1960) forbids "unnatural carnal knowledge" with anyone. While it does not explicitly illegalize homosexual practices, it has been used to prosecute homosexual men. In 2003, four young men were sentenced to two years in prison each for engaging in homosexual acts.[13] In 2007, a British tourist was charged with "unnatural carnal knowledge" after police searching him at the airport found pictures of him having sex with a Ghanaian. He was held in jail and fined.[14] More recently, Ghana has gained the reputation of being a bit of a gay destination, and many Ghanaian gay men post profiles on the Internet on Web sites like gaydar.co.uk.

In addition, gays and lesbians receive little or no support, or even recognition, from the government. Moreover, they are often not granted equal protection under the law, nor are gays and lesbians given protection from crime if the perpetrators of the crime accuse the victim of being homosexual. When the government banned the planned 2006 gay and lesbian conference in Ghana, Information Minister Kwamena Bartels claimed that organizers and those who approved the conference would be prosecuted and punished, but it was not made clear what law they broke.[15] While the conference did not take place, in the end, no one was officially prosecuted for any crime.

The incident involving the cancelled conference reveals a more recent trend in Ghanaian politics. In general, there is silence on the subject of homosexuality, and many in Ghana, including the government, seem to prefer that gay Ghanaians remain a silent minority. However, when the issue does arise, often by gays and lesbians themselves, the condemnations are vociferous and extreme. Articles on *www.ghanaweb.com* either condemn homosexuality or appeal for an end to silence by recognizing that homosexuality is a disease and problem afflicting the country, although there are also voices for toleration.[16]

RELIGION AND SPIRITUALITY

A majority of Ghanaians belong to an organized religion. Almost 70 percent are Christian, 15 percent are Muslim, and over 8 percent practice traditional religion, usually some form of animism.[17]

Regardless of one's religions, many Ghanaians freely combine Christianity or Islam with more traditional beliefs, like ancestor veneration or animism. For many Ghanaians, there is no contradiction. Likewise, many who practice polygamy see no contradiction with their own Christian beliefs. In spite of these more inclusive attitudes toward traditional beliefs and polygamy, many Christians take a very traditional stance towards homosexuality. African Anglican leaders, including those in Ghana, expressed outrage at the Protestant Episcopal Church of America's consecration of the openly gay bishop Eugene Robinson.[18] It is reported that some groups, like the Pentecostals, exorcise homosexuals to rid them of the demon that they believe has caused homosexuality.

VIOLENCE

In general, Ghana is not a violent society, and it has much lower levels of violent crime compared to other West African nations like Cote d'Ivoire and Nigeria. Gays and lesbians claim that they are frequently the victims of violence and that they are afraid to go the police for fear that they will be the victims of more violence, or be charged with some other crime.

OUTLOOK FOR THE 21ST CENTURY

Ghana is on the cusp of positive change in many ways. It is one of Africa's most successful and stable democracies. It has experienced steady economic growth.

As a healthy and stable democracy, it has the potential to become a place where gays and lesbians can openly assert their place in society and demand civil rights. While same-sex unions may not be approved as they have been in South Africa, Ghana may very well become the next country in Africa to completely decriminalize homosexual acts. Gays and lesbians in Ghana are beginning to pursue community organization, and are beginning to assert their identity. At the same time, there has been a backlash by more conservative forces in Ghanaian society who do not want any recognition for gays and lesbians in Ghana, or who want to continue to claim that homosexuality is a Western problem. While the coming decades promise struggle and continuing discrimination, the end to the silence is seen by many as a positive development.

RESOURCE GUIDE

Suggested Reading

Aart Hendriks, R. Tielman, and E. van der Veen, eds., *The Third Pink Book: A Global View of Lesbian and Gay Liberation and Oppression* (Buffalo, NY: Prometheus Books, 1993).

J. O. Murray and W. Roscoe, eds., *Boy-Wives and Female Husbands: Studies of African Homosexualities* (New York: St. Martin's Press, 1998).

Web Sites

Ghana: Golden Anniversary, http://journalism.berkeley.edu/projects/mm/luckie/index.html.

> Report by American journalism student who spent time in Ghana researching the LGBT community.

Ghanaweb, www.ghanaweb.com.

> Web site for and by Ghanaians covering many issues concerning Ghana. Includes news stories, editorials, and blogs on the subject of homosexuality. Includes personal ads from Ghanaian gays and lesbians in the classified section.

NOTES

1. All statistics are from Ghana (2008). CIA World Factbook. https://www.cia.gov/library/publications/the-world-factbook/geos/gh.html (accessed on May 16, 2008).

2. J. O. Murray and W. Roscoe, eds., *Boy-Wives and Female Husbands: Studies of African Homosexualities* (New York: St. Martin's Press, 1998).

3. Nii Ajen, "West African Homoeroticism: West African Men who Have Sex with Men," in *Boy-Wives and Female Husbands: Studies of African Homosexualities,* ed. J. Murray and W. Roscoe (New York: St. Martin's Press, 1998), 128.

4. Prince, "Gay in Ghana: From Gay Bashing to Aids," *The Gully,* June 24, 2004, http://www.thegully.com/essays/gaymundo/040623_gay_life_ghana.html (accessed May 16, 2008).

5. "Ghanaian Gay Conference Banned," *BBC News,* 2006, http://news.bbc.co.uk/2/hi/africa/5305658.stm; and "Ghana Turns Down Homosexuals' Bid for Recognition," *afrol News,* September 5, 2006, http://www.afrol.com/articles/21080.

6. Prince, "Gay in Ghana."

7. Orla Ryan, "Ghana's Secret Gay Community," *BBC News,* March 14, 2007, http://news.bbc.co.uk/2/hi/africa/6445337.stm (accessed May 16, 2008).

8. Murray and Roscoe, *Boy-Wives and Female Husbands.*

9. Ryan, "Ghana's Secret Gay Community."

10. "Fact Sheet: Male Circumcision and HIV," UNAIDS, July 2005, http://data.unaids.org/Publications/Fact-Sheets04/FS_Male_circumcision_26Jul05_en.pdf (accessed May 20, 2008).

11. Prince, "Gay in Ghana."

12. Conversation of the author with native Ghanaians during Peace Corps Volunteer Service, 1999–2001.

13. Mark S. Luckie, "Somewhere over the Rainbow," Ghana Golden Anniversary, 2007, http://journalism.berkeley.edu/projects/mm/luckie/rainbow.html (accessed May 20, 2008).

14. Alexandra Topping, "Briton Charged over Gay Sex in Ghana," *The Guardian,* November 7, 2007, http://www.guardian.co.uk/uk/2007/nov/07/world.gayrights (accessed May 17, 2008).

15. "Ghanaian Gay Conference Banned," *BBC News,* 2006, http://news.bbc.co.uk/2/hi/africa/5305658.stm (accessed May 16, 2008).

16. Dossier: Homosexuality, 2008, Ghana Home Page, http://www.ghanaweb.com/GhanaHomePage/NewsArchive/dossier.php?ID=120.

17. CIA, "Ghana: Statistics," *World Factbook,* 2008, https://www.cia.gov/library/publications/the-world-factbook/geos/gh.html (accessed May 16, 2008).

18. "Ordination of Gay Anglican Bishops—'Ghana cannot comment,'" 2006, Ghana Home Page, http://www.ghanaweb.com/GhanaHomePage/NewsArchive/artikel.php?ID=110387. Despite the title, in the article the Archbishop of Ghana explains that the church cannot make an official pronouncement like the Nigerian church because it is not an independent province. However, the archbishop stated that the Nigerian church represented the opinion of all Africa in its condemnation of the consecration of Eugene Robinson.

KENYA

Nancy Nteere and Tom Ochieng Abongo

OVERVIEW

Kenya is located in the eastern part of Africa. It is bordered by Sudan and Ethiopia to the north, Tanzania and the Indian Ocean to the south, Uganda to the west, and Somalia to the east. Kenya has an area of 219,788 square miles, stretching from sea level in the east to 17,057 feet at the peak of Mount Kenya in the west. Between these two points is what is known as the Kenya Highlands, over 2,952 feet above sea level. The highlands are generally cooler and agriculturally richer than the lowlands, and are divided into two sections by the Great Rift Valley. Mount Kenya is on the eastern side. The Amboseli Game Reserve and Tsavo National Park, both rich in wildlife, are situated in the drier, lower belt of the Kenya Highlands. The coastline of Kenya is approximately 333 miles long. Kenya's approximate flying time from major European cities is 8–10 hours and approximately 16–20 hours from North American cities.

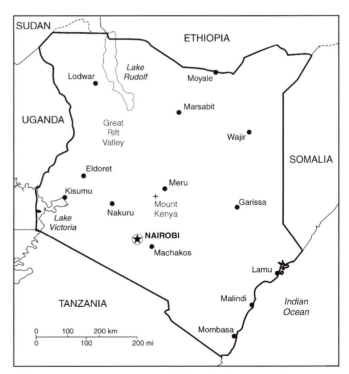

The major cash crops of Kenya are coffee, tea, wheat, corn, and pyrethrum. Livestock farming is also practiced. Kenya's natural resources include limestone, soda ash, salt, barites, rubies, fluorspar, garnets, and wildlife. The currency used in Kenya is the Kenya Shilling (KES).

As of 2007, Kenya has a population of approximately 36.7 million[1] with a higher concentration of people living in the urban areas compared to the rural areas. Traditionally, settlement has been preferred in places where water was easily found. Today, there has been a steady rise of migration from rural to urban areas, as more people are opting to go to the city in search of opportunities and employment.

The population growth rate is 2.8 percent, and the birth rate is 37.89/1000. As of 2008, the estimated infant mortality rate is 56.01/1000 and the estimated life expectancy is 56.64 yrs.[2]

In rural Kenya, the birth rate has increased due to the lack of sexual and reproductive health education. In the urban centers, families opt to have three children on average, as the cost of living is considerably rising. Over 60 percent of Kenyans are under 30 years of age, with 32 percent of the entire population between 15 and 30 years old.[3] In general, the population is slowly declining with the increasing rate of HIV/AIDS, which has in some instances wiped out entire families.

There are approximately 42 tribes in Kenya. The Kikuyu make up the majority of the population at 22percent, followed by the Luhya (14%), Luo (13%), Kalenjin (12%), Kamba (11%), Kisii (6%), and Meru (6%). The combined total of other African tribes makes up 15 percent of the population, while non-Africans compose only one percent.[4] Each tribe has an indigenous language, however English and Swahili are the official languages of Kenya and are most commonly used.

Forty-five percent of Kenyans identify themselves as Protestant, and 33 percent identify as Roman Catholic. Of the remaining population, 10 percent are Muslim, 10 percent practice indigenous beliefs, and two percent practice other religions such as Hinduism or Sikkhism.[5]

Before becoming an official colony in 1920, Kenya was a British protectorate dating back to 1895. By the 1940s, British settlers had acquired a great deal of fertile land in Kenya, commonly known as *the white highlands*. In 1944, Jomo Kenyatta formed the first national organization that gave rise to the Mau Mau rebellion in 1952. The legislative council elected African members in 1957 and lifted the state of emergency in 1960. The Kenya Africa National Union (KANU), and the Kenya Africa Democratic Union (KADU) were formed after Kenyan political parties were legalized. KANU won the general elections that were held in 1961, but refused to form a government until the release of Kenyatta, who had earlier been tried and sent to jail for being a member of the Mau Mau Society, though no proof was determined to support the claim.

Kenya gained its independence from Great Britain in 1963, with Kenyatta becoming the prime minister. In 1964, Kenya became a republic, KADU dissolved itself, and Jomo Kenyatta became the first president. For the remainder of Kenyatta's rule, Kenya remained a one-party state, as he banned an opposition party in 1969. Kenyatta died in 1978 and Daniel Arap Moi became the second president. In 1991, a multiparty system was restored, with several opposition parties. In 2002, the presidential candidate of the National Rainbow Coalition Party, Emilio Mwai Kibaki won the national election. Elections in 2007 were disputed following discrepancies in presidential vote tallying results by the ECK (Electoral Commission of Kenya). The two leading presidential contenders, the incumbent President Mwai Kibaki (Party of National Unity), and Raila Odinga, leader of the ODM (Orange Democratic Movement) agreed to form a coalition government. This coalition resulted in a unique political dispensation where the incumbent, Kibaki, retained his presidential seat and Raila Odinga became the Prime Minister. The next general elections will be held in 2012 and a number of reforms are under way under the auspices of the National Peace and Reconciliation Accord to bring equity, fairness, and justice to all levels of government. President Kibaki is serving his last term, which will end in 2012.

There are three branches in the Kenya military force: the Kenya Army, Kenyan Navy, and the Kenyan Air force. Due to the stigma associated with homosexuality, there has been no mention of same-sex relationship in the military. The military service age is between 18–49 for both men and women, with an obligation bracket of nine years.

OVERVIEW OF LGBT ISSUES

Former president, Daniel Arap Moi has verbally attacked homosexuals and lesbians on various occasions. Moi has said, "Kenya has no room or time for homosexuals and lesbians. Homosexuality is against African norms and traditions, and even in religion it is considered a great sin." In 1999 he also stated that, "it is not right that a man should go with another man or a woman with another woman. It is against African tradition and Biblical teachings."[6] Kenya outlaws homosexuality, especially sexual activities between men. If two gay men are caught together, they are charged with indecent behavior, as the law states they can only be arrested if they are caught in the sex act itself. If there is evidence of homosexual behavior, a penalty of 5–14 years imprisonment, or a cash fine of up to KES 30,000 ($400) is administered. (There is no mention of lesbian relations, but it is assumed that the law applies to them as well.) There have been a few cases in which men have been charged in court for alleged homosexual behavior, but there has not yet been a lesbian who has been arrested with a charge of homosexual activity. It is, however, very unlikely for the police to take action against a suspected homosexual male or female unless some other offense had been reported.

Homosexuality in Kenya has not drawn national attention nor has the topic received much attention from the government. The country assumes that the LGBT community is too small to give it time and attention, so there is very little said about it by the police or politicians. The LGBT organizations and groups are very discreet; a person will not know of them unless he or she is well-connected, which also makes it very rare for police to raid any gay parties. The LGBT groups and organizations rarely disclose involvement in any of their activities, as the general society is quite homophobic, and they may face condemnation or imprisonment. Although there is often a strong negative response from family members or church communities against individual instances of homosexuality and lesbianism, it is unlikely for discreet homosexuals to face prosecution or persecution.

The World Social Forum, held in Nairobi in January 2007, was a major arena where human rights activists, religious leaders, and Kenyan society as a whole came forward and challenged the existence of homosexuals in the country. For the first time in the history of Kenya, a gay man and a lesbian appeared in the media and declared their sexual preferences. At the same time, two of the gay male participants in the forum were chased away from their homes and are currently seeking asylum in different countries. LGBT organizations now operate so as not to antagonize the government.

EDUCATION

There is an unspoken hostility towards homosexual behavior in Kenya. Although the country is struggling with HIV/AIDS, the Kenyan government has excluded any subject or topic that touches on sex education in the school curriculum.

In August 1995, in the quest of spreading knowledge on sex education, the Roman Catholic Archbishop of Nairobi and the Imam of the Jamia Mosque in Nairobi led their congregation in the burning of condoms and sex education books.

According to interviews that were conducted within the LGBT community, most lesbian relationships in Kenya start in boarding schools.[7] The heads of schools have occasionally been summoned to expel a student who showed any homosexual behavior, but due to the fear of losing prospective students, administrations often opt to turn a blind eye to the activities. However, some students have been periodically suspended for a short time if they are suspected of homosexual behavior.

In the curriculum of Kenya, there is recognition of two types of families, the nuclear and extended family. Despite the emergence of single parenthood, there is stigma attached to a family with only one parent. No nongovernmental organizations are geared to assist LGBT children. The children are referred to counseling or seek psychiatric help.

Immediately after independence, the government of Kenya promised free primary education to all children, but this did not come to pass until 2003 due to lack of funding. The education system that was promised was "7-4-2-4." This meant seven years in primary school, four years in high school, two years in upper high school, and four years in university. In 1985, the system changed to 8-4-4, which meant eight years in primary school, four years in high school, and finally four years in university for the students who qualified. This system ensures that all students in Kenya receive basic knowledge to sustain them in their lives, even if they choose to drop out of school.

There are four types of primary schools in Kenya: government-owned, missionary-run, private, and harambee schools. (*Harambee* is a Swahili name that means "pulling together.") Harambee schools are established by communities coming together and raising funds to establish a school in their neighborhood, village, or wherever there is a need. Harambee schools account for almost 80 percent of the schools in Kenya. Seventy-five percent of the secondary schools exist through the harambee effort. Private primary schools are normally more expensive than the other three options, but their students also perform better on final exams. Private schools also typically have fewer students compared to the government schools because of the tuition costs, and the fact that the majority of the government-owned schools provide boarding facilities. At the end of primary school, students traditionally take the final exam known as the Kenya Certificate of Primary Education (K.C.P.E), and the results obtained determine their placement in secondary education.

Depending on the score attained in the K.C.P.E, students opt to study in either private, government, missionary, or harambee secondary schools. In most schools, the students are guided by their career counselors on what subjects to choose, so as to determine their careers. At the end of four years in high school, the students sit for their final exam to earn their Kenya Certificate of Secondary Education (K.C.S.E). The final exam grade determines whether the student can go to university or their choice of career or vocation.

There are eight public universities and 18 private universities in Kenya. The first public university was established in 1970. Grades from the K.C.S.E exams determine acceptance into the public universities. Every year, the grades are raised as more students qualify for free public university due to the introduction of free primary education in 2003. There has been a steady rise in the establishment of private universities as more Kenyans seek higher education. Parents who can afford to do so send their children to different countries to pursue their higher education, as there is still some congestion in the local universities. Basic facilities such as computers and boarding facilities are often lacking in public universities.

Through various acts of parliament, colleges and polytechnic schools have been established by the government to offer technical skills to students who do not attend universities. These institutions offer two or three year diplomas and certificates for technical and professional skills.

Distance learning is also becoming an option for higher education in Kenya. Most universities in Kenya have formed affiliations with universities overseas, and have developed online degree programs in which Kenyan students can study like their counterparts abroad. This trend is gaining popularity with the older generations who never got the chance to attend university, or those who are working full time and need a degree to earn a promotion at work or simply for self achievement.

The government of Kenya is slowly coping with the higher demand for education, despite the overcrowding of classrooms since the introduction of the free primary education and the constant strikes of teachers demanding higher salaries for their services.

The literacy rate in Kenya is 61.5 percent. According to a survey conducted by the Kenya National Bureau of Statistics between June 8 and August 18, 2006, 7.8 million Kenyans still have not acquired the minimum literacy levels and cannot read or write. The survey shows that Kenyans are more familiar with numbers than reading; the percentage of Kenyans who can do basic arithmetic stands at 67.9 percent. This is attributed to the fact that mathematics is a life-supporting skill that even a basic vegetable vendor needs to learn. The urban centers, such as Nairobi and Kisumu record the highest literacy levels, while the coastal areas have the lowest. One of the reasons cited for such low literacy rates in the coastal areas is a tradition of using the Swahili language, as opposed to English.[8]

EMPLOYMENT AND ECONOMICS

The economy of Kenya is dependent on agriculture. At the same time, only four percent of the land is arable. The country is divided into eight provinces: Nairobi, Central, Eastern, North-Eastern, Western, Rift-Valley, Nyanza, and Coast. The three major cities in Kenya are Nairobi, Mombasa, and Kisumu. Employment opportunities in Kenya are scarce due to a slow pace of industrialization, thus the majority of Kenyans are mainly dependent on the informal industrial sectors known locally as the *Jua-Kali* or "Hot Sun" industries, where all forms of work such as vehicle repair, sale of imported second hand clothes, sale of imported second-hand cars, and the sale of handicrafts are done in open grounds. There is a large influx of people migrating from rural to urban areas in search of job opportunities, contributing to the growth of shanty towns within major cities. As the population of young Kenyans who are graduating from high school, middle-level colleges, and universities increases, so too does an increasing scarcity of employment opportunities. Many young people are, in turn, turning to crime, prostitution, and illegal trade as a means of earning a living.

There is currently no recorded statistic of the percentage of the population employed by the government, civil service, or the military. LGBT people in Kenya are more affected than their heterosexual counterparts by lack of employment opportunities. Those who cannot find employment must remain dependent on family members or guardians for sustenance, and often suffer abuse. This situation reduces the self-worth of LGBT people who are faced with having to accept and submit to the demands and conditions of living with relatives and family members.

Employed LGBT individuals in Kenya also face a number of tribulations in the workplace due to homophobia. In Kenya, most organizations and companies do adhere to an equal employment opportunity clause to have equal representation of male and female employees. This clause is actually not based on any national legislation, and is used more as a publicity statement. The biggest challenge, however, has been to fully practice inclusion of LGBT individuals. As such, there is always a silent policy of intolerance towards any person who is seen or suspected to be a homosexual. This is more so in the multinational companies, the civil service, and the electronic media organizations where one's profile might be viewed as being representative of a company's policy. The lack of a basic legal framework to protect the human rights of LGBT people in all sectors of the economy has led to many cases of abuse or assault against LGBT people in the workplace going unreported.

Gay men and lesbians who are independent professionals such as lawyers, doctors, or engineers prefer to keep their sexual orientation secret in order not to lose out on lucrative contracts or clients.

SOCIAL/GOVERNMENT PROGRAMS

The government of Kenya does not recognize the presence or the rights of LGBT people. Therefore, none of the programs and services for its citizenry include a component targeted to the LGBT community. The legal position, as stated in Section 162–165 of the Penal Code, outlaws all homosexual behavior. It is with this in mind that all services provided by the government do not address any issues specifically affecting the LGBT community. The National AIDS Control Council has occasionally involved the LGBT community in workshops that center around HIV/AIDS prevention programs.

SEXUALITY AND SEXUAL PRACTICES

The churches, as well as traditional cultures, have a great influence on sexual practices and on determining what is morally right or wrong. Abortion is illegal in Kenya, except in instances where the pregnancy places the life of the mother in danger. Most clinics, however, operate under the pretense of offering reproductive health services and do offer abortion as a choice of family planning method with the risk of being shut down if discovered. Although the Catholic Church came out strongly and denounced the act of abortion, there are still debates among pro-life and pro-choice activists, and the government has not enforced anti-abortion laws.

In the rural parts of Kenya, sexuality is still a taboo subject especially in communities in which cultural practices override religion. Sex is not discussed between people of the same age-group. Circumcision, which was mandatory in some communities for both boys and girls, was regarded as the passage through which the young men and women would receive sex education from their elders. However, with urbanization and intermarriages some of these customs have been forfeited as there has been a merge of cultures and westernization. For example, in the Kalenjin community, a girl was forced to go through female genital mutilation in order to belong to the community. This was also necessary before she could be married off and also to reduce her urge for sex, which would theoretically help her remain faithful to her husband. However, a community-based organization called *Tumndo Ne Leel* Support Group has introduced sex education among the girls without the cut, thereby encouraging woman to seek education rather than undergoing genital mutilation.[9]

With the emergence of Christianity, the traditional Kenyan cultures have been forced to consider homosexuality as an immoral behavior and yet during the pre-colonial era homosexuals were not shunned or looked down upon. Peer education programs have been initiated by the government in different organizations in order to reach out to youth in fighting the HIV virus.

Religious institutions have not been supportive of introducing sex education in schools and have instead chosen to focus on the morality that surrounds it. There has been continued debate on whether it is the duty of the school, the religious leaders or the parents to educate children on sexuality issues. As a result of the silence that surrounds sexuality, the LGBT community has consequently kept their sexual orientation silent. The draft constitution was rejected by the religious leaders as they cited that it was encouraging homosexuality and yet it should condemn the behavior.[10] For example, Emmanuel Kamau, a gay Kenyan man, confided in his priest about his sexual orientation and the priest recommended him to a church retreat in order to change his lifestyle; after the church realized he would not change his sexual orientation he was kicked out of the church.[11]

FAMILY

According to Kenyan law, marriage is described as a union between a man and a woman and there is no reference to a family consisting of two people of the same gender. There is also no law legalizing two people of the same gender living together. A person who deviates from the societal expectation of a heterosexual relationship is viewed as a hooligan or a rebel against society.

There is limited research and statistics in regard to family, marriage, and divorce in Kenya; this may be attributed to the assumption that a marriage is a solid institution that does not need to be researched.

Setting up a family is highly regarded in the Kenyan culture. A typical family is a nuclear family or single-parent family in the urban setting; however in the rural parts of the country the extended family is common. The number of children per family varies in urban and rural settings. In the urban centers the cost of living is higher, and consequently families opt for fewer children as compared to the rural areas where the cost of living is considerably cheaper.

From the 1960s, a family that did not have a boy child was regarded as incomplete, as a boy was seen as the pillar to a family and the only way of sustaining the family name. In the 21st century, however, there has been a change as more families accept children of either gender with equal love and value. In some cases the girl child has proven to be more of an asset compared to the boy child, because girl children will eventually get married and, as a result, bring a bride price to the family either in the form of cattle or money.

The Kenyan adoption policies are quite stringent in regard to adoption. Currently the Kenya Children's Society is the only licensed adoption agency in Kenya.

The adoption laws prohibit homosexuals or single people from adopting children, and they also give preference to married couples who are financially stable. A marriage certificate is a prerequisite for adoption to be considered.[12]

COMMUNITY

Community is very important in rural Kenya. From the early 1960s, there were certain regions of the country that were designated for different tribes and communities. As such, it was believed that certain groups of people could easily describe the character of a person based on the region they came from.

Each tribe has its own culture, customs, and clans. The clans consist of people who are from the same tribe and share the same customs. In the clan there is a subgroup of people who belong to the same age group. These groups perform activities together, such as cattle grazing, seasonal dances, or arranging for parties in the said community. The clan is an important part of the community, as it is also responsible for punishing any member of their community who does not adhere to the laws that have been set by the council of elders. The elders also participate in organizing ceremonies such as circumcision, harvest dances, and marriage ceremonies.

In the traditional community, an elder is at liberty to punish any young person who is not considered moral. The community is, by itself, a family. In the urban centers the community is a cosmopolitan one. People from different tribes live together and share different cultures and customs. The urban community is not as close-knit as it is in the rural areas; the integration of different cultures, nationalities, religions, and tribes has led to a more diverse and accommodating atmosphere in the cities.

In the northern part of Kenya, the Pokot have accepted as pseudo-hermaphrodites men whose penises are too small to be circumcised. These men are not mocked, however, they are not assigned any gender roles in the community because they are regarded as neither male nor female.

Gay issues are discussed more prominently in Nairobi than in other urban centers. The gay community is quite discreet in its activities; however, among their own groups, they have many activities including parties, tournaments, training, and community services. However, the Penal Code, societal expectations, and homophobic social mores, restrict homosexuals from publicly announcing their events or activities.

Despite the social pressure against homosexuality and lesbianism from the society at large, a number of small LGBT organizations have been formed to fill up the void that currently exists in order to articulate issues affecting homosexuals. However, most of the organizations operate discreetly so that they will not be discovered by the government and will not fall foul of the law that prohibits any form of homosexual practice.

There are several LGBT organizations in Kenya. However they are not registered and some have only a few seasonal members. The first LGBT organization in Kenya was Ishtar, which was formed in 1997. However, due to the lack of support from government and nongovernmental organizations, Ishtar does not have programs or projects as an organization. The Gay and Lesbian Coalition of Kenya (GALCK) was established in 2006 and is the umbrella body of all the independent LGBT organizations. GALCK represents the LGBT organizations in Kenya in national and international forums and offers support services for the LGBT community.

HEALTH

The Ministry of Health has established provincial hospitals in Kenya's eight provinces, which are charged with the responsibility of providing subsidized health services to its citizens. There are also various public health centers run by the government, and church organizations are based at the district level to ease congestion at the main provincial hospitals. Independent private hospitals are also competing to provide health services to the public, though their fees are out of reach for the majority of Kenyans. Despite the efforts of the government to bring medical care to citizens, diseases like malaria, typhoid, tuberculosis, cholera, dysentery, and HIV/AIDS are still proving to be a big challenge to contain in both the urban and rural areas.

The first reported case of HIV/AIDS in Kenya was in September 1984.[13] The notification of the disease was by a Ugandan journalist who made this public knowledge through the East Africa medical journal. Since 1984, HIV has spread rapidly nationwide. The University of Nairobi has occasionally initiated successful programs that target female sex workers in order to curb the spread of the virus and improve their social status. The Population Council of Kenya has, however, gone a step further in advocating for voluntary counseling and testing centers and providing follow-up activities on their effectiveness.

Kenya has declared the HIV/AIDS scourge as a national disaster and various measures have been in place to contain this fast spreading disease. The national HIV prevalence rate in Kenya between the ages of 15–49 is 6.1 percent, the population between the ages of 0–49 living with HIV at the end of 2005 was 1.3 million, and AIDS deaths in both adults and children were reported at 140,000 in the same year.[14] In reality, HIV/AIDS is an issue that is affecting both the heterosexual and homosexual community in Kenya. However, government programs for HIV/AIDS, which are run by the Ministry of Health, do not have any information targeting the LGBT community in terms of prevention and treatment. This has amounted to the LGBT community being ignored in policy decisions made by Ministry of Health officials. There is also a lack of interest by health practitioners to try and understand the health needs of LGBT people.

Little research has been done in Kenya on the health needs of the LGBT community. However, there have been a number of nongovernmental organizations that have made strides in trying to ensure that health services reach the LGBT community. However, these organizations only exist in a few urban areas, leaving the rural LGBT community out of reach.

In August 2005, three GLBT groups organized 25 participants to complete a survey in order to establish existing gaps in regard to access to sex education and sex-related health services among men who have sex with men (MSM) in Kenya. The survey was also designed to form a strong network in addressing health concerns among the MSM. This was a ground breaking dialogue organized by GALEBITRA and Gay Kenya.[15]

The serious health problems that the LGBT community faces in Kenya are sexually transmitted diseases due to inadequate, or lack of, access to specific gay-oriented safe sex materials and improper use of the same where available. The ignorance that is displayed by health officials and staff concerning homosexual practices are always based on stereotypes and traditional beliefs. In most health institutions, LGBT people are ridiculed by homophobic nurses and doctors. This has resulted in a majority of LGBT people using the only option available of visiting quacks and traditional healers for their health needs, leading to many hazardous results. This insensitivity displayed by the health authorities towards health issues affecting LGBT people has compounded the STD/HIV/AIDS problem in Kenya.

A research targeting 500 gay men, conducted between 2004 and 2005 by the National AIDS Control Council indicated an HIV/AIDS prevalence rate of 47 percent.[16] The fight against HIV/AIDS on the part of the government has been one-sided and only targets the heterosexual community. There has not been any attempt to have HIV/AIDS information that educates LGBT people about safe sex, nor are there any provisions of LGBT safe-sex materials. This has resulted in ignorance on the part of the LGBT community in Kenya regarding how to avoid becoming infected with HIV/AIDS. The lack of response by the government in addressing issues affecting the LGBT community in its HIV/AIDS programs defeats much of the effort to reduce the spread of HIV/AIDS as a whole (considering the tendency of LGBT individuals to lead a double life by officially marrying a person of the opposite sex while maintaining secret affairs with partners of the same sex). This is a common trend in Kenya due to the dilemma that many adult LGBT individuals find themselves in while trying to conform to traditional societal norms.

According to leading Kenyan psychiatrist, Frank Njenga, homosexuality cannot be classified as a mental disorder. Njenga further stated that female genital mutilation and homosexuality receive the same moral judgment due to deep cultural beliefs and a lack of understanding of underlying factors.[17]

POLITICS AND LAW

Kenya is a multiparty democracy with presidential and legislative elections held every five years. The president has two term limits of five years each. No political parties currently represented in the legislative assembly have any LGBT representation. Many political leaders avoid openly supporting the LGBT cause for justice. It is always safer for political leaders to use gay bashing language in order to gain political mileage and votes from their supporters and constituents. Politicians in Kenya are, as a whole, against homosexuality, and if a politician makes a stand in support of LGBT people, he or she is sure to lose favor with the electorate.

In June 2007 an intersex inmate in one of the maximum-security prisons in Kenya sued the government for exposing him to ridicule, threats of rape, and molestation in the prison due to his sexuality. The inmate had been charged with a violent robbery. The Kenyan Constitution does not have provisions for the intersexed to receive special facilities and identifies their gender according to their behavior.[18]

Currently, the law does not protect any basic human rights of LGBT individuals. The Penal Code, under Section 162–165, outlaws any homosexual relations in Kenya and defines homosexuality as an "unnatural practice" with a penalty of 5–14 years in prison. There is no mention of lesbian relations in the stipulated law. The law, as currently constituted, makes no distinction between consensual sodomy and rape, and the determination is left at the mercy of legal experts who may apply their own personal view points to arrive at a decision.

The clamor for review of the Kenyan Constitution has been ongoing since 2000. However, the original constitution remains. The constitution review process has been stalled by politicians who want statutory changes made only to enhance their powers, thus denying the common citizen of Kenya the chance of having a constitution in place that would guarantee human rights and freedom. At various forums that were set up to collect views from the public by the government-run Constitution Review Commission, a number of LGBT activists presented their views on the need to have in place a clause in the bill of rights that ensures that no one should be discriminated against because of his or her sexual orientation. The draft that was put through a public referendum in November 2005 was rejected; yet it was devoid of any mention of LGBT rights. This illustrates the apathy that LGBT people face in trying to bring forth issues that are paramount to their welfare as a community.

RELIGION AND SPIRITUALITY

The majority of Kenyans adhere to a Christian faith, while the rest of the population identifies as Muslim, Hindu, Sikh, or they adhere to the traditional African belief system. The largest single Christian institution in Kenya is the Catholic Church, followed by the Anglican Church and other Protestant churches. Religious leaders of all mentioned affiliations have come out strongly to condemn any form of homosexuality in Kenya. The Anglican Church in Kenya has been more vocal against homosexuality than other churches, especially after it broke away from the U.S. Episcopal Church after the consecration of openly gay bishop Eugene V. Robinson.[19] Strong condemnation by church groups has had an impact on the treatment of gays in Kenya. For example, in Kisumu, a city in western Kenya of approximately one million people, cases of abuse against LGBT people have been on the rise following the stand taken by the Anglican Church.

Most gay people who need spiritual nourishment simply disguise themselves and attend church in order to be safe. This has been a source of mental anguish for LGBT people, many of whom seek spiritual guidance from their church but are afraid to openly admit who they are for fear of admonishment.

VIOLENCE

In general, same-sex relations attract negative reactions in Kenya. Gay bashing is a common occurrence in Kenya and many LGBT people have faced the wrath of unruly mobs who are misguided by proclamations made by political and religious leaders against gays. At the family level, many gays and lesbians suffer abuse at the hands of immediate family members who believe that they are bewitched and need cleansing through correctional rape, eviction from home, forced marriage, physical assault, and public humiliation.

Lesbians face more violence than gay men due to the nature of Kenya's patriarchal society. A man in traditional society is supposed to be the head of the family and, by the age of 25, should be ready to pay the price for a bride. A woman, on the other hand, should be ready to be married off between the ages of 18 to 23 years old. Any reverse role for a woman is shunned and not tolerated by immediate family members or the extended family, who believe that the bride price is a source of wealth for them. A woman is always under pressure to be seen to be in courtship with a male partner. The same applies to a man but to a lesser degree, though eyebrows will start to be raised if a man is not seen courting a partner of the opposite sex. Any transgression from the normal channel is a cause of great concern and one is bound to suffer the consequences. A man cannot show affection to another man in public without provoking a reaction. If two men are seen holding hands or kissing in public, epithets such as *shoga* or *msenge*—abusive Swahili words meaning a person of loose morals—are thrown at them.

Emmanuel Kamau, a gay Kenyan activist, appeared on the television and on radio advocating for gay rights during the World Social Forum in 2007. Consequently, he received death threats and was forced to seek asylum in the United States.[20]

OUTLOOK FOR THE 21ST CENTURY

During the 1990s, Kenya had one forum that addressed homosexuality and gay rights. Still, homosexuality still remains a taboo topic not to be talked about in public. The World Social Forum, which was held in Nairobi in January 2007, allowed the gay community in Kenya to come out and declare their existence in the country and to the world. LGBT Kenyans hope the government will review the Constitution and include a draft supporting their rights of association. There are eight key organizations advocating for LGBT rights in Kenya. With the opening up of dialogue and democratic spaces in all spheres in the Kenyan community, the expectations are high among the LGBT community that their voices will be heard.

RESOURCE GUIDE

Suggested Reading

Ed Aarmo, E. Blackwood, and S. E. Wieringa, *How Homosexuality became un-African: The Case of Zimbabwe, Female Desires, Same Sex Relations and Transgender Practices Across Cultures* (New York: Columbia University Press, 1999).

J. Gay and E. Blackwood, *Mummies and Babies and Friends and Lovers in Lesotho: The Many Faces of Homosexuality, Anthropological Approaches to Homosexual Behavior* (New York: Harrington Press, 1986).

Cary Alan Johnson, *Off the Map: How HIV/AIDS Programming is Failing Same-Sex Practicing People in Africa* (New York: International Gay and Lesbian Human Rights Commission, 2007).

Scott Long, A. Widney Brown, and Gail Cooper, *More Than a Name* (New York: Human Rights Watch Publication, 2003).

Ruth Morgan and Saskia Wieringa, *Tommy Boys, Lesbian Men and Ancestral Wives: Female Same Sex Practices in Africa* (Johannesburg: Jacana Media Publisher, 2005).

G. M. Shepherd and Patricia Caplan, eds., *Gender and Homosexuality: Mombasa as a Key to Understanding Sexual Options* (London: Tavistock Publications, 1987).

Web Sites

CLARION Kenya: Center for Law and Research International, http://www.clarionkenya.org. In collaboration with the Human Rights Foundation in Oslo, seven human rights organizations in Kenya have collaborated to initiate a Human Rights House in Kenya. The Human Rights House has in the past addressed issues dealing with gay rights and serves as a vital hub in accessing information concerning gay rights.

Behind The Mask, www.mask.org.za.

> Behind the Mask is an interactive e-zine involving LGBT communities in Africa in the debates surrounding homosexuality issues.

Gay and Lesbian Coalition of Kenya, http://galck.org/.

> The Gay and Lesbian Coalition of Kenya (GALCK) is an umbrella body for gay and lesbian organizations in Kenya. GALCK represents the gay and lesbian organizations at international and local forums and also organizes conferences and workshops nationally. GALCK hosts nine LGBT organizations: Gay Kenya, Minority Women in Action, Ishtar MSM, Equality Now Development Group, Diverse Outing, GALEBITRA Kenya, Kenya Gay and Lesbian Trust, Changing Attitudes and The Other Men In Kenya (TOMIK)

Organizations

Nongovernmental Organizations

Family Health Options Kenya (FHOK), www.fhok.org.

> Established in the 1950s, FHOK was the first family planning movement in Kenya. It encompasses other organizations and aims at establishing safe sex programs and a planned parenthood program in Kenya.

Kenya Association of Professional Counselors, www.kapc.or.ke.

> KAPC provides guidance and counseling to people who are in a transition or change. They also train counsellorship in various fields such as HIV/AIDS and peer educators.

Kenya Human Rights Commission, Tel: 254–020–3874998/9, 38746065/6: www.khrc.or.ke.

> The Kenya Human Rights Commission provides protection and enhancement of basic human rights in the political spheres, social structures, and cultural dimensions of Kenyan culture.

Liverpool Voluntary Counseling and Testing, www.liverpoolvct.org.

> Liverpool VCT has been in partnership with the government of Kenya through the Ministry of Health's National AIDS and Sexually Transmitted Infections Control Program in addressing HIV/AIDS by providing counseling and testing services. In the past they have introduced a program that incorporates men who have sex with men.

Young Women Leadership Institute, www.ywli.or.ke.

> YWLI provides a forum for young women to be sensitized on community issues. They have a wide range of programs that include human rights, advocacy, and organizing intergenerational dialogue forums.

Community-Based Organizations (CBO)

Equality Now! Development Group.

> E-mail: equalitytoday2003@yahoo.com
> Equality Now! is a peer group of LGBT people aspiring for equal access to information, education, health care, and to overcome all forms of discrimination in Kenya based on sexual orientation.

Governmental Organizations

Kenya National Commission on Human Rights, www.knchr.org.

> The commission was established by the government of Kenya to promote, enhance, and fight for basic human rights for Kenyans. It was mandated in 2002 by an act in parliament.

National AIDS Control Council, www.nacc.or.ke.

> The council acts as a support mechanism by providing resources and support for both the HIV infected and affected people. They set up policies that are adhered to by different organizations.

NOTES

1. Population of Kenya: 2007 Country Profile, *Infoplease,* www.infoplease.com/ipa/A0107678.html.

2. CIA, "Kenya: People of Kenya," *The World Factbook,* 2008, https://www.cia.gov/library/publications/the-world-factbook/geos/ke.html.

3. Population of Kenya: 2007 Country Profile.

4. CIA, "Kenya: People: Tribe Statistics," *The World Factbook,* 2002, http://www.faqs.org/docs/factbook/geos/ke.html.

5. CIA, "Kenya: People: Religions," *The World Factbook,* 2002, www.faqs.org/docs/factbook/geos/ke.html. (A large majority of Kenyans are Christian, but estimates for the percentage of the population that adheres to Islam or indigenous beliefs vary widely.)

6. Gay Kenya News & Reports 1998–2006, "Kenya's President Jumps on Anti-gay Bandwagon," October 1, 1999, Globalgayz.com, "Kenya has no room or time for homosexuals and lesbians. Homosexuality is against African norms and traditions, and even in religion it is considered a great sin" and "It is not right that a man should go with another man or a woman with another woman. It is against African tradition and Biblical teachings," http://www.globalgayz.com/kenya-news.html.

7. Mokaya Migiro, "Kenya Girls Together," *Saturday Magazine Home,* July 5, 2003, http://www.globalgayz.com/kenya-news.html.

8. "Literacy Levels in Kenya," Kenya National Bureau of Statistics, 2009, http://www.cbs.go.ke/home.html.

9. "Common Beliefs on Sex Outside Marriage, Homosexuality, Masturbation and Female Genital Mutilation (FGM) in Kenya," *Sexuality in Africa Magazine* 4, no.1 (2007): http://www.arsrc.org/publications/sia/mar07/researchnote.htm.

10. Ibid.

11. Galebitra Kenya: Gay blogs Kenya, 2005, http://www.galebitra.blogspot.com/.

12. "The Virus in Kenya: History of the Virus," Kenya AIDS Watch Institute, http://www.kenyaaidsinstitute.org/aboutthevirus.html.

13. "Kenya Children's Society," Adoption Laws and Requirements for Adoption of a Child in Kenya, *Africa's Angels,* http://www.africasangels.org/Organizations/KenyanChildrensSociety.html.

14. "2008 Country Profile: Kenya," The United States President's Emergency Plan for AIDS Relief, 2008, http://www.pepfar.gov/documents/organization/81664.pdf.

15. Galebitra Kenya: Gay blogs Kenya.

16. "Horror as Kenyan Hermaphrodite Shares Cells with Male Inmates at Kamiti, Now Sues," June 2007, *You Missed This,* http://kumekucha.blogspot.com/2007/06/horror-as-kenyan-hermaphrodite-has-both.html.

17. Sally Sue, "Living in the Q Side of Nairobi," *Haiya!* 2008, http://www.haiya.co.ke/node/625.

18. Frank Njenga, "The Concept of Mental Disorder: An African Perspective," *World Psychiatry* 6, no. 3 (2007): http://www.pubmedcentral.nih.gov/articlerender.fcgi?artid=2174593&tool=pmcentrez.

19. Mike Mwaniki, "Kenyan Bishop Pulls Back from Fete Linked to US Episcopal Pro Gay Bishop," *Daily Nation,* February 10, 2004, http://www.virtueonline.org/portal/modules/news/article.php?storyid=320.

20. Sue, "Living in the Q Side of Nairobi."

LIBERIA

James Daniel Wilets

OVERVIEW

Liberia is a democratic republic located on the Atlantic Coast in West Africa, bordered by Sierra Leone on the northwest, Cote D'Ivoire on the southeast, and Guinea on the north.

The first Europeans to explore what is now Liberia were the Portuguese in 1461. Beginning in 1822, the area that is now Liberia was settled by freed American slaves, subsequently called *Americo-Liberians*. This migration was sponsored by the American Colonization Society, consisting of slave owners, abolitionists, and clergy. The Republic of Liberia was established by the Americo-Liberian settlers on July 26, 1847. This group also established a constitution and a style of government that was loosely based on that of the United States. The Liberian government was dominated from 1847 until 1980 by Americo-Liberians, who formed a one-party state under the True Whig Party. Indigenous Liberians, who comprised a large majority of the population, were denied the right to vote and were denied citizenship until 1904.

In 1980, the regime was overthrown in a violent military coup led by Master Sergeant Samuel K. Doe, who established an authoritarian regime for approximately nine years. Despite the poor human rights and undemocratic record of the Doe regime, it enjoyed close relations with the United States, and President Doe met two times with President Ronald Reagan. The dominance of the Krahn tribe in the Doe administration exacerbated ethnic tensions within the

country. In 1989, Charles Taylor led a rebellion against Doe's rule, resulting in Doe's death. This rebellion led to a lengthy and violent civil war between Taylor and the forces of the Liberian successor government to Doe, resulting in more than 200,000 Liberian civilian deaths. The Liberian government was supported by the United Nations, the international community, the United States, and the Economic Community of West African States (ECOWAS), and its military counterpart, ECOMOG. Taylor's forces committed many atrocities against civilians, such as inducting children into his forces and committing murder and rape on a systematic basis. Nevertheless, in 1997, Taylor won a national election and became president, largely based on public fear of continued civil war if he lost. Nevertheless, because of Taylor's continuing human rights atrocities, civil war broke out again in 1999. In 2003, Taylor resigned and fled into exile in Nigeria. He was subsequently indicted by the International Criminal Court in The Hague for atrocities committed by his forces in neighboring Sierra Leone and is standing trial in the International Criminal Court for his alleged crimes.

A transitional government established a functioning democracy in Liberia, and in 2005, Ellen Johnson-Sirleaf won the presidency in an election deemed by international observers as largely free and fair. The current government has taken affirmative steps to rebuild the society and disarm more than 100,000 ex-combatants and has benefitted from substantial international aid in its reconstruction.

Nevertheless, Liberia's violent and turbulent recent history has resulted in an ongoing reconstruction of basic societal, economic, and political institutions. Thus, many social institutions including those of relevance to the LGBT community, are absent.

OVERVIEW OF LGBT ISSUES

Same-sex relations are illegal in Liberia, and LGBT individuals are subject to widespread societal discrimination and social animus.[1] Animosity towards LGBT individuals is rooted in Christian and Muslim religious traditions, and the history of severe legal persecution of gays and lesbians is traditionally characteristic of other former English colonies in Africa, Asia, the Americas, and until recently, the United States.

There is no gay movement, gay organizations, or organized gay society in Liberia. There are no gay social clubs or prominent openly-gay individuals. A 2006 report filed by the United Kingdom Home Office stated that there were no known reports of any homosexual culture in Liberia.[2] This lack of a LGBT community is a result of three factors: (1) Liberia's nearly three decades of violent civil war, which resulted in severe social upheaval and the elimination of the most rudimentary legal and civic institutions that could provide any protection to LGBT individuals; (2) widespread societal animus towards LGBT individuals, which prevents gay individuals from being openly gay; and (3) legal persecution as reflected in the longstanding criminalization of homosexual acts.

EDUCATION

Although primary and secondary education is supposed to be universal, compulsory and free, in practice there is not a fully functioning educational system.[3] There are no educational programs particular to the LGBT community. LGBT students are prevented from expressing their identity or opinions regarding LGBT issues because of the widespread societal animus towards LGBT individuals.

EMPLOYMENT AND ECONOMICS

The principal economic activities in Liberia are mining and rubber plantations. One of the principal foreign investors in Liberia's mining operations is Pat Robertson, a well-known U.S. Christian fundamentalist leader and longtime foe of LGBT rights.[4] Because of the Liberian Civil War, and Charles Taylor's involvement in the Sierra Leone conflict, the United Nations imposed sanctions on Liberian export of diamonds and timber. Those sanctions have now been removed. There is no employment protection for LGBT employees, and LGBT individuals are effectively silenced in the workplace as in other aspects of society.

SOCIAL/GOVERNMENT PROGRAMS

The destruction of the Liberian economy and societal institutions has meant that there are no social or governmental programs beyond the provision of the most basic, still inadequate, social services.

SEXUALITY/SEXUAL PRACTICES

Because of the invisibility of the LGBT community, there is no information available on sexuality or sexual practices in Liberia.

FAMILY

Liberia, along with Sierra Leone, suffered an unprecedented destruction of the family as large numbers of children were recruited as soldiers from as young as eight years old; Taylor's forces frequently forced children to commit atrocities against their own families in order to destroy the children's ability to identify with their tribe in the future. Taylor's forces also committed widespread sexual atrocities, using rape as a tool of war. As a result of this history, Liberians are extremely sensitive to the integrity of the family. To the extent that homosexuality is perceived as a threat to the integrity of the family unit, the preexisting anti-LGBT animus is heavily aggravated by Liberia's wartime history.

COMMUNITY

The Immigration and Refugee Board of Canada, charged with researching the human rights situation of homosexuals in Liberia, concluded that "[n]o information on the availability of... organizations that help homosexuals could be found among the sources consulted by the Research Directorate."[5]

HEALTH

In a 2004 report, the Family Planning Association of Liberia documented a "glaring inadequacy of services to address the unmet national sexual and reproductive health needs."[6] According to the report, nearly two-thirds of the population does not have access to health care and only half have access to clean water.[7]

POLITICS AND LAW

Male and female homosexuality is criminalized in Liberia.[8] Under Section 14.74 of the Penal Law, voluntary sodomy is categorized as a first-degree misdemeanor.[9] Voluntary sodomy is defined as "deviate sexual intercourse."[10] With the exception of one presidential nominee who was rejected by the Interim Legislative Assembly for his reputed homosexuality,[11] there is no documented participation by LGBT individuals in Liberia's political or legal systems.

RELIGION AND SPIRITUALITY

There are strong religious justifications given in Liberian society and political discourse for criminalization of homosexuality and discrimination against LGBT individuals. To a large extent, this reflects the prevalent Christian ethos from the time that the first Americo-Liberians came to Liberia, and in part this reflects a perception by those who practice indigenous African spirituality and believe that homosexuality is a Western importation. In fact, extensive historical documentation demonstrates that homophobia is largely a product of antihomosexual attitudes among Western colonialists rather than African indigenous culture.[12]

VIOLENCE

Liberia endured an extraordinarily violent and brutal civil war, lasting from 1989 to 1996, and again from 1999 to 2003. One unique aspect of the war was Taylor's extensive use of thousands of children to commit horrendous human rights atrocities. Although an attempt is being made to integrate these child warriors into Liberian society, the culture of violence is still prevalent in Liberian society. Because there are very few openly LGBT individuals in Liberia, there is no documentation of violence against LGBT individuals.

OUTLOOK FOR THE 21ST CENTURY

Despite the dismal recent history of Liberia, the advent of democracy and a current government that generally supports human rights bodes well for all Liberians, including LGBT Liberians. Although progress for the LGBT community is far from being realized, even to a small degree, it can be expected that as Liberia becomes a more stable country, it will follow the path of other countries in developing, at a minimum, some kind of LGBT community.

RESOURCE GUIDE

Suggested Reading

Stephen Ellis, *The Mask of Anarchy: The Destruction of Liberia and the Religious Dimension of an African Civil War,* 2nd ed. (New York: New York University Press, 2006).
Mary H. Moran, *Liberia: The Violence of Democracy* (Philadelphia: University of Pennsylvania Press, 2008).

NOTES

1. See, for example, United Kingdom: Home Office, "Country of Origin Information Report—Liberia," UNHCR Refworld Section 6.67; U.S. Citizenship and Immigration Services, "Response to Information Request Number LBRO1008.ZAR. Liberia: Information on the Treatment of Homosexuals," April 26, 2006, http://www.unhcr.org/refworld/docid/447aabcd4.html.

2. United Kingdom: Home Office, "Country of Origin Information Report—Liberia."

3. Ibid.

4. Colbert I. King, "Pat Robertson's Gold," *Washington Post*, September 22, 2001, http://www.washingtonpost.com/ac2/wp-dyn?pagename=article&node=&contentId=A7124-2001Sep21.

5. Immigration and Refugee Board of Canada: Country of Origin Research, "Liberia," July 21, 2006, http://www.unhcr.org/cgi-bin/texis/vtx/refworld/rwmain?page=country&docid=45f147652f&skip=0&coi=LBR&rid=456d621e2&querysi=gay&searchin=fulltext&display=10&sort = date.

6. International Planned Parenthood Federation, "Country Profile: Liberia," April 29, 2004, http://www.ippf.org.

7. Ibid.

8. International Lesbian and Gay Association, Behind the Mask, "Liberia," http://www.mask.org.za/index.php?page=liberia.

9. U.S. Citizenship and Immigration Services, "Response to Information Request Number LBRO1008.ZAR."

10. Daniel Ottosson, "State-Sponsored Homophobia," International Lesbian and Gay Association, 2008, http://www.ilga.org/statehomophobia/ILGA_State_Sponsored_Homophobia_2008.pdf; see also, U.S. Citizenship and Immigration Services, "Response to Information Request Number LBRO1008.ZAR."

11. U.S. Citizenship and Immigration Services, "Response to Information Request Number LBRO1008.ZAR."

12. See, for example, James Wilets, "Conceptualizing Private Violence against Sexual Minorities as Gendered Violence: An International and Comparative Perspective," *Albany Law Review* 60 (1997): 1020; Rob Tielman and Hans Hammelburg, *World Survey on the Social and Legal Position of Gays and Lesbians* (New York: Prometheus Books, 1993), 251; James Wilets, "International Human Rights Law and Sexual Orientation," *International and Comparative Law Review* 1 (1994): 5.

MOROCCO

Jen Westmoreland Bouchard

OVERVIEW

Morocco is a constitutional monarchy with King Mohamed VI as the head of state. Morocco is located in North Africa and is considered to be part of the Maghreb, along with Tunisia and Algeria. Morocco is approximately one-tenth larger than the state of California. The country is bordered by the Strait of Gibraltar on the Mediterranean side and the Atlantic Ocean on the northwest corner. Algeria is located to the southeast. Morocco is bordered by the disputed territory of Western Sahara. The Atlas Mountains extend northeastward from the south of Morocco to the Algerian frontier. The average elevation of the mountains is 11,000 feet (3,353 m). Because of the geographical challenges of mountains and desert, the majority of Morocco's population is grouped in the major cities of Tangiers, Casablanca, and Rabat.

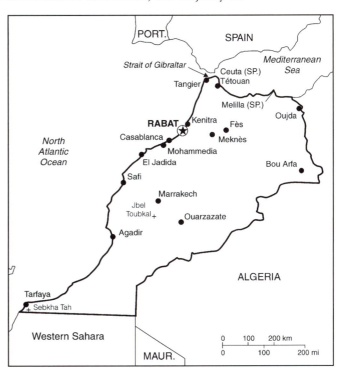

Morocco gained independence from France in 1956, at which time Rabat was established as the capital city. The Moroccan *dirham* is the official currency. Morocco has an estimated population of 33,241,259 inhabitants. Arabic is the official language, yet many Moroccans speak Berber and French. Ninety-eight percent of the country is Muslim, Christians comprise 1.2 percent of the population, and there is a very small minority of Jewish citizens.[1]

OVERVIEW OF LGBT ISSUES

Despite the fact that Islam strongly disapproves of sex between members of the same sex, Muslim societies, in general, have historically been tolerant of homosexual practice. This is especially true if such relationships are discreet and out of the public eye. Numerous poets of classical Arabic literature indulged in homoerotic activities, yet they were viewed as no less successful than their heterosexual counterparts. In fact, the relatively liberal attitudes concerning homosexuality in much of the Arab world both fascinated and shocked the protestant European travelers of the 18th and 19th centuries. Homosexuality was often referred to as a contagion or an illness by European travelers in the 1800s. French visitors to Morocco during the 18th century often claimed that Arabs were bisexual in nature. Many male European authors wrote of *licentiousness* (lesbianism) among Moroccan women in public bath houses. Throughout this time period, the British considered homosexuality to be a *Persian* vice.[2]

Many Arab countries are becoming increasingly conservative concerning social issues.[3] As is the case in most predominantly Muslim countries, homosexuality is a topic that most Moroccans are reluctant to discuss. Homosexual practices are considered to be un-Islamic, unnatural, and are typically viewed as a Persian or a Western import. As a result of this conservative trend, homosexual Moroccan men and women are often doubly oppressed within social, religious, and familial systems that simultaneously protect and inhibit them from living openly homosexual lives.

During the 1950s-1980s, Tangiers was home to numerous American and European homosexual celebrities such as Allen Ginsberg, William Burroughs, Truman Capote, Paul Bowles and the Frenchman, Jean Genet.[4] However, since the 1980s (and continuing into the 21st century), there has been a conservative backlash in both Tangiers and Casablanca. Tangiers, in particular, has lost its appeal for homosexual celebrities. Somewhat contradictory to this development is the fact that the government often ignores the various forms of pederasty and homosexual prostitution that are still commonly practiced in Tangiers.[5] Today, there exists a double standard regarding outward expressions of affection (heterosexual and homosexual) in Morocco and other Muslim countries. Heterosexual Muslim men are often seen walking hand-in-hand or kissing in public to express their friendship. However, homosexual men may not profess their sexual love for each other or express it in any way in the public eye. Same-sex relationships often happen behind closed doors. Outsiders who know of such relations ask few questions, and most do not protest if the couple is discreet. It is thought that if homosexual relationships are not talked about or written about, they do not exist according to Moroccan societal norms.[6]

Terminology, or the ways in which gays identify themselves (or are identified by others) linguistically, plays an important role in community formation in Morocco. In Arab and Muslim societies, the use of the word *gay* is loaded with a myriad of Western connotations. The term *homosexual* carries with it images of a certain lifestyle that only Western gays assume (and that Arab gays may try to emulate). The Arabic language has no accepted and used equivalent of the word *gay*. The Arabic term for homosexuality is *al-mithliyya al-jinsiyya*, which translates as "sexual sameness." This term is used mostly in academic and literary circles. The shortened version of the term, *mithli*, is beginning to be used as a more commonplace word for gays. Both of these terms are relatively neutral and many Arab gays accept them. Religious conservatives and popular media publications often use the term *shaadh* (which translates as "queer," "pervert," or "deviant"). Thus, the term *shaadh* is a heavily loaded and pejorative term. The conventional term for lesbian is *suhaaqi-yya*. There are many lesbians who argue this term has inaccurate connotations, and therefore prefer *mithliyya* (the feminine version of *mithli*).

There exist no positively connoted terms in Arabic to express the complex interactions of sentimental and physical relations between two people of the same sex. Most of the expressions in classical Arabic carry pejorative connotations. The term *shouzouz jinsi* means "abnormal sexuality" and *loowat* is an insulting way of referring to a homosexual act among men. This term refers to the Biblical fable of Lot, or Lut, in the Koran. *Sihaq* is a derogatory term for homosexual acts among women. The term bisexuality has no positive translation in Arabic. The lesbian publication, *Bint el Nas* uses the expression *mozdawijat el moyool el jinsiya* to express female bisexuality and *mozdawij el moyool el jinsiya* to express male bisexuality. The working term for hermaphrodite or intersex, or a person who has both male and female reproductive organs, is *izdiwaji el jins.*

In regard to transsexual or transgender individuals, Arabic provides two terms. The negative term is *khanis.* A more positive option is *moghayir el jins.* An individual who is born with male reproductive organs but identifies as female is termed *moghayirat el jins* (male-to-female transgender). This term uses feminine adjectives out of respect for the way in which these individuals identify themselves, whether they have undergone gender transformative surgical procedures or not. An individual who is born with female reproductive organs but identifies as a male is called *moghayir el jins* (female-to-male transgender).[7] Since homosexuality and various forms of *queerness* are generally not accepted in Muslim societies, it is nearly impossible to meet in gay support groups, much less attempt to celebrate one's sexuality in the form of a gay pride festival. In interviews, numerous Moroccan gays have reported feeling extremely lonely, isolated, and pressured to conform to a traditional, heterosexual lifestyle.[8] However, from the 1990s on, more gay social venues have appeared in larger Moroccan cities such as Rabat, Casablanca, and Tunis. However these establishments often experience an imposing police presence, precluding a comfortable sense of community.[9]

EDUCATION

There is no formal LGBT education in Moroccan schools.

EMPLOYMENT

There is no specific information on employment rates and homosexuality. However, many known or suspected homosexual Moroccans are discriminated against during the interview process and in the workplace.

Lesbians have a particularly difficult time in this arena. An unspoken norm is that any young woman who is not married or engaged will receive unsolicited sexual or romantic attention from her boss. Lesbians who do inform their bosses of their sexual identity are often fired. The only justification given by the boss is that lesbians are not employed at their establishment. Due to the complex political and societal relationship with lesbianism in Morocco, these women have very little legal recourse.[10]

SOCIAL/GOVERNMENT PROGRAMS

The Moroccan government does not provide funding for any social programs specifically for homosexuals. This is common in most predominantly Arab countries.

SEXUALITY/SEXUAL PRACTICES

Though contemporary Morocco is no longer the gay *mecca* it was known to be in the 1950s and 60s, sexual tourism persists. The current government often ignores prostitution because tourism of any kind boosts the economy in general, which is viewed as a positive outcome by most politicians.

Modern views and constructs of sexuality in Arab countries are impacted by the Western notion of sexuality, which came to fruition in the late 19th century. The construct of sexuality is centered on the notion that sexual behavior determines a person's identity, and therefore defines (to a certain extent) his or her lifestyle.[11] Therefore, a person who defines him or herself partly or entirely by his or her sexuality is considered to be under the influence of Western gay culture. Thus, he or she is considered an outsider on many levels.

Lesbians have a particularly difficult time in Morocco. In a patriarchal society built on heterosexual relationships, lesbians are often ignored or invisible. However, lesbianism is more common than one might expect in Arab countries, Morocco included. Many married women engage in homosexual activities as a way of combating boredom or dissatisfaction (sexual or otherwise) in their marriages. Other lesbians are well aware of their sexual preferences and chose to get married anyways (to conform to social or family expectations). These women often keep female lovers on the side. Given marital expectations in Morocco, these relationships are quite easy to maintain. So many Moroccan husbands are paranoid that their women are cheating on them with other men that they suspect nothing when their wives say they will be spending an evening with other women. In fact, most men are relieved that their wives would prefer to spend time with female friends instead of in the company of other men. One popular lesbian meeting place is the public bath, where women go for hair removal by a traditional Moroccan technique called *halawa*. However, authorities became aware of lesbian relations in many of these places and they have since been closed.[12] As for homosexual male meeting places, there exists no official gay infrastructure of bars, restaurants, or hotels anywhere in Morocco. However, many gay men identify each other through glances on the street, which lead to encounters in alleyways and private residences. Married gay men often keep one or multiple lovers and a separate apartment on the side for their homosexual rendezvous.[13]

FAMILY

In traditional Islamic families, homosexuality is usually either denied or ignored. At worst, homosexuals who come out to their families are treated with psychological and physical violence. In Morocco and other Arab societies, there are countless testimonials of homosexual sons being attacked by their fathers and brothers or forced to leave home. Others are subjected to intensive therapy sessions or forced to undergo electroshock treatment.

In many well-educated and affluent households, homosexuality is treated as an illness. It is considered to be curable with the right and appropriate length of treatment. Parents in this situation often believe that their child has been seduced or forced into homosexual behavior. To avoid these various forms of family-induced trauma, many gay men take on faux girlfriends or even arrange marriages for themselves with lesbians who are similarly seeking safety within the confines of cultural convention.[14]

Marriage is obligatory in most Arab households. Marriages are commonly arranged by parents. In cases where a gay or lesbian marries an arranged partner,
many pursue homosexual relations outside the marriage.[15] Many never reveal their
sexuality until after one or both parents have died. Some simply live in secrecy or
move to another country where they can live out their homosexual lives honestly
and relatively safely.

COMMUNITY

In Morocco, young homosexuals find most of their information about homosexual lifestyles on the Internet. At times, this knowledge is also passed on from
more experienced friends. The majority of the Web sites used as resources are in
French or English, thus literacy in these languages (and access to a computer) is
required. Many young Arab gays find general safety or sexual information on the
Internet that may be useful. However, most of the psychological references found
online are geared toward a Western audience and do not offer advice on how to
live as a homosexual in an Arab country.[16]

Moroccan lesbians face certain challenges when using the Internet as a way of
connecting with other women. The fellow lesbians they find online (who are allegedly looking for lovers or friendship) frequently end up being men (sometimes even
the suspicious boyfriends or husbands of lesbian women). Therefore, many lesbians
use caution and judgment when looking for companionship online. Street-smart
homosexual women arrive early to an agreed upon meeting place and keeps a safe
distance so that they can observe who shows up before he (or she) sees them.[17]

Despite the obvious negative aspects of being gay in Morocco, one positive trend
is that local publications are beginning to provide more information to Moroccans
about gay culture. In March 2002, *L'Indépendant Magazine* published a feature
article entitled "Les gays marocains font leur coming-out" ("Moroccan Gays Come
Out"). In 2004, Casablanca's *Tel Quel* published "Etre homosexuel au Maroc,"
("Being Homosexual in Morocco") an article outlining the numerous difficulties
associated with being gay in Morocco.[18] Though not a topic commonly broached by
authors, homosexuality has been discussed in several highly controversial Moroccan
novels of the second half of the 20th century. In the 1950s, Driss Chraibi criticized
Morocco's sexual value system in *Le Passé Simple*. More recently, Abdelhak Serhane
attacked cultural phobias surrounding gay sex in *L'amour Circoncis* (1995).

There also exist organizations such as the Gay and Lesbian Arabic Society (GLAS)
that serve Arab homosexuals worldwide. Established in the United States in 1988,
GLAS is an international organization that aims to promote positive images of
gays and lesbians living in both Arab and non-Arab communities. Another goal of
GLAS is to provide a network and educational resources for members of homosexual Arab communities.[19] Another notable organization is *Bint el Nas. Bint el Nas* is
an international Arab lesbian association that maintains an informational Web site
and publishes a biannual literary journal. In their mission, they state that they are
designed to provide information and social assistance to "women who identify as
gay, lesbian, bisexual, transgender, and/or queer (including female-to-male and
male-to-female transgender people in any state of transition), and who are identified ethnically or culturally with the Arab world, regardless of where they live."[20]
Bint el Nas is an Arabic expression that translates to "daughter of the people."
In Arab cultures, this phrase means "a girl or woman of good social standing."

HEALTH

Many gay Arabs report feeling lonely or isolated. This correlates directly to a lack of familial and communal acceptance and support. Consequently, mental illness is prevalent among both gay men and women and many become suicidal. This issue is complicated by the fact that Islam (like Christianity) considers suicide to be a mortal sin.

Homosexual individuals living in Islamic countries also find it difficult to receive adequate health care. In 2006, the Moroccan Association for the Fight Against AIDS launched a fund-raising campaign to support AIDS research and awareness. Instead of receiving widespread support, the association is now fighting conservative Muslims who accuse it of endorsing "the culture of the condom."[21] This privately funded organization states that about 19,000 people in Morocco have either HIV or AIDS, mainly transmitted through heterosexual activity. Opponents of this initiative believe that AIDS is a divine punishment for homosexual activity.

Traditional Muslims blame practices associated with sexual tourism for the spread of HIV/AIDS in Morocco. The Moroccan economy depends heavily on tourism and hopes to have 10 million visitors per year by 2010.[22] This conservative backlash will certainly have a negative effect on the reputation of the tourism industry. In the past several years, conservative Muslims have taken over beaches and demonstrated against sunbathing and swimming by engaging in collective prayers. This series of events came to be known as "the war of the beaches." In light of the recent controversy over protection against AIDS, many Moroccans believe there is a looming "war of the condoms."[23] There are currently 19,000 living with HIV in Morocco. Rates of HIV infection are especially high among at-risk demographics (sex workers and drug users). Thanks to the intervention of UNAIDS and their work with local governments, antiretroviral medications are available at a reasonable cost to those living with HIV.[24]

POLITICS AND LAW

In the minds of many Moroccans, attitudes towards male homosexuality (and also women's rights) are intertwined with international politics. Homosexuality is considered yet another form of Western imperialism. Thus, political and cultural discussions of homosexuality are inextricably linked to the opposition of various forms of Western cultural invasion.[25] In a tenuous era of neocolonialism, many Arab societies have turned to traditional customs and practices as a way to bolster national morale and solidify a common identity. Thus, homosexuality is not only viewed as a Western creation, it is also considered to be decidedly un-Arab and culturally offensive. Conversely, lesbian relationships are not typically viewed as signifiers of cultural degradation or Western imperialism. When invoked in contemporary Arab discourse or literature, they tend to be discussed as a natural, logical recourse for a woman who has not been satisfied by her husband.[26] Therefore, lesbian relationships have become a sort of shameful warning sign to married Arab men.

Somewhat paradoxically, the Moroccan government has historically turned a blind eye to the use of homosexual prostitution (even among the youth) to earn money, a visa, or travel opportunities. These young gays are extremely knowledgeable when it comes to international gay codes and norms. Many know how to attract homosexual tourists' attention by emphasizing certain physical characteristics, strategically placed jewelry, or the wearing of certain fashions.[27] In 2004, a 66-year old Englishman was arrested in Rabat after engaging in homosexual activities with a known prostitute. He was sentenced to one year in prison and forced to pay 500 dirham (the equivalent of about US$60). He claimed to have visited Morocco as a sexual tourist many times since the 1980s and had never been arrested before this incident. Later that year, nine adolescent boys were killed in Taroudant. Both of these events ignited debate over homosexual prostitution in the press and among government officials. The man who was arrested for the killings reportedly committed the murders after engaging in pedophilic activities. The press surrounding this case strengthened the Moroccan government's resolve to eradicate homosexual prostitution.[28]

Homosexuality is criminalized under Section 489 of the country's Penal Code. Currently, the legal penalty for sexual relations between people of the same sex is between six months and three years in prison, in addition to fines from 120 to 1,000 Dirhams (US$30–70).

RELIGION AND SPIRITUALITY

Islam is the dominant religion in Morocco. In the main book of the Koran, homosexuality is strictly prohibited: "And as for the two of you who are guilty thereof, punish them both. If they repent and mend their ways, let them be. God is forgiving and merciful" (4:16). Another important Islamic source is the *Shari'ah* (meaning "path" in Arabic). The *Shari'ah* is, in essence, a divinely created code of conduct (expressing God's will) that all Muslims must follow.[29] According to the Shari'ah, homosexual behavior is strongly prohibited.

The *Shari'ah* contains information on sex and the regulation of it. The basic premise is that sex is natural and condoned. In fact, most Muslim sects believe that sex in paradise leads to the fulfillment of the spiritual and bodily self.[30] However, because of human imperfection, sex on earth has become corrupt and must be regulated. Sex within marriage is encouraged. However, a partner of the same sex is considered to be an illicit partner because he or she could never be a spouse and because a homosexual act threatens the natural order. In more conservative sects, homosexual activities are considered a revolt against *Allah* (God).[31] More commonplace is the notion that deviant sexual acts produce illness, such as AIDS.

Therefore, according to Muslim law, these thoughts must be repressed and never acted upon. If a Muslim admits to having homosexual thoughts, religious leaders encourage them to ask Allah to rid them of these feelings and never to get physically involved with a person other than his own heterosexual spouse. He will be further advised to seek medical treatment and religious support from a local *imam* (religious leader).[32]

An important distinction between Islam and Christianity is that Islam addresses homosexual acts but does not address homosexuality as an identity or lifestyle. Christianity tends to view homosexuality (the lifestyle, acts, and identity) as a sin and preaches that this lifestyle is indeed a choice. The reasons for this distinction are clear if one bears in mind that homosexuality is perceived as a Western construct. The term homosexuality embodies the notion that sexual behavior determines a person's identity, and therefore defines (to a certain extent) his or her lifestyle.[33] Particularly in Morocco, homosexuality is viewed as a form of Western decadence.

In a more general sense, the term and concept of homosexuality also refers to the public transgression of moral codes and behaviors. In Islam, homosexuality often becomes representative of unnatural, disorderly conduct that will eventually lead to chaos and social decay. Likewise, homosexuals themselves are seen as deviant members of society and as such, they are a direct threat to social order. Therefore, the category of homosexuality can easily (and dangerously) become extended to incorporate anyone who disturbs the mores of Islam, including criminals, political opponents, outsiders, or foreigners.[34]

Traditional Islamic law prescribes harsh punishments for homosexual behavior. Since homosexual behavior is considered to be a form of adultery, the same guidelines hold true as for heterosexual adulterers. The penalties consist of physical violence: stoning to death for married peoples and 100 lashes for unmarried people. These extreme punishments, meant to deter homosexual activity, are often performed in the public eye.

However, Islam recognizes that humankind is intrinsically fallible. Therefore, practice is gentler than theory. Therefore, for corporal punishment to be carried out, there must be an eyewitness to the homosexual event or a direct confession. If the person who has made the transgression seeks to repent and reform, punishment may be delayed or simply never occur.

A somewhat contradictory historical Moroccan cultural belief is *baraka* (religious good luck). Historically, it was believed that saintly or blessed men could transmit his *baraka* to another man through anal intercourse (fellatio was not considered an effective form of transmission).[35]

VIOLENCE

Violence against homosexuals in Morocco is related to the perception of homosexuality in general. Homosexuality is viewed as a foreign illness, one that must be eradicated in order to maintain stasis in Moroccan life and Muslim values. Since homosexuality is viewed as just one of the many ways in which Western cultures are trying to dominate the world, much of the violence against homosexuals is driven by this fear of neocolonialism.

As a result of both family and random acts of violence, gays who have the financial means to leave Morocco move to European countries or the United States; places in which they can continue their lives in peace. On several occasions, Moroccans have been granted asylum by the United States Government after undergoing beatings from family members and other members of Moroccan society as a result of their sexuality.

Violent reactions from family members are especially common in traditional parts of Morocco. In these regions, the notion of family honor is of the utmost importance. Any type of deviance, homosexuality included, brings shame upon the household and also shames past generations. Such emotional reactions often result in fathers killing their homosexual sons to preserve the family's honor. In the heterosexual context, brothers have been known to collectively kill a sister if she becomes pregnant before marriage in order to maintain the family name and reputation. They have been threatened by honor killings by family members if they return to their towns.[36]

OUTLOOK FOR THE 21ST CENTURY

The rise in antihomosexual events in Morocco in the past decade reveal a conservative trend away from accepting homosexuality. In the past, Arab societies were much more tolerant of homosexual activity if it was kept private. Now, public displays of homosexuality are viewed as a Western illness that must be cured through various techniques including psychotherapy, electroshock therapy, social exclusion, and violence. This mentality is also entangled in international politics. The perceived threats of Western imperialism and modernity in general have spawned an overwhelming return to traditional Islamic values as a cultural defense mechanism. However, these traditional values are much less universal than the majority of Arabs realize. As proven by historical writings, these conservative sexual values were not wholly respected or observed in the past. However, there still exist numerous conservative Muslims who portray the battle of sexual orientation as a Western crusade against Islam.

As a result of these complex and layered antigay and anti-Western ideologies, it will be a long time before homosexuals will feel safe living openly gay lives in Moroccan society. Over the past 10 years, much scholarly work as been done on identity and community formation among gay Arabs. This scholarly attention is a positive phenomenon in that it informs a Western audience of the challenges faced by gay Arab populations. By bringing cases of injustice and hidden acts of violence into the light, academics and human rights organizations can help to eventually create a safe environment and sense of community for Arab homosexuals in Morocco and worldwide.

RESOURCE GUIDE

Suggested Reading

Abdul Aziz Al-Fawzan, "The Evil Sin of Homosexuality," 2004, http://www.islamweb.net/english/family/sociaffair/socaff-84.html.

Abdelwahab Bouhdiba, *Sexuality in Islam,* trans. A. Sheridan (London: Routledge and Keagan, 1985).

G. H. Bousquet, *L'éthique sexuelle de l'Islam* (Paris: Maisonneuve, 1966).

Bruce Dunne, "Power and Sexuality in the Middle East," *Middle East Report,* Spring 1998.

Abderrahim El Ouali, "Morocco: War Over Condoms in the Battle Against AIDS," *Inter Press Service English News Wire,* 2006.

Madelaine Farah, *Marriage and Sexuality in Islam: A Translation of al Ghazzali's Book on the Etiquette of Marriage* (Salt Lake City: University of Utah Press, 1984).

Matthew Link, "Under Morocco's Sheltering Sky: The Timeless Magnetism of the Desert Lures Modern Travelers into the Mysticism of an Ancient North African Land," *The Advocate,* 2005.

Valentine M. Moghadam, *Modernizing Women: Gender and Social Change in the Middle East* (Boulder, CO: Lynne Rienner, 2003).

Vincenzo Patané, "Homosexuality in the Middle East and North Africa," in *Gay Life and Culture: A World History,* ed. Robert Aldrich (New York: Universe Publishing, 2006).

Geoff Puterbaugh, "North Africa," in *The Encyclopedia of Homosexuality,* vol. 1, ed. Wayne Dynes (New York: Garland Publishing, 1990).

Staff Writer, "Briton Jailed for 'Homosexual Practices' in Morocco," *AP Worldstream,* 2004.

Serge Trifkovic, "Islam's Love-Hate Relationship with Homosexuality," *Front Page Magazine,* 2003.

UNAIDS, "Morocco Country Profile," 2007, www.unaids.org.

Brian Whitaker, *Unspeakable Love: Gay and Lesbian Life in the Middle East* (Berkeley: University of California Press, 2006).

Brian Whitaker, "Behind the Veil: Lesbian Lives in the Middle East," *Diva Magazine,* July, 2006, http://www.divamag.co.uk/diva/features.asp?AID=1677

Brian Whitaker, "Let's Talk about Sex, Habibi," *The Guardian,* June, 2006, http://commentisfree.guardian.co.uk/brian_whitaker/2006/06/the_history_of_sex.html.

Web Sites

Bint el Nas Association for Arab Lesbians, www.bintelnas.org.

Bint el Nas is an international Arab lesbian association that maintains an informational Web site and publishes a biannual literary journal.

The Gay and Lesbian Arabic Society, www.glas.org.

Established in the United States in 1988, GLAS is an international organization that aims to promote positive images of gays and lesbians living in both Arab and non-Arab communities. Another goal is to provide a network and educational resources for members of homosexual Arab communities.

Gay Middle East, www.gaymiddleeast.com.

A comprehensive and diverse news source for those interested in homosexual issues in the Middle East. This site provides links to articles from a variety of Middle Eastern, American, and British news sources. Gay tourism information is also available.

NOTES

1. "Morocco," 2006, www.countryreports.org.

2. Serge Trifkovic, "Islam's Love-Hate Relationship with Homosexuality," *Front Page Magazine,* 2003.

3. Geoff Puterbaugh, "North Africa," *The Encyclopedia of Homosexuality,* vol. 1, ed. Wayne Dynes (New York: Garland Publishing, 1990), 19–22.

4. Ibid.

5. Ibid.

6. Brian Whitaker, *Unspeakable Love: Gay and Lesbian Life in the Middle East* (Los Angeles: University of California Press, 2006).

7. Bint el Nas, http://www.bintelnas.org.

8. Whitaker, *Unspeakable Love;* Brian Whitaker, "Behind the Veil: Lesbian Lives in the Middle East," *Diva Magazine,* July 2006, http://www.divamag.co.uk/diva/features.asp?AID=1677; Brian Whitaker, "Let's Talk about Sex, Habibi," *The Guardian,* June 2006, http://commentisfree.guardian.co.uk/brian_whitaker/2006/06/the_history_of_sex.html; Staff Writer, "Briton Jailed for 'Homosexual Practices' in Morocco," *AP Worldstream,* 2004.

9. Vincenzo Patané, "Homosexuality in the Middle East and North Africa," in *Gay Life and Culture: A World History,* ed. Robert Aldrich (New York: Universal Publishing, 2006).

10. Whitaker, *Unspeakable Love.*

11. Maarten Schlid, "Islam," in *The Encyclopedia of Homosexuality,* vol. 1, ed. Wayne Dynes (New York: Garland Publishing, 1990), 615–20.

12. Whitaker, *Unspeakable Love;* Whitaker, "Behind the Veil"; Whitaker, "Let's Talk about Sex, Habibi."

13. Matthew Link, "Under Morocco's Sheltering Sky: The Timeless Magnetism of the Desert Lures Modern Travelers into the Mysticism of an Ancient North African Land," *The Advocate,* 2005.

14. Whitaker, *Unspeakable Love*.
15. Ibid., 25.
16. Ibid.
17. Ibid.
18. Patané, "Homosexuality in the Middle East and North Africa."
19. The Gay and Lesbian Arabic Society (GLAS), www.glas.org.
20. Bint el Nas, www.bintelnas.org.
21. Abderrahim El Ouali, "Morocco: War Over Condoms in the Battle Against AIDS," *Inter Press Service English News Wire,* January 2006.
22. Ibid.
23. Ibid.
24. UNAIDS, "Morocco Country Profile," 2007, www.unaids.org.
25. Whitaker, *Unspeakable Love*.
26. Ibid.
27. Patané, "Homosexuality in the Middle East and North Africa."
28. Staff Writer, "Briton Jailed for 'Homosexual Practices' in Morocco."
29. Schlid, "Islam."
30. Ibid.
31. Ibid.
32. Whitaker, *Unspeakable Love*.
33. Schlid, "Islam."
34. Ibid.
35. Puterbaugh, "North Africa."
36. Whitaker, "Behind the Veil: Lesbian Lives in the Middle East."

NAMIBIA

Nancy Nteere

OVERVIEW

Namibia is located on Africa's southwest coast and covers 318,261 square miles. It is the second least populated country in the world with a population of only 20,550,080 people (2007). The life expectancy for women is 41.8 years and for men it is 44.4 years. The fertility rate (2007) is 2.94 children born per woman.[1] There is a high rate of HIV/AIDS in the country with a total of 230,000 people living with the virus.[2]

Namibia is bordered on the east by Botswana and South Africa, on the west by the Atlantic Ocean, on the north by Angola and Zambia, and on the south by South Africa. Deserts occupy most of Namibia—namely the Kalahari and Namib deserts. There is scant vegetation in the deserts and grasslands, which are used by livestock and game animals to graze. The semi-arid central plateau is covered by woodland savannah. The forests in the northeast region of Namibia are home to game animals such as zebras, lions, giraffes, rhinoceros, and hartebeests.

Namibia was formerly known as South West Africa. German settlers discovered diamonds in the region in 1908, which encouraged an influx of European settlers. Namibia is a rich source of minerals and the primary exports are diamonds, copper, gold, zinc, lead, and uranium, as well as a variety of game meat. The Okavango River generates more hydroelectric power than all other rivers in Southern Africa. The Namibian climate is typically hot and dry. The average rainfall, which ranges from the Namib

Desert to the coast, is two inches a year. The summer (October-March) is the rainy season. In the mainland to the south, the average rainfall is six inches annually. To the north, rainfall is 22 inches per year. The average temperature in the mainland is 70 degrees Fahrenheit, and at the coastline it is 62 degrees Fahrenheit.

Namibia's population is comprised of a variety of ethnic groups. More than half the population consists of the *Ovambo* tribe. The other groups are the *Kavango, Herero,* and *Damara* peoples, mixed race (*colored* and *rehoboth*), white (German, Afrikaans, and Portuguese), *Nama, Caprivian,* Bushmen, and *Tswana*. Most of these groups share similar home languages, but the black and white Namibians are distinctively different in their communal identities. The *Ovambo, Kavango* and *East Caprivian* people work as herders and farmers and are settled in the well-watered and fertile parts of the country. However, urbanization, industrialization, and the zest to find jobs elsewhere in different regions have resulted in integration of the different communities in the urban centers such as Windhoek (the capital city). There is a minority white population that is descendant from South Africa, Britain, Portugal, and Germany.

More than half of the white population speaks Afrikaans, a language derived from the 17th-century Dutch settlers. Each ethnic group has a chief or a queen to govern the traditional acts in honor of democracy. Most communities elect women since it is believed they embody strong leadership skills and, ultimately, respectable traditional homes. The oldest community in Namibia was known as the *San,* who lived in the Kalahari Desert; however the Kalahari is now divided between Botswana, Namibia, Angola, and South Africa.

OVERVIEW OF LGBT ISSUES

In the rural parts of Namibia, gays and lesbians are forced to marry and have children. As in many African countries, once the community suspects or discovers someone is gay, he or she is ostracized or physically attacked without the protection of law. Shortly before Namibian independence in 1990, gays in Namibia had the freedom to hold hands in public without much repercussion. However, that changed as the economy faltered. Namibian leaders and government officials looked for any scapegoat to attribute the slow economic growth—and homosexuality was blamed. In 1996, the debate on homosexuality prompted the former president Sam Nujoma to give his first antigay speech in which he encouraged government officials and ministers to discriminate against gays. This negative stance has been repeated by other government officials. For example, approximately ten years ago, the Deputy Minister of Land, Resettlement, and Rehabilitation was interviewed and advised gays and lesbians to be operated on to remove some of the "unnatural hormones" that made them homosexual. It is no wonder that LGBT people in Namibia are afraid to come out.

According to the national AIDS policy that is under consideration, homosexuals will be included as an identified group. If the draft is approved, it will intervene to help with the prevention of HIV among gays and lesbians. This is an important step forward in bringing national awareness to gay issues.

Due to the high number of hate speech and crimes directed towards LGBT people, a large percentage of the gay population prefers to stay silent and closeted, and are expected to do so for the foreseeable future. However, gay organizations have slowly formed in the major cities and members have openly declared their sexual orientation. These organizations have also held workshops and visited schools and churches to spread their message of tolerance. Even with the negative government position, the overall climate in Namibia has become less hostile in recent years.

EDUCATION

As in most African countries, higher education is paid for by the students; however, the Namibian constitution guarantees that primary education is free and compulsory. Formal primary education is made up seven years, grades one through seven. The secondary education consists of three years of junior secondary school and two years of senior secondary school. Students of primary education vary between the ages of six to 16 years. The language of instruction chosen by government-sponsored schools is English due to various reasons including: Pan-Africanism, unity, wider communication with the outside world, and greater access to science and technology. The government began teaching about HIV/AIDS transmission using age-appropriate sex education materials in schools in order to curb the prevalence among Namibia's youth.

Just after independence and through the intervention of President Sam Nujoma, a commission was established to review the higher education needs. The result of the commission was the elimination of tertiary education and the inclusion of a university and polytechnic institutes. The University of Namibia was established in 1992. In 1994, the polytechnics of Namibia were established as institutions of higher learning, along with four teaching universities.

Namibia boasts of being one of the countries with the highest literacy level in sub-Saharan Africa. The Namibian government claims to have achieved almost a 100 percent literacy rate except for a small population found mostly in the *San* community. For the *Sans*, informal education facilities have been established to accommodate their special living conditions. Many academics challenge the official literacy rate and claim it is much lower as evidenced by the large population of unskilled unemployed workers.

EMPLOYMENT AND ECONOMICS

A fairly large portion of Namibia's population is either unemployed or under-employed. The majority of the unemployed manage to eke out a living in the informal sectors, such as by hawking goods or working in family owned farms to produce food crops. The working force is comprised of 820,000 people. Overall, unemployment stands at 35 percent of the population.[3] Agriculture employs almost half of the total work force. A large number of the work force still remains illiterate and unskilled, prompting the government to enroll more people in education and training.

Namibia's per capita gross domestic product (GDP) is US$7.781 billion (2008 est.; $7,478 [2005 est.]). The growth rate is 3.5 percent (2005 est.) and the inflation rate is 2.3 percent (2005 est.).[4]

A large number of Namibia's imports originate in South Africa. The two countries' economies remain dependant on the South African currency as the rand (ZAR) can be used to trade in both countries.

Former president Sam Nujoma's government has generally diversified Namibia's economy by introducing Export Processing Zones, increasing fishing, mining and tourism incentives, and also by improving the infrastructure. Mining is Namibia's chief export sector. A small percentage of the population is employed in the mining sector. In Africa, Namibia is the fourth largest exporter of nonfuel minerals. Ranked as the world's fifth-largest producer of uranium, Namibia also exports lead, zinc, tin, silver, and tungsten. Coupled with the micro and macro economic policy, mining has stabilized the inflation rate, economic growth, and interest rates.

Corruption is rampant at all levels of government. Consequently, there are a lot of uncertainties and unjustified dismissals in the labor force.

There have not been any reported cases of unlawful dismissal from employment due to sexual orientation. Most of the LGBT organizations employ gay and lesbian employees. There have not been any notable cases of discrimination at work places due to sexual orientation, but many workers also remain closeted to their employers.

SOCIAL/GOVERNMENT PROGRAMS

According to Namibia's new labor laws, discrimination based on sexual orientation has been eliminated. Yet, the laws are not enforced, leaving a gap concerning the labor rights of the LGBT community. The country is conflicted between asserting basic rights while at the same time government officials (including the president) are making discriminatory remarks. For example, key ministers in the government have made varied homophobic statements. These in turn led to outright discrimination by government officials and others. As such, the new labor laws are rarely enforced.

As a result of homophobic statements from key people in government posts, gay organizations such as The Rainbow Project, Legal Assistance Center, and Sister Namibia have developed programs in which they incorporate gay activists and encourage gay people to speak out. Members of these pioneer gay groups visited schools, churches, television and radio shows, and human rights organizations in order to educated people and gain recognition for tolerance. Allying with other African countries, Namibia has had programs that have incorporated other lesbian, gay, bisexual, and transgender groups. Among the programs that are organized by the government are those that involve the sensitization of both genders on basic human rights education through workshops targeting traditional teachers, counselors, parents, and the youth.

Half of the population works in agriculture. The government has issued farm policies concerning the use of titled land as security in banks and government institutions. As such, small- scale farmers and women have benefited from this program since 1994. However, married women require consent from their husbands in order to access the loans. Since gays and lesbians cannot marry, these important credit programs are unavailable to same-sex couples.

SEXUALITY/ SEXUAL PRACTICES

The first debate on the legalities of homosexuality in Namibia was initiated in 1995. The debate centered on the recognition by law of lesbian couples who lived together. The High Court termed the union a "Universal Partnership," which granted the same recognition as given to a cohabitating heterosexual couple.

In the urban setting, a small percentage of LGBT people come out to their families and rarely experience homophobia. There are some organizations and shelters that offer counseling services for members of the LGBT community. However, most gays and lesbians still remain closeted. Some actively participate in workshops and events that promote self-awareness and acceptance.

Namibia, like most other African countries, considers homosexuality as un-African and taboo. Although there is a history of some ethnic groups being aware of the existence of gay people and go so far as to give them special tribal names, the names chosen usually have a negative connotation to them. For example, Namibia's largest ethnic group is the *Ovambo*. They are deeply rooted in patriarchy and believe homosexuality makes gay sons unacceptable for inheritance of land from their fathers. In contrast, the *Damara* is one of the communities that is more accommodating towards homosexuality.

Namibia's LGBT community operates discreetly. The official status of homosexuality remains illegal, therefore the gay community meets in places that are determined to be safe, such as in offices that are gay friendly. Same-sex dating is not accepted by Namibian society, which forces same-sex couples to camouflage their relationships as friendships in order to divert attention. However, there are cases of house parties that are organized by the LGBT community where there is open interaction and pairing up of same sex couples. The National HIV/AIDS policy was adopted in parliament; however gay, lesbian, bisexual and transsexual people were left out of the policy, and thus receive no recognition.

FAMILY

It has been preached all over Africa that homosexuality is un-African and a Western influence, and Namibia is no exception in terms of spreading this type of rhetoric. The former president, Sam Nujoma, often made remarks supporting antigay culture, values, and morality, and called for the eradication of same-sex relationships. Nujoma repeated the claims that homosexuality was promoted by Europeans and, as such, was a deviancy to be stamped out. He gave permission to parents and traditional leaders to discipline young people who refused to follow cultural norms, including gay and lesbian children. However, Nujoma allowed lesbians to practice their rights in their homes but not in public.

All African languages have specific terms denoting the practice of homosexuality. This history counters the idea that homosexuality did not exist until European colonialization. In each of the Namibian indigenous languages, there existed a tribal word for homosexuality.

Namibian law recognizes customary marriages as a legal union between a man and a woman so long as all the customs are adhered to. Different communities have different traditions of solemnizing marriage. Even still, the marriage traditions need to conform to constitutional law. As such, same-sex customary marriages are not acceptable as they are still unconstitutional. Traditional marriage also does not allow for divorce. Women are forced to endure promiscuous husbands until "death do us part." Polygamy in a household mostly depends on the available wealth, since the man is required to pay for the bride's price and take care of the new wife and family. There are, however, some harmful traditional marriage customs. In some communities, blood relatives of a deceased man are allowed to confiscate his property from the widow and children. This leaves the widow and

children homeless and destitute. In such cases, the local chief is obligated to offici-
ate over the matter.

COMMUNITY

Due to homophobic outbursts from members of parliament concerning homosexuality, South African lesbians and gays have teamed up with lesbian and gay
citizens of Namibia to set up an active LGBT community. LGBT organizations
have come to the support of the gay communities of these countries. Additionally, in Namibia's urban centers, many people in the general population have also
been in support of LGBT organizations. Behind the Mask, a South African LGBT
organization and Web site, has sponsored conferences and talks in Namibia. The
organization offers support to the victimized LGBT groups in Namibia. The two
key feminist organizations that address gay and lesbian issues in Namibia are Sister
Namibia and The Rainbow Project.

HEALTH

Namibia has one of the highest HIV infection rates in the world. The government has introduced strategies in prevention and treatment, and supplies free antiretroviral to people who are living with the infection. By the end of 2005, there
were 230,000 adults and children between the ages of 0–49 living with HIV. The
HIV prevalence rate among adults between the ages of 15–49 is 19.6 percent.
Compared to other health care systems in Africa, Namibia has one of the best in
both its population-to-doctor and its population-to-hospital-bed ratios.

Namibia's national HIV/AIDS policy excluded issues concerning the gay and
lesbian community. In many ways, the policy assumes that homosexuals do not
exist in the country. This oversight may be caused by the status of homosexuality
as illegal, and also due to the fact that many Namibians associate AIDS with male
prostitutes.

Most of the programs related to health rights are geared towards heterosexuals
and, therefore, very few address the issue of same sex relationships. In most African
countries, women take the role of being celibate and monogamous in marriages
and men are sanctioned to be promiscuous. Gay men in Namibia are faced with
the decision of being celibate or monogamous to their partners in order to curb
sexually transmitted diseases and HIV/AIDS.

There has been little effort by national or regional HIV/AIDS prevention education campaigns to address issues related to same-sex sexuality. An example of
this negligence is found in the Namibian prisons. Security wardens are provided
with condoms while the inmates who are involved in same-sex relationships have
no provision of them. It is assumed only heterosexual sex is the main transmission
of HIV/AIDS, and this misconception has led to sky rocketing HIV rates among
inmates.

POLITICS AND LAW

Male homosexuality remains illegal in Namibia; however lesbian sexual acts
are not mentioned in the law. It is normally assumed lesbian acts are also illegal

although no woman has ever been prosecuted under the law. The labor laws prohibit discrimination based on sexual orientation, but this is not enforced. Once a person is suspected to be a homosexual they are often subjected to verbal and physical violence. There have been a few incidents where the former president used the term *homosexuality* as an epithet to attack his political enemies. This encouraged other gay bashings. Due to the antigay remarks by key politicians in the government, gays have received sexual assaults in homes, schools, prisons, and police cells. In the rural parts of Namibia, lesbians sometimes are forced to marry older men or are married off as second wives to retain the community's culture or traditions.

There were threats in 1998 by the Minister of Home Affairs, who planned to introduce new legislation against homosexuals. He stated that gay rights would never qualify as human rights and should be regarded as human wrongs. He claimed that authentic Namibian culture and religious institutions ranked homosexuality as a sin against God and country. However, the new legislation was never introduced.

Since independence, there have been many discussions concerning human rights for Namibians. Only one legislation touched on the issue of same-sex sexuality issues. The labor law was modified to criminalize discrimination based on sexual orientation.

RELIGION AND SPIRITUALITY

Being gay in Africa leads to being called un-Godly or un-Christian. Homosexuality is often characterized and smeared as a European import. However, this strategy can backfire since Christianity was an European import. Colonization obliterated Namibia's cultural traditions and religions. For example, in northern Namibia, homosexuals historically served as spiritual leaders and healers. Thus, there is confusion over the veneration of traditional beliefs, imported Christian values, and nationalism.

LGBT Namibians often turn to their churches for help in their struggle for equal rights, but the response has been varied. Christians account for the highest population in Namibia, Protestants make up 38 percent, Roman Catholic 28 percent, indigenous beliefs 26 percent, Muslim 7 percent, and others 1 percent.[5] Most Christian churches have been antagonistic toward gays but Lutheran churches have been more accepting.

VIOLENCE

There have been few reported cases of physical violence against the gay community in Namibia, but reports are hard to find as most gay people are closeted. There was, however, a notable case of gay bashers who attacked three gay men. Additionally, a case was reported on the Web site run by Behind the Mask on the July 19, 2005, on a case of a student who was sodomized by a male teacher. Sister Namibia, an organization supporting gay rights, has had their offices gutted by fire and their library burned to ashes.

In Namibia, antigay policies and beliefs have been made into a political platform. In the past, politicians including former president Sam Nujoma, made verbal attacks against homosexuals. Nujoma clearly stated that homosexuality was un-African and ungodly. He ordered that once homosexuals are found, they were to be arrested, imprisoned, or deported. He instilled the notion that homosexuality was a foreign ideology and that Europeans were diluting the Namibian culture.

In a speech made by the former president's Home Affairs Minister, the minister asserted that the police had been ordered to rid Namibia of gays and lesbians, and equated their relationships to unnatural acts, including murder. He blamed gays for the rising HIV infection rate. He also ordered the killing of *gay dogs* (i.e., dogs owned by gay people). Further, the Deputy Home Affairs Minister equated homosexuals to patients with psychological and biological deviations and who should be cured of their sickness.

There have been some brutal attacks on gays and lesbians. For example, families of lesbian daughters have arranged to have the daughters raped in order to teach them the *right* way to have sex. Similarly, gay men have had their earrings ripped off from their ears by the police. Some gay students have dropped out of school because they have been outcast or are subjected to violent "cures." In an article written by *Chicago Tribune* foreign correspondent Laurie Goering, a leading government official was reported as issuing a treatise on the cure of homosexuality.[6] It advocated sawing off the top of the skull and using a chemical solution to cleanse off the homosexual tendencies.

OUTLOOK FOR THE 21ST CENTURY

In Africa, no church or religion has taken a pro-gay stand or offered support for the LGBT community. In rural regions of Namibia, there are many hurdles in accepting homosexuals as equal members of society. However, the gay-friendly Lutheran church may be instrumental in helping other religious groups learn and accept gays and lesbians as equals. These other religious groups dominate the national discourse and play the greatest role in national politics. South Africa has played a significant role in Namibia's gay rights struggle by intertwining LGBT organizations from both countries.

Urban centers like Windhoek will continue being central to the struggle for LGBT rights. Many lesbians and gay men have migrated there with the hope of recognition and assistance in the fight for their rights. Although progress has been slowed by verbal attacks from political leaders, there is hope that with new leaders the situation will change for the better. Although homosexuality is still deemed illegal in Namibia, the Namibian LGBT community in the 21st century is hopeful of achieving equality and a peaceful life.

RESOURCE GUIDE

Suggested Reading

Barry D. Adam, Jan W. Duyvendak, and Andre Krouwell, *The Global Emergence of Gay and Lesbian Politics* (Philadelphia, PA: Temple University Press, 1999).

William Beinart, *Twentieth Century South Africa* (Oxford: Oxford University Press, 2001).

Ken Cage, *The Language of Kinks and Queens* (Johannesburg: Jacana Media, 2003).

Cary Alan Johnson, *Off the Map, How HIV/AIDS Programming is Failing Same-Sex Practicing People in Africa* (New York: International Gay and Lesbian Human Rights Commission, 2007).

Ezekiel Kalipeni, *HIV/AIDS in Africa* (Oxford: Blackwell Publishing, 2004).

Scott Long, Widney A. Brown, and Gail Cooper, *More Than a Name* (New York, Human Rights Watch Publication, 2003).

Fatima Mernissi, *Beyond the Veil: Male-Female Dynamics in Modern Muslim Society* (Bloomington, IN: Indiana University Press, 1985).

Ruth Morgan and Saskia Wieringa, *Tommy Boys, Lesbian Men and Ancestral Wives: Female Same Sex Practices in Africa* (Johannesburg: Jacana Media, 2005).

Robert Morrell, *Changing Men in Southern Africa* (London, Zed Books Limited, 2001).

Jennifer Ellen Robertson, *Same Sex-Cultures and Sexuality: An Anthropological Reader* (Oxford: Blackwell, 2005).

Shaun Waal and Anthony Manion, *Pride, Protest and Celebration* (Johannesburg: Jacana Media, 2007).

Veit Wild-Flora, *Body, Human in Literature- Body Sexuality and Gender,* ed. Dirk Naguschewski (Amsterdam: Radopi Publications, 2005).

Web Sites

Behind the Mask, www.mask.org.za.

> Behind the Mask gives a voice to the African LGBT community by publishing an online magazine and by providing a platform for exchanging and debating issues relating to the LGBT community in Africa.

The Gay & Lesbian Alliance Against Defamation (GLAAD), www.glaad.org.

> The Gay & Lesbian Alliance Against Defamation (GLAAD) works to eliminate homophobia and discrimination based on gender identity and sexual orientation by ensuring accurate and inclusive coverage of events in the media.

Legal Assistance Center of Namibia, www.lac.org.na.

> The LAC's five broad themes are advocacy, law reform, research, education and training, information, and advice and litigation. The main objective is to protect the human rights of all Namibians.

Organizations

Nongovernmental Organizations

Khomas Women in Development (KWID)

> KWID is a good resource for women in Namibia to seek information, education, and support while learning new skills and developing confidence to promote their advancement.
>
> P.O. Box 7061
> Katatura, ERF 682, Windhoek, Namibia
> Ph: 264-61 218723

Legal Assistance Centre, E-mail: dianne@iwwn.com.na.

> The center works on law reform issues, compiling statutes on rape and domestic violence in Namibia.
>
> Namibian Women's Association (NAWA)
> P.O. Box 3370
> John Knox Street, Maroela, Katutura
> Ph: 061 262 461

National Society For Human Rights, www.nshr.org.na.

Sister Namibia, E-mail: sister@windhoek.org.na or sister@iafrica.com.na.

> Sister Namibia focuses its efforts on addressing issues such as lesbian rights, media and communications, reproductive rights, sexuality, and violence against women.
>
> P.O. Box 40092, Windhoek 9000, Namibia
> Ph: 264 61 230 618/230 757

The Rainbow Project, http://overland.naomba.com/rainbow.html,
> Advocates for Lesbian, Gay, Bisexuals and Transgendered rights in Namibia. Orga-
> nizes programs, projects, advocacy education in various communities and churches
> in support of GLBT issues.
> P.O. Box 26122, Windhoek, Namibia
> Ph: 09–264–61230710
> E-Mail: madelene@trp.org.na or trp@mweb.com.na

Governmental and Religious Organizations

Department of Women's Affairs, Office of the President, E-mail: women_affairs@namibia.
com.na.
> Tre Building, 1st Floor, Private Bag 13339, Windhoek
> Ph: (264–61) 226 842 / 226 637

Ministry of Women's Affairs and Child Welfare (MWACW), E-mail: women_affairs
@namibia.com.na.
> Corner of Independence Avenue and Juvenis Building
> Private Bag 13359
> Private Bag 13339, Windhoek, Namibia
> Ph: (264-61) 2833111/2833204

NOTES

1. Namibia Statistics, globaledge.msu.edu/countryinsights/statistics.asp?.

2. United States President's Emergency Plan for AIDS Relief, "2007 Country Profile: Namibia," http://www.pepfar.gov/documents/organization/101659.pdf.

3. Ibid.

4. "Namibia," Worldpress.org, http://www.worldpress.org/profiles/namibia.cfm.

5. Namibia Statistics; "Namibia Facts and Figures," *Encarta*, 2009, http://encarta.
msn.com/fact_631504824/Namibia_Facts_and_Figures.html.

6. Laurie Goering, "Africa's Gays Persecuted as Cause of Ills," *Chicago Tribune*.

NIGERIA

Unoma N. Azuah and Leo Igwe

OVERVIEW

Nigeria is a West African country that is bordered in the north by Chad and the Niger River. To the east it is bordered by the Republic of Benin. Nigeria spans approximately 356,700 square miles—about the size of Arizona, California, and Nevada combined. The geographic terrain is a mixture of tropical forests, open woodland, grassland, and then coastal swamps in the south, and semi-desert in the far north. The annual rainfall along the coast is 150 inches, compared to 25 inches or less in the north. Nigeria obtained its independence from Britain in 1960 and, after 33 years of military leadership, adopted a new constitution in 1999 and held democratic elections.

During the same period, a transition to a civilian rule was concluded. Nigeria's largest economic base is petroleum, but corruption and gross mismanagement have caused the waste of most of its oil revenues. Consequently, with a population of about 140 million, over 70 percent of the Nigerian populace is categorized as poor. Out of the 140 million, there are about 20 million that make up the LGBT community in Nigeria; this is according to Reverend Jide Macaulay who runs one of the very few nongovernmental organizations in Nigeria for homosexuals. Further, the Nigerian LGBT community cuts across the multiethnic and religious beliefs that exist in Nigeria. The diversity of ethnicities and religions in Nigeria has caused ethnic and religious strain, however, the problems that occur due to this strain are not

manifested through any specific persons with specific sexual orientation. Besides, most of Nigeria's LGBT community are in the closet and do not openly reveal or talk about their sexual orientation because of the backlash that may occur. Most Nigerians, for example, would rather deny the existence of homosexuality in Nigeria. However, among the 140 million that make up the population of Nigeria, 20 million make up the LGBT community. There are about 250 ethnic groups in Nigeria; the *Hausa-Fulani, Igbo, Yoruba* and *Ijaw* are the largest. Nigeria's official language is English, even though Nigerian indigenous languages include, *Igbo, Hausa, Yoruba, Tiv*, and *Ijaw*. Nigeria's LGBT community consists of people from these various ethnic communities.

OVERVIEW OF LGBT ISSUES

Because Nigeria acceded to the International Covenant on Civil and Political Rights in 1993 to protect the rights to freedom expression, conscience, assembly, and freedom of association, it would have no option but to keep to the rules it has agreed to maintain. It also underscores an international legal obligation to fundamental freedoms. The African Charter on Human and Peoples' Rights also asserts the equality of all people.

Even though Nigeria's LGBT community is said to be more than 20 million, its penal system criminalizes homosexuality, thus hampering any form of debate or progress on LGBT rights. It also legalizes intolerance and discrimination against gays and lesbians. However, the constitution provides for a wide range of human rights. These provisions have been used to argue and lobby the government on LGBT issues.

EDUCATION

Even though the European style of education is wide spread and the dominant form of education in Nigeria, there are two other educational systems, namely the indigenous system and the *Quranic* system. In the indigenous educational system practiced mostly in the rural areas, children learn skills that range from farming, cattle herding, blacksmithing, textile, trading, and fishing. They also learn skills that would aid them as adults and contributors to their communities. Some of these skills include an apprentice scheme, a craft that involves leather and mat-making among other hand crafts.

Part of the religious duties of Muslims in Nigeria is to receive an Islamic education. Before children get to the age of six they are required to learn two chapters from the Koran, and are taught by a religious teacher or a *mallam*. The curriculum of the Islamic education comprises of copying and reading the Arabic alphabet and the ability to read and copy texts needed for daily prayers. Most instructions for this system of education are carried out in mosques, under a tree or in a religious teacher's house. The primary level of education is the most common. However, a limited number of young children who further their education are usually from well off homes; they go as far as scrutinizing the interpretations of the Arabic texts, including jurisdiction, rhetoric, syntax, arithmetic, grammar, and even theology at a much advanced level. The next level of schooling sees students moving on to famous Islamic learning centers. Nonetheless, most of the Islamic education is offered through *mallams*, or religious scholars whose specialties are in religious studies and teaching. Most of the Muslim schools set up during the colonial period were situated in Kano. Missionaries brought the western system of education to Nigeria in the 19th century. The Methodists found the first missionary schools in 1843, but the Missionary Society of the Anglican Church aggressively created a series of mission schools in 1850, which was closely followed by the Roman Catholics in the later part of 1850. By 1887, an education department that started forming requirements for curriculum and the administering of grants to mission societies was created in Southern Nigeria. When northern and southern Nigeria were amalgamated in 1914, 59 government and 91 mission primary schools existed in the south, and all the schools except for one were mission schools. In the same year there were 1,100 primary school students in the north, compared to 35,700 in the south.

Additionally, the north had no secondary schools while the south had eleven. In 1950, based on the British replica, Nigeria established the three-tier system of education consisting of primary, secondary, and higher education. The heels of independence were followed by a 10-year period of outstanding growth in education. Consequently, a movement for universal education was born in Western Nigeria. Primary school enrollment in the north sky rocketed from 66,000 in 1947 to 206,000 in 1957. Within the same period in western Nigeria the figures jumped from 240,000 to 983,000. In the east, it went from 320,000 to 1,209,000. Because of the importance of formal education, this became the largest program of the Nigerian government. By 1984–1985, more than 13 million students were enrolled in mostly public primary schools. Approximately 3.7 million children attended 6,500 schools, and about 125,000 were enrolled in postsecondary schools, including 35 colleges and universities. The enormous growth in education came with its own problems. The final examination method adopted from the British for one to earn a degree and economic hardship introduced widespread corruption among students, staff, and faculty in higher institutions; plus there were no incentives for research, and writing added to a lack in needed materials like required texts. Some measures were introduced to rectify these problems. For example, private universities and colleges were established to encourage healthy competition. The LGBT community was heavily involved in all of these attempts to improve the educational system in Nigeria. Despite their active role, they remain invisible, especially with the absence of LGBT organizations in these institutions. Homophobia dominates most, if not all the educational system in Nigeria.

In general, the Nigerian educational system is estimated to have 32 percent of men enrolled in secondary education, while 27 percent represent female students. These percentages include teenagers and adults who are members of the LGBT community in Nigeria. The general literacy rate is between 39 to 51 percent; this also does not exclude LGBT members. Across the country, about seven million children are out of school, though enrollment is gradually increasing. These seven million un-enrolled children include children that are being raised by lesbian and homosexual parents, and often living in the closet.

Early in the 21st century, formal education in Nigeria remains in the control of religious bodies, faith-based institutions, and states who often use it as a weapon of evangelization and proselytizing. Schools are often covert churches, and both mosques and the educational modules are infused with religious indoctrination. Students are made to embrace the religious ideologies of their schools, including the conservative and antagonistic stance on LGBT issues. The religion-laden education and instruction that Nigerians receive at home and in schools continue to undermine progress and national debate on LGBT rights. Because most students in Nigerian universities and high schools are guided by their religious beliefs, a good number of them are homophobic.[1] For instance, as recent as the 1990s, a male homosexual student was beaten to death at the University of Ife in Oyo State, Nigeria. The students that attacked him were under the impression that he was trying to make passes at one of them. Additionally, there have been cases where homosexual high school students have been punished by being lashed and expelled from school. According to the British, Danish fact-finding mission on human rights in Nigeria, there was a recent case where two lesbians were discharged from the University of Enugu.

EMPLOYMENT AND ECONOMICS

Nigeria's estimated economic growth of six percent in 2004, primarily from the oil industry, conceals the fact that Nigeria has a high unemployment rate. The oil industry in Nigeria is capital-intensive and does not entail a lot of labor. Fifty-five percent of the unemployed population are high school graduates. Additionally, more than half of the population is under the age of 35, and they are mostly unskilled. As such, it is speculated that Nigeria's unemployment rate is approximately 17 percent.

A privatization program that was formed in line with the IMF and World Bank's conditional policies, aided in changing the attitude of some employees in the public sector, however, there is no proof that privatization works or benefits citizens.[2] Yet another sector that is a challenge to the Nigerian economy is the electricity supply. Its power capability is about 20 percent of a country like Egypt. Improving the electrical supply has remained a top priority for the Nigerian government, who expects to improve its capacity by ten-fold in the year 2010.[3]

Nigeria's nominal gross domestic product for 2007 was estimated to be $175 billion; their 2006 date revealed that 26.8 percent of this revenue came from agriculture; 48.8 percent came from industry, while 24.4 percent came from services. The actual gross domestic product rate was estimated to be at 6.3 percent; oil growth was between five and six percent, and non-oil growth was at 9.6 percent. Further, Nigeria's per capita gross domestic product was estimated to be $1,158, with inflation at the rate of 5.4 percent.

There are no known records of how the Nigerian LGBT community contributes to the economy, but they make up the vast majority of workers and executive directors who are more or less living closeted lives. Nigeria's natural resources, which include oil and natural gas, were estimated to be 37 percent of the 2006 gross domestic product. Apart from petroleum, other natural gas resources include: tin, columbine, lead, limestone, coal, zinc, and iron ore. Nigeria's agricultural products include cocoa, groundnuts, yams, millet, livestock, rice sorghum, cassava, palm oil, and cotton. Nigeria's top industries consist of textiles, car assembly, detergents, cement, footwear, metal products, lumber, beer, and food products. In regard to trade, Nigeria's exports are valued at $59 billion; petroleum alone provides for 95 percent of the revenue. Other export products are comprised of rubber and cocoa. Nigeria's trade partners are the United States, which imports about 52.5 percent of its product, followed by Spain, which imports 8.2 percent, and Brazil at 6.1 percent. The value of Nigeria's imported products is $25 billion, and these imports are mostly machinery, manufactured goods, chemicals, and transport equipment. Nigeria's main import partners are China, the United States, United Kingdom, and the Netherlands.[4]

Nigeria's oil reserves total approximately 36 billion barrels, while its reserves of natural gas are estimated to be over 100 trillion cubic feet. Nigeria is a member of the Organization of Petroleum Exporting Countries (OPEC). By 2006, its crude oil production came to an average of about two million barrels per day. However, destruction of oil infrastructure ensued because of an unfortunate relationship with the indigenes. Added to this were harsh ecological damage and the government's inability to secure lives and property in the Niger Delta oil producing region. This epidemic haunted the oil industry. One of the programs created to remedy these problems was the Niger Delta Development Commission-NDDC, to assist with economic and social development of the area. The Nigerian economy is trending in a positive direction, especially with the 2005 summit of the G 7 where its external debt was reduced from 60 percent to barely five percent. The hike in oil prices around the world could also boost its revenue and reserve.

LGBT persons face systemic discrimination and exclusion in the area of employment. Anybody who is identified to be a gay or lesbian in most cases is automatically fired.[5] So, LGBT persons are forced to hide or disguise their identities in order to get or keep their jobs. From time to time, the Nigeria Army and local police expel officers alleged to be homosexuals. However, with the emergence of many privately owned companies, limited involvement of the state on employment and job creation, is generating hope for gays and lesbians in Nigeria to live and work with dignity in the years ahead.

SOCIAL/GOVERNMENT PROGRAMS

Though Nigeria witnessed a boom in almost all of its sectors in the 1970s, when it had a prosperous period in its economy because of the oil windfall, in subsequent years, especially within the past two decades, its general infrastructure has gradually depreciated. The downward trend of services like health and education is mostly due to poor management, lack of required work materials, inadequate, and disenchanted staff.[6] Further evidence that show the downfall in social services is revealed in the decline in school enrollment and the decline in the use of public health facilities since the 1980s. Poor quality in services and facilities force people to look elsewhere; many people tend to utilize private health services. Also, family planning services are not offered in over 70 percent of public health facilities.[7] The figures in the location of social services tend to be disproportionate. For example, in both the public and private health services more than 80 percent of hospital beds are in southern Nigeria, which leaves about a mere 20 percent for the north. The disproportionate allotment of services also affect the LGBT community because they are considered invisible, and as such are mostly treated the same way heterosexuals are treated. Their peculiar needs are not often taken into consideration, even when very few build up the courage to publically reveal their sexual orientation.

The Nigerian government is not oblivious to the problems that exist within the homosexual sector of social services. It has, therefore, gone ahead to introduce wide-ranging national guidelines for improvement in health, education, and population. Part of the plan for the introduction of these programs is to reduce poverty among the citizenry, even though the peculiar problems of the LGBT community are not taken into account. Some of the developed and published policies that are aimed at improving social services include the National Policy on Education, the National Health Policy, and the National Policy on Population. The National Policy on Education aims to achieve a universal, free, and mandatory education for all; it takes care of all educational functions and actions. The National Health Policy underscores the importance of health care as the best way to enable Nigerians to live lives that are rich and productive. In the meantime, the National Policy on Population concentrates on ways to check the mortality and reproductive rates of mothers and their children; here, family planning is emphasized. There are also efforts being put in place to build up the National Policy on Nutrition. Though these policies have been described as bogus and impractical,[8] and constant changes in government have threatened the success of these policies, the current government is determined to see them succeed. Again, disregarding the needs of the LGBT community, consequently there is no public health and social programs for the LGBT community in Nigeria, though some nongovernmental organizations work underground with LGBT persons. Some of these organizations include SMAN (Sexual Minorities Against Aids in Nigeria) Alliance Rights, INCREASE (International Center for Reproductive and Sexual Rights), the MCC church headed by Pastor Jide Macaulay, and the Humanist Society of Nigeria.[9] These organizations organize lectures and seminars in numerous schools, both at the university and high-school level, in the cities where they have their central offices. The focus of their seminars is mainly safer sex, AIDS, STDs and encouraging the Nigerian LGBT community to be proud of their sexuality as one way of curtailing homophobia.

SEXUALITY/SEXUAL PRACTICES

The International Center for Reproductive Health and Sexual Rights in Minna, Nigeria, conducted research that affirms the existence of nontraditional sexual choices in Nigeria and found that the Nigerian environment is very homophobic or at least appears to be.[10] According to the study, there is an outward expression of homophobia in the dominant culture although among the general population, there is greater understanding and tolerance that the practices exist. It is difficult for gays and lesbians to come out and admit to others that they are gay, bisexuals, or lesbians. They are therefore forced into heterosexual relationships. They marry to give a semblance of belonging to the widely accepted sexual orientation—heterosexuality—while they continue to meet their same sex partners secretly. This trend is additionally validated by Oludare Odumuye, one of the founders of the first openly gay association in Nigeria. He attests that, "because of the stigmatization of homosexuality, many gay men have girlfriends and even marry to be seen to conform to cultural and societal norms. It is not uncommon . . . for men to insist on using a condom with a woman but not bother with a male lover since they do not always realize that AIDS can be caught from sex with another man."[11] This phenomenon occurs because homosexuality is illegal in Nigeria; it is proscribed both in its penal code and the Muslim law. In northern Nigeria, a predominantly Muslim region, same sex relationships can get the harshest sentence: death. Under the penal code, homosexuality carries up to 14 years in prison. In January of 2006, the Nigerian Federal Executive Council was presented with a proposal that attempted to ban relationships between people of the same sex. This would not only criminalize such relationships or unions but also punish groups of persons or organizations that supported homosexuals and their activities. The proposed law entailed a five-year imprisonment for people who go "through the ceremony of marriage with person of the same sex, performs, witness, aids or abets the ceremony of same sex marriage, or is involved in the registration of gay clubs, societies and organizations, sustenance, procession or meetings, publicity, and public shows of a same-sex amorous relationship directly or indirectly in public and in private." These would include anyone like a cleric helping or supporting such unions. These people would also be liable to get the same prison sentence. The bill consisted of outlawing the adoption of children by homosexuals. The nullification of approved same-sex marriages conducted abroad was inclusive in the bill. Conversely, the United States Department of State reviled the law. Additionally, 16 human rights groups from all over the world wrote a letter to the government of Nigeria expressing disapproval of the bill and insisted that among other harms the bill will do, it will jeopardize the fight to stop or put a check on the spread of AIDS, especially when Nigeria has the world's third highest population with AIDS, with more than three million infected with HIV.

Chapter 42, Section 214 of Nigeria's criminal code punishes consensual homosexual sex among adults with a 14-year jail term. Added to that is the Sharia punitive code that was introduced in 1999 in northern Nigeria; it proceeds to criminalize sodomy. This is reflected in Chapter 111 "Hudud and Hudud related offences." There is also the Part 111 "Sodomy (Liwat)," Section 128–129 of the Kano State Sharia Punitive Code Law 2000. Further, as homosexuality is a capital crime in Islamic law, a married homosexual man faces a death penalty if caught, while a single man faces up to 100 lashes. Homosexuals who live in bigger cities have less reason to be afraid because most of them are in the closet and do not flaunt their sexuality. However, rich or well-known homosexuals who are either in government or in the public eye are often able to bribe their way through in order to escape the penalty. There are also situations where some homosexuals in cities like Kano and Lagos were caught by the police and they were disgraced by the Nigerian police force. They were asked to perform homosexual acts as a means of being implicated. Photographs of the act were taken and used by the Nigerian police as exhibits in court. Fear of being ostracized has kept majority of the Nigerian gay population underground. This fear may have been responsible for the fact that it was only in the year 2004 that a homosexual rights group was formed in Nigeria.[12] This group, known as Alliance Rights Nigeria (ARN), revealed themselves when the fourth national AIDS conference was held in Abuja. They were and still are working to spread the message of tolerance. They insist on the need for the country to acknowledge and defend the LGBT community because the secrecy attached to their lifestyle has consequently led to the astronomical rise in the number of AIDS victims, especially among homosexual men. To make matters worse, a broad spectrum of Nigerians deny that homosexuals exist. According to the late Oludare Odumuye, the president of Alliance Rights Nigeria, "It means that, for most of the Nigerians, [men who have sex with men] MSMs are not human beings-they simply don't exist." Odumuye continued by revealing that, "Recently, some of us have been arrested by the police, thrown into jail and raped in cells." Odumuye further disclosed during the AIDS conference in Abuja that "One out of 50 lawyers we have contacted has accepted to defend their interests. The others were too afraid to be associated with homosexuals, even if they were homosexuals themselves."[13]

The basic human rights of homosexuals are being threatened, especially as shown in the Nigerian government's attempt to introduce a bill that would render it nearly impossible for homosexuals to enjoy rights as every other Nigerian citizen. The witch-hunting by the government of Nigeria makes it obvious that their agenda is to strengthen the hate toward those with homosexual sexual orientation; particularly, when there exist laws that already prohibit homosexuality. So far there have been arbitrary arrests and sentencing of homosexuals and persons suspected to be homosexuals. In July 2007, in northern Nigeria, a Sharia court sentenced a man to death by stoning.[14] The man had admitted to having homosexual sex, even though he was accused of committing sodomy. He has remained on death row for months waiting to be put to death.[15] In August 2007, 18 men in northern Nigeria were arrested and are facing 10 years imprisonment; they are to receive 120 strokes of the cane. They have been accused of cross-dressing at a private a party.

These current events are in contrast with centuries of acceptance by Nigerians of homosexuals. For example, in northern Nigeria, there have been men referred to as *Dan Daudu*. They had been accepted and have remained part of the *Hausa-Fulani* culture until the Sharia Islamic law was introduced.[16] *Dan Daudus* are men who cross dress and act like women. They perform roles and acts considered traditionally to be women's. Even party organizers hire them as entertainment crews for their guests. However, Islam, as an alien religion to Nigeria, has threatened and continues to threaten that part of the culture. For example, in April 2008, Abubakar Hamza, a 19-year-old cross-dressing man in Kano, also known as "Fatima Kawaji," his female identity, was jailed and fined for what was described as "immoral behavior."[17] Also, in April 2008, a lesbian couple in Kaduna, northern Nigeria, was sentenced to six months in prison plus 20 strokes of the cane for homosexual activities.[18]

These homophobic stances seem contrary to the African cultural standards because African traditional tenets have been based on the needs of the communities, on what they thought was best for them. Africa was made up of independent ethnic communities, monarchies, and people with varied cultural traits and philosophies, before Western and Arab colonists arrived. Groups of people were governed by caucus, mutual consents, and laws handed out by traditional rulers, elders and priests. Because of the high mortality rate, a great emphasis was placed on reproductive sex and procreation, and not necessarily on any other kind of sexual practices. Therefore, heterosexuality was the medium; it served the need for sustaining land and offspring. Yet, that heterosexuality was considered typical did not mean that homosexuality was rejected or considered nonexistent.

Traditionally, Africans did not perceive same sex relationships as a vice. Rather, people were punished by being exiled, lashed, or stoned to death for murder, rape, kidnapping, and larceny. Nobody was, however, penalized for same-sex relationships or acts. However, with the introduction of foreign religions like Islam and Christianity, the abhorrence of homosexuals entered into the social consciousness. This debunks the myth that homosexuality is alien. Homophobia can therefore be said to be alien to Africa, not homosexuality.

In spite of the terrorization homosexuals confront in Nigeria, there remain some who are outspoken for equal rights, like Jide Macaulay. Macaulay became well-known after he spoke out against the same sex bill on the floor of the Nigerian House of Representatives in Abuja in February of 2007. Macaulay is a 42-year-old gay minister and the pastor of House of Rainbow, a church in the outskirts of Lagos. His church is one of the very few institutions in Nigeria that provide counseling for sexual health among gay men and lesbians. They also provide safe-sex resources. Macaulay emphasizes the need for partners to be faithful in their relationships. Through his ministry, he has created a space and a safe haven for about 30 Christian homosexual males who have lost their means of livelihood, endured some kind of mistreatment from friends and family members, or have been harassed by the police. He has additionally reaffirmed the place of homosexuals as children of God, especially for those who left the church because of their sexual orientation.[19] He restates this when he says that the mission of his church is to get, "gay men and women to reconcile their sexuality and their spirituality. The tragedy is that many people cannot do it because of historical interpretations of the scriptures."

FAMILY/COMMUNITY

Acceptance and accommodation of same-sex relationships existed in precolonial Nigeria.[20] Among the *Igbos* of Eastern Nigeria, same-sex marriages were (and still are) practiced. Women marry women; an only female child could choose to marry a woman to have children in most cases to keep her father's lineage. For the purpose of procreation, she arranges with her wife to have sex and have children with a man outside of their marriage. Because the African culture is matrifocal, emphasis is placed on procreation particularly for working the land. There was an emphasis placed on reproductive sex for childbirth, and homosexuals in Africa were constrained to live and express themselves privately and secretly, but this was not without the awareness of the other members of the community. So, homosexuals engaged in heterosexual marriages; this was to fulfill the social and not necessarily individual-need for children.

Nigeria is a very family oriented society. Their definition of family is not restricted to the nuclear type of family where only a mother and a father and their children are found. A sense of family to Nigerians would include extended family members; this will include uncles, aunts, cousins, nieces, nephews, and in-laws. In other words, relatives, regardless of how distant, can be considered a family member. This pattern is also obtained even in polygamous homes. This system is inclusive, especially in situations where two lesbians or two gay men can raise a child or children. Yet they will likely need to live a closeted life.

Children are very important to Nigerians. The need for children is so vital that a childless woman or man is looked upon as unfortunate. This is yet another reason why the Nigerian LGBT community is looked down upon, as they are not able to naturally bear children. Because there is a general love and desire for children, many Nigerians have a lot of children. Consequently, children are raised with the belief engrained in them that they will grow up to have wives in the case of men, and in the case of women, to have husbands. Therefore, observances like child naming are highly essential to most families. A child is typically given a name after seven days of his or her birth; this comes often with an elaborate celebration. Another factor responsible for the need for children is based on the importance placed on the male child; he is seen as the inheritor of the patriarchy and therefore maintains the genealogy of the patriarchal line. When a family lacks a male child, there is usually a tendency for the family to keep having children until they eventually get a male child. It is seen as a misfortune for any family or woman not to have a male child. However, there is a growing trend among some Nigerians (mostly in cities) not to have more children than they can care for. This is mostly due to economic reasons. Further, there is a tendency for most Nigerians to refer to their extended family members who are of their parent's age and related to their parents as "uncle," "aunt," "mother," or "father."

In most *Igbo, Ijaw,* or *Yoruba* communities for example, parents are usually acknowledged by the name of their first-born child. In other words, if a parent has a first child or a child called "Dada," he or she would be known as "Mama Dada"— Dada's mother or "Papa Dada"—Dada's father: The calling of parents Mama or Papa is not restricted to birth parents. Members of the Nigerian LGBT community who inherit children, mostly their relatives' children, still have the status of being called a Mama or a Papa. In most instances their sexuality is not revealed. The possibility of a lesbian couple or a gay male couple raising children is further affirmed in the African proverb that states, "it takes a village to raise a child." Almost everybody in a community is involved in raising a child because when a mother or father is not home, a neighbor automatically assumes that role. The communal life that exists in Nigeria also helps in the sense that a neighbor will usually feel free to run into a neighbor's house to ask for a pinch of salt, some water, or anything he or she runs out of unexpectedly. This relationship is usually symbiotic. It involves and affects most aspects of Nigerian life. For example, a neighbor can baby sit, help out in the farm, cook, and even take care of a sick neighbor when immediate family members are not around. Also in Nigeria there are unconventional family arrangements such as female same-sex couples, and single motherhood. These unorthodox family configurations are chosen and embraced by individuals to satisfy family needs and aspirations. However, with the rise in education, urbanization, and globalization, many Nigerians are abandoning the traditional ideas of the family relationship and are gradually embracing novel family values and configurations like those formed on the basis of LGBT rights and identities.

HEALTH

In 2007 52 deaths occurred for every 1,000 live births. There are 102.44 deaths among male infants compared to 1,000 live births. Meanwhile, female infants are at the rate of 88.38 deaths to 1,000 live births.[21] These occurrences affect both the heterosexual family and the closeted homosexual family.

Life expectancy for Nigeria's total population is at an average of 47.44 years. As of 2007, the average life span for Nigerian men was age 46.83, while women have 48.07 years of life expectancy. The fertility rate is 5.45 children born/woman. The prevalence of HIV/AIDS among adults is at 5.4 percent as far back at the year 2003. In the same year, 3.6 million Nigerians were living with HIV/AIDS, and about 310,000 people died from HIV/AIDS-related deaths.[22]

Because the LGBT community in Nigeria is largely ignored, they do not get the health care they need. For example, there are no known hospitals or clinics in Nigeria that accept openly gay men and women. It has been noted that if gays "announce to the doctor that they have anal wounds, you can be sure that they won't get proper care."[23] This finding is alarming considering that about 40 percent of men who have sex with men are married men. As Odumuye further observes, it has also been noted that "they continue to have sex with male partners, covertly-putting their wives and families at the risk of HIV infection." The Nigerian government's per capita spending on health is speculated to be one of the lowest in Africa. Consequently, there is a lack of workers in the health care field. Most of the qualified health workers migrate to the west, especially to Europe and America for better opportunities. About 21,000 Nigerian doctors have migrated to the United States alone. These doctors include doctors who are members of the Nigerian LGBT community, thereby limiting the chances of homosexuals to have access to a doctor that may be sympathetic to their peculiar situations. The Nigerian budget deficit in the health division is a primary cause for the lack of adequate health care. This problem acerbates the spreading of the AIDS epidemic. For example, Nigeria has about one million orphans due to AIDS; there are three million people living with HIV. Yet, there are less than 20 doctors accessible for every 100,000 people in Nigeria. The shame associated with AIDS has, for many years, limited the open acknowledgement of the disease. However, the Nigerian government has established organizations like the National Action Committee on AIDS (NACA); this organization coordinates the building of centers that specialize in offering gratis testing, treatment, and care. At least a quarter of those in need of antiretroviral drugs, or about 135,000 patients, received the drugs through the more than 200 centers in Nigeria by the last part of 2006.[24] Yet in all these arrangements, homosexuals, particularly men who sleep with men (MSM), are not seen as a fundamental group of people to work with in this respect.

Due to the fact that homosexuality is a crime, it is difficult to know the health situation including the prevalence if HIV/AIDS among the Nigerian LGBT community.[25]

POLITICS AND LAW

Nigeria's laws are modeled after the British Common Law, and in northern Nigeria there is an influence of Islamic law. There is also the traditional law based on the traditional tenets that existed before the colonization of Nigeria. Nigeria adopted a new constitution on May 5, 1999, which became effectual on May 29, 1999. Nigeria's government is referred to as the Federal Republic of Nigeria. It consists of 36 states, of which is included Abuja, the Federal Capital Territory. Nigeria also contains 774 local government areas. The Nigerian government has overhead costs that exceeds $13 billion, as reflected in its 2006 budget.

Some of the political parties that make up the Nigerian political organizations include Action ANPP, or All Nigeria People's Party, PSP or People's Salvation Party, FDP or Fresh Democratic Party, LP or Labor Party, PRP or Peoples Redemption Party, Accord Party or AC, APGA or All Progressive Grand Alliance, UNPP or United Nigeria Peoples Party, AC or Action Congress, AD or Alliance for Democracy, MRDD or Movement for the Restoration and Defense of Democracy, NDP or National Democratic Party, PPA or Peoples Progressive Alliance, and the ruling party, which is called the PDP, or Peoples Democratic Party. Some members of the Nigerian LGBT community are well-known politicians who are constrained to hide or deny their sexual orientation in order to keep a positive image for the public eye; they need to do this to enable them win votes. Nobody in Nigeria would vote for an openly gay politician. Some of their secret lovers who were willing to be interviewed, even though they refused to give their names, revealed that these politicians have arranged marriages to give the impression that they are heterosexuals. They are paid handsomely to keep these affairs a secret.

In spite of the turmoil that was witnessed in the 2003 and 2007 presidential elections, in 2008 Nigeria has come to embrace its longest period of civilian leadership since achieving independence in 1960. For example, the April 2007 elections became the first civilian-to-civilian handover of power in the history of the country. Politically, the LGBT community is excluded from politics. In fact, no openly gay person can take part in politics. Nobody who openly support gay rights can succeed politically in Nigeria. A gay identity is a weapon of blackmail. The laws criminalizing homosexuality remain in place and there seems to be no indication that they would be reversed any time soon. However, the recent suspension of the Anti-Gay Marriage Bill (initially sent to the parliament in 2006) by the federal government is a sign that the end of state-sanctioned homophobia may be drawing near.

RELIGION AND SPIRITUALITY

The religious practices in Nigeria include Islam, Christianity, and indigenous religions. Muslims make up 50 percent of the population, and about 40 percent are Christians. Indigenous believers equal about 10 percent of the population. African traditional religion did not record any hatred for homosexuals or homosexuality but with the infiltration of foreign religious practices, especially Islam and Christianity, the detestation and persecution of homosexuals began entering into the culture. Christian leaders, such as Anglican Bishop Peter Akinola, are some of the religious figures who are intensely homophobic. Because religion is taken very seriously in Nigeria, most Christian leaders encourage homophobia. Further, the severe Islamic Sharia Laws introduced in northern Nigeria have made the atmosphere impossible for homosexuals in the north to live and express themselves freely. There is no record of homophobia in the Nigerian indigenous religion.[26]

Indigenous religion involves the worship of deities like water spirits called *Mammy Wata*. The worshipers of water spirits are offered good fortune in return for some form of relationship with the spirits. These spirits can also inflict mayhem in an individual's life. Worshipping of *Mammy Wata* is well-known in the water areas of south and southeastern Nigeria. Also in southeastern Nigeria is what is known as traditional worship; it consists of two forms of worship: the routine worship and the occasional worship. Routine private worship is comprised of offerings given to ancestors through the head of a family at an ancestral shrine. The offerings are usually kola-nuts, white chalk, prayers for general good health of the family, success, and protection. Occasional private worship is done when a diviner asks an individual or a family to carry out the wishes of the gods or ancestors. This is usually after a family or an individual had consulted the diviner. There are no known records that indicate a person's sexual orientation excludes him or her from participating in these rituals. There are also rare occasions where a diviner conveys a message to a total stranger on a street. He gives the stranger a message, and often times the message is a request from the gods or ancestors asking for a sacrifice, and no emphasis is placed on sexual orientation as a means of being qualified to be a part of this belief. The LGBT community in Nigeria practices either the traditional religion, Christianity or Islam; even though Islam and Christianity as practiced in Nigeria directly or indirectly promote homophobia. Some Nigerian Christian Bishops, like Archbishop Peter Akinola, have been in the forefront in condemning homosexuals, not only in Nigeria but also throughout the world. In Akinola's words, homosexuality is "an aberration, unknown even in the animal kingdom."[27] He also describes homosexuals as "strange, two-in-one humans."

VIOLENCE

There are three primary sources of violence in Nigeria: Inter-ethnic conflicts, religious fights, and rebellion in the oil producing region of the Niger Delta. Apart from the three main ethnic groups in Nigeria—the *Igbos, Yorubas,* and the *Hausas,* there are more than 250 ethnic communities that exist in Nigeria. Many of them live in dire circumstances. Some of them are also excluded from their land rights because almost everything is perceived as property of the Nigerian government. On occasion, rancor arises between neighbors due to land disputes or inter-ethnic family brawls.

Since the introduction of the Islamic Sharia law in 12 northern states of Nigeria, religion has remained a major basis for violence, particularly between the predominantly Islamic north and minority Christians living in the north. As a result, the Christian dominated south has, on occasion, rallied to avenge the deaths of their relatives killed in the north by attacking and killing Muslims living in the south. Therefore, the number of people killed in religious/ethnic clashes dating as far back as 1999 has exceeded 13,000. The government has not been successful in controlling these clashes, nor has it been able to hunt down the people responsible to charge them for their crimes.

Further, the discovery of oil in Nigeria dating back to the 1950s became a mixed blessing for the country; it has remained the major source of Nigerian revenue. Oil produces about 95 percent of the country's foreign exchange, but it has also remained the major source of violence in the Delta region. In spite of the four-fold increase in oil revenue, the region still remains in abject poverty and there is still a severe lack of services. This situation gave rise to the sprouting of rebellious groups like the Movement for Emancipation of the Niger Delta (MEND). These groups focus on pressurizing the government to implement environmental justice and the development of the region's infrastructure. Additionally, some of the rebel groups engage in vandalizing, damaging installations of the oil refineries and kidnapping expatriates and some traditional leaders.

Violence against LGBTs in Nigeria is common and widespread.[28] Many have suffered physical attacks, personal harm, and injuries. Some have been beaten and roughed up. Some years ago, a mob attacked an openly gay person in Ile Ife, which is in southwest Nigeria, and forced a stick into his anus.[29] Such violent crimes against LGBTs go unaddressed and unpunished because gay sex is illegal.

OUTLOOK FOR THE 21ST CENTURY

The outlook for Nigeria in the 21st century is uncertain, as its quadruple gain in oil revenue does not translate into better lives for its citizens. Over 70 percent of its people live on under one dollar a day. Even with adequate food production, an international agency called ActionAid suggests that at least one-third of the citizens are starving. Nigeria is the fifth largest exporter of oil to the United States; it also has the largest population (about 140 million) in Africa.

Nigeria's unsuccessful attempt to leave any significant mark in the Millennium Development Goals (MDGs) has led the United Nations to conclude in 2007 that the MDGs will possibly not be reached in sub-Sahara Africa. Nigeria, on the other hand, has not given up on improving. For instance, some of the government programs established to check poverty include what is called the National Economic Empowerment and Development Strategy (NEEDS) and this program has an ancillary branch in all of the 36 states in Nigeria. Even though some administrative flaws threaten to slow the initiative down, the government of Nigeria has remained optimistic. In addition, the Nigerian Ministry of Finance has recorded a notable five percent growth in the Nigerian economy. Though it may cost Nigeria $5 billion to sustain and achieve the MDGs, it has not given up on working towards the goals. The situation may be worse for the LGBT community because they have to live an invisible life as members of an unacknowledged sexual minority. Nigeria may not accept homosexuality in the near future. However, the country is under pressure to uphold and respect the free and democratic choices of the citizens and to make its laws compatible with international human rights standards. This type of social progress portends a hopeful and promising future for LGBTs in the country.

RESOURCE GUIDE

Web Sites and Organizations

Global Right Nigeria, http://www.globalrights.org/site/PageServer?pagename=www_afr_index_42.
House of Rainbow Metropolitan Community Church, Nigeria, http://houseofrainbowmcc.blogspot.com/2009/03/house-of-rainbow-metropolitan-community.html.
The Independent Project for Equal Rights, Nigeria, http://www.ysm-rightsorg.page.tl/.
International Center for Reproductive Health and Sexual Rights (INCRESE, Nigeria), http://www.increse-increse.org/.
Lawyers Alert, Nigeria, www.lawyersalert.org/about.php.
Nigerian Humanist Movement, Nigeria, http://www.iheu.org/node/1472.
Queer Alliance Nigeria, http://queeralliancenigeria.blogspot.com/.
Youths Together Network Nigeria, http://projects.tigweb.org/YES-Nigeria?langrand=1854860841.

NOTES

1. Personal interview with E. Y. Otubelu, a graduate of the University of Ife, conducted by Unoma Azuah and Leo Igwe, February 1998.
2. Akande Adebowale, "Nigeria Guide," OneWorld.Net, 2008, www.uk.oneworld.net/guides/Nigeria/development.
3. Ibid.
4. A. H. Ekpo and O. J. Umoh, "Growth and Direction of External Trade," Online Nigeria, 2008, http://www.onlinenigeria.com/links/economyadv.asp?blurb=488.
5. Personal interview with a lesbian lady that worked with the Ministry of Education in Nigeria, interview conducted by Unoma Azuah, May 2008, Lagos, Nigeria.
6. Adebowale, "Nigeria Guide," 2008.
7. Ibid.
8. Ibid.
9. Behind the Mask, Allaince Rights, SMAAN, Sexual rights nongovernmental orgnizations.

10. Unoma Azuah, "Emerging Lesbian Voice in Nigerian Feminist Literature," in *Body, Gender and Sexuality,* ed. Flora Veit-Wild and Dirk Naguschewski (Kenya: Matatu Press, 2005).

11. Oludare Odumuye, IRIN NIGERIA (Integrated Regional Informational Network), "Persecuted Gay Community Cautiously Seeks a Voice," May 7, 2004.

12. According to the NGO Behind the Mask: "Alliance Rights Nigeria is a gay welfarist association and was formally launched on July 2, 1999, in Lagos, Nigeria," "About Nigeria: Gay Community Claim a Voice, 2004," www.mask.org.za.

13. Integrated Regional Information Network (IRIN).

14. "Death Sentence for a Homosexual Act in Nigeria," *afrol News,* April 2008, www.afrol.com/articles/16722.

15. "Clash Over Nigeria Cross Dressing," *BBC News: Africa,* August 21, 2007, http://news.bbc.co.uk/2/hi/africa/6956848.stm.

16. Nosa Olotu, "Nigerian Men that Like to Dress Up as Women," February 22, 2008, http://www.nigeriavillagesquare.com/.

17. Tony Grew, "Nigerian Sharia Court Punishes Lesbian Couple," *Pinknews,* April 11, 2008, http://www.pinknews.co.uk/index.php?s=Nigerian+Sharia+Court+Punishes+Lesbian+Couple.

18. Ibid.

19. Waldimar Pelser, "God Also Loves Gay People," *City Press,* March 15, 2008, http://jv.news24.com//City_Press/Features/0,186-1696_2289015,00.html.

20. Ifi Amadiume, "Female Husbands, Male Wives" (Zed Books, 1987).

21. Adebowale, "Nigeria Guide," 2008.

22. Ibid.

23. Odumuye, IRIN NIGERIA.

24. Ibid.

25. Immigration Service, "Report on Human Rights Issues in Nigeria-Joint British Danish Fact Finding Mission to Abuja and Lagos, Nigeria," October–November 2004, www.ecoi.net/.../470_1161611888_joint-british-danish-fact-finding-mission-to-abuja-and-lagos.

26. Leo Igwe, "Homophobia in Africa," April 2007, *culturekitchen,* http://culturekitchen.com/leo_igwe/story/homophobia_in_africa.

27. Pelser, "God Also Loves Gay People."

28. Ibid.

29. Personal interview with five male homosexuals, Nat Gwalaga, Cyprus Eneh, Ndudi White, Fola Williams, and Orseer Gyste (not their real names). This interview was conducted by Unoma Azuah at Abuja in July 2008.

SOUTH AFRICA

Johan H. B. Smuts

OVERVIEW

The Republic of South Africa is located on the southern tip of the African continent. It borders Namibia, Botswana, Zimbabwe, and Mozambique to the north while facing the Atlantic Ocean to the west, and the Indian Ocean to the south and east. South Africa also surrounds the two small nations of Lesotho and Swaziland.

South Africa has the largest economy and most developed infrastructure on the African continent, and ranks 26th in global GDP. This ranking does not diminish the fact that South Africa, with its dual economy, high unemployment rate, and underdevelopment in the rural areas, remains a developing country. Economically and politically there are major divides in the population. Poverty is the norm among all races, becoming even more pronounced due to privatization and disinvestment. The white middle class remains the most homogenous and represented population group, although there is a rapidly expanding black middle class.

South Africa has a population of around 47 million people. The majority of the population are black Africans (80%), while white and mixed-race Africans, as well as South Africans of Asian descent comprise the remaining 20 percent. South Africa has 11 official languages, including English, the only official language to be spoken outside of the continent. Nearly 80 percent of South Africans identify as Christian, belonging to denominations found only in South Africa, which are heavily influenced by African traditional religions. The majority of the white population identifies as Protestant, Charismatic, Anglican, or Catholic, in that order.

South Africa is diverse in its geography and people. It is noted for its multi-cultural, multiracial, and multilingual society. Communities are rural and urban, rich and poor, conventional and modern. Every major religion, including African traditional religions, is practiced. All of these differences influence the way people think about and interpret social issues such as gender and sexuality, and it is difficult to give a comprehensive account of all LGBT issues across all South African communities.

Until 1994, an oppressive regime of white leaders descended from European colonists represented mostly white South Africans, controlled all politics, economy, and law. Their moral motivation was rooted in Christian Nationalism, the ideology of the ruling class, which stripped nonwhite, nonheterosexual, and some non-Christian people of their rights as citizens of the Republic. Nonwhites were sent to live in *cultural homelands* called Bantustans, which were actually segregated townships and suburbs. This race-based discrimination, known as apartheid, extended to the separate use of public amenities such as transportation, toilets, and shops. Despite their policy of freedom of religion, the white government still attempted to control the morality of the general population.

Under the laws of apartheid, intimate interracial relationships were deemed illegal, as was the practice of homosexuality. After the relatively peaceful transition of rule from the all-white government to a demographically representative, democratic government in 1994, these laws were revoked, and in 1996 the Bill of Rights was accepted as central to the Constitution of the Republic. The Bill of Rights included a detailed antidiscrimination clause that included gender and sexual orientation, and with that clause penned in, South Africa became the first country in the world to outlaw discrimination against sexual orientation in the Constitution. In South Africa there exists no institutional discrimination; however, this has not curbed infrequent homophobic acts and attitudes. Homosexual South Africans neither automatically assumed equal footing with their heterosexual neighbors, nor did the Constitution change the way homosexuality was understood and practiced in rural areas, towns, and cities. Despite the extreme variation in culture, class, and race, homosexual people and their practices are found in all communities.

OVERVIEW OF LGBT ISSUES

Officially, it appears as if the struggles of the LGBT community in South Africa is over and victorious. Full recognition is officially given to alternative sexualities and relationships, and recently the Civil Union Act (Act 17 of 2006) of Parliament placed civil unions on a legal par with heterosexual marriage. The term civil union remains a bone of contention, as some activists believe that true equality would culminate in an amendment of the Marriage Act.

In the private sector, examples of individual discrimination and victimization can be identified, yet there is not an extensive record of homophobic acts and violence perpetrated against members of the LGBT community. This may be due to individual fears about reporting incidents to the police while having to continue living within communities that may not hold the same attitude as the Constitution in regard to the equality of people with alternative sexualities.

Amongst theorists and academics in South Africa, sexuality is consistently equated with gender, a problem not only for their peers in the academy, but also for the subjects about whom they theorize. The tenacious conviction that gender is sexuality remains, even among members of the South African LGBT community. Another inherent dilemma facing social scientists and commentators is the backlash by black African intellectuals and traditional leaders who deny the *Africanness* of homosexuality, claiming it was a vice imported by European colonials.

HIV/AIDS is the single largest crisis facing South Africans in the 21st century. It is a problem primarily associated with heterosexual people in lower income or poor communities, more so than with gay men. Even among men who practice homosexual sex, HIV infection is most often found among transitory laborers and sex workers.

A concern not always considered by the LGBT community is their previous history under an oppressive, discriminatory legal system. Homosexuality, sodomy, and cross dressing all led to incarceration under the nationalist regime. Furthermore, homosexual individuals conscripted into the defense force during the 1970s and 1980s were subjected to a number of faux-therapies that did not keep up with the growing acceptance of homosexuality in the rest of the world.

LGBT South Africans, for the most part, seem to be satisfied with the legal recognition they enjoy under the liberal Constitution, but this does not mean that the experience of individuals in communities are simplified. Politically there is no rallying point for LGBT people in South Africa, which is an ongoing struggle for those concerned with having a political voice.

EDUCATION

The South African educational system was unified from different departments of education that had previously catered to specific racial groups under the former nationalist government. Now a single department is responsible for all education in South Africa. Primary and secondary schools are administered by provincial departments of education, while colleges and universities remain under the authority of the national department.

The current education policy gives more responsibility to individual communities for running and funding their own schools. This means that the unification of the educational system did not close the breach that existed between previously disadvantaged schools and middle-class schools. Even if most schools are public schools, those located in more affluent areas still have a financial benefit over those in the rural areas and poorer settlements. This inequality results in some schools having very good access to educational technologies and resources, while many others are without basic necessities such as running water and electricity.

In general, public institutions, such as schools, respect the Bill of Rights as applied by the Constitution. Schools cannot discriminate against LGBT learners in any way. Some provincial departments even run programs in their schools to develop attitudes of equality and tolerance. There are a number of examples of high school seniors who have, with the support of their schools, attended school functions with their same-sex partners. This atmosphere of tolerance does not always extend to less privileged schools. Very few of the poorer schools allow for the formation of student associations, and so there is a shortage of approved school associations for LGBT students. Although schools are governed by liberal constitutions and policies, some students experience homophobic acts and attitudes from other students.

Colleges and universities, on the other hand, have always been at the forefront of liberalism in South Africa; most of them have been supportive of political and institutional transformation. Many universities have organized LGBT societies that cater to the needs of their student bodies. Many universities also teach courses dealing with sexuality and gender and continue to research and publish on the topic. A conservative, resistant element still remains in institutions that used to be solely for those who spoke Afrikaans.

EMPLOYMENT AND ECONOMICS

Due to the disparity of wealth in South Africa, the country has the unique characteristic of having a dual economy, a formal economy, and an informal economy. These separate economic superstructures are estimated to be of about equal size, but this is difficult to prove as the informal economy is completely without record. The size of the informal economy can be ascribed to poverty among most South Africans. High interest rates and unemployment force many individuals to engage in informal, untaxed labor, as well as trade in unregulated commodities that are easier to afford. The government is trying to curb what they call the "second economy," as massive turnover results in a notable loss of tax revenue. Due to the unregulated nature of the informal economy, the issues surrounding sexuality in this economy, including the proliferation of sex work—most of which is illegal—remains unrecorded.

Like most other sectors of society, discrimination in the workplace based on sexual orientation is prohibited by the Labor Relations Act (Act 66 of 1995). The situation had improved even more when the Employment Equity Act (55 of 1998) classified diverse sexual orientation and race as a characteristic that should be represented in all corporate and employment structures. In spite of Act 66, many South Africans remain hesitant to disclose their sexual orientation in such a public way. The application of Act 66 is primarily geared toward the advancement of black Africans in the workplace.

The currency of South Africa is the South African Rand (ZAR). Marketers and retailers have realized the value of the *pink rand,* that is, money from the LGBT community. This can be seen in the many ad campaigns geared toward LGBT consumers in both the gay and mainstream press. Apart from poverty, marginalization from the formal economy in labor and consumption is not an everyday experience for the majority of LGBT people.

SOCIAL/GOVERNMENT PROGRAMS

A number of social programs, both privately and publicly funded, are geared towards the LGBT community in South Africa. The vast majority of programs for LGBT South Africans are operated by nongovernmental organizations (NGOs). In rural and poor areas, programs attempt to inform people about sexual health issues, and strive to create safe environments within which LGBT individuals can socialize and express themselves. There seems to be less community critique of homosexuality, or of those who are in same-sex relationships, when people do not self-identify as gay or lesbian. Most public money is spent on sex education and HIV/AIDS centers, and on research for a predominantly heterosexual population.

In the more affluent parts of South Africa, funding for social projects aimed at LGBT people also comes from both the public and private sectors, most notably philanthropists from the European Union and the National Lottery. A number of community centers, pride parades, festivals, and film festivals cater to individuals who can afford to attend these events, each run by independent organizations that include health education and activism in their agendas.

SEXUALITY/SEXUAL PRACTICES

In South Africa, the nature of sexual practice depends on its social context. Some communities may be very tolerant of homosexuality, while others are not. In some communities, such as single-sex institutions like prisons and labor compounds that house transitory laborers, the practice of homosexuality is a viable expression of sexuality. The Department of Corrections has gone as far as supplying condoms to prisoners in an attempt to minimize HIV and STD transmission. The expression of same-sex affection in places such as these is structured according to social norms that may not exist outside those institutions.

Homosexuality among people not living in single-sex environments is also not limited to men and woman who self identify as LGBT. Most cities and towns have areas such as public toilets and cruising areas where anonymous sexual encounters between individuals, especially men, take place. Public sex is not heavily policed. Anonymous sexual encounters between women are not well documented.

In South African LGBT communities where homosexuality is not a taboo topic, anonymous sexual encounters among gay and lesbian individuals are less frequent. LGBT people are prone to more intimate homosexual interactions than heterosexuals, even if these interactions do not lead to relationships.

A popular misconception remains about the nature of gay and lesbian sex. Most people believe that gay and lesbian sex is similar to the traditional heterosexual model in that one partner should assume a dominant or "masculine" role, while the other should assume a passive or "feminine" role. This may be the case in some relationships, while others are based on equality, mutual respect, and synchronicity.

FAMILY

Family structure is another example of the diversity found in the South African population. Families and the relationships that structure them can be divided into three broadly defined categories: The first and most visible category would be the Western nuclear family model, although they are decreasing due to a rise in divorce and the acceptance of single parent households. This kind of family is most likely found in urban areas and parts of the privileged rural populations.

The majority of rural South African communities consist of extended families, many of which are centered on polygamous households where one man, when he can afford it, has more than one wife, and children with each of those wives. These marriages are not illegal in South Africa; the Constitution allows for the recognition and practice of traditional law in as much that traditional law has to be considered in courts. Not all people are allowed to have polygamous marriages, however; only a person who functions and resides in a community where traditional law is practiced may have more than one wife. The rules that govern these relationships are different from community to community, and even when permitted by law, not all people in those communities practice polygamy.

The third category of family is family-households that consist of people who choose to live together without being biologically or legally related. The majority of LGBT households in South Africa would fall into this group. Family households living together by choice have the benefit of domestic and economic cooperation among individuals. Family households of this nature are neither limited by the nature of the relationship between its members, nor the number of people who participate in these households.

A new household pattern has arisen due to the prevalence of HIV/AIDS in South Africa. In many communities, so many adults succumb to AIDS-related illnesses that there is an increase in child-headed households. These households, for lack of the presence of healthy adults, are run by and provided for by underage children as young as their early teens. The government has responded to this social problem by lowering the age of legal adulthood to eighteen.

COMMUNITY

The many different kinds of communities in South Africa affect the lives and social interaction of LGBT individuals. The 1980s saw the first attempts of homosexual South Africans to organize politically. The effect it had on social policy was minimal, and catered primarily to the social needs of interested participants. This was to be the life story of many South African LGBT movements in the following decades. The liberation struggle against apartheid benefited on a number of levels from the contribution of LGBT people, like Justice James Cameron, a human rights lawyer, who now resides on the bench of the Constitutional Court; their contribution created a sentiment fostered by the new government of equality and tolerance. Gay liberation was inherent to the Constitution of the Republic, and further struggles against public institutions were deemed unnecessary unless institutions infringed on the right of the LGBT community.

A number of organizations geared toward LGBT services operate in most major cities, but the social relevance exerted by these organizations is limited to devoted members. Social clubs and events are more successful in mobilizing the LGBT community to participate. Currently, LGBT lobbying and pressure is controlled by a select number of NGOs.

HEALTH

In South Africa, any citizen can seek medical assistance and treatment from the state, as there are currently hundreds of hospitals and thousands of community clinics available. The standard of service provided by state health care providers has degraded to such an extent that those who can afford it would rather use expensive medical services provided by the private sector. Private sector health care is comparable to health care in the first world. The state does not provide health services that cater specifically to the needs of the LGBT community. It would appear that the services required by the LGBT community in South Africa do not differ from the needs of mainstream society at all, as no incidents of unfair treatment due to sexual orientation have been reported.

HIV/AIDS is the largest health issue in South Africa, followed by tuberculosis. The combination of these two epidemics taxes the public health system to its extremes. The government, initially loath to agree to the relationship between HIV and AIDS, chose to ascribe the occurrence of these diseases to poverty. Under pressure from activists, the government has started the mass supply and distribution of antiretroviral treatments. This program aims to increase the life expectancy of the population at large, as demographic change prompted by the pandemic shows a reduction in economically active age groups. Some medical service providers dedicated to LGBT health issues exist, primarily run by private health care professionals and NGOs. Health issues among men-who-sleep-with-men differ from group to group; in labor compounds and prisons the incidence of HIV and STD transmission is higher than in other contexts, while some communities have more information about safe sex practices than others. Health issues among lesbians and women-who-have-sex-with-women are not well researched.

POLITICS AND LAW

Laws dealing with LGBT issues are comprehensively governed by the Constitution. The Constitution, in turn, is subject to the Bill of Rights and the Constitutional court, both of which are champions of LGBT rights. Not only were the laws that criminalized homosexuality and its practice rescinded by the National Assembly, but laws governing sexual expression were also revised in favor of more liberal approaches. These changes came about through the lobbying of some LGBT organizations, but a ready path existed in the freedoms offered in the Constitution. One of the major LGBT lobbying victories though was reducing the age of male sexual consent to 16 years old, which is the same as the age of consent for females. The most recent legal change in favor of the LGBT(I) community was the institution of same sex marriages, known by the term civil unions. Some activists think that the act is still discriminatory by making a distinction between same-sex and opposite-sex relationships, and excluding same-sex unions from the definition of marriage.

Parliament consists of two houses. In the lower house, also known as the National Assembly, the people are represented by elected political parties. Currently the party with the ruling majority (African National Congress) and the official opposition (Democratic Alliance) have a very good record of supporting LGBT rights. At the same time, a number of minority parties have politically and religiously conservative policies regarding sexuality, and these parties are often outspoken and critical of the positive attitude that the government has toward the LGBT community.

RELIGION AND SPIRITUALITY

All major religions, as well as the moral reservations they have about homosexuality, are practiced and recognized in South Africa. About 80 percent of the population identifies as Christian, but many local interpretations of Christianity are closely related to African Traditional Religions (ATRs), and much of the theological interpretation and iconography may seem strange to western Christians. These churches are outspoken in their disapproval of homosexual lifestyles and identities.

White South African churches are divided on LGBT issues. Afrikaans Dutch Reformed denominations have changed their attitude from outright damnation to a more enlightened attitude of "hate the sin and not the sinner." The Charismatic churches follow the trend set by the Christian right of the United States, and thus view homosexuality as a curable disease. The Anglican Church in South Africa has set itself apart from Anglicans on the rest of the African continent by having a positive attitude towards LGBT issues. Some South African Anglican priests are even willing to bless same sex unions in the church, even if civil union liturgy has not yet been created. The Catholic Church in South Africa follows the doctrine of the Vatican. Most Christian LGBT people remain in the closet, or they leave the church entirely. Some of the major metropolitan areas have churches that are dedicated to serving the LGBT community.

Jewish and Muslim communities thrive throughout South Africa, with Islam having more devotees. Both of these communities make their policies under strict guidance of religious scripture. South African Jews and Muslims seem to be less outspoken and critical of LGBT issues, but that may simply be due to underrepresentation. Organizations that serve LGBT individuals in the Jewish and Muslim communities exist and are active in improving the lives of the LGBT community and other social issues.

African Traditional Religions (ATRs) are practiced by many South Africans, most of whom are black. These religions originated in the rural areas, but are still practiced all over modern South Africa. The leaders of these religions are traditional healers, practitioners of magic, and *sangomas* (shamans), all of whom rely heavily on the intervention of the ancestors in the lives of individuals. ATRs do not deal with LGBT politics and policies. In many ATRs however, the sexual orientation of a man or woman is considered an indication of the ancestors calling such people to service. The practice of homosexuality is not prohibited in ATRs, but LGBT people who practice these religions may choose not to self-identify as gay or lesbian. Religion in general does not have a major influence on national politics because South Africa is a secular state.

VIOLENCE

South Africa is one of the most violent countries in the world. Much of the violence can be ascribed to crime. South Africa has a very high crime rate and many people are murdered, raped, robbed, hijacked, and assaulted daily. Some theorize that this is because of the extreme divide between rich and poor in the country, and that some poor people commit crime in order to survive. The violent nature of crimes, however, is not explained by this theory; practically no research is being done on the subject. Violence committed against members of the LGBT community also takes place, but very little proof exists to illustrate that they are singled out because of their sexual orientation.

Violence against homosexual women and men in affluent communities rarely goes beyond homophobic statements and bullying. For homosexual people in more traditional communities, the situation can be much worse. Some lesbians are raped by men in order to "make them straight again". Much of the violence committed against LGBT(I) people comes from within the LGBT(I) community itself in the form of domestic violence. Domestic violence among same-sex partners is also prohibited by the Domestic Violence Act (Act 116 of 1998).

OUTLOOK FOR THE 21ST CENTURY

LGBT communities in South Africa are some of the most fortunate in the world. They get full recognition and protection from the state when they demand it. LGBT people in South Africa hope to contribute to the future of their country by participating in its economy and nation building. There is a concern that LGBT rights may be infringed upon in the future, because even if the government is liberal on LGBT issues inside the Republic, it remains quiet in regard to the legal oppression of homosexual people in its neighbor states of Botswana, Namibia, and Zimbabwe. Few organizations have tried to pressure government into discussing the issue with the governments of these countries, but larger political issues overshadow these concerns and government policies of silent diplomacy are ineffectual.

It is the hope of the LGBT communities in South Africa that mainstream society will become less sensitive to their presence, and be more informed about the myths created by LGBT stereotypes. This will not happen unless the LGBT community rallies itself around desensitization campaigns, aimed not at institutions and government, but at people in general.

RESOURCE GUIDE

Suggested Reading

Edwin Cameron and Mark Gevisser, eds., *Defiant Desire: Gay and Lesbian Lives in South Africa* (London: Routledge, 1995).

Paul Germond and Steve de Gruchy, eds., *Aliens in the Household of God: Homosexuality and Christian Faith in South Africa* (Northampton, MA: Interlink Publishing Group, 1997).

Gordon Isaacs and Brian McKendrick, *Male Homosexuality in South Africa: Identity Formation, Culture and Crisis* (Capetown: Oxford University Press Southern Africa, 1992).

Herb Klein, *South African Sons* (London: Prowler Press, 1998).

William J. Spurlin, *Imperialism within the Margins: Queer Representation and the Politics of Culture in Southern Africa* (New York: Palgrave Macmillan, 2007).

Saskia Wieringa and Ruth Morgan, *Tommy Boys, Lesbian Men and Ancestral Wives* (Johannesburg: Jacana Media, 2005).

Video/Film

Apostles of Civilized Vice. Directed by Zackie Achmat, 2000.

Apostles of Civilized Vice: Part I: Questions of a Queer Reading History. Directed by Zackie Achmat, 2000. Wits Gay Library.

Cold Stone Jug. Directed by Cedric Sundstrom, 2003. CMS Film Productions: Johannesburg, South Africa.

Everything Must Come to Light. Directed by Mpumi Njinge and Paulo Albertson, 2003. Coproduced by The Gay & Lesbian Archives of South Africa, and Out in Africal Gay & Lesbian Film Festival.

Four Rent Boys and a Sangoma. Directed by Catherine Muller, 2004. Documentary filmed in the streets of Johannesburg, South Africa.

Metamorphosis: The Remarkable Journey of Granny Lee. Directed by Luiz DeBarros, 2000. Underdog Entertainment; South Africa.

My Son the Bride. Directed by Mpumi Njinge, 2002. Documentary filmed for M-Net pay channel.

Out in South Africa. Directed by Barbara Hammer, 1995. Barbara Hammer Productions; South Africa.

Property of the State: Gay Men in the Apartheid Military. Directed by Gerald Kraak, 2003. Coproduced by GALA, Out-in-Africa, and the National film and Video Foundation.

Proteus. Directed by John Greyson, 2003. Pluck Productions; Canada and South Africa.

Pussy. Directed by Stanimir Stoykov, 2004. South Africa.

Quest for Love. Directed by Helena Nogueira, 1989. Distant Horizons: South Africa.

Simon and I. Directed by Beverly Ditsie and Nicky Newman, 2002. South Africa.

Web Sites/Organizations

Cape Town Pride, www.capetownpride.co.za.

Gay and Lesbian Archives, www.wits.ac.za/gala.

GEM: Gay issues in the media, www.gemsouthafrica.org.

Gender DynamiX, www.genderdynamix.org.za.
  Transgender issues.

RainbowUCT, www.rainbowuct.org.
  Student group at the University of Cape Town.

SA Bears, www.sabears.co.za.
  A gathering of large masculine men who self-identified as "bears."

Triangle Project, www.triangle.org.za.
  Counseling, mental health, HIV support, and advocacy.

Up & Out, http://www.up-and-out.co.za/.
  GLBT student society at the University of Pretoria.

TANZANIA

Tom Ochieng Abongo

OVERVIEW

Tanzania is a united republic comprised of two independent states: Tanganyika on the mainland and Zanzibar on the island in the Indian Ocean. Tanganyika attained independence from the British Empire on December 9, 1961, and one year later it became a republic. Likewise, Zanzibar became independent on December 10, 1963, and after the revolution of January 12, 1964, the People's Republic of Zanzibar was established. These two independent republics finally merged on April 26, 1964, to form the United Republic of Tanzania. However, the two republics maintain a distinct governing autonomy.

Tanzania is bordered by both Kenya and Uganda to the north, thereby making up the East Africa region. Tanzania is a secular state with a diverse religious composition; the main religions are Islam, Christianity, and Hinduism. The official language in Tanzania is Swahili, though English is also used widely in most urban areas.

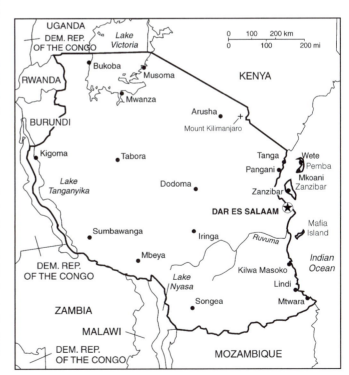

OVERVIEW OF LGBT ISSUES

Homosexuality is frowned upon in Tanzania, and all of the religious followings condemn any behavior that does not conform to the perceived law of nature. The definition of sexual intercourse under Tanzania's Sexual Offenses Act of 1998, is given as penile-vaginal penetration, and any sexual act that does not conform to this is an offense that can incur a prison term of up to 30 years, along with corporal punishment in jail.

EDUCATION

The education system in Tanzania is based on a "7-4-2-3" system, in which seven years is spent in primary school, four years in secondary school, two years in high school, and three years in university. Public schools are funded by the government. All lessons in public schools are conducted in the Swahili language. However, there are a number of private schools and academies that conduct their school curriculum in English; these are preferred by the middle- and high-income earners who want their children to be taught in an internationally recognized language.

In schools, same-sex relations abound but are always kept secret out of fear of expulsion. Gays in school struggle to identify with their sexuality due to homophobia. School authorities have clamped down on homosexual relations, and anyone suspected of engaging in homosexual behavior is put through the worst punishment available.[1]

The safety of LGBT students in school is not guaranteed and gay organizations are not permitted. Sexual harassment against gays is a common occurrence that goes unreported in most schools.[2] On the other hand, teachers in public schools in Tanzania are not trained to handle the psychological trauma of a young teenager who is struggling to identify with his or her sexual orientation.[3] Lack of counseling in schools has led many gay youth to abuse drugs and alcohol, and has often led to suicide.[4]

EMPLOYMENT AND ECONOMICS

The economy of Tanzania is based on agriculture. The first president of Tanzania, the late Mwalimu Julius Nyerere, introduced socialist policies in all sectors of the economy after independence from colonial rule. Socialism, however, did not work well for the economy of Tanzania, and instead of growth there was a decline in many areas. The economies of neighboring Uganda and Kenya, which followed capitalism after gaining independence, grew in leaps and bounds, leaving Tanzania behind. This prompted Nyerere to officially admit in the early 1990s that socialism had failed in Tanzania. Following this humble admittance, Tanzania soon embraced capitalism and a free-market economy that has tremendously improved the country's economic performance. The current government of Tanzania, under H.E (His Excellency) President Jakaya Mrisho Kikwete, has pursued consistent and predictable national economic policies with low inflation rates, thus attracting major foreign investments that have boosted the economic growth rate, improved infrastructure (including roads, electricity, water supply, and communication facilities), spurred industrial growth, reduced donor aid dependency, and has led to the establishment of well-equipped public health facilities.

However, the major challenge of the government has been an increase in people moving from rural to urban areas in search of jobs and a better life. This has resulted in the mushrooming of shantytowns or informal settlements, accompanied by high levels of crime, illicit trade, commercial sex work, and other vices. This trend is visible in all urban centers across the country, with private entrepreneurs taking advantage of rural immigrants and paying low wages—a factor that has contributed to poverty across the country. LGBT people are also affected by the same lack of employment crisis.

SOCIAL/GOVERNMENT PROGRAMS

The government funds public health hospitals and clinics countrywide. In conjunction with international nongovernmental organizations (NGOs), the government has put in place HIV/AIDS intervention measures countrywide.

However, there are no programs targeting the LGBT community specific, due to denial on the part of the government of the existence of homosexuals in their areas of jurisdiction. Organizations that have supported gay people are often forced to operate discreetly in order to avoid being penalized under the Sexual Offences Act, which prohibits homosexuality.

SEXUALITY/SEXUAL PRACTICES

The effect of HIV/AIDS in Tanzania has prompted the government to introduce sex education in schools with the intention of encouraging young people to change their behaviors and to promote safer sex practices. Free condoms have been distributed widely in recreational areas, hospitals, higher education institutions, and both public and private offices. However, sexual health education in Tanzania is biased and only addresses heterosexual activity. The LGBT community has been left out of all safe sex programs that have been implemented by health authorities. Safe sex materials specific to the needs of LGBT people are hard to come by and, if they are available, it is always at a high cost. A number of LGBT groups have been formed to fill the void left by health authorities, but their programs are often hampered by the legal system. To date, no research has been done by government health officials on matters of health concerning homosexual people in Tanzania.

FAMILY

The family unit in Tanzania consists of a husband, wife, and children. An adult male and female are, according to cultural norms, expected to marry by the age of 25. Single families and childless unions are frowned upon. Most widowers and widows are pressured to remarry by family members and friends. In most rural areas, people live in small village enclaves where the surrounding land is shared communally. Such a setup confines people to follow the traditional family structure without wavering. In the family unit, the man is the sole earner, and the wife is supposed to stay at home and take care of the house and children. Same-sex relations are unheard of, and if they do exist the couple lives a secretive life away from relatives or friends.

COMMUNITY

Despite the Sexual Offenses Act's prohibition of any same-sex relations, a number of independent gay activists have been vocal in championing the rights of LGBT people in Tanzania. Some courageous activists have even mobilized gays to form organizations that represent the interests of gays in local and international forums. Such organizations have been instrumental in providing LGBT people with health information, safe sex information, access to antiretroviral drugs, legal advice, and voluntary counseling and testing (VCT). Workshops and conferences have been held in the main city of Dar es Salaam, where attendees advocate for the human rights of LGBT people.

HEALTH

It is estimated that 22.5 million people in Africa are living with HIV/AIDS, making this epidemic one of the major health concerns of the continent.[5] In Tanzania, the HIV/AIDS scourge has affected the entire population equally. HIV/AIDS programs run by the government in conjunction with local and international NGOs only target the heterosexual community. There are no programs specific to the health needs of the LGBT community. Despite the fact that health services are subsidized by the government through public clinics and hospitals, the cost of health care is still too high for the majority of people. Health services in private clinics and hospitals are also beyond the reach of low-income earners, who form the majority of the population. Homophobia in health institutions has made it difficult for LGBT people to visit hospitals or clinics. LGBT people are often forced, under these circumstances, to visit traditional healers and medical quacks for their health needs, thereby exposing themselves to even more health risks. Common ailments like syphilis, tuberculosis, herpes, and various STDs have been a challenge to control due to the tendency of LGBT people to shy away from hospital treatment and instead rely on nonsanctioned medicine for their health care needs.

POLITICS AND LAW

When Tanzania gained independence in 1961, its constitution required presidential and parliamentary elections to be held every five years, a practice that has been followed by all governing authorities to date. The fourth president of Tanzania, H.E. (His Excellency) President Jakaya Mrisho Kikwete, emerged as the victor in the presidential and parliamentary elections held on December 14, 2005. On December 21, 2005, the President of the United Republic of Tanzania was sworn into office for a five-year term. The Constitution of Tanzania was amended in 1985, giving presidents a limit of two terms in office.

The Constitution presently guarantees the human rights of every citizen of Tanzania. However, same-sex relations are criminalized by the same legal framework that guarantees the protection of human rights for all citizens.

RELIGION AND SPIRITUALITY

The two main religions in Tanzania are Islam and Christianity. Leaders and followers of these two faiths generally agree that homosexuality is against the will of God. Attempts by LGBT activists to protest have been met by stiff resistance and violence from followers of the two religions. For example, following the move by the Episcopal Church in the United States to accept gay priests, the Anglican Church in East Africa and Tanzania vocally condemned homosexuality.[6] Christians have often used biblical verses to stir the public's anger against homosexuals. However, in the coastal regions of Tanzania, where the Islamic faith is more predominant, homosexuality is silently acknowledged, especially on

Pemba and Zanzibar islands, whose inhabitants are mostly Arabs from the Far East.[7]

VIOLENCE

LGBT people face violence at almost every level in Tanzania—in school, at work, and even at home. The patriarchal culture makes it virtually impossible for a gay person to come out openly. This situation has forced many LGBT people to live a double life in which one is officially married to a partner of the opposite sex but maintains a secret affair with a same-sex partner.

A practice known as bride price has become one of the major causes of violence against gay women. The family assumes that their daughter is ready to be married off to a willing suitor as soon as she turns 18. Poverty has been a contributing factor; parents are forced to marry their daughters in order to get a dowry payment. Parents may inflict violence on their daughters who refuse to get married, and in many cases evict them from the home. Likewise, gay men are scorned if they do not honor the family by bringing home a bride when they are expected to.

The police have fallen short of their duties by being un-cooperative when dealing with the LGBT community. Threats of arrest are used to force gay people to follow unwarranted demands by the police. Cases of rape committed against gay people in prison, though they may be reported, are never investigated.[8]

Most LGBT people suffer in silence because a majority has assumed, correctly, that LGBT people do not have legal grounds to challenge any abuse of their human rights.[9] As such, many political leaders have taken advantage of this by giving hateful, gay bashing lectures, contributing to discrimination against gay people.

OUTLOOK FOR THE 21ST CENTURY

The gay movement in Tanzania is gaining strength and visibility due to the growth of membership in a number of established gay organizations in both the urban areas and rural regions. A foundation to challenge the cultural, religious, and legal framework that denies gay people in Tanzania a chance to fully express their identity and enjoy their sexuality has been established. This is being developed further through cooperation of the local gay movement with regional and international gay organizations in capacity building initiatives, facilitating research work, resource sharing, and participation in exchange programs and general support. This foundation is a first step toward achieving human rights for all Tanzanians, regardless of sexual orientation.

RESOURCE GUIDE

Suggested Reading

Peter Drucker, *Different Rainbows* (London: Millivres, 2000).
GALZ, *Understanding Human Sexuality and Gender* (Harare: Gays and Lesbians of Zimbabwe, 2005).
Jody Kollapen, *An ABC of LGBTI* (Johannesburg: Joint Working Group, 2004).
Ruth Morgan and Saskia Wieringa, *Female Same Sex Practices in Africa* (Johannesburg: Jacana Media, 2005).

Organizations

Community Peer Support Services (CPSS), cpss91@yahoo.com.
>   CPSS aims to provide health services to gay men in all regions of Tanzania.
>   Private Bag
>   Dar-es-Salaam, Tanzania

Talesa (Tanzania Lesbian Association), talesa2000@yahoo.com.
>   Talesa was founded by two young women who felt that Lesbian issues were not represented in mainstream women civil organizations. Lesbians in Tanzania are faced with even more challenges than those women in general face and TALESA has taken the task of reaching out to lesbians to help tackle issues affecting them.
>   P.O. Box 106178
>   Dar-es-salaam, Tanzania

NOTES

1. Ruth Morgan and Saskia Wieringa, *Female Same Sex Practices in Africa* (Johannesburg: Jacana Media, 2005).

2. TALESA (Tanzania Lesbian Association), "Project Reports 2001–2005."

3. Ibid.

4. CPSS, "Community Peer Support Services Newsletter," January 2004.

5. UNAIDS, "2003 HIV/AIDS Human Rights and Law Geneva," http://www.unaids.org/en/default.asp.

6. Nation Media Group, www.nationmedia.com.

7. Peter Drucker, ed., *Different Rainbows* (London: Millivres Ltd., 2000).

8. CPSS (Community Peer Support Services), "Project Reports 2002–2005."

9. Ibid.

TUNISIA

Benjamin de Lee

OVERVIEW

Tunisia, sandwiched between the much larger countries of Libya and Algeria, is the smallest country in North Africa. It is slightly larger than the U.S. state of Georgia.

Tunisia was made a French protectorate in 1881, and became independent in 1956. Habib Bourguiba, the first president of Tunisia, ruled for 31 years in a strict one-party state. While political conformity was demanded, other civil liberties were granted. Complete equality was given to women, and a secular constitution and legal system, modeled on France, were adopted. Investments were made in infrastructure and education, and great advances in literacy and education were achieved. Zine el Abidine Ben Ali led a bloodless coup in November 1987 and continues to rule the country today. Ben Ali has continued Bourguiba's policies and still honors the now deceased former president as the father of the country.

Tunisia's constitution guarantees complete equality to all citizens and grants universal suffrage to citizens over the age of 18. Ninety-eight percent of the population is Muslim, while one-percent is Jewish, and another one-percent is Christian or other.[1] In spite of having a working constitution, the government of Tunisia has been accused of using threats of terrorism and Islamic fundamentalism to crush peaceful dissent.[2] President Ben Ali and his Constitutional Democratic Assembly dominate the political life of the country, although small opposition groups are tolerated if they do not support the overthrow of the government in favor of an Islamic regime. While there are independent media outlets in the country, criticism of the government, although not illegal, is unheard of in major outlets.

Tunisia has a healthy and diverse economy, though it lacks the oil wealth of its neighbors. It has a well-developed agricultural, mining, tourism, and manufacturing sectors, and it has paid particular attention to developing its tourism industry. The country itself has enjoyed greater stability and economic growth than other countries in the region, in spite of its lack of petroleum resources like neighboring Libya. The gross domestic product in 2007 was over $77 billion, with a 6.3 percent growth rate. Still, unemployment is high at 13.6 percent. France and Italy are Tunisia's two biggest trading partners. Tunisia has an army, navy, and an air force, although the military is relatively small. Military expenditures are only 1.4 percent of the GDP.[3] Tunisia has avoided international conflicts, seeking mediation in a border dispute with Algeria in 1993. In the 1970s, relations with Libya were strained, but Tunisia avoided armed conflict then as well. The *gendarmerie* and police presence in Tunisia are more significant than the military.

OVERVIEW OF LGBT ISSUES

As in many Arab countries, one might say there are no LGBT issues, as homosexuality is largely invisible. Sodomy is still punishable with up to three years in prison under Article 230 of the Penal Code (est. 1913, revised in 1964); yet homosexual acts are common between men. Society turns a blind eye to homosexual acts, yet homosexuality as a concept or identity is thought to be repugnant, a Western vice and immoral. Thus, there is no discussion of sexual identity as such. HIV infection rates are some of the lowest in the world. There are no specifically gay or lesbian organizations. Gay and lesbian issues are not part of the national dialogue in any way. Efforts to address gay and lesbian issues, as in Nouri Bouzid's film *Bezness* (1992), have met with government censorship. This film is an indication that things may be changing in Tunisia. More and more gay Tunisian men and lesbian women are asserting a sexual identity. Pan-Arab gay and lesbian organizations like the Gay and Lesbian Arab Society (GLAS) provide resources for Tunisian gays and lesbians, although these resources are available mostly to an educated, urban population group with internet access.

EDUCATION

Tunisia has worked consistently to improve and expand its education system since gaining independence from France. The school system is based on the French model but has abandoned mandatory French for complete Arabicization, but with a focus on learning international languages like English and French. Primary school is now compulsory. The Ministry of Education oversees primary and secondary schools, while the Ministry of Higher Education oversees the university and advanced technical school system. There are no programs that address sexual or LGBT issues.

EMPLOYMENT AND ECONOMICS

Tunisia needs high rates of economic growth to accommodate its large population of young people, especially the increasing number of university graduates. Economic growth is healthy, but unemployment numbers are still high. Gay and lesbian Tunisians can be found in all areas of employment, but they are frequently found in the tourism industry. Gay men may work in the tourism industry directly or may work in tourist-frequented areas as sex workers.

SOCIAL/GOVERNMENT PROGRAMS

There are no government-funded or social programs for LGBT people. The Association Tunisienne de Lutte Contre le Sida (the Tunisian Association against AIDS) works to educate all members of the population about the risks of HIV transmission. It is a small organization that works to confront the taboos of Tunisian society.[4]

SEXUALITY/SEXUAL PRACTICES

Attitudes concerning sexuality and sexual practices in Tunisia are similar to those throughout the Islamic world. Although it is rare to see a veiled woman in Tunisia, sexual contact between unmarried heterosexual couples is quite rare. In contrast, sexual contact between unmarried young men is quite common, and such experiences are not considered part of a homosexual identity. Indeed, in particular, males who assert themselves as the dominant and penetrative role (top) are unlikely to consider themselves homosexual. Regardless of role, the vast majority of Tunisian men and women marry, although many married men continue to engage in homosexual practices.

HIV-AIDS has not become a major issue in Tunisia because there is a very low rate of infection, although as mentioned there is now an NGO that is attempting to confront the issue. However, Tunisia, like much of North Africa, has had something of a reputation as a gay travel destination. Tunisia is a popular tourist destination with a well-developed tourist infrastructure. Young single men often attach themselves to European travelers of either sex. While the young men would never consider themselves prostitutes, they function as a local guide and gigolo for the wealthier traveler. Safe-sex practices are not well known, discussed, or encouraged in Tunisia since it would mean a certain level of openness about sexuality and sexual practices. Thus, the population is potentially vulnerable if HIV infection rates begin to rise.

FAMILY

Tunisian families follow the traditional model of heterosexual marriage. Polygamy, although allowed in Shari'ah Law, is illegal. Gender roles are traditional, although a large number of Tunisian women in urban areas have careers. Marriage is a civil institution, with both partners having complete equality and the right to initiate divorce, although divorce rates are very low. Same-sex unions are not recognized. The extended family is still important, and in rural areas, especially in the south of the country, the rhythms of village life have scarcely changed.

Whether Tunisian families are supportive of their gay and lesbian children is hard to know. The upper classes of Tunisia tend to be very Westernized, and those that can afford to send their children to the West for education, usually France, do so. Such families often have Western views and attitudes. In Nouri Bouzid's film *Man of Ashes*, the protagonist, a gay man, feels pressured to marry by his family. Adult children tend to live with their parents until they marry, and marriage is expected of most adults at some point.

COMMUNITY

There is no identifiable gay and lesbian community in Tunisia.

HEALTH

Public health care in Tunisia is adequate but understaffed and underfunded. In more rural areas, facilities and resources are less available than in urban centers. AIDS cases are at less than 1,000, and no specialized treatment for HIV-AIDS exits, although there are large number of private hospitals and clinics with staff and resources comparable to those in the West.

POLITICS AND LAW

Article 230 of the 1913 Penal Code (revised in 1964) states that anal intercourse between men is illegal and carries an imprisonment up to three years. In reality, this law is rarely enforced, but there are no political movements seeking to overturn this law. In 1993, the Appeal Court of Tunis refused to grant a change in gender status for a transsexual. The court ruled that the surgery was voluntary, and therefore the government was not obliged to recognize the plaintiff's new gender. What limited political opposition exists in Tunisia, the political structure has never addressed gay and lesbian issues. Islamic parties would no doubt prefer a crack down, as has occurred in Egypt, while liberal parties are more interested in a completely free press and free elections.

RELIGION AND SPIRITUALITY

Tunisia's population is overwhelmingly Sunni, with very small Christian and Jewish minorities. Islamic law forbids anal intercourse between men, but Islamic society has a surprising history of toleration of homosexuality. However, in recent years fundamentalist movements have targeted gays as a sign of Western decadence. Tunisia is not a very religious country, and while almost everyone identifies him or herself as Muslim, it is unusual to see any overt religiosity in public.

VIOLENCE

There are no specific complaints of violence against gays and lesbians in Tunisia. On the whole, Tunisia has very low rates of violent crime. Reports of violence against tourists are rare. In recent years, there has been one terrorist attack against a synagogue (2002) on the island of Djerba. Tourists are targets for petty crime, usually theft, and gays and lesbians who are tourists are equal targets. Gay men who have sexual encounters with Tunisian men have reported that their sexual partner has threatened to call the police as a way to elicit money, but there have been no reports of violence or actual prosecution of a tourist.

OUTLOOK FOR THE 21ST CENTURY

The situation for gays and lesbians in Tunisia is unlikely to change in the near future. The government, while maintaining its pragmatic, secular stance, is unlikely to encourage any level of liberalization and openness, especially since that might provoke Islamic fundamentalists to become critical of the regime. At the same time, the crack-down on gays and lesbians, such as in Egypt in 2002 with the mass arrest of 52 gay men at a nightclub, appears unlikely as it might affect the tourism industry and tarnish Tunisia's reputation as an appealing, laid-back, and liberal Mediterranean vacation destination.

However, there are signs that a sense of sexual identity is spreading. Web sites such as *www.gaydar.co.uk* show a growing number of personal profiles in Tunisia. Organizations like the Gay and Lesbian Arab Society and Web sites like *www.kelma.org* offer a forum to gay Arabs throughout North Africa and the Middle East. Films such as *Bezness* are also provoking a greater openness on the issue of sexuality. There are also gay couples in Tunisia who say that they are happy and content, but there are others who say they are a persecuted minority.[5] It is hard to say what the 21st century will bring for gays and lesbians in Tunisia. Historically, Muslim societies have been tolerant, yet silent, about gays and lesbians. Many colonists and Europeans in the 19th and 20th centuries found North Africa to be a relative haven where sexual expression, which was repressed in Europe, was allowed. This local tradition of silent toleration, however, is coming under increasing pressure from Islamic fundamentalists who want to end all tolerance, as well as from gays and lesbians who want an end to the silence.

RESOURCE GUIDE

Suggested Reading

Abdelwahab Bouhdiba, *Sexuality in Islam* (London: Routledge and Kegan Paul, 1985).
Bruce W. Dunne, "Homosexuality in the Middle East: An Agenda for Historical Research," *Arab Studies Quarterly* 12, nos. 3/4 (1990): 55–82.
Albert Memmi, *Pillar of Salt,* trans. Edouard Roditi (New York: Criterion Books, 1955).
Stephen O'Murray and Will Roscoe, *Islamic Homosexualities: Culture, History, and Literature* (New York: New York University Press, 1997).
Arno Schmitt and Jehoeda Sofer, eds., *Sexuality and Eroticism among Males in Moslem Societies* (London: Routledge, 1992).

Videos/Films

Bezness. DVD. Directed by Nouri Bouzid. Tunisia: CTF, 1992.
 A film about a Tunisian hustler in Sousse who is engaged to a Tunisian woman. Roufa, the hustler, seeks to go to Europe through a German client, while he demands that his fiancée remain a virgin until they are married.
Man of Ashes. DVD. Directed by Nouri Bouzid. Tunisia: Cinétéléfilms, 1986.
 The film follows the story of three boys who were molested in a Tunisian village. One immigrates to France, another is driven from home, and the third faces his own homosexual identity.

Web Sites

Ahbab, http://www.glas.org/ahbab/.
 Web site of the Gay and Lesbian Arab Society. Another site for valuable news updates, HIV/AIDS awareness, and links to other gay and lesbian sites.
Gay and Lesbian Arabs, http://www.al-bab.com/arab/background/gay.htm.
 A valuable database of resources for gay and lesbian Arabs. Includes links to films, literature, and Web sites.
Kelma, http://www.kelma.org/.
 Includes links to social events in Paris, pornography, and personal ads. Also includes news stories, education, and culture. Significant because it is the only Web site devoted exclusively to gay francophone Arabs.

Middle East Research Institute (MEMRI), http://www.memri.org/bin/articles.cgi?Page=
    countries&Area=northafrica&ID=SP117006.
    Includes a summary of various articles and interviews on homosexuality in Tunisia.
    Most of the links are to the Tunisian weekly *Réalités*.

NOTES

1. CIA, "Tunisia," *The World Factbook*, https://www.cia.gov/library/publications/
the-world-factbook/geos/ts.html.
2. "Universal Periodic Review of Tunisia," *Human Rights Watch*, 2008, http://hrw.
org/english/docs/2008/04/11/global18514.htm.
3. CIA, "Tunisia."
4. Alasdair Soussi, "Interview with Tunisian Association Against AIDS," *New Internationalist*, 2008, http://findarticles.com/p/articles/mi_m0JQP/is_408/ai_n24940314.
5. Sonia Ounissi, "HIV and Gay in Tunisia: A Twin Taboo," *Reuters*, March 7,
2008, http://www.reuters.com/article/lifestyleMolt/idUSL077623120080307.

UGANDA

James A. Wilson Jr.

OVERVIEW

Uganda is a landlocked equatorial country located west of Kenya, south of Sudan, north of Tanzania, and east of the Democratic Republic of the Congo. As of 2007, the population of Uganda was estimated at 30.9 million people living in a country roughly the size of Oregon. The capital city of Uganda is Kampala, which is located just seven miles from the great Lake Victoria. There are four other major cities in Uganda—Gulu, Jinja, Mbale, and Mbarara, but a majority of Uganda's population lives in rural developing communities.

Uganda, like many countries in Africa, is an amalgamation of different ethnic groups, cultures, religions, languages, and identities. There are three primary lin-

guistic groups that make up most of the population: *Bantu, Nilotic,* and *Nilo-Hamitic.* The southern region of Uganda is the highest populated region and home to the *Baganda* people, who constitute the largest ethnic group in Uganda, representing 18 percent of the population. Other *Bantu* ethnic groups in the southern region include the *Bahima* and *Banyankole* people, who make up 10 percent of the population; the Bakiga people (8%); the Banyarwanda people (6%); the Bunyoro people (3%); and the Batoro people at three percent. The *Nilotic* and *Nilo-Hamitic* ethnic groups are located in the northern region of Uganda and they include the *Langi* people (6%); the Acholi people (4%); the *Lugbara* people (4%); and the *Karamojong* people, who largely occupy the driest pastoral section of the northeast Uganda.

In the eastern region of Uganda, two ethnic groups primarily occupy this region: the *Basoga* people, who make up 8 percent of the population, and the *Bagisu* people. In addition to the African citizens of Uganda, there are also Europeans, Asians, and Arabs—communities that make up roughly one percent of the Ugandan population.[1]

The rich precolonial history of these well-established ethnic groups shaped the political and cultural structures in Ugandan societies for centuries. The southern region of present-day Uganda had centralized states with powerful kings, as well as established hierarchies of chiefs and laws that governed the relationships of the various communities. The northern and eastern regions of present-day Uganda, however, were not organized like the southern region because centralized states did not evolve. As a result, the north and eastern regions were more isolated from the political and cultural developments of the southern region. This stark contrast in development among the various ethnic groups played an important a role in the amalgamation of different African cultural, social, and political traditions when the British declared its protectorate over Uganda in 1894. The British then immediately employed the classic divide and conquer method to increase division and disunity in Uganda by creating a Buganda state within a state. That is, the British encouraged European missionary societies to introduce Christianity to the *Baganda* people, who were indeed the largest and most powerful ethnic group, thus creating a mini-state within the protectorate. Of course, the other smaller ethnic groups did not receive the same type of political, cultural, economic, religious, or educational opportunities as the Baganda people, and over time this political division among ethnic groups in Uganda has created major problems for modern, postcolonial political development in Uganda.[2]

The evolution of modern African politics in Uganda began in 1952 with the first political party, the Uganda National Congress (UNC). With the guidance of both the British colonial state and the influences of the Church Missionary Society, the UNC was formed in Buganda with a majority of Baganda leadership. Moreover, all of the Baganda leaders were Protestant, which was a minority religious identity among the more popular Catholic majority throughout the country. Nonetheless, the Baganda Protestant leadership dominated the UNC and other political parties, creating a pattern of Baganda dominance over national and local institutions such as the press, local newspapers, educational leadership positions, religions agendas, and public discourses. Eventually, resentment and division was the reaction to Baganda leadership instead of unity and cooperation to form a united African party for all black Ugandans.[3] Ten years later, on October 9, 1962, Uganda declared its independence from the British colonial government.

Many African countries emerged as newly independent states during the early 1960s. However, the political process and transformation of powers was not an easy transition. Uganda's postcolonial political evolution was no exception. By 1966, four years after receiving its independence, the Ugandan military supported a political activist, Milton Obote, who abrogated the 1962 Constitution of Uganda and placed himself as ruler and dictator of the state. In 1971, Obote's army commander, Idi Amin, overthrew him in a bloody coup d'état to declare the presidential throne for himself.[4]

From January of 1971 to April of 1979, Idi Amin ruled Uganda with the forceful tools of oppressive authority, harsh dictatorial governance, and physical cruelty to suppress any form of resistance, which ultimately restricted all expressions of political freedoms, citizenship rights, or social and economic liberties. The British colonial government had recruited railroad workers from India to build the infrastructures in many African countries, and after two centuries, many of the Asian citizens were born in Uganda, Kenya, Tanzania, Zimbabwe, Zambia, and South Africa. Nonetheless, Idi Amin wanted all Asians out of Uganda. In 1972, Amin expelled the Asian population of Uganda from the country and denied them citizenship. He then targeted the Israelis living in Uganda and blamed them, alongside the Asians, for the deterioration of the Uganda economy. To counter any criticism from the West regarding his anti-Semitic decisions, Amin joined forces with Libya's Muammar Qaddafi to support "the struggle of the Arab people against Zionism and imperialism."[5] As a result of Amin's radical positions to remove Asians and Jews from Uganda in 1973, the United States quietly decided to withdraw and evacuate all U.S. Peace Corps volunteers from their various grassroots projects in Uganda.[6] The Peace Corps reestablished programs in Uganda in 1991 and continued to develop its programs until 1999 when it was suspended for political reasons and safety concerns. However, in 2000, the Peace Corps reestablished volunteers in Uganda once again, and the programs are all moving forward.

Uganda experienced many economic, social, political, and cultural hardships during Amin's political reign, and many Bugandan intellectuals were targeted and murdered because of their decisions to expose to the world the injustices of Amin's policies. With the uncertainty of safety and security, eventually many Ugandan intellectuals managed to cross the borders into Kenya and Tanzania to reestablish their lives. In April of 1979, Amin was removed from power by a combination of Tanzanian army members and exiled Ugandan political groups. However, the revolving political cycle continued with Yusufu Lule, who held on to the presidential power for only 68 days until the National Consultative Council removed him, supported by the Uganda National Liberation Army.[7] The next several Presidents of Uganda all had military support to sustain their leaderships, and this particular type of governance has maintained a continual succession of fragmented leadership in Uganda. Ultimately, the never-ending political crises to create a sustainable governing body at the national and local levels have hindered Uganda's potential to develop economically, politically, and culturally.

OVERVIEW OF LGBT ISSUES

The issue of sex, sexually transmitted diseases, and sex education has recently emerged as part of a national discourse in Uganda because of the HIV/AIDS crisis. Like many African countries, the people of Uganda realized a radical change was needed to address the enormous death rates of Ugandans from AIDS. By 1995, Uganda's President Yoweri Museveni, local political leaders, Christian ministers, international NGOs, medical researchers, school teachers, local Ugandan women's groups, and concerned citizens throughout Uganda all began to organize a public campaign to talk about sex and HIV/AIDS. However, the issue of homosexuality was not included in the body of literature disseminated nationally to educate Ugandans about sexuality and sexual education. Because of the conservative influences of Christianity, first introduced by European and American missionaries in Uganda, many African religious leaders completely disregard the idea and existence of LGBT Ugandans.

According to a recent report on Health and Gay/Lesbian affairs in Uganda, "the national HIV/AIDS program [made] no provisions for sexual minorities, despite scientific evidence that gay men are more susceptible to HIV transmission than any other group."[8]

The report illustrated the disconnect between the innocence of gay Ugandan men and the ignorance of HIV/AIDS health administrators responsible for addressing all issues related to sexual practices, transmissions, and identities related to the spread of HIV/AIDS in Uganda. The report acknowledged that, "many gay men in Uganda remain unaware of the risk of contracting sexually transmitted infections through unprotected sex."[9] This might seem difficult to imagine given Uganda's overwhelming success with the (ABC) policy that called attention to the ideas of "Abstinence" for A, "Be Faithful" for B, and "Condoms" for C as a comprehensive strategy to reduce the spread of HIV/AIDS. However, this report also demonstrated just how invisible the LGBT community is by highlighting the experiences of one 20-year-old gay Kampala resident: "Joel said, 'some boys believe that to sleep with a man is safe because all the billboards around town show heterosexual couples, with messages. Nothing is said about homosexual couples using a condom, so they think it is safer to sleep with each other than a girl.'"[10]

The LGBT community is small and responsible for organizing educational materials to correct much of the misinformation and mixed messages about HIV/AIDS for gay citizens in Uganda. The main objective of LGBT Uganda is to transform the sodomy laws and to protect gay and lesbian Ugandans from discrimination, violence, blackmail, and unlawful abuses of civil rights, harassments, and lengthy jail sentences. At present, a conviction for sodomy in Uganda carries a life sentence in prison. Additionally, legal support and assistance for gay, lesbian, bisexual, or transgender Ugandans is extremely difficult mainly because of the stigma associated with being constructed as different from the conventional heterosexual norms. Yet there is a need to address basic ignorance about terms and identities such as gay, homosexual, bisexual, lesbian, and transgendered. Often government ministers, religious leaders, and members of the Church Interfaith Family Culture Coalition Against Homosexuality use these terms incorrectly as part of their public antigay campaigns. With the help of the Internet there is a website entitled *Gay Uganda,* which provides an overview of definitions, history, legal rights, organizations, and other important links.[11] Without question, the most challenging issue the Ugandan LGBT community faced in 2005 was the antigay campaign led by President Museveni to constitutionally ban gay marriage.[12]

EDUCATION

Throughout Africa, formal education is a major priority for everyone; however, for many people the cost to obtain an education is very expensive and competitive. The Ministry of Education has improved the overall educational system to offer Ugandans more opportunities. The original blueprint and educational concepts, established by European missionaries, introduced a national curriculum that reflected the values of European history, religion, philosophy, and culture. However, the Ministry of Education in Uganda has consistently transformed the once European-focused educational system. One of the legacies of the colonial system is an emphasis on educating male students over female students; this is still a major concern of Uganda's current educational program that must be improved. Gender equality is a significant problem in many African countries, and education is the best way to eliminate gender discrimination for future generations. Like its East African neighbors Kenya and Tanzania, Uganda has a long way to go to ensure that girls and women will have equal and abundant opportunities.

Today, the educational system in Uganda is based on a 7-4-2 system, which means seven years of primary education, four years of secondary schooling, and two years of high school before attending university. At present, Uganda has 13 universities, with Makerere University in Kampala as the oldest and most prestigious university in Uganda and East Africa respectively.[13] The political inconsistency of Uganda's Presidency has created many years of closed universities, but President Museveni has supported the development of more universities with more degree plans. There are LGBT organizations on some of the university campuses in Uganda, but gay and lesbian students must maintain very discreet profiles because university administrators and professors support a more conservative, Christian climate for student activities on campus. Increasingly, LGBT organizations have appeared in student newspapers and in public discourses, but with little support these organizations struggle to exist as part of the university culture to assist gay students.

The issue of AIDS and increasing death rates is a major concern for educators in Uganda because of the number of orphaned children and dying teachers. Uganda's HIV/AIDS crisis, however, is relatively contained in comparison to other African counties. All the same, the Ugandan population has actively responded to the AIDS crisis as it relates to new educational initiatives to secure opportunities for orphans and families to attend all levels of education.

EMPLOYMENT AND ECONOMICS

Uganda's economy is one of the poorest performing financial systems in the world, primarily because of the erratic political system the country has endured for many years. However, since 1986 when President Museveni took office, Uganda's economy has slowly improved. The fragile infrastructure of the country is one of the priorities President Museveni has worked to expand. Both the IMF and the World Bank supported this necessary rebuilding in 1987 to allow Uganda opportunities to regenerate its local and foreign markets. One positive aspect of Uganda's economic growth is the production of agricultural exports such as coffee. Following the success of Kenya in coffee production, Uganda is the second largest producer of coffee in Africa.[14]

With regards to Uganda's external debts, for the past decade President Museveni has worked steadfastly with donor countries to postpone and/or cancel sizeable percentages of outstanding debts. One financial concern that has generated lots of support to Uganda is HIV/AIDS research. In 2002 the Uganda Virus Research Institute in Entebbe, Uganda was the second trial site in Africa to receive over $94 million dollars from the International AIDS Vaccine Initiative or IAVI for two years to establish academic labs, clinical trails, and tests to produce an HIV vaccine. In addition to the IAVI program, in 2004 the Bill and Melinda Gates Foundation also invested in this partnership to research a possible vaccine.[15]

There was no inclusion of LGBT research issues as part of the IAVI partnership with the Uganda Virus Research Institute. In fact, the Uganda government and economy benefited from establishing partnerships with the global AIDS medical community to come to Uganda to conduct research. On the other hand, in 2005 the issue of corruption regarding this mismanagement of research grants by three Ugandan ministers of health resulted in the suspension of more than $200 million dollars from the Global Fund. Even worse, between $400 to $500 million dollars worth of antiretroviral medicines stored at the national medical stores in Entebbe, Uganda, were destroyed due to expired dates.[16]

Employment opportunities and a measurable development in the standard of living for Ugandan citizens have improved increasingly over a 20-year period. For example, in 1987, the inflation ran at 240 percent and in June of 1992 it was 42 percent. However, in 2003 inflation was 5.1 percent and it only recently increased to 7.7 percent in 2007 as a result of recent rising food prices.[17] Indeed, employment in both local and foreign export industries has created jobs for Ugandans.

There are no antidiscrimination laws to protect LGBT Ugandans.

Under President Museveni's administration, the LGBT community has endured many homophobic attacks launched by religious and political leaders to forbid basic civil rights to gay and lesbian Ugandans. Overall, the work environment in Uganda does not provide LGBT workers, as well as women in general, with much legal recourse against sexual harassment, discrimination, and physical violence.

SOCIAL/GOVERNMENT PROGRAMS

There are no existing programs in support of the LGBT community in Uganda. In fact, the Ugandan government has consistently set a tone of disapproval for homosexuals and has supported public campaigns of harassment of gays and lesbians. In August of 2006, a tabloid newspaper entitled *Red Pepper* published a story about 45 alleged homosexuals and expressed concerns about the government's harsh and unfair treatment of LGBT Ugandans. In 2002, this same tabloid published a story about a lesbian couple's decision to get married. As a result of the story, the two women were later arrested and detained by the government.[18]

SEXUALITY/SEXUAL PRACTICES

In many African countries, Christianity and Islam are the formal institutions that set the cultural norms to express the limits of sexuality. According to these religions, marriage is the proper and legitimate social contract that allows people to express love and human sexuality. Hence, the idea of alternative sexual identities is simply not discussed or presented as an option. In Uganda, like many African countries, homosexuality is illegal, and the only acceptable sexual practice that is acknowledged and supported is heterosexuality. The evolution of women's sexuality is a very recent movement, and in many African cultures, women do not have many options to express their own sexual independence outside of getting married and producing children. Of course, prostitution is one obvious deviation from the normal sexual expectation for African women, but prostitutes are often regarded as immoral and dirty sinners who deserve no protection or respect. As a result of this limited expression of sexuality, there are no legal rights for homosexuals to fight discrimination, harassment, violence, or rape. Nonetheless, homosexuality has existed in African cultures for centuries, and the diversity of sexual identities will continue to emerge as human beings continue to express themselves sexually. Uganda is no exception to this reality.

FAMILY

The African family unit is the backbone of every African society and the important transmitting institution of traditions, cultures, languages, customs, laws, land tenure, food production, and local economies. All of these factors depend on the development of the family. In Uganda, like many African countries, the importance of marriage between a man and a woman, as well as the high expectation placed on procreation to create large families, is the general standard of normative behavior and morality.

Hence, the diversity of the Ugandan family unit might include a close network of extended family members, but the presence and celebration of gay and lesbian family units would not be openly accepted or encouraged. Divorce is also a relatively new option for African families mainly because of the inequality that African women face if they elect to divorce their husbands. As a result, the divorce rate in Uganda is comparatively lower than most western countries that award women property and resources as part of divorce settlements.

Unlike the newly constructed gay and lesbian family units in Europe and North America, Ugandans would view nontraditional gay family units with condemnation, and religious leaders alongside the powers of the Ugandan government would condemn such arrangements. In fact, in 2005 Uganda became the only country in the world to include in its constitution the meaning and limitations of what constitutes a legal marriage. Perhaps the recent HIV/AIDS crises in Africa have reconstructed the "normative construct" of the family unit because of the devastations caused by massive deaths. Nonetheless, the emergence of LGBT family constructs is still not acknowledged as an acceptable option.

COMMUNITY

The LGBT community in Uganda emerged publicly as organized groups began to demand their rights as equal citizens in 2003. The term *Kuchu* means a gay Ugandan, and members of the LGBT community and neighboring Kenya decided their voices and opinions needed to be heard loud and clear on issues involving the HIV/AIDS crisis, the dissemination of medicines and treatment, claims to family properties, adoption of orphans, demands to end discrimination and harassment, and their rights to organize and assemble. One LGBT group called Freedom and Roam, Uganda (FAR-Ug) is an alliance of lesbians in Uganda who formed their organization in 2003. FAR-Ug's main objective is to function as the advocacy group for LGBT (*Kuchu*) rights. In 2004, another LGBT group called Sexual Minorities, Uganda (SMUG) emerged as an umbrella organization to unify and coordinate advocacy rights for the LGBT community. Both FAR-Ug and SMUG have worked with Rainbow Uganda, a gay men's organization in Uganda that is registered as an NGO. All three organizations have received biting criticisms from Ugandan religious and political leaders, but increasingly, increasing numbers of gays and lesbians in Uganda have committed themselves to fight to end all forms of sexual discrimination, harassment, and exclusion.[19]

HEALTH

Uganda has made significant contributions in the fight against the spread of the HIV virus in Africa, and President Museveni's strategy to mobilize both the Ugandan society and the global community to communicate effective methods to reduce the death rates due to AIDS is one of the more positive outcomes of this health crises. Educating the public about sexual risk factors is a sure way to curve an epidemic, but there are additional issues such as providing a sense of national security and continuity to those affected by poverty and disease, as well as the empowerment of African women so they are not completely dependent on men economically and politically. Moreover, the educational and health sectors of Uganda had deteriorated for over 30 years as a result of political conflicts, and this environment has had to be corrected to stop the susceptibility to the spread of HIV/AIDS.[20]

The positive health accomplishments achieved in Uganda have indeed served as a model for neighboring African countries Kenya, Tanzania, Rwanda, Burundi, and the Democratic Republic of the Congo, as well as other countries in Africa struggling to curb the AIDS crisis. However, many gay Ugandans continue to die of HIV/AIDS because doctors will not provide medical treatment to homosexuals. In a 2000 Global UNAIDS report, researchers concluded, "AIDS and men who have sex with men found that the risk of HIV transmission by unprotected anal sex was several times higher than the next most high risk category."[21] This blatant disregard for human life and rights is a challenge the Ugandan government must address. As the ministers of health establish new health priorities and initiatives for Ugandans, a critical objective should focus on the health of sexual minorities.

POLITICS AND LAW

In 2005, the Ugandan constitution was amended to explicitly state that "marriage is lawful only if entered into between a man and a woman" and "it is unlawful for same-sex couples to marry."[22] This specific amendment made Uganda the first and only country in the world to legally forbid homosexuals from marrying one another. This was the beginning of several public crackdowns on the LGBT community initiated by President Museveni. In 2007, the government denied LGBT representatives to speak before the Commonwealth Heads of Government Meeting in the capital city of Kampala, and this denial was met with resistance. As a result, Ugandan police beat and physically removed LGBT members who were trying to attend the meeting.[23] This confrontation only encouraged SMUG (Sexual Minorities of Uganda) members to work harder to organize demonstrations and to expose to the world the inhumane treatment of gays and lesbians in Uganda. For example, the legal punishment for sodomy or any sexual act between members of the same sex in Uganda is several years to life imprisonment for any practicing gays and lesbians.

RELIGION AND SPIRITUALITY

Religion in Uganda is an important part of the national culture. Both Christianity and Islam are the dominant religions followed throughout the country, but three out of every four Ugandans are believers of one denomination of Christianity. Religious leaders in Uganda, like in many African countries, are important figures in their communities, and often their conservative views about society play a part in influencing local and national politics.

In 2007, the Interfaith Rainbow Coalition against Homosexuality in Uganda launched their first antigay campaign to encourage the government to crack down on the freedom of speech exercised by organized gay and lesbian groups. Without question, this antigay rally commended the attention of the entire country, and one summarized statement pronounced by one of the religious organizers captured a singular message for all to consider: "The Government should learn from the Church of Uganda, which has withstood international pressure and had to do without donor funds in order to uphold morality."[24] The response to the rally created a public discourse about the evils of homosexuality and how "immoral" the practice of same-sex relationships are to the Ugandan family, the union of marriage, and to the future of innocent children. Religious interpretations about homosexuality, sin, and immorality are political bandwagon issues that the clergy have expressed directly to President Museveni's administration, and because of the fear of sexuality diversity, religious leaders have become the primary antigay campaign organizers to criminalize members of the LGBT community in Uganda.

VIOLENCE

The political history of postcolonial Uganda involves multiple cycles of violence related to presidential election campaigns, the civil war conflicts in northern Uganda between citizens of southern Sudan, the Ugandan government, and the Lord's Resistance Army (LRA) over land and settlement. In addition, there have been repeated reports of violence against refugees in Uganda, violence against women, and the physical harassment and ostracism of LGBT people in Uganda.[25] Amnesty International's 2007 *Human Rights Report on Uganda* concluded that "attacks on freedom of expression and press freedom continue to be a problem, as well as the torture of detainees and the harassment of people on account of their sexual orientation."[26]

OUTLOOK FOR THE 21ST CENTURY

Uganda is a developing country with many internal challenges to overcome. It has been an independent country for only 45 years, and it is expected to take at least 100 years to fully recover from an unstable past. At present, the life expectancy of a Uganda citizen is roughly 45.3 years, and the HIV/AIDS crisis continues to shorten the lives of millions of Ugandans. On the other hand, there are promising signs that progress is ongoing to expand the life expectancy of HIV-positive Ugandans. Although President Museveni has played an active role in amassing international medical support to research and fight against the spread of HIV/AIDS, he has consistently orchestrated antigay campaigns against members of the LGBT community.

The future of gays and lesbians in Uganda will be a long, difficult fight because the combination of political and clergy antihomosexual public discourse will continue to alienate and harass the LGBT community until the international community decides to step in and expose this injustice. However, Uganda is no different from many African countries, and the intrusion of international pressure to address a loaded issue of homosexuality will only aggravate this political discourse even further. The key strategies to transform Uganda's societal biases against gays and lesbians will require brave local and national leaders, an educational campaign to teach a new generation to value diversity and difference, and time for these transformations to develop.

RESOURCE GUIDE

Suggested Readings

Tade A. Aina, "Patterns of Bisexuality in Sub-Saharan Africa," in *Bisexuality and HIV/ AIDS*, ed. R. Tielman, M. Carballo, and A. Hendriks (Buffalo, NY: Prometheus Books, 1991).

T. Barnett and M. Haslwimmer, *The Impact of HIV/AIDS on Rural Livelihoods and Farming Systems in Eastern Africa* (Rome: United Nations FAO, 1993).

T. Barnett and A. Whiteside, *AIDS in the Twenty-First Century: Disease and Globalization* (New York: Palgrave MacMillan, 2002).

I. Bergstrom, "A Second Life," *African Woman* (Kampala), April, 2006.

H. Hansen and M. Twaddle, eds., *Changing Uganda: The Dilemmas of Structural Adjustment and Revolutionary Change* (London: James Currey, 1991).

R. Hyam, *Empire and Sexuality: The British Experience* (New York: Manchester University Press, 1990).

T. Melady and M. Idi Amin Dada, *Hitler in Africa* (Kansas City, KS: Sheed Andrews and McMeel, 1977).

A. Molnos, ed., *Cultural Source Material for Population Planning in East Africa: Beliefs and Practices* (Nairobi: East African Publishing House, 1973).

N. Monk, "A Study of Orphaned Children and their Households in Luweero District, Uganda," Research for the Association Francois-Xavier Bagnoud, 2001.

S. Murray and W. Roscoe, eds., *Boy-Wives and Female Husbands: Studies in African Homosexualities* (New York: Palgrave, 1998).

S. Nolen, *28 Stories of AIDS in Africa* (New York: Walker and Company, 2007).

G. Okiror, A. Opio, and J. Musinguzi, "Change in Sexual Behaviour and Decline in HIV Infection among Young Pregnant Women in Urban Uganda," *AIDS* 11, no. 1 (1997).

J. Sachs, *The End of Poverty* (New York: Penguin, 2005).

M. Southwold, "The Baganda of Central Uganda," in *Cultural Source Material for Population Planning in East Africa: Beliefs and Practices* (Nairobi: East African Publishing House, 1973).

R. Tanner, "The East African Experience of Imprisonment," in *African Penal Systems,* ed. Milner (New York: Praeger, 1969).

Web Sites

AIDS Support Organization of Uganda (TASO), www.tasouganda.org.

Behind the Mask, http://www.mask.org.za.

DATA: Debt, AIDS, Trade, Africa, www.data.org.

Gay Uganda, http://www.geocites.com/gayuganda/general/htm.

Global Fund to Fight AIDS, TB, and Malaria, www.theglobalfund.org.

National AIDS Commission in Uganda, http://www.aidsuganda.org.

NOTES

1. U.S. Department of State, Bureau of African Affairs, "Background Note: Uganda," April 2008, http://www.state.gov/r/pa/ei/bgn/2963.htm.

2. Mutibwa Phares, *Uganda since Independence: A Story of Unfulfilled Hopes* (London: Hurst and Company, 1992), 1–3.

3. Ibid.

4. Holger Bernt Hansen and Michael Twaddle, eds., *Changing Uganda: The Dilemmas of Structural Adjustment and Revolutionary Change* (London: James Currey, 1991), 230.

5. Thomas and Margaret Melady, *Idi Amin Dada: Hitler in Africa* (Kansas City, KS: Sheed Andrews and McMeel, Inc., 1977), 59.

6. Ibid.

7. Hansen and Twaddle, *Changing Uganda*.

8. *afrol News*, "Uganda's gays left out of HIV/AIDS Strategy," March 20, 2007, http://www.afrol.com/articles/18781.

9. Ibid.

10. Ibid.

11. See Gay Uganda, http://www.geocites.com/gayuganda/general/htm.

12. Ibid., 3; Gay Uganda: The Law of Uganda.

13. "Uganda—Education," My Uganda, www.myuganda.co.ug/edu/universities.php.

14. U.S. Department of State, Bureau of African Affairs, "Background Note: Uganda," April 2008, http://www.state.gov/r/pa/ei/bgn/2963.htm.

15. Stephanie Nolen, *28 Stories of AIDS in Africa* (New York: Walker and Company, 2007), 206–7.

16. "Uganda: Events of 2006," Human Rights Watch, http://hrw.org/englishwr2k7/docs/2007/01/11/uganda14719.htm.

17. U.S. Department of State, Bureau of African Affairs, "Background Note."

18. "Uganda: Events of 2006."

19. See Gay Uganda http://www.geocites.com/gayuganda/general/links.htm.

20. Tony Barnett and Alan Whiteside, *AIDS in the Twenty-First Century: Disease and Globalization* (New York: Palgrave MacMillan, 2002), 116.

21. *Afrol News*, "Uganda's gays left out of HIV/AIDS Strategy."

22. Gay Uganda: The Law of Uganda.

23. "Anti-gay Movement: Maroon He Gays Elaborate Plan by the Ugandan Government to End LGBT Activities," *New Internationalist* 408, no. 1 (2008).

24. "Religious Groups Demonstrate against Homosexuals," *The New Vision*, August 21, 2007, http://www.newvision.co.ug/.

25. Amnesty International, "Report 2007, Uganda: The State of the World's Human Rights," http://thereport.amnesty.org/eng/Regions/Africa/Uganda.

26. Ibid.

ZIMBABWE

Derek Matyszak and Keith Goddard

OVERVIEW

Zimbabwe is a landlocked country in central southern Africa occupying 150,871 square miles. The territory was occupied by the British in 1891 and named Southern Rhodesia after its founder, Cecil John Rhodes. In 1896, the local *Shona* and *Ndebele* inhabitants rebelled against the invaders in what became known as the First Chimurenga (struggle). The rebellion was crushed and the two spirit-medium leaders, Kaguvi and Nehanda were hanged.

Rhodesia became a self-governing colony in 1923 although, in 1953, the British government joined Southern Rhodesia to the territories of Northern Rhodesia (now Zambia) and Nyasaland (now Malawi) to form the Federation of Rhodesia and Nyasaland.

After World War II, Britain began to divest itself of its colonies in Africa. The Federation was dissolved in 1963, and Northern Rhodesia (Zambia) and Nyasaland (Malawi) attained independence and majority rule. Fearing that independence and majority rule might also be extended to what was now called Rhodesia, the then prime minister, Ian Smith, led the white minority in rebellion against the British crown and declared a Unilateral Declaration of Independence (UDI) from the United Kingdom in 1965.

UDI was a devastating blow to black nationalists who had hoped that the days of white minority rule were at an end. The result was a civil war known as the Second Chimurenga. The Zimbabwe African National Union (ZANU), representing the *Shona* people, formed an armed wing (ZANLA); the Zimbabwe

African Peoples Union (ZAPU), representing the *Ndebele* people, formed a separate military wing (ZIPRA).

The war ended in 1979 after the British brokered a peace agreement between the parties at Lancaster House in London. Independence was formally granted on April 18, 1980, with President Robert Mugabe as the first prime minister under a Westminster-style of government. Canaan Banana, who was subsequently tried in the Zimbabwean High Court for 11 counts of sodomy, became the first ceremonial president.

Although the 1980s were marked by growing prosperity and improvements in education and health services for the majority of Zimbabwe citizens, a series of attacks on farms in Matabeleland by groups dubbed by the government as dissidents, resulted in Operation Gukurahundi (or "drive out the chaff"). North Korean soldiers were brought in to command a brutal suppression of the Ndebele people, in which at least 20,000 civilians, including women and children were massacred. A unity agreement was finally signed with the Ndebele leader Joshua Nkomo in 1987. In the same year, the government amended the national constitution abolishing the office of prime minister and introducing an executive president. Mugabe was duly elected to this office in January 1988.

In 1990, Zimbabwe adopted an Economic Structural Adjustment Program inspired by the International Monetary Fund. Severe drought and other factors caused the program to flounder and inflation to rise. A series of disastrous policy decisions, including an enormous and unbudgeted payout to war veterans in November 1997 (which caused the Zimbabwe dollar to crash), an ill-advised and expensive military adventure into the Democratic Republic of Congo, and an even more economically catastrophic radical land redistribution policy have put Zimbabwe into a state of severe crisis. Since 2003, inflation in Zimbabwe has spiraled out of control and in July 2008 the Zimbabwe dollar collapsed and reached an all-time world record of 231 million percent. By the end of February 2009, the U.S. dollar, the South African rand, and the Botswana pula had entirely replaced the Zimbabwean dollar as units of currency. Unemployment now stands at over 80 percent[1] with most people eking out a living through informal trading. Foreign investment is minimal, and while other countries in the region are enjoying growth rates of around six percent annually, Zimbabwe's growth has declined by the same percentage every year since 2000. As a result, an estimated three million people have sought employment outside of the country, leaving a depleted population of about 12 million.

Food riots in 1997, the formation of an effective opposition party, the Movement for Democratic Change (MDC) under Morgan Tsvangirai, and the rejection of the government's proposed new national constitution in a referendum in February 2000 have led to increasing militarization of the state as the ruling party tries to cling on to power. The official Zimbabwean army has around 30,000 troops, with an additional an air force of around 5,000; but a militia of so-called war veterans, many of them too young to have fought in the liberation struggle, is estimated at over 20,000 and is the force most closely linked to the intimidation of the populace.

A 2005 census showed that life expectancy in the country had dropped dramatically from 67 years in 1990, to 37 years old (34 for women) making it the country with the lowest life expectancy in the world. In 2001, the HIV prevalence rate was set at 26.5 percent, but by the end of 2007 it was said to have dropped to 15.6 percent.[2] This may explain the recent small increase in life expectancy to 39.7 years old.[3]

Zimbabweans place great value on education, although the system tends to be highly conservative and oriented towards the passing of examinations. Children go through seven grades of primary education and six forms of secondary education. 'O' (Ordinary) level and 'A' (Advanced) level national examinations are taken in November and are also offered in June.

Adult literacy is estimated at 90.7 percent,[4] which is significantly higher than any other country in the region, with the exception of neighboring South Africa where it is 86.4 percent.[5] School education was made free in 1980 but fees were reintroduced in 1988 and have now become unaffordable for many. Falling standards in education, as qualified teachers leave the country, have meant that parents who can afford it now send their children to the more expensive private (or independent) schools.

Zimbabwe is generally a conservative society. Around 75 percent of people are either purely Christian or practice a mixture of traditional beliefs rooted in the ancestral spirits and Christianity.[6]

OVERVIEW OF LGBT ISSUES

Virtually nothing is known about homosexual activity in ancient Zimbabwean society, although it has been suggested that a *San* (Bushman) painting of between 1,000 to 11,000 years old depicts the act of a sick man anally penetrating a healer.[7]

The view that homosexuality is a phenomenon alien to Africa, therefore, there are no grounds for homosexuals and lesbians to be defended against discrimination has prevailed through much of Africa until the Gays and Lesbians of Zimbabwe (GALZ) emerged, prompting harsh negative reaction from President Mugabe that was soon echoed by other African leaders including Sam Nujoma of Namibia, Yoweri Museveni of Uganda and others.

According to the Zimbabwe National AIDS Council (ZNAC), "the main mode of HIV transmission in Zimbabwe is heterosexual contact." However, the denial of the existence of homosexuals in Zimbabwean culture, strong social disapproval of homosexuality that pushes LGBT people underground, and a lack of research mean that transmission rates among men who have sex with men (MSM) and women who have sex with women (WSW) remain largely unknown.

Zimbabwe inherited a Roman Dutch law from South Africa. Sexual relations between men were criminalized under common law. Sexual relations between women are not an offence. In 2006, Zimbabwe codified its common law replacing common law crimes with statutory ones. This has resulted in an increase in penalties for sexual acts between men.

The protection of freedom of speech is enshrined in the national constitution, but, in reality, oppressive legislation and extra-judicial practices severely limit the ability of Zimbabweans to meet in public space and to freely receive and impart information. Despite a High Court ruling in 1996 that the Gays and Lesbians of Zimbabwe (GALZ) had the right to exhibit at the Zimbabwe International Book Fair (ZIBF), the organization has systematically been prevented from doing so by unknown agents since 2005.

EDUCATION

The traditional roles of uncles and paternal aunts in educating children have been seriously diminished in modern Zimbabwe, and so many children receive little or no sex education within the family. There is no education around same-sex sexuality in schools, not even in HIV/AIDS education. There are reported cases of LGBT young people being expelled from school. For example, in 2003, 45 suspected lesbian pupils were expelled from Langham School.[8]

In the past, there was also little sex education in schools, but with the onset of HIV/AIDS children are now regularly taught basic life skills in the classroom, although homosexuality remains a taboo subject. *Aunty Stella,* a pack of discussion cards dealing with issues facing teenagers, is one initiative that has sought to fill this gap by including two cards on gay and lesbian issues.[9]

At the tertiary level there is limited but more balanced inclusion of homosexuality in certain degree courses, for example in the Bachelor of Science Degree in Counseling of the Zimbabwe Open University. GALZ (Gays and Lesbians of Zimbabwe) has also hosted internships to students doing research for courses at the Midlands State University and the School of Social Work.

EMPLOYMENT AND ECONOMICS

Zimbabwe had one of the most developed economies in Africa based largely on agriculture and mining. Even sanctions imposed by the United Nations against the white settler regime in 1966 did little damage to begin with and in fact encouraged diversification of the economy and the development of the manufacturing industry.

After independence in 1980, Zimbabwe was generally referred to as the *breadbasket of Africa.* However, overspending, general mismanagement, and disastrous policies of land reform have brought Zimbabwe's economy to a state of crisis.

The historical economic disparity between wealthier whites and poorer blacks is also reflected in the country's LGBT community. In the early years of GALZ, the membership was largely made up of both whites and blacks, most of whom were concerned primarily with attending recreational activities. From the mid-1990s, as the membership started to become predominantly black, many whites left and the focus of the GALZ, besides becoming more political, turned towards serving the needs of a community that was far less well resourced.

There has been no debate around LGBT people in the workplace. Although strict laws exist making it difficult to fire employees, with 80 percent or more unemployment, LGBT people are understandably concerned about losing their jobs if they are outed at work. That said, no case of dismissal on the grounds of an employee's sexual orientation has come to the attention of GALZ or the Zimbabwe Congress of Trade Unions. However, like many other Zimbabweans, a large number of LGBT people have fled the country to take up employment or seek asylum in South Africa, Canada, the United States, Britain or elsewhere.

SOCIAL/GOVERNMENT PROGRAMS

There are no government services targeting LGBT people in Zimbabwe. However, some voluntary testing and counseling centers are welcoming to nonheterosexuals, and the Zimbabwe Institute for Systemic Therapy includes discussion on homo-sexual relationships as part of its training courses even though there is no specific mention of these relationships in any of its manuals.

GALZ is also well embedded within the HIV/AIDS network, but there are still very few AIDS Service Organizations (ASOs) that make any effort to include MSM and WSW in their programming. GALZ members have also received legal support from organizations such as the Legal Resources Foundation, The Zimbabwe Human Rights NGO Forum, and Zimbabwe Lawyers for Human Rights in cases of arrest, intimidation or extortion.

SEXUALITY/SEXUAL PRACTICES

In Zimbabwe, many taboos exist around sex and sexuality, in particular homo-sexuality. This is slowly beginning to change, however, as ASOs and others encourage people to be open about their HIV status and not to encourage stigma.

In general, Zimbabwean men have a reputation for holding extremely narrow, sexist views about gender and sexual roles. A small but significant research project among 1,688 men and women throughout the country indicated that the majority of Zimbabwean men and male youths believe that women are inferior to men and that "a woman's thoughts, feelings, aspirations and needs must, uncompromis-ingly, serve those of the man."[10] The study also showed that 80 percent of men and 84.2 percent of women believe that "there is something wrong with a woman who does not want to marry and raise a family."[11]

In terms of sexual roles, there is a common belief that "if a man is penetrated, he is being used as a woman and is, therefore, demeaned."[12] Even in homosexual prison relationships, gender roles are rigidly enforced in that "the bigger, stron-ger partner (*mhondoro*) provides protection to the often younger, weaker partner (*kapoto* or small-pot wife) in return for domestic duties and sex."[13]

The lack of proper social education on issues of sexual orientation and gender identity has led to numerous confusions and misunderstandings, most of it based on the stigma encouraged by state-instigated propaganda that is the only source of information for many.

Many are also thought to believe that unprotected anal sex carries with it no risk of contracting HIV. This may have something to do with the focus of the Zim-babwe National AIDS Council on penis-to-vagina intercourse and the barring of GALZ from conducting any public education on safer-sex.

FAMILY

Before the arrival of Christianity, Zimbabweans practiced polygamy and many still do. In the past, families tended to be large but have tended to become smaller owing to the general downward trend in child mortality and the cost of supporting and educating children. There is also a growing trend towards the nuclear fam-ily system, especially in urban areas, although it is common for men to engage in extramarital relations.

There is heavy pressure on both men and women to marry and have children. This means that many gay men and lesbian women feel obliged to fulfill their social obligations to their families. Many also marry in order to disguise their sexual orientation and, for this reason, it is commonly believed that there is probably a significant number of MSM and WSW who are hidden within the general population.

Many LGBT do not come out to their families for fear of being violently punished and/or evicted from home. There are even reports of families organizing curative rape of lesbian family members.

There is no possibility of gay marriage being legalized in Zimbabwe in the near future. In 2006, at a celebration in Mutare to mark Mugabe's 82 birthday, Mugabe threatened to have arrested any clergy who performed gay marriages.[14] Despite this, there are a number of examples of lesbian and gay couples living together and bringing up children, in particular children who have been orphaned by AIDS.

COMMUNITY

Formed in 1990, GALZ is the only organization exclusively serving the needs of LGBT people in Zimbabwe, and since 1995 it has tended to draw its membership largely from black townships and peri-urban areas. GALZ operates from Harare but in 2007, opened a second office in the city of Bulawayo. An important function of GALZ is to provide safe spaces for its members to meet and socialize. It also organizes the annual Miss Jacaranda Queen Drag Pageant, which takes place in October. Legal support is also provided to members, in particular to victims of blackmail.

In recent years with the increasing economic meltdown, GALZ has offered sponsorship to members for vocational training through its Skills for Life and Women's Scholarship Programs. The motivation behind these initiatives is that "family members who are discovered to be lesbian, gay or bisexual, are less likely to be evicted from home if they are income generators. And should this happen, a person is more likely to have the means to be economically and socially independent. In addition, lesbian and gay people who are earning generally have a greater sense of self-esteem which motivates them to take better care of their health needs."[15] An additional fund, the GALZ Safety Net, provides emergency relief to members who, for example, have been made homeless or need urgent medical attention.

The GALZ health department provides counseling and organizes activities around HIV/AIDS prevention and support. Under the Positive Image Health Scheme, all members living with HIV are guaranteed access to affordable health care, including antiretroviral drugs.

The gender department ensures the visibility of lesbian and bisexual women at all levels within the organization and has done much to include the voices of lesbian and bisexual women within the women's movement.

The organization produces a regular monthly magazine, *Whazzup,* and the quarterly *GALZETTE,* which contains more scholarly articles meant for wider distribution. A Web site, http://www.galz.co.zw, was launched in February 2005.

GALZ has done much to embed itself within the broader human rights network and is a member of a number of important coalitions, including the Women's Coalition and the Zimbabwe Human Rights NGO Forum to which GALZ sends reports on human rights violations against its members.

HEALTH

Although the health care system in Rhodesia was fairly adequate for blacks, there was dramatic improvement in postindependent Zimbabwe with the development of policies to prioritize the provision of primary health care and build more clinics, especially in rural areas. However, with the economic meltdown and the strain put on the health care system by HIV/AIDS, the system has all but collapsed and many qualified doctors and nurses continue to leave the country.

The first Zimbabwean case of AIDS was identified in 1985 but, in line with many other African countries, the Zimbabwean government was relatively slow to respond to the epidemic. The National AIDS Co-ordination Program was launched in 1987, followed by the formation of the Zimbabwe National AIDS Council in 1990, but it was only in 1999 that a national HIV/AIDS policy was put in place.

The policy makes no mention of the LGBT community except to acknowledge that homosexual practices occur in prisons and that there is "consensual and forced sexual activity in crowded prisons."[16] The policy is entirely silent on the distribution of condoms to prisoners but suggests that prisoners have the right to counseling and information about HIV/AIDS.

The Zimbabwe Prison Service has consistently refused to distribute condoms to prisoners. In 1993, Edna Madzongwe suggested that prisoners be given condoms so as to curb HIV. The suggestion was rejected because it was seen as tantamount to legalizing homosexual acts in prisons.[17] In November 2007, the Chief Prisons Officer, Gertrude Musango, told ZimOnline: "Homosexuality is an offence in Zimbabwe. ZPS [Zimbabwe Prison Service] would not consider providing inmates with condoms but would rather embark on more measures to stop inmates from engaging in these illicit activities."[18]

Recently, the Zimbabwe National AIDS Council acknowledged men who have sex with men (MSM) as a vulnerable group in its Strategic Plan 2006–10,[19] and also acknowledged that "adopting punitive approaches will only serve to drive MSM and reduce opportunities to dialogue with this group."[20] At present, GALZ is the only organization in Zimbabwe exclusively performing HIV/AIDS intervention work among the LGBT population.

POLITICS AND LAW

Between 1892 and 1935, approximately 450 cases of male on male sexual crimes were processed in the colonial courts, of which only 39 involved whites,[21] suggesting that homosexual activity is not as foreign to Africa as has been suggested. However, throughout the colonial period there was little mention of homosexuality in the media and it was never part of general public discourse.

The 1914 Immigration Act of Southern Rhodesia declared that "any persons convicted for sodomy or unnatural offenses" would be prohibited from immigrating to the country. In the 1954 Immigration Act and subsequent editions up to 1996, prohibition was extended to anyone engaging in prostitution or homosexuality.

Until the 1990s there was little organized activity around LGBT issues in Africa outside of South Africa. Government leaders were either silent on the issue or denied the existence of homosexuals in their countries.

This was certainly true in the first 15 years after Zimbabwean independence, where the 1990 formation of the Gays and Lesbians of Zimbabwe (GALZ) went unnoticed by the government, until 1994 when GALZ tried to advertise its counseling services in the press and on the radio.

In 1995, having been barred from the media and subjected to a barrage of antigay propaganda, GALZ decided to enter the Zimbabwe International Book Fair (ZIBF), which had as its theme that year, Human Rights and Justice. It applied for and was granted permission to operate a small stand exhibiting materials on LGBT rights and its counseling services. When the government learned of GALZ's intention to be at the ZIBF, it placed enormous pressure on the trustees of the ZIBF and successfully coerced them into revoking GALZ's permission to exhibit. This solicited strong protest from writers, Wole Soyinka and Nadine Gordimer, who were present at the fair's *indaba* on freedom of expression. Mugabe reacted to the resultant furor, which received international coverage, with a series of extreme and homophobic statements. At a press conference during the ZIBF, he responded to a question on LGBT rights with the pronouncement that "I don't believe they should have any rights at all." Later, in a speech, he said: "[Homosexuality] degrades human dignity. It is unnatural and there is not a question ever of allowing these people to behave worse than dogs and pigs."[22] Elsewhere he has stated: "Let the Americans keep their sodomy, bestiality, stupid and foolish ways to themselves, out of Zimbabwe. Let them be gay in the U.S., Europe, and elsewhere. They shall be sad people here." Further, on another occasion, he stated: "What we are being persuaded to accept is sub-animal behavior, and we will never allow it here. If you see people parading themselves as lesbians and gays, arrest them and hand them over to the police."

His homophobic statements were repeated in almost every public speech he delivered thereafter for the next few years. Mugabe's ministers competed with each other, hoping that their sycophant, homophobic statements would be rewarded by Mugabe in accordance with their extremity. One parliamentarian referred to homosexuality as a "festering finger'" on the body of Zimbabwean society that needed to be cut off. The government-controlled press followed suit:

> Painful experience reminds us Zimbabweans and other Africans on the continent of moves orchestrated by colonialists to wipe out anything that had to do with African culture as constituted mainly by customs and traditions…many years after decolonization, attempts to wipe out cultural values are still being made—and made with a vengeance in some cases. Witness the shrill outcries over the refusal by the Government of Zimbabwe to allow the Gays and Lesbians of Zimbabwe to peddle its ideas by exhibiting at the recent Zimbabwe International Book Fair in Harare in Harare—a refusal that all Africans who cherish their cultural identity—or what remains of it—should support unflinchingly.[23]

In fact, as a number of recent books have shown, including *Unspoken Facts: A History of Homosexualities in Africa* that homosexuality was accommodated and tolerated in traditional precolonial society. The traditional values that were, and are still lauded as African, are, in reality, the values brought by Christian missionaries. The vast majority of Zimbabweans now identify themselves as Christian, and 62 percent are active churchgoers. When encountering Zimbabweans in public, be it the clerk in a building or government department, a bible is often open on the desk, a biblical quotation may be photocopied and stuck to the wall of the office, and gospel or religious music often plays in the background. Most public meetings begin with a Christian prayer.

In 1996, GALZ, undaunted, again applied to exhibit its publications at the ZIBF. Although the main state-owned daily newspaper carried a front-page headline proclaiming "GALZ banned from ZIBF," the trustees refused to bow to government pressure a second time. When the government sought to deploy the

Censorship Act to exclude GALZ from the ZIBF, GALZ successfully applied to the High Court for an order allowing it to exhibit. The GALZ exhibits generated a huge amount of attention at the ZIBF, but on the last day, after several hours, under threat of physical violence from a group that announced itself as the protectors of Zimbabwean culture, GALZ made a tactical retreat.

This event was important in the history of not only the LGBT struggle in Zimbabwe but for human rights in the country as a whole. For the very first time the Mugabe government had been successfully and publicly defied using the Bill of Rights within the Constitution. GALZ had initiated what is now a vibrant nongovernmental organization (NGO) human rights advocacy movement in Zimbabwe and has gained the respect of other human rights organizations. GALZ has overcome the initial reluctance of most of these NGOs to embrace LGBT rights as human rights. Furthermore, Mugabe's vilification of the LGBT community had caused such outrage internationally that supportive funding poured in from around the world, helping to build GALZ into the established and well-respected organization it is today. The furor from Mugabe also awarded GALZ far more publicity than it could have achieved through being allowed to advertise in the smalls columns of the state-controlled media.

GALZ's outing and its raised profile were not without negative repercussions. Blackmailers proliferated, seeking to take advantage of the homophobic backlash, and GALZ began to deal with two to three cases of blackmail of its members monthly. Other LGBT people, intimidated by the homophobic hysteria, retreated back into the closet. Some African leaders, most notably Sam Nujoma of Namibia began to parrot Mugabe's homophobic statements.

In 1997, a second and important development for the LGBT community unfolded. Also seeking to take advantage of the homophobic climate was the former *aide de camp* of the erstwhile ceremonial president, Canaan Sodino Banana, Jefta Dube, who shot and killed a person who had taunted him in public as being "Banana's wife." Seeking to mitigate the sentence after a conviction of murder, the aide pleaded posttraumatic stress consequent upon repeated nonconsensual sodomy by Banana while he was president (an allegation that sat rather awkwardly with Mugabe's pronouncements that homosexuality was un-African). As a result, Banana found himself facing several counts of sodomy. Although Banana's sexual orientation was openly known (at least to the LGBT community), he denounced homosexuality as un-African and denied all charges. He pleaded that if sodomy had taken place in regard to one count, then it was consensual. This opened the way for a challenge to the constitutionality of anti-LGBT legislation in Zimbabwe, and specifically the validity of the common law against sodomy. Counsel argued the matter without any reference to GALZ and thus without input from GALZ, which would have proved beneficial.

This was also precisely the wrong kind of case and the wrong moment to argue the point. Counsel first made the argument that the common law proscribing lesbian behavior had been "abrogated by disuse," there being no records of any prosecutions in this regard. The argument was accepted by the judges of the Supreme Court without comment. Same-sex sex for women was thus quietly decriminalized. The milestone was not immediately realized by the LGBT community, lost as it was in the media's lurid reporting. Nor was it appreciated by several blackmailers whose extortionate attempts on several women thereafter were coolly rebuffed. Acceptance of this point allowed the further argument that it constituted discrimination on the grounds of sex or gender to allow same-sex sex for women but not for men. The court split three to two, with the majority upholding the validity of legislation criminalizing sodomy between consenting adult males. The minority essentially adopted the argument that had earlier been accepted in the South African courts. Justice McNally, a practicing Catholic, wrote the judgment for the majority. He determined that while laws proscribing consensual sex for adult males and not women were technically discrimination on the basis of sex, he held that this was "chop logic." The real discrimination was against homosexual sex. It had to be assumed that, since Zimbabwe's Constitution did not prohibit discrimination on the basis of sexual orientation, as did South Africa's, this omission must be deemed to be deliberate and designed to permit such discrimination. As to whether such discrimination was "reasonably justifiable in a democratic society," he glibly noted that America has similar sodomy laws in 25 states (using the figure in *Bowers v. Hardwick*), and since America is a democratic society such laws could not be regarded as being undemocratic. This judgment effectively precluded any further challenge within Zimbabwe to the validity of sodomy legislation.[24]

In 1998, at the height of the Banana scandal, GALZ again became the center of a media frenzy when, at the invitation of the World Council of Churches (WCC), it applied to participate at the human rights and cultural forum (*Padare*) of the WCC's 8th Assembly, which took place in December in Harare. Despite the resistance of the Zimbabwe Council of Churches, GALZ was required to obtain an endorsement from a local church in order to take part, which, naturally, it was unable to do. In the end, GALZ managed to slip in under the umbrella of a loose coalition of human rights organizations that had come together to create awareness around the 50th anniversary of the signing of the Universal Declaration of Human Rights.

In 1999, GALZ made a submission to the government-led Constitutional Commission calling for the inclusion of sexual orientation in the Bill of Rights, and again this became big news in the press. In the end, although the term *sexual orientation* did not specifically appear, the phrase *natural difference or condition* was widely believed to include LGBT people.

In 2000, the draft constitution was rejected in a national referendum, not because it provided protection to homosexuals but because it provided too much power to the Executive Branch.

In July 2006, Zimbabwe codified its criminal law, effectively replacing common law crimes with statutory ones. This has resulted in substantial changes to the laws affecting LGBT people. Most importantly, whereas previously consensual and non-consensual anal sex between men was regarded as sodomy, sodomy now only refers to consensual sex between men. In addition, sodomy previously only referred to anal sex. Other sexual acts aside from anal sex fell into a residual category called "unnatural offenses." Sodomy now includes any sexual contact between men and is defined as:

> Any male person who, with the consent of another male person, knowingly performs with that other person anal sexual intercourse, or any act involving physical contact other than anal sexual intercourse that would be regarded by a reasonable person to be an indecent act, shall be guilty of sodomy and liable to a fine up to or exceeding level 14 or imprisonment for a period not exceeding one year or both.[25]

Due to rampant inflation in Zimbabwe, fines are now set at various levels, from one to fourteen, the monetary sum of which is then altered periodically by regulation. The fines stipulated for sodomy are the maximum possible and should only be imposed by the court for the gravest infringement of the legislation. In practice, a lesser sentence will likely be imposed. It has yet to be seen if the courts follow the precedent prior to codification of imposing fines in the region of level three or less for sodomy. Nonetheless, rather than simply codifying the common law, the penalties for consensual anal sex appear to have increased. Previously, offenses of this nature have tended to attract a small fine, whereas a term of imprisonment is now provided.[26] It is anomalous that nonconsensual sexual acts falling short of anal sex attract a lesser fine of level seven.

According to GALZ, most cases are reported to the police as being nonconsensual, which is usually contrary to the facts. The law relating to nonconsensual sexual acts is such that nonconsensual anal sex between men is now called "aggravated indecent assault," which is defined as:

> Any person who, being a male person, commits upon a male person anal sexual intercourse or any other act involving the penetration of any part of the other male person's body or of his own body with indecent intent and knowing that the other person has not consented to it or realizing that there is a real risk or possibility that the other person may not have consented to it, shall be guilty of aggravated indecent assault and liable to the same penalty as is provided for rape.[27]

The penalty provided for rape is a maximum of life imprisonment, though generally the sentence is usually between seven and ten years. Any other nonpenetrative, nonconsensual sexual act between men is now called "indecent assault," which is defined as:

> A person who, being a male person, commits upon a male person any act involving physical contact that would be regarded by a reasonable person to be an indecent act, other than anal sexual intercourse or other act involving the penetration of any part of the male person's body or of his own body with indecent intent and knowing that the other person has not consented to it or realizing that there is a real risk or possibility that the other person may not have consented to it, shall be guilty of indecent assault and liable to a fine not exceeding level seven or imprisonment for a period not exceeding two years or both.[28]

The Banana judgment effectively foreclosed the possibility of a further constitutional challenge to the legislation prohibiting consensual sex between two adult males. However, this does mean that the possibility of pursuing a similar challenge under the African Charter on Human and Peoples Rights (which requires that domestic remedies be exhausted first) is now an option.

The Africa Charter, drafted at a time when African nations were at pains to emphasize their difference from Western liberalism in the form of a communalism, is unusual as a human rights instrument in including "duties'" as well as "rights." Hence it contains clauses such as Article 17(3): "The promotion and protection of morals and traditional values recognized by the community shall be the duty of the State." The Charter is replete with similar such clauses, indicating a different approach will be required under the African Charter than that adopted under Western liberal instruments.

Nevertheless, GALZ along with other African LGBT organizations, has cautiously started looking into working around the African Commission and was part of a 15-member LGBT delegation to the 38th session in Banjul, The Gambia in October 2005. The delegation was encouraged to find that there was no open hostility to its presence and it was able to make a statement before the Human Rights Forum protesting the imprisonment of homosexuals in Cameroon. In May 2009, GALZ was again part of an African LGBT delegation to the commission's 45th session where the NGO Forum preceding the main session divided into 14 groups to discuss human rights issues. Group 12 was devoted to gays and lesbians.

RELIGION AND SPIRITUALITY

The conservative and often religious views of many Zimbabweans mean that most disapprove of homosexuality and are shamed by the existence of any homosexuals in their families. There are a number of reports from GALZ members about families taking them to church to be prayed for or to traditional faith healers (*n'anga* or *sangoma*) since they believe that homosexuals are possessed by evil spirits (*ngozi*). Despite the homophobic rhetoric preached from many pulpits in Zimbabwe, many LGBT are practicing Christians. In an unpublished survey of its membership GALZ found that 64.7 percent of its membership identified as Christian, which is slightly higher than the national average. Although no church leaders are openly supportive of LGBT rights, some quietly try to understand and help their LGBT parishioners.

While some religious leaders, such as the Roman Catholic Archbishop Pius Ncube have been openly critical of the Zimbabwean government, others such as the former head of the Zimbabwe Council of Churches, Anglican Bishop of Harare Jonathan Siyachitema, have supported Mugabe especially in his antigay stance. Siyachitema's successor, Nolbert Kunonga, even called Mugabe a prophet.[29] Kunonga was dismissed and finally excommunicated from the Anglican Church in 2008 after trying to withdraw the Diocese of Harare from the regional synod on the grounds that the Anglican Church was too lenient towards homosexuals. His successor, Bishop Sebastian Bakare, showed a welcomingly tolerant attitude by calling for a church that is inclusive and accepts all people.[30]

VIOLENCE

Although incidents of violence do take place against LGBT people, they tend to be sporadic and there are no systematic campaigns of gay-bashing. In terms of the state, antigay campaigns have taken the form of virulent hate-speech but this has not translated into any witch hunts. GALZ operates openly from its premises in the Milton Park suburb of Harare and in Bulawayo and has never been invaded or attacked by a militia.

OUTLOOK FOR THE 21ST CENTURY

Although there are a number of pressing human rights and humanitarian issues that urgently need to be addressed in Zimbabwe, and that LGBT people also face, it is clear that gradual progress is being made towards the normalization of LGBT people in society. With the restoration of democracy and the rule of law and the drafting of a new constitution, GALZ will be better able to integrate itself into broader society and educate the broader public about LGBT issues.

At the end of 2009, a Government of National Unity (GNU) between ZANU-PF and the two factions of the MDC is in place after ZANU-PF heavily lost political ground in the 2008 parliamentary and presidential elections. A national constitutional review process is now underway, which GALZ is involved in.

RESOURCE GUIDE

Suggested Reading

C. Dunton and M. Palmberg, "Human Rights and Homosexuality in Southern Africa," *Current African Issues* 19 (June 1996).

M. Epprecht, *African Heterosexuality: The History of an Idea from the Age of Exploration to the Age of AIDS* (Athens: Ohio University Press, 2008).

M. Epprecht, *Hungochani: The History of a Dissident Sexuality in Southern Africa* (Montreal: McGill-Queen's University Press, 2004).

GALZ, *Sahwira: Being Gay and Lesbian in Zimbabwe* (Harare: GALZ, 1995).

GALZ, *Unspoken Facts: A History of Homosexualities in Africa* (Harare: GALZ, 2008).

K. Goddard, "A Fair Representation: The History of GALZ and the Gay Movement in Zimbabwe," *Journal of Gay and Lesbian Social Services* 16, no. 1 (2004): 75–98.

C.A. Johnson, *Off the Map: How HIV/AIDS Programming is Failing Same-Sex Practicing People in Africa* (New York: International Gay and Lesbian Human Rights Commission, 2007).

R. Kilalea, "Mea Culpa," in *Writing Still* (Harare: Weaver Press, 2003).

S. Long, *More Than a Name: State-sponsored Homophobia and its Consequences in Southern Africa* (New York: HRW and IGLHRC, 2003).

D. Marechera, *Mindblast!* (Harare: College Press, 1984).

C. Mungoshi , "Of Lovers and Wives," in *Walking Still* (Harare: Baobab, 1997).

S.O. Murray and W. Roscoe, eds., *Boy Wives and Female Husbands: Studies in African Homosexualities* (New York: St. Martin's Press, 1998).

O. Phillips, "The Invisible Presence of Homosexuality: Implications for HIV/AIDS and Rights in Southern Africa," in *HIV/AIDS in Africa: Beyond Epidemiology,* ed. E. Kalipeni (Cambridge, MA: Blackwell, 2004).

Web Sites

Behind the Mask, http://www.mask.org.za.
    A source for information on LGBT activities throughout Africa.
GALZ, http://www.galz.co.zw.
The NGO Network Alliance Project, http://www.kubatana.net.
    Internet hub for organizations working in the field of human rights in Zimbabwe, including GALZ.

NOTES

1. "Zimbabwe Unemployment Rate," Index Mundi, http://www.indexmundi.com/zimbabwe/unemployment_rate.html.

2. "Zimbabwe: HIV Rate Down to 15.6 Percent," *The Herald,* November 1, 2007.

3. "Zimbabwe Demographics Profile: 2008," Index Mundi, http://www.indexmundi.com/zimbabwe/demographics_profile.html.

4. "Zimbabwe Literacy," Index Mundi, http://www.indexmundi.com/zimbabwe/literacy.html.

5. "South Africa Literacy," Index Mundi, http://www.indexmundi.com/south_africa/literacy.html.

6. "Zimbabwe Demographics Profile: 2008," Index Mundi, http://www.indexmundi.com/zimbabwe/demographics_profile.html.

7. GALZ, *Unspoken Facts* (Harare: GALZ, 2008), 42.

8. GALZ statement, February 3, 2003.

9. *Aunty Stella: Teenagers Talk about Sex, Life and Relationships* (Harare: TARSC, 2005), cards 9 and 34.

10. P. Chiroro, et al., *The Zimbabwean Male Psyche with Respect to Reproductive Health, HIV, AIDS and Gender Issues* (Harare: Centre for Applied Psychology, University of Zimbabwe, 2002), viii.

11. P. Chiroro, et al., *The Zimbabwean Male Psyche*, 11.

12. *Understanding Human Sexuality and Gender* (Harare: GALZ, 2005), 21.

13. Ibid., 27.

14. "Mugabe Attacks Gays and Threatens Pro-gay Clergy with Prison," *Pink News* February 26.

15. GALZ, http://www.galz.co.zw/index.php?option=com_content&task=view&id=16&Itemid=35.

16. *National Policy on HIV/AIDS for Zimbabwe* (Harare, Zimbabwe: National AIDS Council, 1999).

17. "Zimbabwe-prisons-AIDS-health: Homosexuality Rampant in Zimbabwe's Prisons: Report," *Agence France-Presse*, October 14, 2003.

18. *ZimOnline*, November 6, 2007.

19. *Zimbabwe HIV and AIDS Strategic Plan 2006–10* (Harare: National AIDS Council), 13.

20. Ibid., 20.

21. M. Epprecht, *Hungochani: The History of a Dissident Sexuality in Southern Africa* (Montreal: McGill Queens University Press, 2004.)

22. This quote and those that follow appear in Dunton and Palmberg's article, "Human Rights and Homosexuality in Southern Africa," *Current African Issues* 19 (June 1996). This issue also contains a detailed account of the Book Fair furore.

23. See Dunton and Palmberg, footnote 1, *The Chronicle*, August 9, 1995.

24. See *S v. Banana* 2000 (1) ZLR 607 (S).

25. Criminal Law (Codification and Reform) Act 9:23 section 73(1).

26. See, for example, *S v Roffey* 1991(2) ZLR 47 HC.

27. Criminal Law (Codification and Reform) Act 9:23 section 66.

28. Criminal Law (Codification and Reform) Act 9:23 section 67.

29. Ceclia Dugger, "Zimbabwe Unleashes Police on Anglicans," *The New York Times,* May 16, 2008, http://akinolarepent.wordpress.com/2008/05/15/nyt-zimbabwe-unleashes-police-on-anglicans/.

30. Ibid.

THE MIDDLE EAST

IRAN

Brandon L. H. Aultman

OVERVIEW

The Islamic Republic of Iran is a nation-state with a complex sociopolitical and religious history dating back roughly 2,500 years. Currently one of the largest Islamic states in the Middle East, Iran was traditionally ruled by a single executive, a shah, whose power was infinite, dictated only by the monarch's personal ambition. The Islamic Revolution of 1979 solidified the end of monarchical control that had existed in Iran for nearly 2,500 years, supplanting it with a system of religious leaders vested with constitutional power based on traditional law. Sexuality, however liberal throughout Persian history, became deeply shrouded with the inauguration of stricter, Sharia-based penal codes.

Between the late 18th and early 19th centuries, the Qajar Dynasty made major concessions to the invading British and Russian powers. Compounded by the loss of two wars with the latter that led to two separate treaties in the early 19th century, Iran's fiscal crises were solidified. With a strategic battle between Russia and Britain over access to Afghanistan and India, Iran was battleground for external hegemonic control. The tobacco and oil concessions granted to these powers at the close of the 19th century called the fiscal machinations of the Iranian ruling elite into question. An increased social awareness among the Iranian laity of the relative ease with which the Iranian elites laid down to foreign power led to a call for constitutional reform.

One major cultural shift occurred as a result of this rapid political change.

As clerical power was diminished during the period, so too did the moral under-pinnings of the Iranian culture. This provided the basis of Ayatollah Ruhollah Khomeini's campaign for revolution: a major moral shift to reassert Islamic tradition. The outcome was the Islamic Revolution of 1979.

An incipient constitutional government was formed in the early 20th century, which sought to reassert popular sovereignty yet maintain certain vestiges of the monarchy, but it met its demise not long after creation. Due to a lack of an ideological core, Tehran's newly formed government fell victim to the overwhelming influence of the British and Russian political forces, whose sole concern rested on whether the newly formed Iranian government would disrupt their steady influence in the region. Along with the rise of Reza Shah, monarchical rule had been reinstituted—this time with despotic force. For a period spanning nearly 20 years, Reza Shah worked to take power from foreign influence, industrialize Iran, and bring the nation into modernity.

Following the abdication of the despotic monarch in 1941 and the end of World War II (in which Iran remained neutral), the nationalist movement for free elections received a pendulum-like power swing once again. Party politics took root, but by the mid-20th century, Iranian nationalism hit its peak. After centuries of external influence on Iran's socioeconomic and political independence, the Islamic Revolution of 1979, led by Ayatollah Ruhollah Khomeini, cemented these deep feelings of nationalism, with Muslim culture at its core. As a result, Iran's legal structure heavily incorporated traditional Islamic Sharia Law. As a result, strictures pertaining to sexual relations permitted little deviance. Outside of heterosexual intercourse within the auspices of marriage, sex is strictly forbidden. Sexual acts between members of the same gender are punishable by death or prison time. Finding open LGBT people in Iran is a difficult task; however, many find avenues for socializing in an underground atmosphere, through cinemas, online access, and social gatherings.

Iran has a current population of nearly 70 million people, and a gross domestic product of $852.6 billion as of 2007. As the second most populous country in the Middle East, boasting the second largest economy, Iran's major export is oil (nearly 80%). Although the Islamic Revolution was intended to strengthen the family and Iranian citizenry through a variety of human development programs, social protections, and a brand of social justice, sexual minorities often experienced the brunt of persecution.

OVERVIEW OF LGBT ISSUES

The antigay moral climate of Iran is directly related to the attention Islam pays to sexual behavior. The Qur'an, the holy document that ensconces the basic religious tenets of Islam, mentions homosexuality only briefly. In a number of scriptural references, homosexual acts are categorized as a sin. However, much like its Christian counterpart, the Bible, the Qur'an's interpretation is left up to the religious hierarchy's discretion. Traditionally in Iran, LGBT people have been persecuted as a result of conservative interpretations of these various references.

The prominent international LGBT organization, the International Lesbian and Gay Association (ILGA), stated in 2005 that homosexuality is considered a crime in Iran. ILGA refers to the traditional Iranian Islamic Penal Code that can be used against sexual minorities. The offense can range from something as innocuous as two members of the same gender lying under the same sheet, to acts of physical intimacy. The accused, if found guilty, has the option of choosing the punishment—hanging, stoning, being halved by a blade, or plummeting from such a height as to render death. The judge presiding over the case has discretion—he may commute the sentence to a period of time in prison or enforce a specific death mechanism.

The LGBT Persian magazine, *MAHA* (distributed from within Iran via online subscription only) suggests that the situation for LGBT Iranians is not as terrible as international bodies report. There are many meeting grounds at which LGBT people congregate, like cinemas and parks—places that the majority of individuals recognize as gay hotspots. The regime, *MAHA* reports, does not persecute gays as readily as it would appear externally. Although Iranian law provides for the punishment of homosexual offenses, it is understood that the government seldom enforces this sanction on private activities. It takes particular umbrage to the reportage that exists concerning the deaths of two Iranian youths in 2005, as they were found guilty of rape, not purely homosexual conduct. Scholars agree, stating that the international community is quick to judge Iran for its overtly religious stance and fundamentalist attitudes. However, LGBT people choose to live quiet lives out of the public eye.[1]

Critics of Iran's social landscape suggest that its policies toward LGBT peoples should not be underestimated. In response to many the assertions that gays and lesbians in Iran face limited persecution, a representative from the Iranian Queer Association stated that many gay men are continuously found guilty of sexual crimes in the obviously homophobic penal code. A police raid in late 2007 resulted in the arrest of 85 men who were privately consorting for *deviant purposes*.[2] From those afflicted with HIV/AIDS, openly gay men to preoperational transsexuals, many people still face a variety of political and legal obstacles and punishments. As being gay is seen as a crime, many seek out sex reassignment surgery as a means of overcoming the social hardship associated with being openly gay.

EDUCATION

Iran's traditional educational system was predicated on religious institutions. The clergy from both Shi'a and Sunni sects were charged with the responsibility of educating Iran's youth. As with most monarchical societies, the children of political and social elites tended to have access to the best education. Because of foreign influence during the late 18th century and throughout the 19th century, educational models became decidedly European. During the constitutional reforms on the early 20th century, a shift from religious-oriented schools to a secularized government-funded policy took place. A number of public schools opened, but a nationwide system was never fully realized.

By the inception of the Islamic Revolution, schools had become a secular institution. The Islamic Revolution saw to a de-secularization process. Revisions to, and removal of, textbooks that contained references to atheism or that were disparaging in any way to Islam became commonplace. Removal of teachers who did not demonstrate an adequate, and decidedly political, understanding of Islam was also a common practice. The revolution did not uproot the organization of the public school system per se, but significant alternations to its core curriculum were made to ensure heightened religiosity.

The modern Iranian higher education system originated from initiatives in the 1920s. These universities have often been at the epicenter of conflict and controversy following the Islamic Revolution. Currently, intellectuals and students who participate in demonstrations against the Iranian regime fall victim to a variety of legal mechanisms seeking to limit expression that might deride the government. Professors and students at public universities in the 1980s, for instance, who were deemed to lack sufficient understanding of the state-endorsed precepts of Islamic code, were removed from the school. Moreover, student enrollment at the University of Tehran, in one account, dropped from 17,000 to little more than 4,000 by the mid-1980s.[3] Because of the religious nature of schools and the strict moral interpretations of the Iranian government, LGBT students remain silent and meet in secret.

EMPLOYMENT AND ECONOMICS

Following the Islamic Revolution of 1979, Ayatollah Khomeini took to reforming his country. Included in his policies were various *jihads,* or religious calls to action, to fight illiteracy and to rebuild the country that, up to that point, was perceived to have been ravaged by foreign influence. Among his many policies were socialized medicine, low-income housing, and food subsidies. Upon his death a decade after the advent of the revolution, another political sea change took place. Khomeini's Islamic socialist stance disintegrated and Iran began a slow process of liberalization, cutting many of the programs that wove the revolution together. The 1990s put a particular crunch on the Iranian poor, as more and more social programs were cut.

A conservative upswing in the last decade has inaugurated a number of changes economically; however, the state itself is in control of most employment. The private sector is generally made up of small-scale workshops, with minimal agricultural activities. Iran has an unemployment rate of nearly 11 percent, as of 2007 estimates.[4] Receiving most of its revenue from oil transactions (nearly 85%), Iran's $70 billion in oil exchanges have reportedly done little to ease economic tension and high rates of inflation (17%). Iran has an estimated 18 percent of its citizenry living below the poverty line.

These figures do little to elucidate the continuous trials facing LGBT peoples in the workplace. There are currently no employment protections for LGBT people. Since homosexual conduct is a crime, and the state regime controls most access to employment, one could lose one's job on the sole basis of deviant sexual orientation.

SOCIAL/GOVERNMENT PROGRAMS

There are currently no public policies in explicit support of LGBT rights. However, there are nearly 20,000 documented Iranian transsexuals who underwent gender reassignment surgery. Iran offers roughly $4,500 in government grants for the surgery and postsurgical hormone therapy.[5] The *fatwa* authorizing this political stance toward transsexuals came from the religious leader Ayatollah Khomeini during the Islamic Revolution of 1979.

SEXUALITY/SEXUAL PRACTICES

The first reported case of HIV in Iran was identified in 1987. The Islamic clergy tends to perpetuate the image that Iran's citizenry engages in strictly heterosexual marital sexual relations, and the statistics seem to bolster this view. Nearly 57 percent of cases named intravenous drug use as the primary vector of transmission, whereas sexual contact accounted for only seven percent of reported cases (the remaining 34% is registered as "unknown").[6] Even the state's HIV/AIDS prevention program is divorced from overt references to sex, including depictions of condoms. The World Health Organization places the number of registered cases of HIV infection at a ceiling of 30,000. However, these statistics do no reflect the totality of cases. Since premarital sex is frowned upon, large numbers may report drug abuse or remain silent altogether to avoid disgrace.

Iran is situated along a major narcotics transportation route (with neighboring Afghanistan, a leading producer of narcotics) and there are high levels of intravenous drug use. Furthermore, neighboring countries are experiencing increased rates of HIV/AIDS infections, contributing to Iran's number of infections through immigration. HIV/AIDS infections are also quite prevalent in the prison population. Iran has taken several steps to combat these rates; however, social stigma applied to infected individuals still keeps many from seeking help. Iran currently offers information and educational material concerning HIV, ongoing HIV surveillance, voluntary testing and access to counseling, and HIV care and treatment.

Although LGBT peoples find it difficult to lead open lives in Iran, those afflicted with HIV/AIDS carry on even more isolated lives. Fearful that they will be further driven from their families, not to mention from their jobs, HIV-positive Iranians may choose to remain silent, and actual numbers of HIV-positive Iranians may be as high as 70,000, which is much larger than the reported statistic of 12,000. Other critics have suggested that the government has traditionally done little to ease the pains of those afflicted with AIDS, who are mostly turned away by hospital administrators who refuse to treat them.[7]

FAMILY

The concept of family is intrinsic to the foundations of Islam and the Islamic Revolution. Moral pretexts, especially sexual, are based on the notion of committed marriages, solemnized by the clergy. Sexual behavior is therefore monopolized by religious institutions. Marriage is strictly defined as a union between a man and a woman in the eyes of Allah and as a means of procreation. Infertility can be grounds for divorce. Shi'a Islam, the predominant religion in Iran, allows for a fixed period of marriage, in which those involved may be wed for several days or for decades.[8] The move emanated from a policy desire to encourage youths to marry and not live in sin (i.e., premarital sex).

The Iranian Queer Organization (IRQO), formerly the Persian Gay and Lesbian Association, reports that honor killings, often filicides initiated by the father of an alleged homosexual son, occur to prevent disgrace on the family. Reports of teen suicides, drug use, and prostitution are often linked to LGBT youths who have found nothing but persecution in their homes, places of work, and other social spheres of their lives.[9]

To avoid these hardships, many gay men and women have turned to sex reassignment surgery as a means of being with those whom they love. Indeed, transsexuals are more welcomed than overt homosexuals.

COMMUNITY

Because of the rigidity of the Iranian legal system with regard to sexual conduct, a cohesive LGBT community is difficult to locate. Reports of a flourishing LGBT underground are common, with many stating that numerous traditional laws pertaining to homosexuality are rarely, if ever, enforced. Conflicting accounts of how often these laws are executed occur frequently. For instance, scholars have gone on record to indicate that the LGBT community simply does not want a social movement for political change. They simply want international and national politics out of their lives, choosing to lead a quiet existence instead.[10]

Gay men and women mostly converse online, attend parties, or congregate at local cinemas. However, it is reported that government monitoring has stifled most avenues for social interaction.[11] Gay men may find that the other person responding to their e-mails is actually an agent of the Department of Intelligence enforcing the various aspects of Iranian Penal Code that criminalizes sodomy. Because students receive a disproportionate share of surveillance, LGBT university life is not always as openly flourishing as in many other contemporary university systems.

HEALTH

Iran offers its citizens substantial access to health care, with a large percentage of its GDP going toward that effort. HIV/AIDS programs have been reported to be among the most effective in the world, according to many sources.[12] Although references to sexual transmissions are missing from many of the state-sponsored pamphlets distributed to individuals regarding HIV/AIDS, references to intravenous drug use (with drawings of syringes) are explicit. In 2006, the Iranian government allocated nearly $30 million to HIV/AIDS-related programs to increase awareness. Within Iranian prisons, inmates are receiving condoms and syringes in an effort to promote safer sexual and drug practices.[13] Iran is among only six or seven countries promoting these efforts in the world.

Two brothers, Arash and Kamiar Alaei, after having obtained their medical degrees, began conducting research and shedding light on the HIV/AIDS crisis affecting small groups of Iranians.[14] HIV/AIDS is often considered a Western disease, and many believe that Iranians simply do not contract the disease. Most often, prisoners contract the disease through unprotected sexual practices and intravenous drug use. It took years before the Iranian government became comfortable with the notion of sexual education. However, President Ahmadinejad condones the practice of disseminating syringes, condoms, and methadone for heroine addicts. Iran has set up Triangular Clinics to address the growing heroin problem among its citizenry and to treat individuals suffering from HIV/AIDS, should these individuals come forward for treatment.

POLITICS AND LAW

A theocratic republic, Iran has three distinct branches of government. The 1979 Constitution defines both popular sovereignty and the supreme rule of sectarian authority. The highest authority is an elected figure, the Supreme Leader, chosen by an Assembly of Experts. This leader oversees the three divisions of state: a popularly elected executive, a legislature, and an appointed judiciary. The Assembly of Experts is generally comprised of learned scholars of Islam. Thus, Islamic moral code is infused throughout the structure of governance. Generally finding homosexuality a sin, Iranian officials have voiced their opinion concerning homosexuality. For instance, Iran's chief executive, President Mahmud Ahmadinejad, appeared at New York's Columbia University in 2007. When asked about the current situation of LGBT people in Iran, the Iranian President responded that, "In Iran, we don't have homosexuals, like in [the U.S.]." He later suggested that homosexuality is a phenomenon that Iran does not experience.

Much of Iran's legal framework is guided by the monotheistic religion, Islam. Following the end of Reza Shah's despotic rule, Iran's push for nationalism (one that stemmed from the early 20th century but was quashed) reached its apogee in 1979, when the Islamic Revolution instigated a sea change of policy strictly guided by moral absolutes. As a result, explicit condemnation of homosexuality (and sodomy) is evident in Iran's penal code, specifically in Articles 108 through 140, in which direct references to homosexuality are made and provisions of proper punishment are elucidated. Some of these punishments include 74 lashes (Articles 108 to 113) and, depending on the extent of physical contact, duration, and repetition, can include death. Since criminal proceedings are overseen by a single member of the judiciary, who prosecutes, investigates, and eventually decides the case, further discriminatory action is ineluctable. Most of these laws are predicated on the concept of Sharia Law, the traditional code that has been passed down through centuries of scholarly interpretation. Literally translated, Sharia means "path" or "way." The adoption of Sharia Law is, in most cases throughout Islamic states, mandatory.

Freedom of Expression

There are no overt constitutional protections for expression in Iran. The Press Law, passed in 2000, for example, has tight restrictions on the expressive content of the press. Articles 6, 24, and 32 of the Press Law expressly forbid the publication of atheistic articles or other missives that might be critical of Islam. On more individual, less journalistic grounds, Articles 498 and 499 of the Penal Code prescribe punishment of up to 10 years for individuals who seek to associate with groups that would disrupt the republic or form propaganda against the state. Those who publish falsehoods, defamation, and other materials deemed to incite a negative reaction to the state may be held criminally accountable and sentenced to a set prison term.

As a result, a variety of journalists and intellectuals have been prosecuted according to some stipulation of the Press Law and Penal Codes, creating a climate of anxiety and fear.[15] Students also bear the brunt of investigations, as student activities are monitored invidiously. In July 1999 and again in 2003, a number of students were attacked, arrested, and prosecuted for having participated in demonstrations that called for a variety of reforms to the republic. In 2003, photojournalist Zahra Kazemi was arrested, detained for four days without access to council, and eventually taken to the hospital unconscious, where she later died. Her crime was taking pictures of protests outside Evin Prison in Tehran.

In 1987, Iran's embassy wrote that "homosexuality in Iran, treated according to Islamic law, is a sin before the eyes of God and a crime for society."[16] However, transsexuals are treated differently under Iranian law than are homosexuals. Considered to have a mental disorder that can be potentially cured through an operation—contrary to homosexuality's criminalization without "cure"—transsexuals are actually encouraged to undergo gender reassignment surgery. Reports suggest that Iran has the second highest number of such operations in the world, next to Thailand. Estimates place the number of transsexuals residing in Iran to be between 15,000 and 20,000.[17]

International Human Rights Obligations and Constitutional Protections

Iran is a signatory to several human rights conventions, some of which ensconce basic tenets protecting LGBT political freedoms. One of these conventions is the International Covenant on Economic, Social, and Cultural Rights (est. 1975) and the International Covenant on Civil and Political Rights (1975). Yet, the Iranian Constitution states that, "all citizens of the country, both men and women, equally enjoy the protection of the law and enjoy all human, political, economic, social, and cultural rights, in conformity with *Islamic criteria*." As homosexuality is deemed a crime under Iranian law, LGBT groups are not viewed as a suspect class meeting equal protections criteria. Furthermore, although the class explicitly protects gender rights, discrimination on the basis of gender is still widespread. Only recently have there been major shifts, as a result of globalization, in the nature of the patriarchal system that has historically subverted political rights of sexual minorities.

RELIGION AND SPIRITUALITY

Religion is a guiding principle in nearly all industrialized nation-states. Iran's religious background is varied, but spirituality often dictates its legal structure. Before Arab occupation, Zoroastrianism pervaded Iranian culture and the core set of beliefs are still held today by less than two percent of the population. However, Islam is the dominate religious force impacting the sociopolitical structure of modern Iran.

Iran's adoption of Shi'a Islam seems to run contrary to the more popular Sunni sect among most Arab nations. With 89 percent of the population adhering to its beliefs, Shi'a Islam has guided the basic legal frameworks of Iran, especially following the Revolution of 1979. However, aside from their divergence regarding who constitutes the heir apparent of Muhammad, Sunni and Shi'a Islam's tenets often blur. Islamic scholars throughout the centuries created various interpretations of the Qur'an by which Muslims should live. After centuries of such interpretations, numbering nearly 600,000, it was only natural that many of these contradicted. The Hadith, as it is known, has many contradictory accounts concerning what is to be done with perpetrators of homosexual acts. However, final determinations as to punishments are left to the single judge presiding over the case.

VIOLENCE

Iran has a long history of gender-related violence, as gender inequality is an inherent aspect of Iranian culture. Violence typically takes place in the form of domestic abuse, where the victim rarely reports the assault.[18] Familial violence is ingrained in a culture that has historically viewed women as a subservient class in many respects. Deemed honor killings, women are often brutalized at the hands of their husbands, fathers, or brothers for a variety of social infractions. The death penalty, the most extreme form of judicable retribution, and ardently held as a violation of basic human rights norms by a number of international bodies, is a mainstay for a variety of offenses. Permutations of violence exceed gender boundaries as LGBT people are subject to a variety of brutal punishments.

Most notably, in July 2005, two Iranian youths were executed over the alleged rape of a 13-year-old boy. The conviction, and the news coverage surrounding the execution, left many human rights organizations skeptical. Many headlines covering the executions read, "Lavat beh onf." Literally translated, this statement means, "sodomy by coercion." The two boys were reportedly tortured until a confession was rendered from them. The boys were unaware of the penal code's prohibition against homosexual conduct, claiming that many boys their age are engaging in such activity. Although many sources, including contemporary LGBT groups, reported that the deaths of these two boys were predicated on their committing rape, many others remained skeptical. According to one source, over 4,000 separate executions of homosexuals have been reported since 1979.[19]

The executions caused an international outcry. European LGBT organizations, especially Outrage!, published stories that worked to immediately shed light on the executions and place valuations behind the convictions and sentencing. Assertions were immediately made that, although other LGBT and human rights organizations were urging individuals not to count the executions as a strictly gay issue, the charges of rape were insidious. Reiterating that the penal code makes explicit the "crime" of homosexuality, Outrage!, noted that the confession of these boys was rendered through torture and that the executions were carried out as a means of removing homosexuals from the population.[20] Although blogs and other online sources of information described the executions as hate-motivated, Iran's official response was that these two boys were not homosexuals, but rather they were rapists who were tried and convicted accordingly.

However, another execution in 2007 may have more overtly considered sexuality in the adjudication of the case. On June 11, 2007, days after a U.N. tribunal on human rights asked Iran to place a moratorium on the death penalty, local officials at the Kermanshah Central Prison hanged Makvan Mouloodzadeh. Found guilty of sodomy in a district court, the decision was later upheld in an appellate court. Mouloodzadeh appealed to the Iranian Chief Justice, who commuted his sentence. The decision held that the death penalty was antithetical to Islamic teaching, but the decision itself was later ultimately disregarded.

OUTLOOK FOR THE 21ST CENTURY

Iranian LGBT culture exists in secret, through preordained meeting places like private parties and online interaction. However, homosexuality is still not overtly tolerated. Although there are conflicting accounts concerning the extent to which sodomy laws are enforced, the consensus from the IRQO is that numerous arrests are still made with the intent to punish sexual deviance.

International jurists and Iranian nationals entreat countries and individuals alike to avoid quickly judging Iranian law. However, human rights abuses, arbitrary arrests, and police entrapment are nothing new, even in 2008. With President Ahmadinejad's statements at Columbia University last year, the outlook for LGBT people moving forward seems uncertain, at best. Law enforcement is disproportionately carried out depending upon the crime and gender of the assailant, and the United Nations has continuously called Iran's administration of justice arbitrary and in violation of numerous international standards of legal conduct and accepted human rights norms. As a result, Persian gays and lesbians find themselves caught in a culture of silence, where "coming out" can lead to imprisonment or death. The 2009 presidential elections in Iran declared Ahmadinejad the "people's choice," but not without high levels of civil violence contesting the results. The re-elected president's statements promising "change" may certainly not apply to the LGBT population, which he claims does not exist.

RESOURCE GUIDE

Suggested Reading

Hannah Allam, "Iran's AIDS-Prevention Program among World's Most Progressive," Common Dreams News Center, April 14, 2006, www.commondreams.org.

Keyan Keihani, "A Brief History of Male Homosexuality in the Qur'an, Saudi Arabia, Iran, and Arab-Islamic Culture," *Middle Eastern Studies* (2005): 150.

Michael Luongo, *Gay Travels in the Muslim World* (New York: Harrington Park Press, 2007).

Will Roscoe and Stephen Murray, *Islamic Homosexualities: Culture, History, and Literature* (New York: New York University Press, 1997).

Brian Whitaker, *Unspeakable Love: Gay and Lesbian Life in the Middle East* (Berkeley: University of California Press, 2006).

Videos/Film

A Jihad for Love. DVD. Directed by Parvez Sharma. New York: First Run Features, 2008.

Web Sites

Gay Middle East, www.gaymiddleeast.com.
>	Gay Middle East is a leading forum of discussion and media for LGBT youth in the Middle East. Includes access to a variety of materials ranging from video screening to locations of lectures and news conferences; highlights Middle Eastern countries and policies affecting the LGBT community.

International Lesbian and Gay Association, www.ilga.org.
>	A leading international organization dedicated to the dissemination of materials highlighting the various LGBT-policies of specific countries worldwide.

Iranian Queer Organization, www.irqo.net.
>	A leading resource for Persian LGBT peoples offering a variety of links to personal resources, press releases, and news coverage of Middle East LGBT activity.

The Middle East Gay Journal (gay Middle East blog), www.gaymiddleeast.blogspot.com.
>	A site dedicated to the free marketplace and exchange of ideas concerning the ongoing battles of LGBT people in the Middle East.

NOTES

1. Doug Ireland, "Gay and Underground in Iran," *Gay City News,* June 7, 2006, http://direland.typepad.com/direland/2005/08/irans_deadly_an.html.

2. Ashley Fitzpatrick, "Gay Rights in Iran a Complex Battle," *Nova News Net,* January 26, 2008, http://novanewsnet.ukings.ca/nova_news_3588_13739.html.

3. Helen Chapin Metz, ed., *Iran: A Country Study* (Washington, DC: GPO for the Library of Congress, 1987).

4. CIA, "Iran," *World Fact Book,* 2008, https://www.cia.gov/library/publications/the-world-factbook/geos/IR.html.

5. Robert Tait, "Sex Change Funding Undermines No Gays Claim," *The Guardian,* September 26, 2007, http://www.guardian.co.uk/world/2007/sep/26/iran.gender.

6. You and AIDS Online AIDS Encyclopedia, "Iran at a Glance," http://www.unaids.org/en/KnowledgeCentre/HIVData/CountryProgress/2007CountryProgressAllCountries.asp. See also http://hivinsite.ucsf.edu/global?page=cr08-ir-00.

7. Ireland, "Gay and Underground in Iran."

8. Frances Harrison, "Iran talks Up Temporary Marriages," *BBC News,* June 2, 2007, http://news.bbc.co.uk/2/hi/middle_east/6714885.stm.

9. See Keyan Keihani, "A Brief History of Male Homosexuality in the Qur'an, Saudi Arabia, Iran, and Arab-Islamic Culture," *Middle Eastern Studies* (November 2005): 150.

10. Fitzpatrick, "Gay Rights in Iran a Complex Battle."

11. Ireland, "Gay and Underground in Iran."

12. You and AIDS Online Encyclopedia, "Iran at a Glance," http://www.unaids.org/en/KnowledgeCentre/HIVData/CountryProgress/2007CountryProgressAllCountries.asp. See also http://hivinsite.ucsf.edu/global?page=cr08-ir-00.

13. Ibid.

14. Radio Free Europe Web site, "Iran: Brothers Change The Face Of HIV, Drug-Addiction Treatment," (October 2006), http://www.rferl.org/features/features_Article.aspx?m=10&y=2006&id=7A8CEB97–4FB8–4B22-B87C-AD2D304720CB.

15. Ambeyi Ligabo, "Civil and Political Rights, Including the Question of Freedom of Expression," UN Commission on Human Rights, January 12, 2004.

16. See Keihani, "A Brief History of Male Homosexuality in the Qur'an."

17. Robert Tait, "Sex Change Funding Undermines No Gays Claim," *The Guardian,* September 26, 2007, http://www.guardian.co.uk/world/2007/sep/26/iran.gender.

18. Yakin Erturk, "Integration of the Human Rights of Women and a Gender Perspective: Violence against Women," UN Commission on Human Rights (January 2006).

19. See Keihani, "A Brief History of Male Homosexuality in the Qur'an."

20. Richard Kim, "Witnesses to an Execution," *The Nation,* August 7, 2005, http://www.thenation.com/doc/20050815/kim/2.

LEBANON

Alexandra Sandels and Nadine Moawad

OVERVIEW

Lebanon is a country of 4,035 square miles located in western Asia on the Mediterranean Sea. It borders Syria to the east and north, and Israel to the south. Lebanon has a typical Mediterranean climate, with cool, rainy winters and hot, humid summers. In the country's more elevated areas, temperatures often drop below freezing during the winter with frequent snowfall, while the summers are warm and dry. Lebanon comprises mostly mountainous terrain, except for the country's 140- mile long coastline and the Beqaa Valley in the east.

Lebanon has a population of nearly four million people, of which 95 percent are of Arab origin. Four percent are of Armenian descent. The country is also host to approximately 400,000 Palestinian refugees, and 20,000 to 40,000 Iraqi refugees. It is estimated that seventeen thousand people were displaced during Lebanon's Civil War (1975 to 1990) and the Israeli invasions. During Lebanon's July 2006 war with Israel, more than 200,000 people were reportedly displaced. Today, nearly 18 million people of Lebanese origin are living around the world, approximately 90 percent of them being Christian. Brazil constitutes the world's largest Lebanese community outside of Lebanon, with eight million of the country's citizens being of Lebanese descent. Many Lebanese also reside in Argentina, Canada, and Australia.

Lebanon's official language is Arabic, as stipulated by Article 11 of the National Constitution, although French is considered an administrative

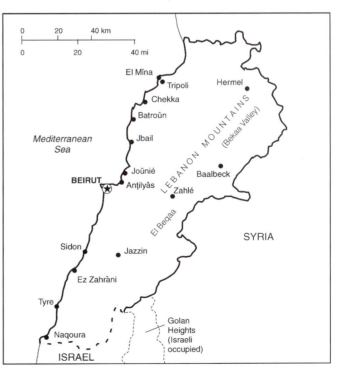

and national language. The majority of Lebanese speak Arabic and either French or English fluently, or both. It is not uncommon to hear Beirut residents use a mixture of Arabic, French, and English, often in the same sentence. In the country's Christian communities, it was previously seen as a mark of status among many to not speak Arabic up until Lebanon's Civil War. Some attribute the reason for this phenomenon to the fact that Christians were generally educated in the country's French school institutions, resulting in the emergence of a Francophone society. In the past two decades, however, English has made headway in the country and has replaced French to a certain extent.

Lebanon is a religiously diverse country comprised of 18 recognized religious sects. Approximately 60 percent adhere to the Muslim faith and belong to either the Shi'a, Sunni, Isma'ilite, Alawite, or Nusayri schools. A minority of Lebanese adhere to the Druze faith, which branched out of Islam. Thirty-nine percent are Christian (Maronite Catholic, Greek Orthodox, Melkite Catholic, Armenian Orthodox, Syrian Catholic, Armenian Catholic, Syrian Orthodox, Roman Catholic, Chaldean, Assyrian, Copt, and Protestant). Lebanon also recognizes the Jewish faith in its personal rights laws, and a very small Lebanese Jewish community is reported to have lived in the south. That community perished and left the country following the eruption of the Lebanese-Israeli War in the late 1970s. A number of religious groups do not enjoy official recognition, such as Bahá'ís, Buddhists, Hindus, and some unregistered Protestant Christian groups. They are disadvantaged under the law in that their adherents do not qualify for certain government positions, but they are permitted to practice their religion freely. All Lebanese citizens were previously required to list their religion on their government documents, but a February 2009 decree has allowed Lebanese citizens to remove their religious affiliation from the identity cards.

Lebanon's military branch, the Lebanese Armed Forces (LAF), is headed by Chief of Staff Jean Qahwaji, and consists of approximately 72,100 active personnel. The Lebanese military is known as highly trained and effective, but suffers from a lack of modern equipment due to the continuous presence of foreign forces, shortage of funds, and political infighting. At the end of Lebanon's Civil War, LAF decided to repair much of its equipment with financial help from other nations. About 85 percent of the LAF's equipment is U.S.-made, with the remaining built by the British, French, and Soviets. The country allocates around 3.1 percent of its $22.01 billion GDP (2006 est.) to military expenditures.

Lebanon was a part of the Ottoman Empire for more than 400 years, in the area of Greater Syria. At the fall of the Ottoman Empire in 1918, Syria was taken over by Anglo-French forces and France received a mandate over the territory of what constitutes current-day Lebanon. In 1920, France formed the State of Greater Lebanon as one of the numerous ethnic enclaves within the Syrian territory. On September 1, 1926, France proclaimed the Lebanese Republic. Lebanon became an independent state in 1943 while French troops remained in the country until the end of World War II. The unwritten National Pact of 1943, between Lebanon and France, stipulated that the country's president needed to be a Christian Maronite, that the prime minister needed to be a Sunni Muslim, and that the head of parliament be a Shiite Muslim. Since gaining independence, Lebanon has experienced shifting periods of stability and political and military unrest while thriving as a regional hub for finance and trade. Lebanon joined the Arab League a few years after its independence but did not participate in the 1948 Arab-Israeli War. The first Palestinian refugees, around 100,000 of them, were living in Lebanon in 1949 as a result of the creation of Israel and the subsequent war.

In 1975, Lebanon underwent a ferocious, multifaceted civil war that ravaged the country for nearly two decades. The conflict became greatly exacerbated by Lebanon's diverse demography, such as the Palestinian refugee influx between 1948 and 1982, inter-religious strife among Christians and Muslims, and the involvement of Syria, Israel, and the Palestine Liberation Organization (PLO) in the war. The 15-year-long conflict resulted in massive human loss and property damage, as well as the complete devastation of Lebanon's economy. More than 150,000 people are believed to have perished in the conflict, and around 200,000 were injured. Thousands of people were displaced and millions of Lebanese emigrated due to the volatile security situation. The war came to an end in 1990 with the signing of a National Reconciliation Accord, known as the Taif Agreement, which was ratified in November 1989. The document, signed in Taif, Saudi Arabia, sought to put an end to the civil war and accommodate a demographic shift to a Muslim majority in Lebanese politics, legitimize deployment of Syrian troops to Lebanon, and reinforce Lebanese authority in the southern parts of the country, which were then occupied by Israel. Israeli troops withdrew from southern Lebanon in May 2000. The passing of UN resolution UNSCR 1559 in October 2004 called for an end to Syrian interference in Lebanese affairs and spurred some Lebanese groups to demand that Syria withdraw its 16,000 troops as well. Following the end of the civil war in 1990, Lebanon enjoyed a period of relative political stability and economic prosperity.

The assassination of former Prime Minister Rafiq Hariri by a car bomb in February 2005 plunged Lebanon into renewed turmoil. The event triggered a chain of mass demonstrations against Syrian's presence in Lebanon, demanding an international commission to investigate the assassination of Hariri and the organization of free parliamentary elections. The uprising became known as the Cedar Revolution. The most notable rally was held in Beirut on March 14, 2005, which attracted 1.5 million people. Syria withdrew its military forces two months later in April 2005. Lebanon held its first legislative elections since the end of the civil war in June 2005, in which the Future Movement Party, led by Saad Hariri, the son of the assassinated prime minister, won a majority. Lebanon's current political arena is comprised of two major blocs, the first being the March 14 Alliance, a group comprised of numerous anti-Syrian and independent political parties, led by Saad Hariri, Samir Geagea of the Lebanese Forces, former president, Amin Gemayel, and Walid Jumblatt of the Progressive Socialist Party. The group's name, March 14, comes from the date of the Cedar Revolution. On the other end of the political spectrum is the March 8 Alliance, a coalition of various sectarian Lebanese political parties in Lebanon. The bloc is considered to be in favor of a Syrian presence in Lebanon. The name, March 8, stems from March 8, 2005, when a number of parties called for a demonstration to thank Syria for its help in bringing the Lebanese Civil War to an end and for supporting Lebanese resistance forces against Israeli occupation. The main parties of the March 8 bloc are Hezbollah, led by Hassan Nasrallah, the Amal Movement led by Nabih Berri, the Free Patriotic Movement led by General Michel Aoun, and the Syrian Social Nationalist Party.

Since the murder of Prime Minister Hariri, Lebanon has witnessed several other politically motivated assassinations, including that of parliamentarian and publisher of the popular *An-Nahar* newspaper, Gebran Tueni, the prominent left-wing journalist and professor Samir Qassir, and the Operations Chief of the Lebanese Army, General Francois Hajj. Despite the establishment of several investigations into the assassinations, no one was charged in any of the cases. Many of the victims were outspoken critics of the Syrian presence in Lebanon.

In the summer of 2006, Lebanon once again became subject to violence. The kidnapping of two Israeli soldiers in July 2006 by the Shiite militant political party Hezbollah produced a 34-day conflict with Israel that resulted in the death of over 1,000 people, mostly civilians, and the displacement of hundreds of thousands. On May 9, 2008, Hezbollah and allying groups seized West Beirut in armed attacks following a number of decisions taken by the government that would curtail the powers of the party. The U.S.-backed government coalition and media reports have referred to the incident as an attempted coup d'etat. At least 65 people died and 200 were wounded in the clashes between progovernment and opposition supporters. The conflicts were referred to as the worst sectarian street fighting since the end of the Civil War in 1990.

In May 2008, former LAF Commander Michel Sleiman was elected President of Lebanon, ending a six-month long political vacuum following the step down of Emile Lahoud from the presidential post in November 2007.[1] In June 2009, the March 14 bloc won the Lebanese parliamentary elections, securing 71 out of the 128 seats in Parliament.

OVERVIEW OF LGBT ISSUES

The beginning of an organized LGBT movement in Lebanon started with the advent of the Internet in 1998. An online mailing list was started on Yahoo Groups and its membership quickly grew to over 300 people within a year. In 1999, a Web site called www.gaylebanon.com (the site is no longer active) was started by the first gay activist in Lebanon, and included information on meeting places, a demand for equality, and a mailing list.

Following the virtual community was the founding of ClubFree, an underground LGBT group headed by a committee of eight gay men and women with the mission of providing community support and social activities. ClubFree would rent out an apartment in Beirut with donations from members and use it as a meeting space for discussions, movie screenings, and meetings for LGBT people. It was in ClubFree meetings that the first ideas for lobbying and advocacy for gay rights in Lebanon took place. Discussion meetings took place to brainstorm strategies for lobbying with the government, including sending anonymous letters to members of parliament and the media, as well as international contacts with ILGA and other international bodies.

In 2002, a small group of LGBT activists registered a nongovernmental organization called *Hurriyyat Khassa* ("Private Liberties"), which aimed at tackling LGBT issues, namely the reform of Article 534 of the Lebanese Penal Code, within and under the umbrella of a larger scope of private liberties. Article 534 criminalizes "sexual acts against nature" with up to a year in prison, and is commonly used to target homosexual activity.

In 2004, a group of activists involved in *Hurriyyat Khassa* decided it was time to register a gay and lesbian organization, and thus was born HELEM (an acronym of the Arabic Himaya Lubnaniya lil Mithliyyeen, meaning "Lebanese Protection for LGBT"). HELEM was first registered in Montreal in 2004 and the members in Lebanon filed an official notification of assembly to the Ministry of Interior in August 2004. The Lebanese rules governing the registration of NGOs decree that a group of five people who have assembled to start an organization must notify the concerned ministry by filling out an application of notification with the objectives and mission of the organization. If the ministry does not reject the application within a period of two months, then the organization is considered officially registered and has the right to meet and develop its projects. Therefore, HELEM became the first officially registered LGBT organization in the Arab world. The government still withholds, however, the license number, which is required to open an official bank account and perform other minor administrative tasks.

HELEM's main programs include work on HIV awareness, testing, and advocacy in Lebanon, in addition to legal and media lobbying for the rights of the LGBT community. HELEM also runs a community center in Beirut open to the public. Every year, HELEM organizes the International Day Against Homophobia in Lebanon and gets increased media coverage every year, attracting more attendees. The program usually involves a discussion panel, film screenings, art exhibits, and publications.

Throughout the history of the LGBT movement, the invisibility of lesbians has always been noticeable. This has been attributed to many social factors, mainly, the oppression of women in general in Lebanon. Lesbians have had less freedom, fewer rights, and harsher economic conditions than gay men, and were therefore, with a few exceptions, marginalized in the activist history.

In September 2006, three women members of HELEM started a women-only mailing list for LBTQ women, and in December 2006, they held the first lesbian-only meeting in a private home in Beirut with 28 women attending. From this meeting was born a new lesbian activism that followed with a few meetings in the first half of 2007 and the creation of Meem (the letter "m" in Arabic that stands for *majmouaat mou'azarat al mar'a al mithliyya,* or "support group for lesbian women") on August 4, 2007. The vision of Meem is a better quality of life for LBTQ women in Lebanon, and the group works with a low-profile strategy to provide support and services, aiming to create a strong grassroots movement where women are empowered and can, in five years, become more visible in their advocacy work. Meem today has 243 members and runs the Womyn House in Beirut, which is an apartment that houses all of Meem's activities and meetings. The Womyn House is open only to members. In March 2009, a group referring to itself as "a bunch of citizens concerned with the escalating level of hatred and ignorance towards homosexuality" formed the people's movement The Gay-Straight Alliance in an effort to spread more awareness and foster understanding of LGBITQ issues in Lebanon. Spring 2009 also saw the birth of the Feminist Collective, a group concerned with enhancing women's rights and feminism in Lebanon. Included on the group's list of causes is acceptance and tolerance of nonheterosexual women.

Media

Recent years have witnessed an upsurge in media coverage of homosexuality in Lebanon. While some reports provide a more balanced view, many still bear negative connotations against LGBT people. Gay-rights organizations and activists across the Arab world have continuously lobbied Arab media to stop the use

of the word "shazz"—a demeaning term still often used by Arabic mass media
to describe homosexuals. Literally, shazz translates as "pervert" or "deviant." Instead of shazz, LGBT activists have sought to introduce the term "mithly," which
loosely translates as "same," and pushed for media adoption of this less disparaging term. In contrast to pan-Arab media, which has appeared reluctant to apply
neutral terminology when referring to homosexuals and still demonizes gays to a
large extent, Lebanese media outlets have increasingly started to abandon shazz
for less demeaning terms such as mithly. But in July 2009, the Lebanese publishing
house Arab Diffusion translated the book *Gay Travels in the Muslim World* into the
Arabic equivalent of *Pervert Travels in the Muslim World,* using the word shazz to
describe gay. It is the first gay-themed book to be translated from English to Arabic. Considering the success story with the Lebanese media, the fact that *Pervert
Travels in the Muslim World* was the prodigy of a Lebanese publishing house came
as a particularly hard blow to gay rights activists in the country. It is unknown at
the end of 2009 whether the translation will be revised and HELEM made a complaint with the publisher.

During the course of 2005 and 2006, an array of media outlets started por-
traying Beirut as the gay paradise of the Arab world. *Agence France Presse* featured a news report entitled "Welcome to Beirut, Sin City of the Arab World,"
on June 23, 2006, describing it as an oasis for Arab homosexuals. In its Winter
2006 issue, the U.S. LGBT travel magazine *Out Travel* featured an article about
Beirut, titled "Arab World's Most Gay-Friendly City Glitters Anew," The BBC
ran the report "Landmark Meeting for Gay Lebanese" on a three-day-long event
organized by *HELEM* marking International Day Against Homophobia in 2006.
In 2005, France's *La Liberation* published an article on gay life in Beirut entitled
"Les gays sortent du placard" ("the gays come out of the closet"). Also in summer 2006, the first Arab adaptation of the renowned theatre play *The Vagina
Monologues,* titled *Hakeh Neswan* ("Women's Talk") took stage in Beirut in front
of sold-out audiences after fierce battles with the censors. Fall 2007 saw the birth
of a new game show on the Lebanese TV channel LBC, led by popular Lebanese
comedian and drag queen Bassem Feghali. *HELEM* currently publishes the quarterly online magazine *Barra* ("Out" in English) for persons in the Arab world
identifying as LGBTIQ. In summer 2008, a number of members from *Meem*
launched the online publication *Bekhsoos* ("Concerning" in English) for LBTQ
women in the Arab world. Half a year later, in January 2009, the Lebanese LGBT
community slammed a talk show on homosexuality in the Middle East that was
aired on Lebanon's satellite LBC channel, claiming it was biased and provided a
distorted picture about gays in the Arab world. Angered members of Lebanon's
LGBT community complained that the show only brought up stereotypical pop-
psychology explanations for homosexuality, including abuse, prostitution, lack of
a father figure, and a strong mother figure that overpowers the masculine figure
in the household. Spring 2009 also saw the birth of the Feminist Collective's new
magazine *Sawt el Niswa* (*Women's Voices*). In late May 2009 Meem published the
book *Bareed Mista3jil* (*Urgent Mail*), featuring the experiences and life stories of
over 40 queer and transgendered women in Lebanon. The book was made available for purchase in Beirut bookstores and over the Internet. The book received
substantive media coverage in Lebanon and was also covered by some foreign
news outlets.

EDUCATION

Lebanon boasts an internationally renowned private educational system at both the school and university levels. The majority of private schools have a long religious heritage and were founded by different (mostly French) missionaries at the beginning of the 20th century. The public school system, however, lacks organization and standards, and has a high dropout rate and few services for students. Both private and public schools are unsafe for gay and lesbian youth, with high rates of homophobic behavior from fellow students, teachers, counselors, and administrators.

Lebanon's private universities are ranked as some of the best in the Middle East and in the world, particularly the American University of Beirut, founded in 1866, and the Université Saint-Joseph, founded in 1875. Most private universities tackle the subject of homosexuality openly and academically in philosophy, sociology, and psychology classes. At the American University of Beirut, for example, every student is required to take an introduction to ethics course that explains the Natural Law Theory and its failure to deem homosexuality as unnatural or immoral. The same university also offers a sociology course in sexuality that is sometimes called queer theory.

Regarding student life outside of academics, homosexuality started to be discussed on campuses since 2006, with student-organized debates and panels. Private universities are generally considered to be safe spaces for homosexual expression. Lebanon's public university, the Lebanese University, suffers from mismanagement, overcrowding, lack of funding, and politicization. There have been, to date, no initiatives to tackle homosexuality or to report homophobic incidents on campuses.

EMPLOYMENT AND ECONOMICS

The Lebanese economy has undergone shifting periods of prosperity and instability due to the repeated political and military unrest in the country. Lebanon's economy marked by private and liberal economic activity with a laissez-faire commercial tradition. Lebanon's economy is largely a service-oriented economy that relies on banking and tourism. The country has strict bank secrecy, and there are no restrictions on foreign exchange, foreign investment, or capital movement. The banking sector is equivalent to more than 2.5 times the economic sector.

The Lebanese labor force is made up of around 1.5 million workers (2005 est.). It is estimated that around one million foreign workers are currently employed in the country (2005 est.). Among them are around 200,000 migrant domestic workers, mainly coming from Sri Lanka, the Philippines, and Ethiopia. A significant number of domestic workers do not possess legal status in Lebanon.

Lebanon's Labor Code of 1946 regulates employment in the country's private sector and prohibits differentiating "between male and female workers in relation to the nature of work, salary paid, employment opportunities, promotion, and technical training." Several working groups are, however, excluded from this law, including domestic workers employed in private houses. The code has been amended numerous times, most recently in May 2000 when modifications to articles concerning equal employment opportunities were introduced. Lebanon does not recognize LGBT employees and therefore there is no law protecting their rights. There are no statistics or data available on homophobia in Lebanese workplaces. LGBT people working in Lebanon have said that civil society groups and creative environments, such as advertising agencies, art studies, and media groups, are usually more open to and accepting of LGBT employees. Lebanon's thriving fashion and film industries are also known to host a significant number of LGBT employees. Hair salons remain a popular workplace among gay men. Some argue that there is less homophobia in workplaces that feature a high number of foreigners or Lebanese employees who have worked abroad. There is no law protecting LGBT people serving in the military.[2]

SOCIAL/GOVERNMENT PROGRAMS

The Lebanese government does not provide funding for any programs for lesbians, gay men, or transsexuals. The groups are, however, recognized by some social health programs. In terms of HIV/AIDS education and treatment, LGBT people are considered a vulnerable group. An increased number of Lebanese NGOs are now featuring sections on the LGBT community in their annual reports. LGBT activist groups tend to receive most of their program funding from international foundations in the United States or in Europe.

SEXUALITY/SEXUAL PRACTICES

Since Lebanon reported its first case of HIV/AIDS in 1984, the country has witnessed a significant surge in both local and international organizations dedicated to prevention, awareness, and education of HIV/AIDS. Despite the HIV programs and the Ministry of Education introducing a section on reproductive health in the national school curriculum, health officials still voice concern over the alleged lack of robust sexual education programs. According to health officials, sexual education programs are not implemented in all school institutions, especially in the country's numerous private religious schools.[3] Following pressure from religious groups, particularly Hezbollah and the Druze Association of the Al-Orfan Al-Tawhidiyyah, the Presidential Decree 2066 ruled in 2000 that the new reproductive health sections should be pulled out from the national curriculum, due to fears that sexual education would lead to promiscuity among Lebanese youth. Religious community groups often stress that reproductive health should be taught by the family and the religious community. The decision sparked outcry among doctors and academics. The lack of functioning sexual education programs has allegedly resulted in young Lebanese consulting the Internet, media, and friends for advice about sexual practices and sexually transmitted diseases (STDs). There are, however, a number of groups teaching sexual education. The Standing Committee on Reproductive Health Including AIDS (SCORA), a group affiliated with the Lebanese Medical Students' International Committee, has reportedly given school talks across Lebanon in an effort to raise awareness about reproductive health, including HIV/AIDS, homosexuality, rape, and abortion. The National Evangelical Institute for Girls and Boys in Sidon provides lessons on HIV/AIDS and STDs for high school students. Many secular schools, including the American Community School of Beirut, have made sexual education a part of their curricula.[4]

FAMILY

Family ties in Lebanon remain the most important social tradition today. This is strongly tied to religious values. The Lebanese family structure is very rigid: a husband, a wife, and their children. Stereotypical gender roles are also just as rigid. Fathers are the breadwinners and mothers stay at home to take care of housework and raise the children. Marriages within families (first or second cousins), as well as within the same village or county, are also very common. Divorce is strongly frowned upon, and no statistics are available on the divorce rates, although it is estimated that the numbers are on the rise in the recent years. Unlike Western traditions, children are not expected to move out of their parents' home when they become adults. On the contrary, it is quite common for men and women to continue to live with their parents until they get married, even throughout their 30s, 40s, and even 50s.

Family pressure and the threat of being ostracized remain the biggest fears facing the LGBT community in Lebanon. Hundreds of cases of LGBT people have reportedly been ostracized from their families in the last 10 years. This form of homophobia is manifested in different ways: gay men commonly get kicked out of their homes, denied inheritance, or in rarer cases sent out of the country by their parents. Lesbians face different problems with their family and are more likely to get put under house arrest or forced into a marriage with a man, but in rarer cases they do get kicked out of their homes as well.

Honor killings, which are murders committed by family members against their own relatives for the sake of saving and purifying family pride and honor, are very rare in Lebanon. A small number of gay men belonging to ultra-conservative families have reported receiving death threats from their brothers and fathers. In 2005, HELEM protected a young man from his family's death threats by flying him to another country for a few weeks, until his family calmed down and he was able to return to Lebanon and move to a different city.

Families who learn about their children's homosexuality also prefer to hide the shame of the news in their communities and villages, so in many cases they refrain from actively expelling their children, and tighten their restrictions on them instead.

COMMUNITY

Lebanon is heavily split into communities based on religion and social class, and the LGBT community is no different. The most visible gay community belongs to a wealthy social class that mainly works in art, graphic design, fashion, or the entertainment industry. They enjoy a certain freedom and public acceptance associated with their involvement in the arts. Internet access, financial ability to travel, and the English language, also limited to upper and middle classes, are components of the formation of communities of LGBT, with less information and reports available on the poorer communities. There is also a noticeable visibility and freedom among the younger generations, who find more acceptance among friends than do LGBT people over 40.

When discussing the situation of LGBT people in Lebanon, it is important to take into consideration those who practice nonheterosexual sex or pursue same-sex relationships without conforming to LGBT labels. While this phenomenon exists throughout Lebanon, it is perhaps most prevalent in less urban areas outside the capital Beirut. HELEM and Meem provide support services to LGBT people across Lebanon.

Gay Men

Gay men living in Beirut can maintain somewhat of a comfortable life style, especially those not residing with their families. Those living outside Beirut tend to maintain a low profile. The government appears to have adopted a policy of tolerance towards LGBT people, and gay men maintain a strong visibility in the capital, frequenting a number of coffee houses, bars, and restaurants known to cater to a gay clientele. Acid, the Arab world's premier gay club, is located in Sin el Fil on the outskirts of Beirut. Other popular hangouts include the restaurant-bars Bardo and Wolf in the Hamra District of Beirut, as well as BO18 and Milk. Additionally, a few gay-owned and gay-oriented businesses operate in Beirut, including the gay-tourism company LebTour.

Lesbians

Lesbianism is generally seen to be more tolerable in Lebanon than male homosexuality, partly because of the eroticism surrounding the idea of two women together and partly because women are simply so marginalized that lesbians are dismissed as sexually frustrated women who want to maintain their virginity and therefore practice sexual play with other women. This tolerance, however, masks multiple layers of discrimination that lesbian and bisexual women face in Lebanon.

Butch women are seen as imitating male behavior, attire, and ambitions because it is natural for one to want to be like men. The term *ikht el rjel* ("the sister of men") is commonly used to describe a woman with a strong personality, strong physique, or butch qualities, and is considered a compliment. The term *Hassan sabi* ("Hassan boy") is the Arabic equivalent of the term *tomboy*, similarly not a derogatory term, and used to describe young girls who have short hair, dress like boys, play sports, or behave in other ways traditionally attributed to the male gender. Lesbians generally follow gay men in frequenting gay-friendly pubs and nightclubs in the Beirut districts of Hamra and Gemmayze.

HEALTH

The Lebanese Ministry of Health runs a National Social Security program that provides free or discounted health care to all employed citizens. In contrast to other Arab countries, Lebanon pursues an open discussion about HIV/AIDS, although health officials stipulate that misinformation about the virus is still prevalent. In recent years, there has been a large influx of organizations concerned with HIV/AIDS issues, following the increase in HIV/AIDS cases after the civil war. In the late 1990s, HIV/AIDS organizations in Lebanon began considering the LGBT community as a vulnerable group.

The United Nations agency UNAIDS estimates that approximately 2,900 people are currently living with HIV/AIDS in Lebanon. There are no reliable statistics on HIV infections in men who have sex with men (MSM) or sex workers in Lebanon. The Lebanese government reports a significantly lower number of HIV cases than UNAIDS, putting the total cases at 756. Health workers believe that the number is considerably higher, perhaps in the range of several thousands. They raise concerns over low condom use among gay men in Lebanon, saying that the easiness to access sex in Lebanon's LGBT community, combined with the low rate of condom use, spur the prevalence of HIV and other STDs in the country. Many HIV patients from the LGBT community contract AIDS along with another STD.

HELEM has an indirect partnership with the Ministry of Health through the subsidiary organization SIDC, with whom HELEM has run a successful prevention program for MSMs. HELEM provides free anonymous HIV testing, and the center is listed in the Ministry of Health's HIV/AIDS information pamphlets.

According to health officials, the Lebanese Ministry of Health buys HIV drugs once a year and distributes them to HIV/AIDS patients for free through the country's Central Drug Warehouse (CDW) and the Drug Distribution Center (DDC) every month. In 1996, Lebanon became the first country in the Arab world to introduce this service. The treatment program involves a combination of three drugs. Among current HIV medicines available in Lebanon are AZT, DDI, and Kaletra. Shortages of at least one of these drugs have been reported several times in recent years. During Lebanon's July 2006 war with Israel, aid convoys carrying medicines apparently had difficulties delivering drugs. It is estimated that approximately 260 people are currently on the governmental treatment program.

There is very little data available on the prevalence of STDs in Lebanon. Specialists in infectious diseases believe that the scarcity of data stems from the taboo status of sex in Lebanese society. To the specialists, STDs are a direct result of the taboo. STD patients usually consult private clinics, pharmacists, or perhaps close friends instead of taking the matter to a public clinic. Those STD cases reported to public clinics are only a fraction of the real number. HELEM refers patients to doctors who are sympathetic to gay patients. Health officials claim that Chlamydia is the most prevalent STD in Lebanon. Warts and herpes constitute the most common STDs among gay men. A recent increase in cases of gonorrhea suggests that the disease is on the rise in Lebanon. Lesbian advocates have raised concern over the lack of gynecologists specialized in treating patients who have sex with other women.[5]

There are no records or studies on lesbian health in Lebanon, and the common misconception is that lesbians are immune to AIDS and other diseases. Women who have sex with women face stigmatization by gynecologists, and efforts are currently being undertaken to create a network of lesbian-friendly gynecologists. Female condoms and dental dams are unavailable in Lebanese pharmacies.

Sex toys including dildos, strap-ons, and vibrators are considered pornographic material and are therefore illegal in Lebanon. Women attempt at times to bring sex toys in their luggage from other countries, and in a few cases have been caught, the items confiscated, and the women released with a warning.

Lebanon's booming psychology field has recently taken a more professional attitude toward the teaching and practice of counseling for homosexuals. While in the past homosexuality was viewed as a condition that needed to be deconstructed and cured, psychologists today have become strong advocates of the normalcy of homosexuality. However, the lack of a union or centralized monitoring institution has led to discrepancies in standards and the opening of many clinics by unqualified therapists. Additionally, little work has been done to study the specific needs of the mental health of LGBT people. Both HELEM and Meem currently offer counseling programs to their members.

POLITICS AND LAW

Gay rights has never been placed on any political agenda nor brought up by politicians or members of parliament. It is generally not seen as a human rights priority in any political context. As politics and religious sectarianism are extremely intertwined, most politicians refrain from approaching the matter because they see it (or their constituents see it) as immoral and against God's will.

Similarly, political parties have not made any statements about homosexuality, although many of them include the Universal Declaration of Human Rights and other articles concerning human dignity in their mission and core values. Almost every political party is run by a religious sect.

Legally, homosexuality is mainly targeted using articles concerning morality in the Lebanese Penal Code, but there have been no legal cases in recent years because of Lebanon's political instability and constant wars since 2005.

Article 534 of the Lebanese Penal Code criminalizes sexual relations that are "against nature" and are punishable by up to a year in prison. This prohibits male homosexuality, along with adultery, sodomy (heterosexual or homosexual), and fornication outside of marriage. Lesbian sexual activities are not illegal in the eyes of the Lebanese law, because they do not involve a penis or penetration. In 2002, local newspapers ran a story about two women who were arrested for having unnatural sex, but they were not charged under Article 534. They were, however, imprisoned for an unrelated incident of theft. In spring 2009, an online petition was launched in an effort to collect 10,000 signatures in support of the scrapping of the law. HELEM is using the summer 2009 parliamentary elections as a spring board for its campaign for the removal of Article 534.

Antidiscrimination Statutes

There are no existing antidiscrimination statutes protecting the rights of LGBT people in Lebanon. Lebanon has, however, signed the Universal Declaration of Human Rights and ratified, with reservations, the Convention on the Elimination of all forms of Discrimination Against Women (CEDAW) in 1996. Lesbian activists in Lebanon have been lobbying the country's women's rights organizations and governmental institutions for the inclusion of the rights of LBTQ women in their programs.

Marriage

Same-sex marriage is illegal in Lebanon. The first chapter of the *Qanun al Ahwal alShakhsiyah* (the "Personal Status Law") mandates that marriage can only occur between two people of opposite sexes. The topic of same-sex marriage has never been addressed in Lebanon by activist groups.

Speech and Association

In contrast to other Arab countries, Lebanon enjoys a high level of free speech and association. Perhaps the main reason why the Lebanese authorities have not shut down HELEM is because of the respect of freedom of association in the country. The highly active Lebanese civil society is divided over the right of gay people to assemble, but the dominant opinion is supportive of this right. In 2006, a member of the Beirut Municipality attacked HELEM in local newspapers, condemning the existence of an organization with the objective of ruining and perverting Lebanese youth. An official complaint was filed against HELEM but was later dismissed on the basis of insufficient evidence.

Lebanese television has featured a few debates on homosexuality, the most important of which happened in 1996 on a show called "El Haki Baynetna" with prominent talk show host Dr. Ziad Njeim. The episode was the last ever of the show and featured gay men behind masks and distorted voices, in addition to Muslim and Christian figures, psychologists, and sociologists. The debate was mostly negative toward homosexuality, but included a few positive responses and made history at the time. Since then, other talk shows have mostly tackled the topic in a sensationalist manner. A major problem is the usage of the term *shaz,* which means perverted, to describe homosexuality in the media. Activist lobbying promotes the usage of the term *mithli,* which is the proper Arabic word for homosexual. This term has been adopted by more progressive newspapers and media outlets, although *shaz* remains more common in translations.

In 2005, HELEM published *Barra,* which means "Out" in English, the first Arab gay magazine. The magazine was mainly in Arabic, with some English and French sections, entirely run by volunteers, and made available in different gay-friendly places in Beirut. HELEM also published a book entitled, *Rihab Al Mithliya: Mawaqef wa Shahadat* (*Homophobia: Attitudes and Testimonies*) in May 2006. The book includes chapters by prominent Lebanese writers discussing homophobia from legal, psychological, and social angles, in addition to personal testimonies and stories. Both HELEM and Meem produce and distribute monthly newsletters containing news on LGBT issues in Lebanon.

Asylum Cases

There have been numerous cases of Lebanese LGBT people, especially gay men, seeking asylum in Europe and North America due to their sexual orientation. In 2005, a number of Lebanese gay men sought asylum in the Netherlands for fears of repercussions and jail sentences. Also in 2005, a U.S. court ruled that Nasser Karouni, a Lebanese HIV-positive gay man from the Shiite-dominated Tyre region fearing persecution from Hezbollah, was to be considered for asylum in the United States.[6] The same year, a man from the northern city of Tripoli sought asylum in Belgium. He said he faced persecution by his work and family due to his sexual orientation. A 34-year-old gay Palestinian man known as "H.C." living in a refugee camp in the outskirts of Sidon fled to Britain in 1998 and subsequently applied for asylum after the video shop he worked in was blown up. "H.C." argued that the shop was attacked because he was gay. In 2001, the *New York Times* reported that a Lebanese lesbian woman was granted asylum in the United States after her family threatened to report her to the police in Beirut.[7] Emigration remains common among Lebanese homosexuals. Meem has emphasized that emigration is very high in Lebanon's lesbian community, especially among women in their mid-20s.

Bisexuals

The ability of bisexuals to enter into relationships with both sexes proves confusing to many people in Lebanon, whether straight or gay. At times, bisexuals face perhaps even more stigma than homosexuals due to their versatile sexuality. When a bisexual forms a relationship with a person of the opposite sex, they are considered heterosexual. When they form same-sex relationships, they are viewed as homosexuals. Some even consider their sexuality as promiscuous. When bisexuals are married to a person of the opposite sex, they receive the benefits provided to married heterosexual couples. When in a relationship with someone of the same sex, they're subject to discrimination from both heterosexuals and homosexuals. Bisexuals remain outcasts of Lebanese society in most aspects.

Transsexuals

Sex changes are permitted in Lebanon and a handful of cases have been reported. The procedure is a long process that requires recommendations from at least three psychiatrists and one doctor specializing in hormone treatment before permission is granted from the court. Once a patient has been granted permission, he or she is entitled to a new identity. Transsexuals who have changed their status legally can maintain a certain level of normalcy in life, while those who do not wish to conduct a sex change face severe hardships in Lebanon. Many are often forced into prostitution due to the difficulty of finding employment. Lebanese employers are required to register the identity cards of their employees after a three-month trial period. Transsexuals often end up losing their employment during this process. Many transsexuals apply for asylum. HELEM is reportedly starting a new support group for transsexuals during the summer of 2008.[8]

Intersexed

Intersexed people are mostly unheard of in Lebanon, as they are born with either partially or fully developed genitalia that are a combination of both male and female genitalia. They face severe, lifelong problems due to their complicated physical situation. For example, they have to note on a form, such as a birth certificate, whether they are male or a female. There have been no reported lawsuits concerning intersexed individuals in Lebanon to date.

RELIGION AND SPIRITUALITY

Religion is very closely intertwined with Lebanese politics, geography, communities, and family structures. Every neighborhood has at least one church or mosque, and the government recognizes all Muslim and Christian celebrations and holidays.

In Lebanon, the age requirement for marriage is 18 years for men and 17 for women. With guardian permission, the ages are 17 for males and 9 years old for women. For Shiites, with judicial permission, it is 15 for males, and 9 for females. For Druze, with judicial permission, the ages are 16 for males and 15 for females.

Interfaith marriages between Muslims and Christians are prohibited. However, if a mixed faith couple marries in another country, their marriage will be recognized as valid in Lebanon. Therefore, most Lebanese couples from different religions get a civil marriage in Cyprus and return to Lebanon, or one of them converts to the other spouse's religion and then they get married.

All 18 religious sects in Lebanon view homosexuality as an abomination and perversion, and call on homosexuals to resist these unnatural tendencies or seek medical treatment and shock therapy from psychiatrists.

VIOLENCE

Not much has been reported about hate crimes in Lebanon outside of the context of civil war and sectarian feuds. No hate crimes against homosexuals have been reported in Lebanon. There are many cases of suicide during the 1990s that were rumored to be gay-related, but these rumors were not confirmed.

Violence against homosexuals is normally manifested in physical abuse, rape, blackmail, verbal abuse, job loss, eviction, and other forms. This happens on the street, in restaurants or coffee shops, at work, in schools and colleges, and other public places. Several incidents of violence against LGBT people have been reported inside the community. Lesbians commonly face verbal abuse and sexual harassment on the street based on their attire, mannerisms, and in case of any minimal public display of affection. However, it is quite common in Lebanon, as in most of the Arab world, for women to walk on the street holding hands or intertwining arms. For men, this is not as common but can still be seen, especially among non-Lebanese Arabs. Common insults for lesbians include *dakar* ("male") or *sharmouta* ("whore"), or a gesture of the tongue.

Gay men, however, especially effeminate men, face much harsher abuse. On the street, they will very probably have *louti* or *foufou* ("faggot") yelled at them, or they will be profanely propositioned for sexual acts. In a few incidents, effeminate men have been beaten up or slapped on the street. They also get fired from their jobs or not hired at all. In schools and colleges, they face strong bullying. Such forms of violence are considered macho behavior by Arab men.

Gay cruising is popular in Lebanon and some areas are well-known to be cruising locations, such as Ramlet El Bayda, a stretch of beach in Beirut. More often than not, gay men who go cruising there are picked up by other men who then steal their money by threatening (with or without weapons) to report them to the police. Gay personals Web sites such as *Gaydar* or *Manjam* are also very popular ways of meeting people online, mostly for sex. These encounters are often highly unsafe and lead to gay men being beaten up and robbed.

The police have made vast improvements in terms of dealing with cases of homosexuality. In the near past, it was very common for police to similarly abuse or blackmail gay men who report cases of robbery or abuse and dismiss them as perverts. In recent years, largely thanks to the work of HELEM, the morality police department, known as the Hobeich police station, has become more aware of violence facing gay men, although it still happens today. In February 2009, however, a publicized gay bashing took place near Sassine square in Beirut's Ashrafiyeh district in which two men allegedly engaging in sexual conduct in the entrance of a building were dragged out onto the Square and severely beaten. Conflicting reports surfaced over the incident and an initial report by the French-language Lebanese daily *L'Orient Le Jour* had it that the beating was carried out by security personnel, while others, including HELEM, claimed the men were assaulted by civilians. A few weeks later, HELEM, along with a number of other Lebanese NGOs, organized the Arab world's first sit-in against violence targeting homosexuals and other minority groups in Beirut's Sodeco square. The demonstration was a direct response to the February beatings at Sassine square.

OUTLOOK FOR THE 21ST CENTURY

While Lebanon constitutes the only country in the Arab world, along with the Occupied Palestinian Territories, that has organizations and groups serving the LGBT community, it will take a long time before LGBT people will become accepted and integrated into Lebanese society and enjoy full rights equal to those of other Lebanese. They lack formal recognition, and although there is certainly space for LGBT people in Lebanon, they are still considered pariahs by many. However, the country's active LGBT organizations, combined with the somewhat- free press and freedom of association, are promising factors for the next generation. The government appears to have implemented an unwritten policy of tolerance toward Lebanon's sprawling LGBT community, but it is important to take into consideration that the state remains weakened and often straddles pressures from religious and liberal groups. The continuous civil unrest and unpredictable political environment stall the legal battles for LGBT groups but leave room for outreach and advocacy. Lebanon's LGBT community can enjoy a certain kind of freedom in Beirut, but they remain behind closed doors in the rest of the country.

RESOURCE GUIDE

Suggested Reading

Robert Aldrich, *Colonialism and Homosexuality* (London: Routledge, 2002).

HELEM Organization, *Rouhab al Mithliya (Homophobia)*. CD in collaboration with HELEM, 2006.

Samer Khalaf and John Gagnon, *Sexuality in the Arab World* (Beirut: Saqi Books, 2006).

Michael Luongo, *Gay Travels in the Muslim World* (New York: Harrington Park Press, 2007).

Josef Maasad, *Desiring Arabs* (Chicago: University of Chicago Press, 2007).

Meem, *Bareed Mista3jil* (Beirut: 2009).

Will Roscoe and Stephen Murray, *Islamic Homosexualities: Culture, History, and Literature* (New York: New York University Press, 1997).

Arno Schmitt, *Sexuality and Eroticism Among Males in Moslem Societies* (London: Routledge, 1992).

Brian Whitaker, *Unspeakable Love: Gay and Lesbian Life in the Middle East* (Los Angeles: University of California Press, 2005).

J. W. Wright, *Homoeroticism in Classical Arabic* (New York: Columbia University Press, 1997).

Videos/Films

A Jihad for Love DVD. Directed by Parvez Sharma. New York: Halal Films, 2007. Filmed in 12 different countries and in nine languages, it is the first feature-length documentary to explore the complex global intersections of Islam and homosexuality.

Caramel (*Sukkar Banat*). Directed by Nadine Labaki. Paris: Films des Tournelles and Roissy Films, 2007. (El Haddad, Rodney, Jihad Hojeily, and Nadine Labaki.) Caramel portrays the everyday life and struggle of five Lebanese women working together in a hair salon. One of the characters is a lesbian.

Organizations

HELEM, www.helem.net.
> Beirut-based organization that works on issues pertaining to LGBTIQ people in Lebanon.

Lebanese AIDS Society, E-Mail ab00@aub.edu.lb (Telephone +961 03 300811).
> Organization that offers education for the prevention of HIV and medical assistance to those living with HIV/AIDS and conducts research on the disease among other activities.

Meem Group, http://www.meemgroup.org/.
> Community group that provides support services to LGBTQ women in Lebanon.

National AIDS Control Program, E-mail: wholeb_nap@inco.com.lb (Tel: (961–1) 566100/1).
> Lebanon's state-run HIV/AIDS program that provides medical treatment for patients living with the virus and conducts research on the disease.

Web Sites

Bekhsoos, www.bekhsoos.com.
> Beirut-based online magazine for LBTQ women in the Arab world.
> The Feminist Collective, http://www.feministcollective.com/.
> Beirut-based feminist group

Gay Lebanon, http://www.gaylebanon.info/.
> Information source on LGBT life in Lebanon

Gay Middle East, http://www.gaymiddleeast.com/.
> Resource and news Web site on LGBT in the Middle East
> The Gay Straight Alliance, http://www.g-sail.org/drupal/?q=node/1.
> Lebanese gay-straight alliance

HELEM, http://www.helem.net.
> Support organization for LGBTIQ people in Lebanon

Lebtour, http://www.lebtour.com/.
> Web site offering travel services to Lebanon and the rest of the Arab world for LGBT people

Meem Group, http://www.meemgroup.org/.
> Community for LGBTQ women in Lebanon

Sawt el-Niswa, http://www.feministcollective.com/?q=category/5/13.
> The magazine published by The Feminist Collective

NOTES

1. CIA, "Lebanon," *The World Factbook,* https://www.cia.gov/library/publications/the-world-factbook/geos/le.html.

2. The International Labor Organization, "The Labor Code of 23 September 2006—Lebanon," http://www.ilo.org/public/english/employment/gems/eeo/law/lebanon/act1.htm.

3. Interview with Jaques Mokhbat, specialist of infectious diseases and director of the Lebanese AIDS Society, April 29, 2008.

4. Zahra Hankir, "Sex in the Classroom," *Now Lebanon,* October 20, 2007, http://www.nowlebanon.com/NewsArticleDetails.aspx?ID=16836.

5. Interviews with health worker Raja Farah on April 20, 2008, and Jaques Mokhbat on April 29, 2008.

6. Robert Dekoven, "Beyond the Briefs: Sex, Politics, and Law," *Gay and Lesbian Times,* May 31, 2005, http://www.gaylesbiantimes.com/?id=4722&issue=901.

7. John Leland, "Gays Seeking Asylum Find Familiar Prejudices in the U.S.," *The New York Times,* August 1, 2001, http://query.nytimes.com/gst/fullpage.html?res=9806E 6D81F3DF932A3575BC0A9679C8B63&fta = y.

8. Interview with HELEM director Georges Azzi on May 5, 2008.

SAUDI ARABIA

Shivali Shah

The Kingdom of Saudi Arabia borders the Persian Gulf to the northeast and the Red Sea to the west. Slightly more than one-fifth the size of the United States, it is the largest country in the Arabian Peninsula spanning 830,000 square miles. The Kingdom's population is approximately 24 to 27 million.[1] The capital city of Riyadh is the largest city with a population of 4,700,000.[2] Saudi Arabia shares borders with Jordan, Iraq, Kuwait, Qatar, United Arab Emirates, Oman, and Yemen. In 1982, a land bridge, the King Fahd Causeway, was built across the Persian Gulf to connect Saudi Arabia to the island country Bahrain.

In 1992, the Kingdom of Saudi Arabia took the lead in forming the Gulf Cooperation Council (GCC), a regional collective security and economic organization. The GCC includes fellow monarchies and sheikhdoms of Bahrain, Kuwait, Oman, Qatar, and the United Arab Emirates. With the King Fahd Causeway, Saudi Arabia is now geographically connected to all the other countries in the GCC.

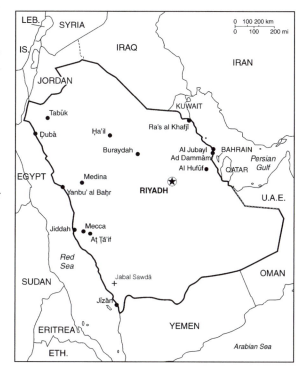

The modern Saudi state was founded in 1902 by Abdul Al-Aziz bin Abd al-Rahman Al Saud, a member of the "Saud" family. In 1932, after a 30-year campaign to unify the Arabian Peninsula, Ibn Saud forcibly formed a unified state from the disparate tribes. Abdul-Aziz bin Saud captured the Al-Saud's ancestral home of Riyadh and, in 1932, the modern Kingdom of Saudi Arabia was established. The leading members of the royal family choose the king from among their family, with the subsequent approval of the *ulema*.[3] Today, as required by Saudi Arabia's 1992 Basic Law, a male descendent of Ibn Saud, rules the country.

The modern day nation-state of Saudi Arabia is the birthplace of Islam. It is home to the two holiest places in Islam: Mecca and

Medina, and is often referred to as The Land of the Two Holy Mosques. Islam is the national religion and religious institutions receive government support. There is virtually no separation of religion and government. The king's official title is Custodian of the Two Holy Mosques.

All Saudi citizens are Arab by ethnicity and Muslim by religion. Arabic is the national language. The vast majority of the Saudi citizens are Sunni Muslims, with a Shiite minority. In the kingdom's southwest, Shiites comprise the majority. They are resistant to the religious oppression and pressure of the official policies intended to convert Shiites to Wahhabism.

Saudi Arabia is the world's leading exporter of petroleum. Saudi's main industries include the production of crude oil and petrochemicals. The export of petroleum and petroleum derived products, including oil, accounts for more than 90 percent of Saudi exports and almost 75 percent of Saudi government revenues. Saudi is a leading producer of oil and natural gas, containing approximately 25 percent of the world's oil reserves. Though most famous for its oil exports, Saudi's industries also include cement, construction, fertilizer, and plastics.

The currency is the Saudi Riyal, which is fixed to the U.S. dollar. Since Saudi Arabia's entry into the World Trade Organization in December 2005, the Kingdom has been pursuing a path of economic reform and diversification, including the promotion of foreign investment. Long-term economic concerns include a booming population with fewer jobs, the depletion of aquifers and oil reserves, global fluctuation of oil prices, and a welfare-state economy largely dependent on its output of depleting petroleum reserves.

The Saudi military has six branches: Army, Navy, Air Force, Air Defense Force, National Guard, and a paramilitary Ministry of Interior Forces. The government spends approximately 12 percent of its GDP on military. The Minister of Defense and Aviation supervises the six branches of the Saudi military while exercising operational control. The National Security Council, or the High Defense Council, is responsible for establishing the country's defense policy. The members of the council include the king, the Ministers of Defense and Aviation, of the Interior, of Foreign Affairs, of Finance and National Economy, and the Chief of Staff of the Armed Forces. As commander in chief, the king makes all final decisions.

OVERVIEW OF LGBT ISSUES

LGBT rights in Saudi Arabia are not recognized. Homosexuality and cross-dressing are widely seen as immoral acts and are treated as serious crimes. In recent decades, there have been numerous reports of an underground LGBT community. While the government has faced criticism from human rights organizations, it insists that it is acting in accordance with Sunni Islamic morality, particularly its Wahhabi influences.

Homosexuality, cross-dressing, and sodomy are considered immoral and illegal acts. Punishment for those convicted of these acts is severe, including stoning, hanging, whipping, and capital punishment. Even those merely suspected of having committed homosexual acts are treated harshly.

Despite the persecution of the gay community, there is a vibrant underground LGBT community. Gay weddings, drag shows, gay beauty pageants, and gay cruising are all activities that many outside the Kingdom are surprised to hear take place within Saudi Arabia's borders. Areas known as stomping grounds for the LGBT community, such as certain streets, Internet cafes, university buildings, and night clubs offer physical spaces for interaction. The sex-segregated country offers many opportunities for same-sex couples to spend time together in public as long as they maintain a platonic appearance. Technology has provided a certain freedom of information and interaction inconceivable 30 years ago.

EDUCATION

When the modern state of Saudi Arabia was established in 1932, only boys from elite families were permitted to receive religious instruction at schools in mosques, or *madrassas,* located in urban areas. Since its founding in 1953, the Ministry of Education has established thousands of primary and secondary schools, as well as colleges, institutes, and universities.[4] Today, public education through high school is free for every Saudi citizen, both male and female. The government offers financial assistance and free housing for university-level education and subsidizes some of the related expenses such as books, transportation and meals. Female university students receive free transportation.

The Saudi government places a high value on the quality of education of its citizens and as such has increased its education spending over the years. In 2004, Saudi Arabia spent 6.8 percent of its GDP on education placing, the Kingdom 28th in the world in terms of percent spent on education.[5] In 2006, 27.6 percent of the government's spending went towards the education of its citizens,[6] placing Saudi Arabia fifth in the world in public spending on education as a percentage of total government expenditure.[7]

Between 1969 and 1996, the number of students at all levels of education increased from 600,000 to approximately four million.[8] Between 1969 and 1995, the number of university level graduates rose from 808 students to 23,074 students.[9] Saudi Arabia has a ratio of 15 students to each teacher, making it one of the lowest student/teacher ratios in the world.[10]

By the 2003–2004 academic year, the Ministry of Education reported that there were approximately 200,000 students attending Saudi universities and colleges, as compared to only 7,000 in 1970.[11] In 2006, 84.3 percent of Saudi adults were literate and 96.6 percent of Saudi youth were literate.[12] In addition to domestic education, the government provides scholarships to Saudi students to pursue graduate and postgraduate education abroad. Thousands of Saudi students are enrolled in universities worldwide, primarily in the United States.

Islam is the foundation of Saudi education and school curriculum must fully comply with Sharia Law. Within Islam, the conservative teachings of the Wahhabi movement[13] are the basis of not only Saudi education but all other aspects of life in the Kingdom. According to Abdulla Muhammad Al-Zaid, the former Director General of Education for the western province of Saudi Arabia, spreading Islam is one of the cornerstones of the Saudi education system: "The purpose of education is to understand Islam in a proper and complete manner, to implement and spread the Muslim faith, to provide a student with Islamic values and teachings."[14] A book published by the Saudi Cultural Mission to the United States underscores the emphasis on the conservative Wahhabi movement in Saudi education, calling for a return to the fundamentals of Islam taught by the Prophet Mohammed.[15]

The government has been making a strong effort to increase female education levels across all levels of education, and over the decades, the education of

Saudi women has been on the rise. According to the Saudi Ministry of Education, today there are approximately an equal number of boys and girls of all age groups enrolled in schools.[16] At the college level, women study among the five universities that now accept both male and female students as well as other colleges that were established exclusively for women. Women made up over half of the 200,000 students attending colleges and universities reported in 2003–2004.[17] The Kingdom's commitment to education for girls is confirmed by UNESCO statistics that show female literacy rates improved over a 14-year period. Between 1992 and 2006, adult literacy for males increased from 80 to 88.6 percent, an 11 percent improvement, as compared to adult literacy for females, which increased from 57.3 to 78.4 percent, a 37 percent improvement.[18] Despite the great strides made by women in education, Saudi women still lag behind other developed nations in comparison. Enrollment in secondary school for males was 70 percent, as compared to 65 percent for females in 2006.[19] In 2006, 88.6 percent of adult males were literate as compared to 78.4 percent literacy among adult females. However, the statistics are higher for the younger generation: among Saudi youth, literacy is 97.7 percent among Saudi boys, versus 95.5 percent literacy among Saudi girls.[20] Despite the progress made, Amnesty International still finds that Saudi Arabia lags behind international standards, stating in 2001 that women are still discriminated against and are routinely denied equal educational and vocational opportunities.[21]

Traditional gender roles in Saudi Arabia also continue to limit women's educational opportunities. Women do not have access to certain subjects in school. While a Saudi man may travel abroad to pursue further studies, a Saudi woman must generally be accompanied by her husband or a male relative. In the case of a single woman, the cost of sending her abroad is compounded by the cost of sending her male chaperone, making such an option prohibitively expensive for all but the wealthiest citizens. Attending school is not a requirement and as a result, over the years, a disproportionate number of girls have been pulled out of school. In 1996, an estimated 61 percent of Saudi children attended school.

Some critics believe that the conservative religious establishment's role in forming school curriculum is not conducive to a modern Saudi workforce. According to Arab News journalist Maha Akeel, "We cannot have 80 percent of our college students graduating in history, geography, Arabic literature, and Islamic studies and we barely have enough students graduating in science, engineering or from the medical schools."[22] Such critics believe that, despite oil wealth, the government is not investing money in the kinds of industries that produce jobs to employ a growing population. Others believe Saudi attitudes towards certain kinds of technical jobs are the primary culprit and the government should work on changing cultural mores. However, others state that it is Saudi Arabia's duty as conservators of the Islamic faith to teach subsequent generations the same form of Islamic lifestyle and to minimize the insinuation of Western culture. Nevertheless, the Kingdom has increased spending on training adult members of the workforce in technical and administrative areas to support the country's growing economic and social needs. The government is paying special attention to providing technical training to its citizens to address the country's shortage of highly skilled workers in technical fields. Similar to many blue-collar jobs, such white-collar job opportunities are currently filled by foreign labor as well.

Although educational researcher Dr. Al Salloom states that the Saudi curriculum undergoes regular reviews to keep up with the changing needs of Saudi society and improves as necessary to keep Saudi students abreast of global technology, it is unlikely that changes will affect its view on homosexuality. As long as homosexuality is banned under Islam, the Saudi curriculum will not recognize homosexuality nor will Saudi universities recognize LGBT student groups. Because homosexuality is a crime punishable by death in Saudi Arabia, there are no protections for LGBT students or even LGBT student groups at the secondary school or university level. Students do not participate in LGBT-related activities in the organized fashion that their Western counterparts would.

These official restrictions, however, do not mean that there is not a gay community among Saudi students. Though there is no visible LGBT activity, there are many reports that gay and lesbian students clandestinely enjoy an active social life. Because all secondary schooling and much of university level schooling is sex segregated, men and women spend all the time they are not among family members, with members of the same sex. Some argue that so much time spent with members of the same sex facilitates gay and lesbian exploration. *Okaz*, a Jeddah-based Arabic-language newspaper, reported that lesbianism was endemic among school-age girls. The article revealed accounts of lesbian sex in the girls' bathroom, with some girls stigmatized for refusing the lesbian advances of other female students, and teachers expressing displeasure that the students involved were unwilling to change behavior.[23]

Such activities are even more prevalent at the university level where students are older, more mature, and are living in the dormitories. It is unusual for Saudi women to live outside the home of their father or husband. As a result, female dormitories are heavily secured, with the movements of the women extremely restricted. Saudi blogger Sabria S. Jawhar reports of unsafe and bleak conditions in Saudi dormitories. From Thursday night to Saturday morning,[24] Jawhar reports, "we would be locked up in our dormitories as prisoners...The steel doors at the bottom of the stairwell that led outdoors were padlocked and an elderly man would guard it in case a crook wanted to break in and attack us."[25]

While ostensibly such measures are to protect the women's virtue and isolate them from the opposite sex, it also leaves them with little to do. A Saudi woman interviewed gave accounts of lesbian activities in the dormitories, as she said, just to explore their sexuality. Farrah,[26] remembers that she and her room partner would sometimes engage in what she understands now to be lesbian activities for lack of other activities and other outlets for their sexual energy. Though happily married to her childhood sweetheart, she says that she was fortunate to have had the opportunity to explore her lesbian tendencies during the one time in her life that she was not living with family members. "If I did not have that chance, I would have always wondered if I would like women better," Farrah said. Farrah also recalls that the girls who lived in the dorms had code words for different sexual activities that they would engage in with one another, and only those considered open-minded enough would be let in on their meanings, whether that person was gay or not.

In *The Atlantic*'s magazine article, "Kingdom in the Closet," by Nadya Labi, several students reveal a gay community in their schools that helped them explore their blooming sexuality:

When Yasser hit puberty, he grew attracted to his male cousins. Like many gay and lesbian teenagers everywhere, he felt isolated. "I used to have the feeling that I was the queerest in the country," he recalled. "But then I went to high school and discovered there are others like me. Then I find out, it's a whole society."[27]

Labi's only source that would openly speak of her lesbian relations was Yasmin,[28] a 21-year-old student, who had briefly had a lesbian sexual relationship with a girl-friend. She recounted how one of the buildings at her college was well-known as a lesbian enclave:

> The building has large bathroom stalls, which provide privacy, and walls covered with graffiti offering romantic and religious advice; tips include "she doesn't really love you no matter what she tells you" and "before you engage in anything with [her] remember: God is watching you." In Saudi Arabia, "It's easier to be a lesbian [than a heterosexual]. There's an overwhelming number of people who turn to lesbianism," Yasmin said, adding that the number of men in the kingdom who turn to gay sex is even greater. "They're not really homosexual," she said. "They're like cell mates in prison."[29]

Despite reports of an underground gay scene at the university level and some forms of acceptance at the secondary school level, the majority of gay students in Saudi Arabia live in silence. As long as public behavior remains platonic, they are left alone, mostly because they are invisible. For students who seek to express trans-gender or transvestite tendencies, however, there is no public outlet. Any behavior that subverts the conventional male/female dichotomy in appearance, manner, or dress is prohibited and therefore, only done in private.

EMPLOYMENT AND ECONOMICS

Saudi Arabia is the world's largest exporter of petroleum possessing approximately 25 percent of the world's petroleum reserves. The government controls most aspects of this oil-based economy. Their economy is centrally planned with a limited number of tightly regulated private companies, including some multinational corporations. In addition to oil, Saudi Arabia also has a strong natural gas industry. In 2007, the Saudi budget recorded a surplus of approximately US$47 billion.

Though oil was discovered in the 1930s, Saudi Arabia did not begin large-scale extraction and production until the 1950s and 1960s. Economic development was funded by accelerated influx of wealth from oil exports in the 1960s and 1970s that converted a country of nomads and small-scale farmers to international businessmen in the span of several decades. Income from oil export comprises over 90 percent of the Kingdom's exports and over 75 percent of the government's GDP.

Prior to the discovery of oil, Saudi Arabia traditionally relied on income from agriculture and fishing. Today, these industries employ less than 10 percent of the population.[30] Though it must import most of its food and other consumables, Saudi Arabia has an export surplus exceeding 100 percent. Government revenues from the oil trade fund economic development within its own borders, as well as provide aid to other Arab and Islamic countries. The majority of food and other consumer items are imported from other countries. Though Saudi Arabia heavily relies on trade, their role in OPEC and vast oil reserves makes them a desirable trade ally.

The Organization of Petroleum Exporting Countries (OPEC) was founded in 1960 to unify the major producers of oil in the international arena. Currently OPEC is comprised of 12 countries: Algeria, Angola, Ecuador, Iran, Iraq, Kuwait,

Libya, Nigeria, Qatar, Saudi Arabia, the United Arab Emirates, and Venezuela. Saudi Arabia has always played a leading role in setting and leading campaigns within OPEC and enforcing OPEC policy. As a result, Saudi Arabia has always been viewed as a desirable trade ally, despite its perceived human rights violations.

The government of Saudi Arabia will not release the numbers regarding their oil reserves. There are a certain number of proven petroleum reserves, but the actual number is kept a government secret, but is acknowledged to be a finite amount. As a result, in recent years, the government has been encouraging diversification of its economy through expanding into nonenergy sectors such as light manufacturing industry, telecommunications, natural gas exploration, and petrochemicals. In 2005, Saudi Arabia became party to the World Trade Organization in an effort to draw in foreign investment and diversify its economy.

Between 2005 and 2007, King Abdullah bin Abdulaziz Al Saud has funded the creation of six new economic cities. These cities, to be created from the ground up in otherwise unused desert lands, and will offer diverse investment opportunities for foreign and domestic corporations. The cities will offer investment opportunities not only in the petrochemical sector, but also in steel, plastic, glass, ceramic, transportation, and even education industries.[31] Amr Dabbagh, Governor and Chairman of the Board of Directors of the Saudi Arabian General Investment Authority (SAGIA) stated that "[t]he impact of these six economic cities by 2020 is $150 billion in contribution to GDP growth, 1.3 million jobs to be created, and to accommodate 4.8 million of the total population."[32]

Despite Saudi Arabia's fast economic growth, the high unemployment rate is of great concern to the government.[33] At the end of 2006, Minister of Labour Ghazi Al-Gosaibi announced that Saudi Arabia's official unemployment rate was nine percent for men and 22 percent for women.[34] In 2008, Saudi male unemployment was at 12 percent, according to local bank estimates, with others placing it as high as 25 percent.[35] The economic cities, along with other government ventures, anticipated foreign investment, and growth in the private sector will create employment for a swelling population. The current population generally lacks the education and technical skills the private sector needs, and the private sector goes to foreign workers to meet its labor needs. With approximately 40 percent of its population under 15 years old, the Kingdom faces a situation in 10 years of having a large, well-educated, but unemployable fleet of Saudi men with nothing to occupy their time. In addition to unemployment creating economic instability, there is an increasing concern that a growing population of unemployable Saudi men will create fertile ground for the rise of religious fundamentalism. Approaching large groups of disaffected, unemployed, and bored youth is a common recruitment strategy for terrorist organizations.

Saudization is another plan to combat unemployment by reserving certain jobs for Saudi nationals. Saudi's Ministry of Labour and Social Affairs has placed a restriction on about forty kinds of positions to Saudi nationals. These jobs include taxi drivers, training and purchasing managers, public relations officers, administrative assistants, secretaries, operators, debt collectors, customer service accountants, tellers, postmen, data handlers, librarians, booksellers, ticket kiosk keepers, auto salesmen, janitors, internal mail handlers and tour guides. Such plans have met with mixed results in other Gulf countries that have tried to implement their own plans favoring their citizens. The private sector in the Kingdom is very resistant to Saudization since it is widely believed by employers that "Saudis are more expensive and less productive than non-Saudis."[36] A combination of cultural attitudes, as well as lack of appropriate skills in its local workforce, make Saudization an unattractive prospect for employers who can find a hard working skilled worker from another country rather than having to train a local citizen.

Many employers skirt the law by paying Saudi nationals to be on the employer's payroll to meet their quota and then by requesting them to remain at home so as not to lower the work ethic at the worksite. There are numerous penalties for subverting this law including fines and bans from applying for government loans and services, however, the financial disincentives are still very high.

The government has increased spending on job training, infrastructure development, and government salaries. It is also working to change attitudes about the kinds of professions Saudis find culturally suitable. Many of the growing industries that require skilled labor are considered appropriate only for foreign workers. Organizations such as ALJ Group are working to change popular attitudes about Saudis performing manual labor and blue collar jobs.

Both the government and private sector prohibit the interaction of men and women in the workplace. Because of the sex-based segregation, even those women allowed to work outside the home are extremely limited in the fields in which they may take up employment. Saudi women primarily work either for the government in clerical positions, work in health care as nurses, lab technicians, and a very few become doctors or teachers. In all cases, they are interacting only with other females.

In 2008, Deputy Labor Minister Abdul Wahid Al-Humaid stated that the high unemployment among college educated Saudi women is due to social factors and the fear of employers that employing women is expensive.[37] Social factors include the fear that having women in the workplace will have a negative impact on the morality, not only of the female workers but the male workers as well. Despite sex-segregated workplaces, the fear of immorality still remains as more women travel outside the home and have opportunities to interact with men to whom they are not related. Recently, the Ministry of Labor enacted regulations allowing women and men to interact in government offices. It is possible that the private sector will follow.

The Saudi government has set aside a large budget for the establishment of advanced vocational academies with the aim of developing Saudi human resources, including training women for vocational occupations. Organizations such as ALJ Group based in Jeddah offer loans to women-run enterprises, opening up avenues that were inconceivable to entrepreneurial women 10 years ago. In 2008, the Public Institution for Vocational Education announced that it would train more than 120,000 women in car mechanics during the next seven years, among other vocations. Such programs, in addition to employing women, help to change cultural attitudes.

Though there are few Saudi women in the workplace, the Shura Council is committed to enacting sexual harassment laws to protect women in the workplace. The Shura Council was created, in part, to address gaps in legislation facing an ever-changing social climate in the country. It is "an institution intended to allow citizens to participate directly in the country policies administration, planning for them, and following up the performance of its agencies. The Shura Council is the place to exercise the multiplicity of opinion, through practicing its tasks and duties with greater openness, objectivity in debate, and aiming at the general welfare of the country and the citizen."[38] There was much excitement in the Arab and international media in 2008 and 2009 with the announcement of a possibility of legally mandated protection for women against workplace harassment.[39]

A wide range of jobs along the socioeconomic ladder are occupied by foreign workers. Professions range from blue-collar work, such as manual labor, construction and domestic work to skilled tradesmen to doctors, nurses, and corporate executives.

The largest sub-population hails from South Asian countries, with an estimated 1.5 million Indians, 1.5 million Bangladeshis, 1 million Pakistanis, 350,000 Sri Lankans, and 400,000 Nepalese. Coming from eastern and southeastern countries are 1.2 million Filipinos, 600,000 Indonesians, as well as Thais and assorted others. Other Middle Eastern countries and North African countries provide a sizeable population with estimates of 1 million Egyptians, 250,000 Palestinians, 150,000 Lebanese, and 100,000 Eritreans, among others. Western Europeans, Canadians, and Americans make up the smallest percentage and typically occupy white-collar professions. There are an approximate 30,000 Americans in Saudi Arabia, with many working for Aramco.

While there is no official protection from workplace harassment for persons who present a nonheterosexual gender identity, the one place where there have been reports of de facto acceptance is among Filipino men in the beauty industry. Hairdressing and related beauty treatments such as facials and massage are considered inappropriate professions for Saudis in general.[40] Because it is perceived as a feminine trade, Saudi men generally steer away from beauty and related care professions. Because it is considered low-skilled work, it is considered inappropriate for Saudi women. Most professions in the beauty industry are practiced by foreign workers. There have been reports that Filipino feminine-leaning men, whether gay, bisexual, transsexual, transvestite or straight, have been generally left alone as long as perceived deviant sexual behavior is not apparent. Because of the perceived feminine nature of hairdressing and related professions in the Arab world, gay Filipino men in these fields are not seen as threatening and are the most visibly gay of any members of the LGBT community in the Kingdom.

Because homosexuality is illegal in Saudi Arabia, there are no figures on the LGBT population within the workplace or their role in the economy. There are currently no protections for members of the LGBT community who are fired, paid less, or looked over for advancement on the basis of their sexual orientation. An employer is not only allowed to fire a gay employee, but can later subject them to extortion and blackmail. Same-sex unions, domestic partnerships or civil unions officiated in other parts of the world do not have legal standing in Saudi Arabia. In fact, evidence of such unions can be used as the basis for criminal proceedings.

While there is a movement towards protecting women from harassment in the workplace by men, it is unlikely that such laws will ever extend either as written or in their application to protect men, whether homosexual, bisexual, transsexual, transvestite or otherwise, from harassment by men on the basis of sexual or gender orientation. At best, such cases could be prosecuted as pure assault and battery. It is equally unlikely that future workplace harassment laws would extend in application to protect women who are being harassed for apparently flouting gender norms from similar type of harassment from other women. However, individual members of the LGBT community will be unlikely to pursue prosecution of perpetrators of gender based hate crimes at work for fear that their own sexual orientation would come into question. The consequences for being labeled queer of any form, whether real or merely perceived are very severe in the Kingdom.

SOCIAL/GOVERNMENT PROGRAMS

The various ministries, as well as the royal family of Saudi Arabia, are working hard to take the Kingdom into the 21st century. The Shura Council, for example, was created, in part, to address gaps in legislation facing an ever-changing social climate in the country. The Shura Council has been a modernizing force in the Kingdom with respect to women's rights.[41] Apart from women, other social groups, including members of the LGBT community, are not served by social or government programs. Current penalties for perceived homosexual activities range from imprisonment, fines, corporal punishment, and execution. As a result, there are no government programs specifically for members of the LGBT community in Saudi Arabia.

HIV/AIDS has only recently been recognized as a problem in the Kingdom. Saudi citizens infected with HIV/AIDS are provided free medical care, including expensive antiretroviral drugs that cost approximately 10,000 Saudi Riyals or US$2,700 per month.[42] Until the late 1990s, information on HIV/AIDS was not widely available to the public, but this has started to change in the last 10 years.

Starting in the late 1990s, Saudi Arabia began to recognize World AIDS Day. The government permitted hospitals and newspapers to disseminate information about the disease. Condoms are available in hospitals and pharmacies, and in some supermarkets as well. According to the Ministry of Health Spokesman, Khaled Marghalani, the Ministry's National AIDS Control Program promotes awareness of HIV/AIDS with approximately 2,000 health centers throughout Saudi Arabia by distributing flyers, putting up posters and educating people.[43] The Saudi government also passed legislation that protects the privacy of Saudi citizens who are ill and furthermore, guarantees their right to work.

While these measures provide some relief and protection for Saudi patients infected with HIV/AIDS, most public and private hospitals will refuse to treat infected patients. Many hospitals and health care workers also refuse to distribute information published by the government about the disease, mainly because of the social stigma attached to the virus.[44] The Saudi Arabia Country Office of the United Nations Development Programme (UNDP-SA) engages in a wide range of activities to help curb the spread and treat those already infected with HIV/AIDS. UNDP-SA has three specialized centers for HIV/AIDS treatment located in the capital Riyadh, as well as in Jeddah and Dammam.[45] It also assists the HIV/AIDS Regional Programme in the Arab States (UNDP-HARPAS) in its work in the Arab region. Activities include awareness workshops and conferences. The Riyadh office has also conducted AIDS workshops for teenagers.[46]

Currently, the UNDP-SA supports the Kingdom's programs to keep accurate records of reported cases and promote health education and awareness. A range of information programs disseminates information about HIV/AIDS, methods of transmission, and preventive measures. The UNDP-KoSA sponsors public service announcements that are broadcast across television stations in the Arab region, including in Saudi Arabia.[47] The preventive programs also include surveying at-risk groups, ensuring safe blood transfusions, and testing of foreign workers.[48] Though members of the LGBT community are considered to be at-risk for contracting

HIV/AIDS, because homosexuality is forbidden in Saudi Arabia, homosexuals are not being surveyed or specifically targeted for preventive programs.

Provisions that protect or treat HIV/AIDS patients only apply to Saudi citizens. To prevent the spread of the virus and to curb the country's health care budget, foreign workers are required to undergo a government-controlled medical examination prior to being issued residency and work permits. In addition to a general health check to flag serious infectious diseases and infirmities, the exam is particularly given to check for HIV and AIDS. The test must be retaken at the time of a visa renewal, usually on a three-year cycle. If a foreigner is found to be positive for the HIV virus or AIDS, entry and visa applications are denied.[49] Foreign nationals already living in Saudi Arabia discovered to be infected with HIV or AIDS are soon deported to their country of origin, sometimes preceded by a period of imprisonment.[50]

SEXUALITY/SEXUAL PRACTICES

Islam, and consequently Saudi society, strictly prohibits nonmarital sex, premarital sex, extramarital sex, and homosexuality.

Chastity, as well as modesty, are highly prized virtues for men and women in Saudi Arabia. While Western media tends to focus on the government enforced veiling of women in public, there is less attention on the fact that even men are to be covered in public. When male children enter puberty, parents teach them to wear the traditional three-piece head covering as a sign for entering manhood. Both men and boys are taught to wear the *thawb,* a loose-fitting ankle-length robe that is typically white and nearly covers the entire body. Young Saudi men are taught to wear loose fitting clothing, whether the traditional Saudi style or Western. They are discouraged from wearing clothing that is too revealing of their physical form including jeans that are too tight or shirts that are low cut, too tight, or otherwise too revealing. Saudi's religious police does not, however, pursue men not adequately covered as rigorously and the requirements are not as all encompassing for men as they are for women.

Veiling women and maintaining sex segregation outside the home are both mechanisms to reinforce and ensure chastity. The only place that sexuality is to be expressed is within the confines of a heterosexual marriage. Because homosexuality is not recognized as a context in which to express sexuality, same-sex sexual relations are also prohibited as being an expression of sexuality outside of marriage.

Women are required to be kept separate from unrelated men. As a result, whenever a woman travels outside the home, she must be accompanied by a male relative or male servant to mediate her interactions outside the home. As an extension of this principle, women are not allowed to drive in Saudi Arabia, though this is mostly enforced in the urban areas. A Saudi woman's dependence on the men in her life to be the intermediaries between her and the outside world continues to perpetuate the patriarchal nature of Saudi society, which places a higher value on her chastity than on the man's chastity.

Arabic literature has a long history with homoerotic poetry as well as prose.[51] Many Islamic jurists have devoted ink to the condemnation, regulation, and prescription of punishment for male homosexuality in the Muslim world.[52] However, the Saudi government, as well as its clergy, denies the presence of homosexuality in the Kingdom. They promote the perception that Saudis only engage in heterosexual sex and only in the context of marriage. As a result, it is difficult to obtain statistics on sexual practices among the LGBT community in Saudi Arabia as distinct from other parts of the Muslim world.

Ironically, the Kingdom's narrowly construed separation of the sexes, allows homosexuals more freedom than heterosexuals. Some report that because Saudi Arabia is sex-segregated, "It's a lot easier to be gay than straight here."[53] It is forbidden for a man and woman who are not related to be traveling alone or even spending time together in one of Saudi Arabia's many modern urban oases: the mall. The religious police will harass or even take in for questioning two people of the opposite sex for spending time together. Two people of the same sex spending hours at a time in public will raise no eyebrows as long as their relationship appears platonic.

Labi reports a phenomenon among homosexual Saudis common in communities as well. Many of the men who have sex with another man do not consider themselves homosexual or gay. As long as they are the one in the dominant position "giving," the gender of the person on whom they are performing is immaterial.[54] In this definition of homosexual, the importance is on the relative position of the actor, not on the orientation of the actors.

Some say that the strict gendered segregation even encourages homosexuality. A gay man told John R. Bradley, author of *Saudi Arabia Exposed: Inside a Kingdom in Crisis* (2005), that he feels quite free to express his homosexuality in public: "We have more freedom here than straight couples. After all, they can't kiss in public like we can, or stroll down the street holding one another's hands."[55] Similarly, because women are confined to interacting mostly with women or male relatives, two women spending hours together and even sleeping in the same room or same bed in a home would not attract as much attention as, for example, an unmarried heterosexual couple.

Most Saudi men are not allowed contact with females outside their families, even after marriage. Even the yet to be married men who identify as heterosexual may engage in gay sex as a way to explore their sexuality without risking a woman's purity, jail, pregnancy, and his family's honor.

"Tariq," a 24-year-old in the travel industry, explains that "many 'tops' are simply hard up for sex, looking to break their abstinence in whatever way they can."[56] Labi's report confirms a practice in Saudi Arabia that is common in other parts of the world, where a heterosexual man engages a homosexual man, transvestite, or transsexual, for sex during the times when his wife cannot provide sex: Francis,' a 34-year-old beauty queen from the Philippines, reported that he's had sex with Saudi men whose wives were pregnant or menstruating; when those circumstances changed, most of the men stopped calling. "If they can't use their wives," Francis said, "they have this option with gays."[57]

Often heterosexual Saudi men will engage in such temporary relations to meet a short-term sexual need or sexual exploration with expatriates to insulate themselves from gossip. Western men will be approached for their apparent open mindedness and experience. Asian men may be approached for the perceived stereotype of their submissiveness or effeminate nature, relative economic disempowerment, and discreetness. In situations where two Saudi men engage in homosexual relations, it is more likely that they are in a relationship offering other relationship benefits such as companionship and emotional support rather than a purely utilitarian relationship.

There are a variety of forums in Saudi Arabia in which Saudi gay youth express their sexuality. The Internet offers the modern Saudi young adult a wide array of information in a private setting. Saudi youth, similar to youth the world over, rely on media and communicating with friends and family members to learn about sexual practices, both heterosexual and homosexual. The university has been a typical site of sexual learning and exploration for youth everywhere and Saudi universities are no exception.

FAMILY

According to the Saudi Constitution, "the family is the kernel of Saudi society, and its members shall be brought up on the basis of the Islamic faith, and loyalty and obedience to God, His Messenger, and to guardians; respect for and implementation of the law, and love of and pride in the homeland and its glorious history as the Islamic faith stipulates.[58]

Being a Muslim, a family member, and a Saudi are the three most important conceptualizations of the self for a Saudi citizen. Family is essential in transmitting and preserving culture and values in Islam.

Despite trends towards modernization, the family, both nuclear and extended, is still the core of Saudi society. Unlike Western families where the role of the nuclear family has become dominant with limited interactions with the extended family, Saudis enjoy a vibrant extended family life. The extended family for many Muslim communities, including Saudi, usually includes aunts, uncles, nieces, nephews, grandparents, great grandparents, in-laws, and cousins. Individuals are often identified through their relationships with family members. One's individual identity can hardly be divested from their place in their extended family. These relationships are reinforced through a combination of social mechanisms. More traditional families live in close proximity or share a family compound or a single house. The Muslim lifestyle provides for frequent meetings at religious ceremonies such as weddings and funerals and related social gatherings such as the breaking of the fast during Ramadan. Extended family relationships are vibrant and part of the fabric of daily life, rather than reserved for special occasion, as evidenced by a small child scarcely perceiving a distinction between her own sibling and a cousin. Oil wealth and Westernization has lessened the centrality of the extended family to an extent. Though social patterns and behaviors may change with time, the fundamental strength of Islamic social values will continue to keep the concept of family as a core value in Saudi life.

In the tribal days of the Arabian Peninsula as well as today, Saudi families are patrilineal, with membership in a family derived from lines of male descendants. While relationships with maternal relatives are important, family identity is established through the father.

Marriages are still mostly arranged. Dating is discouraged, as socializing with unrelated members of the opposite sex is not permitted. The more modern semi-arranged marriage allows the young groom or bride-to-be the freedom to select among a discrete set of choices preapproved by the family.

Marriage is a civil contract, which is signed by witnesses, and for which a stipulated amount of money, called the *mehr*, is paid by the husband to the wife. Divorce is typically initiated by the husband. The marriage contract could also include other stipulations such as the wife's right of divorce if the husband were to take on a second wife or an additional amount to be paid in the event of divorce.

The wife usually keeps her maiden name as well as maintains control over her personal property as per Islamic law. In Saudi Arabia, such provisions in the law were an indication of a woman's independence within the marriage. If a woman were to divorce, her closest male relative, often her father or eldest brother, would be responsible for financially supporting her.

Under Islamic law, men are allowed to marry up to four wives. Polygamy is more common among more the religiously conservative, those from the more rural areas, among the tribal or tribal-leaning communities, as well as the royal family. Though polygamy is legal and practiced in Saudi Arabia, it is a thing of the past among the educated, more Western-oriented elite.

Consanguinity, marrying within one's extended family, has been a common practice in the pre-Islamic Middle East for centuries. Intermarrying was primarily a mechanism to preserve family resources by keeping dowries and inheritances within the same bloodline. Even Mohammed's daughter married her first cousin, a well-respected imam. Its practice in the time of the Prophet has reinforced its place in Saudi society. Saudi Arabia has the highest rate of intermarriage with an approximate 55 to 70 percent of Saudis marrying their first or second cousin.[59] Some medical researchers posit consanguinity as the primary reason for certain genetic diseases occurring in rates almost 20 times higher than in other populations in which consanguinity is not practiced.[60] As a result, some Wahhabi clerics and Saudi government programs have begun to dissuade citizens from intermarrying by educating on the potential health risks as well as encouraging premarital blood tests.

Under Islam, the definition of marriage is limited to a union between a man and a woman. As homosexuality is forbidden under Islam and Saudi law, Saudi Arabia does not recognize same-sex marriages, including ones formed legally in other countries. Because of the strict sex segregation, same-sex couples sometimes find it easy to live together under the radar of the religious police and their own family members.

However, marriage is such an important institution in Saudi society, that a man or woman who is single for too long may also raise inquiries. Saudi society places a premium on having children and grandchildren that the pressure to marry for young gay men and women is immense. Some members of the LGBT community will comply with a family request to marry and start a family, while keeping a same sex liaison on the side. Because of the strict sex segregation in Saudi Arabia and the denial of homosexuality among Muslims, same-sex extramarital affairs are often easier to keep secret for years than heterosexual affairs. Others will enter a heterosexual marriage and give up the chance to express that side of themselves.

A society so conservative as to be slow to change consanguinity practices, despite recorded health risks, will not embrace a union between two members of the same sex for the foreseeable future.

COMMUNITY

Despite the rigid strictures and high cost for being caught, there are still reports that gay life in Saudi Arabia is vibrant. In "The Kingdom in the Closet," Nadya Labi reports that "the kingdom leaves considerable space for homosexual behavior. As long as gays and lesbians maintain a public front of obeisance to Wahhabist norms, they are left to do what they want in private."[61] In the more modern cities of Riyadh and Jeddah, individuals report that one can be picked up any time of the day.[62]

There are various manners in which homosexual activity takes place within the strict conservative lifestyle in the Kingdom. In addition to such interactions taking place through one's existing networks, there are clubs in the larger cities, particularly in Riyadh and Jeddah, which very discreetly have an unadvertised gay night. Information on such activities is highly exclusive because of the danger to the attendees as well as the club owners. Certain nightclubs are known for being exclusively gay or gay-friendly. Because of the sex segregation, some clubs will have all women disco nights to which some of the more conservative families will feel comfortable allowing their daughters to attend. These are often perfect covers for lesbian activity, without raising the suspicion of the religious police.

With the prevalence of the Internet and the relatively high standard of living among Saudi nationals, many gay Saudi nationals are able to find a queer community on the Internet. Students use the Internet to find friendship and opportunities for discussion and in-person meetings.

In past decades, a Saudi looking for a gay community had to be fluent in English to access the Western LGBT community. Now, the plethora of Arab and Muslim Web sites, online chat rooms, and listservs allows Saudi gays to find a community closer to home, and in Arabic. Many of these sites do not specifically divide themselves by geographic borders, but Saudi students participate in these just as students and other young people from other conservative Muslim countries. Though still behind hipper neighboring countries such as the United Arab Emirates, Egypt, and Jordan, in recent years, there has been an increase in gay Saudi Web sites. Some of these Saudi-based sites are specifically designed to help gay Saudis find each other and enable in-person meetings. Internet cafes dot the cities, with some Internet cafes themselves achieving notoriety as locations for singles in the LGBT community to meet.

Government censorship is commonplace. Web sites with content considered un-Islamic are blocked to those accessing the Internet from within the Kingdom. Not limited to homosexual content, there are a wide range of Web sites that are blocked by the government. The censors block these sites within Saudi borders, but software to bypass the government blocks online is easy to procure. Additionally, there are reports that the blocks on some gay Web sites in Saudi Arabia have been lifted by the government amid an international uproar over the 2002 public beheading of three men convicted of homosexuality, rape, and sodomy.[63]

While there are no university clubs that sponsor LGBT activities, some of the Saudi universities are hot spots for gay activity. Whether the student lives in the dormitory or commutes from home, the relatively open environment of campus life affords many young Saudis, both homosexual and heterosexual, a preliminary opportunity to interact with peers without heavy parental or teacher supervision. The universities are also sex-segregated, which again offers opportunity for same sex relationships to go unnoticed.

HEALTH

Saudi Arabia has a national health care system that provides health care free-of-charge to all its citizens. Approximately 11 percent of the Saudi budget is spent on public health care. The government's contribution constitutes 80 percent of all health spending in the Kingdom. The Ministry of Health and increasingly private industry provide a wide range of preventative, rehabilitative, and curative forms of care. The Red Crescent Society provides emergency services all year round and takes on the task of providing emergency health care services for pilgrims during the *Hajj* and *Umrah* at the holy cities of Mecca and Medina.

Employers sponsoring the work visas of foreign workers are required to cover their necessary health care costs. Approximately 70 percent of expatriate health care costs are covered by the employers, with the balance paid for by the employee out-of-pocket.

For many years, the Saudi government has treated the country's number of HIV/AIDS cases as though it were a shameful national secret. In 2003, the Saudi Ministry of Health finally began releasing numbers, reporting that there were 6,700 people infected with the HIV virus or AIDS. In 2004, the Ministry reported 7,800 cases. In 2006, the number of HIV/AIDS patients rose to more than 10,000 cases. This number includes approximately 600 children.[64] Officials account for this increase by better reporting practices. Other doctors, however, state that the actual number is likely to be significantly higher in a country with a population of over 27 million. One physician who regularly treats HIV/AIDS patients estimates the real number to be closer to 80,000 cases in Saudi Arabia.[65]

Because of Islam's ban on nonmarital sex and intravenous drug use and because of Saudi citizenry's relative adherence to the tenets of Islam, the prevalence of HIV and other sexually transmitted diseases is expected to be low. In mosques, imams warn their congregations that AIDS is the "wrath of God" brought upon those who commit sexual deviancy.[66] Consequently, public education on HIV/AIDS and sexually transmitted diseases only focuses on contracting diseases by heterosexual methods or through blood transfusions.

According to the United Nations Development Programme, 78 percent of HIV/AIDS patients are infected through sexual intercourse. Approximately 22 percent contracted the infection through blood transfusions, sharing of needles, and mother-to-child transmission. Men represent three quarters of the cases. Almost four out of five patients are between 15 and 49 years old.[67] Approximately four out of five heterosexual women infected in the Arab world in general are infected by their husbands.[68]

Approximately three-quarters of those infected with HIV/AIDS in Saudi Arabia are foreign workers.[69] Foreigners are not eligible for the government sponsored free health care and once found to have contracted the virus, are deported from the country. The harsh deportation policy of foreign HIV/AIDS patients decreases reporting by foreign workers and strengthens the cloak of silence around the disease.

Though the government has recently begun to implement programs to educate the public about HIV/AIDS, the social stigma and religious taboos around sex and sexuality depresses efforts to curb its spread. The stigma attached to the transmission of the disease contributes to the fact that few public and private hospitals do not offer the free health care services to HIV/AIDS patients paid for by the government. In the government sponsored public education campaign, there is no mention of safe homosexual practices in the prevention of the spread of AIDS. Furthermore, many Saudis view HIV/AIDS as a foreign disease and thus feel less vulnerable to it.

Because of the fear of persecution, there are no available statistics on what percentage of the LGBT population is infected with HIV/AIDS in Saudi Arabia or what percentage of the HIV/AIDS population is gay.

POLITICS AND LAW

The political history of Saudi Arabia is an integral part of the history of the Middle East. By the middle of the 18th century, the House of Saud had joined the Wahhabi sect. In the 1700s, the Wahhabis were a militant and puritanical branch of Sunni Islam. In the early 1900s, with Wahhabism as a catalyzing force, the members of the Al-Saud Dynasty conquered the provinces on the Arabian Peninsula by military force. In 1932, the modern-day Kingdom of Saudi Arabia was established by King Abdulaziz bin Abdulrahman Al-Saud. The Kingdom was built and the provinces unified with Wahhabism as a fundamental pillar.[70] Though today Wahhabism is not as strictly practiced as it was in the 18th and 19th centuries, the Wahhabi doctrine still has considerable influence on modern Saudi life.

The Saudi Constitution provides that the Qur'an and the Sunnah comprise the substantive constitution of the country.[71] Sharia Law is the basis of governance. Article 3 of the Constitution provides that "The Allegiance Institution will abide by the teachings of the Qur'an and the Sunnah. It will also preserve the state's entity, protect the Royal Family's unity and cooperation as well as the national unity and the interests of the people."[72]

Saudi Arabia's central political institution is its monarchy. In 2006, the Allegiance Institution was established allowing a committee of princes to vote on the eligibility of future kings and crown princes.[73] The committee is comprised of the sons and grandsons of King Abdul Aziz. The committee members vote for one of three princes who are nominated by the acting king.

No political, social, religious, or civic group could openly support LGBT rights or the LGBT community in any form without fear of persecution. The Green Party of Saudi Arabia, which promotes the worldwide Green Movement, is the only political group in the Kingdom that has defended LGBT rights. They have also called for the emancipation of women and a greater awareness of gender identity and sexual orientation that goes beyond the binary male/female conceptualization. Because political parties are forbidden, the Green Party of Saudi Arabia is an underground organization functioning outside the bounds of the law. It includes Saudi residents as well as expatriates. Their Web site, including their position papers, is blocked from Internet users in Saudi Arabia.

Sharia Law

The Prophet Mohammed taught Islam as a way of life, governing all aspects of spiritual, interpersonal, and political interactions. As a result, traditional Islam does not recognize a separation between religion and politics, nor does it make a distinction between religious law and secular politics. Sharia dictates rules on one's spiritual and ritual duties, as well as rules of a social, political, and judicial nature, including family law and criminal law. It is divinely ordained and cannot be mutated by the will or intelligence of its followers.

Sharia Law was developed in the first 400 years of Islam by recognized Islamic scholars and clergy to serve as a comprehensive system of laws and principles by which Muslims are to lead their lives. Common sources to all countries' version of Sharia is the Qur'an and the Sunnah.[74] Certain laws are then developed by Islamic scholars, lawyers, and well- established imams. Some laws are considered divine, universal, and timeless, for example, the restriction on drinking alcohol.

Sources of Sharia Law vary among Muslim countries and among sects within Islam. For Sunni Muslims, Sharia can also include popular consensus within a community or state as a secondary source where permitted by the primary sources. In instances where there is no established rule for a particular situation, Islamic scholars use *qiya,* a system of logical reasoning, including by analogy, to come to a decision. Shi'a Muslims, however, have a different approach, for example, rejecting the validity of reasoning by analogy and community will in determining Sharia Law. Local customs and pre- and post-Islamic cultural norms within a particular country often determine Sharia Law. Though some strict constructionist Islamic scholars will debate the validity of this source, more often than not, well-established cultural practices in a community enjoy institutional support regardless of its mention in the Qur'an or Sunnah.

While commonly accepted cultural practices within subcultures of Islam have the opportunity to be incorporated into the Sharia over time, specific practices that are unique to the LGBT community will not be included in the foreseeable future. Because homosexuality is banned in Islam, recognition of practices particular to the LGBT community cannot rise to the level of commonly accepted practices.

Most countries in the Middle East, Asia, and North Africa with majority or significant Muslim populations maintain a secular court system as well as a religious court system. Saudi Arabia, among a few others including Iran, however, has one religious court system that regulates all areas of jurisprudence under Sharia.

Freedom of Speech and Press

Freedom of the press and freedom of speech are not available in Saudi Arabia. All forms of media, as well as private speech, are regulated. Individuals have even been known to be imprisoned for statements made in small private gatherings. Internet, satellite television, radio, and other forms of communication from the outside world are strictly censored. Access to content considered un-Islamic is restricted. Even wire-tapping of phone lines, which are government controlled, is a common concern for human rights activists in the Kingdom.

Saudi and foreign media is replete with articles on the Saudi police and the Mutaween's pursuit of squelching all signs of gay activity in the Kingdom. Other articles report in brief the sentencing or execution of those convicted of homosexuality. Information or material promoting, supporting or even appearing to support homosexuality is prohibited in Saudi Arabia.[75] Stories with in-depth, critical coverage, offering differing view points are found only in foreign media outlets. The Saudi media walks a fine line in reporting such crimes, giving some of the facts, but not providing balanced coverage. Often what is left out of the Saudi media reports are firsthand interviews with the arrested or any statements that contradict official government reports of the events in question. Relevant human rights organizations are not interviewed nor are statistics or any information on the gay community in Saudi Arabia cited. As a result, the Saudi news stories end up serving as iterative cautionary tales for those who might be thinking about engaging in such activities.

Freedom to Assemble

In 2005, the Saudi police raided a hotel that was to be the site of a gay beauty pageant organized by four foreigners and one Saudi national on the occasion of

Eid.[76] The disbanding of many gay weddings by police or the Mutaween are frequently reported. Participants who do not get away in time are arrested and sometimes convicted on a variety of charges. Not only is being party to a gay wedding banned, but merely attending a gay wedding can bring legal trouble to guests. In 2004, 50 persons were held for questioning for "allegedly attending a gay wedding" in holy city of Medina.[77] When the event was raided, guests fled the scene for fear of coming under the scrutiny of the Commission for the Promotion of Virtue and Prevention of Vice. Reports of gay parties being broken up are also commonplace. In 2005, police arrested 92 people in a raid on a gay party in al-Qatif. Many were wearing women's clothes and make-up, and some wore wigs. So far none of them have been sentenced in court."[78] There was little follow up coverage on this case in the media, and little is known about what became of this group.

Legal Restrictions and Sodomy

Homosexuality, though illegal, is not clearly defined in Sharia Law, instead leaving it to local enforcers to make ad hoc assessments often based on spurious evidence and vaguely worded indictments. Not only is homosexuality illegal in Saudi Arabia, but the penalties for being convicted of homosexuality are among the most severe in the world. The Kingdom is one of seven countries in the world that still utilizes capital punishment for convicted homosexuals.[79] Other punishments include imprisonment and flogging.

Under Sharia Law, sodomy is considered a form of adultery and is punished by stoning to death if the convicted is married and 100 lashes and banishment if the convicted is unmarried. To obtain a conviction, Saudi law requires that either four confessions are required on four different occasions or four male witnesses must attest to having witnessed the event.

There are conflicting reports on how often alleged homosexuals are convicted for homosexual acts as opposed to other crimes such as rape, assault, blackmail, and pornography. Other reports conflict on whether Saudi citizens are pursued for their apparent homosexuality: "Some gay foreigners were deported in the 1990s, but no Saudi has ever been prosecuted for being a homosexual."[80] There seems to be no doubt, however, that the laws are applied more harshly towards foreigner laborers from Asia and Africa than Saudi citizens or Western executives.

To enforce Wahhabi rules of behavior, the government established the Commission for the Promotion of Virtue and Prevention of Vice (CPVPV). The Mutaween, or religious police, are the enforcement arm of the CPVPV. The Mutaween are entrusted with enforcing Sharia and have the power to arrest, with force if necessary, unrelated males and females found socializing with one another as well as anyone suspected of violating the sex segregation ban, Muslim dietary restrictions, or the ban on homosexuality, prostitution, and drinking alcohol. They can seize consumer products and media items considered un-Islamic including CDs, DVDs, books, or non-Muslim religious paraphernalia.

Their activities have been widely criticized both by foreign as well as Saudi entities for use of excessive force, creating a KGB-like atmosphere of fear and mistrust, harassing individuals and businesses, and extorting favors and bribes. The gay community particularly lives in fear of persecution. Raids on gay and alleged gay events are routinely conducted, with only a smattering reported in the government controlled media.

Punishment under Sharia has come under heightened scrutiny in the press and by international human rights organization, particularly in cases of extreme physical punishment such as death by stoning, flogging, lashing, and dismemberment. The media particularly focuses on cases in which women and members of the LGBT community, or those suspected of being part of the same, have been subject to harsh punishments.

Saudi Arabia became a signatory to the United Nations Convention against Torture and Other Cruel, Inhuman or Degrading Treatment or Punishment in 1997. However the practice of flogging of convicted criminals, including those convicted of crimes related to homosexuality, continues. According to Human Rights Watch and the International Commission of Jurists: "Saudi Arabia has advertised its contempt for the basic rights to privacy, fair trials, and freedom from torture."[81] In 1996, Saudi Arabia ratified the United Nations Convention on the Rights of the Child. In 2005, however when the UN Committee on the Rights of the Child reviewed Saudi Arabia's record, it condemned them for enforcing the death penalty on juveniles. Islamic scholars and other defenders of Sharia argue that these rules are meant to serve as a deterrent to crime.[82]

Established in 2004 by royal decree, the National Society for Human Rights is the first independent nongovernmental organization created to ensure the Kingdom is implementing provisions in keeping with human rights principles. Reporting directly to the king, one of its goals is to promote human rights as understood by the international human rights community. At the end of March 2009, the society released its 2008 Report to the Shoura Council. In the 100-page report, the society presented a scathing litany of abuses committed by the religious police including physical torture, arbitrary arrests, and a variety of other human rights violations.

However, some subjects covered by international human rights organizations are still taboo for Saudi's National Society for Human Rights. The society does not specifically address the persecution of members of the LGBT community. Additionally, rights that affect the LGBT community's pursuit of decreased harassment and scrutiny in the Kingdom that are not in the society's purview include fair trials for prisoners, the right to assemble as a political party, freedom of press, freedom of speech, and expression. Some believe it is because of its dependence on the government for a business license and patronage as well as the fact that members are current or former members of the government.

RELIGION AND SPIRITUALITY

In the 1960s and 1970s, Saudi Arabia experienced intense economic development, experimentation with liberal policies, and open communication with the West. This liberal trend, however, came to a standstill in 1979 when the Grand Mosque in the holy city of Mecca was attacked by conservative critics of the Saudi monarchy. A small group of zealots laid siege on the Grand Mosque and went on a shooting spree within its walls to call for a return to conservative values. Though the group was numerically insignificant, the message behind the take-over resonated with many clergy and lay people throughout the Kingdom.

The 1980s saw an emergence of politically active conservative movements within Islam throughout the Arab world. In the West, these movements were often referred to as fundamentalist. The primary goal of these movements was the increased institutionalization of Islam within governmental, educational, and political institutions. Though Saudi Arabia already used the Qur'an and Islamic principles as guideposts for the creation of their modern state, the Kingdom also experienced a wave of conservative thought. One of the missions of the Saudi royal family is to spreading Islam. In Saudi Arabia, Wahhabi Islam is practiced.

Since the dawn of Islam, Saudi Arabia has always enjoyed a revered status in the Islamic world. Within its borders are the two holiest cities, the city of Mecca: towards which all Muslims pray five times a day, and the city of Medina: the Prophet Mohammad's home after the Hijrah and the site of his burial. Pilgrimage to the Saudi city of Mecca is one of the five pillars of Islam. Because the two main Islamic holy cities, Mecca and Medina, are located in Saudi Arabia, the government of Saudi Arabia shoulders the great responsibility of being the keepers of Islamic faith. Saudi royalty has viewed guardianship of Mecca, Medina, and the two Holy Mosques within as a primary duty. In the past several decades, the monarchy has increased its allocation of resources towards facilitating a safe and comfortable pilgrimage for Muslim pilgrims. In 1986, to affirm the Saudi monarchy's role in this most important rite of passage for every Muslim in the world, then Saudi King Fahd relinquished the title of His Majesty and adopted in its place the title of Custodian of the Two Holy Mosques.

As keepers of the Islamic faith, the Saudi monarchy holds up Saudi Arabia as a paragon of Islamic living, employing one of the most conservative interpretations of Islam among Muslim countries. Interpretations of traditional Islam and Sharia remain strict, leaving little room for injecting progressive interpretations of the faith. As such, this leaves little chance for members of the LGBT community to make future progress in asserting their presence, accessing rights, or even meeting openly.

The majority of Muslims in Saudi Arabia are members of the Sunni sect, with an approximate 10–15 percent belonging to the Shi'a minority that primarily live in the Eastern Province.[83] The Saudi government strictly enforces a conservative version of Sunni Islam. All Muslims must follow the official interpretation of Islam and deviation can result in revocation of business licenses, fines, corporal punishment, imprisonment, or even harassment for more minor infractions by the religious police, the Mutaween.

Foreign workers comprise the majority of Saudi Arabia's non-Muslim population. Estimates of the Kingdom's foreign population vary from five to eight million depending on the source. The majority of foreign workers are Muslim, but include a range of other religions. Detailed statistics of the religious backgrounds of foreigners in Saudi Arabia are not available, but include Christians, Hindus, Jews, Parsis, Mandeans, Sikhs, and Buddhists.

Despite the merger of religious, political, and social spheres within Saudi Arabia, the country does offer relief to religious groups who do not follow the country's dominant religion of Islam. Members of other religions are allowed to live according to their religious law within their communities if they accepted the position of *dhimmis,* or "protected person." Classic Islamic political and legal texts define a *dhimmi* as a person living within a Muslim state who is a member of an officially tolerated non-Muslim religion. Initially, the term referred to "People of the Book" living under Muslim rule, such as Jews and Christians. Later the term expanded to include other religions such as Zoroastrianism, Mandaeism, Sikhism, Buddhism, and Hinduism. *Dhimmi* status involves the recognition of Muslim authority, special taxes, prohibition on proselytizing to Muslims, and various political restrictions.

Despite *dhimmi* status, freedom of religion for non-Muslims is not a protected right. Non-Muslims are barred from public practice of their religions. Non-Muslims are prohibited from proselytizing in Saudi Arabia and there are extremely severe apostasy laws enforced on those who have chosen to convert out of the Islamic faith.[84] Because proselytizing is illegal, there are restrictions against importing markers of other faiths such as Bibles, rosaries, crucifixes, and items with religious symbols such as the Star of David. While ostensibly non-Muslims are permitted to bring into the country what they need for personal worship, there have been reports that even travelers carrying a single copy of the Bible have had them confiscated at Saudi customs. Because *Dhimmi* is a status given only to religious groups and not members of social or political groups, the LGBT community would not be able to avail themselves of this protected status.

Saudi Arabia's ban on homosexuality in all forms is derived from Islam's rejection of homosexuality. Worse than fornication, homosexuality is considered a sin in Islam and the Qur'an refers to it as an abomination.[85] There are many passages in the holy books of Islam: the Qur'an and Hadith, which have been cited to show Islam's rejection of homosexuality. Most of these passages specifically refer to male-male same-sex behavior. Among these is Qur'an Sura 4:21: "And if two (men) of you commit (adultery), then hurt them both; but if they turn again and amend, leave them alone, verily, God is easily turned, compassionate." This verse seems to recommend physical punishment for men who engage in same-sex sexual activity, but they can be released if they renounce the practice.

Similar to Genesis 19 in the Old Testament, there are a series of passages in the Qur'an that link the sin of same-sex sexual activities among the men of Sodom to God's eventual destruction of the city.[86] When Lot denounces men in Sodom for their homosexual activities warning them in various ways about the terror that will befall them if they continue to sin in this manner, he is threatened with expulsion.

> And Lot, when he said to his people, "Do ye approach an abomination which no one in all the world ever anticipated you in? Verily, ye approach men with lust rather than women- nay, ye are a people who exceed." But his people's answer only was to say, "Turn them out of your village, verily, they are a people who pretend to purity." But we saved him and his people, except his wife, who was of those who lingered; and we rained down upon them a rain;—see then how was the end of the sinners![87]

When God later kills all citizens of Sodom, ostensibly for their same-sex activities, Lot and his family is spared.

The Hadith is a collection of the words and deeds of the Prophet Mohammed that have become important tools for determining the Islamic way of life. In the Hadith, the Prophet Mohammed explains the gravity of the sin of homosexuality: "Allah curses the one who does the actions (homosexual practices) of the people of Lut"[88] repeating it three times; and he states in another Hadith: "If a man comes upon a man then they are both adulterers."[89] In another section, while outlining the punishment for two men engaged in homosexual sex acts the Hadith states: "Kill the one that is doing it and also kill the one that it is being done to."

Effeminate men are not spared in the Hadith with several passages referring to them negatively. One passage states: "The Prophet cursed effeminate men (those men who are in the similitude (assume the manners of women) and those women who assume the manners of men, and he said, 'Turn them out of your houses.'"[90]

There are relatively fewer mentions of lesbian sexual activity in the Islamic holy texts as compared to male-male sexual relations. As in the Hebrew Scriptures, when homosexuality is denounced in the Qur'an, only male homosexual activity is referenced and lesbian practices are not specifically mentioned. The Hadith has several references to lesbian activities. In one Hadith, the Prophet Mohammed is cited as saying: "If a woman comes upon a woman, they are both Adulteresses." Scholars have stated that it is the responsibility of the authorities to punish lesbians in a manner appropriate to the crime.[91]

Terminology for female homosexuality is ambiguous in Arabic and varies by usage. *Sihaq* can mean rubbing, pounding, female masturbation, or even tribadism depending on the context and usage. In the Hadith, the Prophet Mohammed, addresses lesbian activities as a sin: "*Sihaq* (i.e. lesbian sexual activity) of women is *zina* (illegitimate sexual intercourse) among them."[92]

Another term, *musahaqa,* has a variety of meanings that also depend on usage. Some references use it interchangeably with *sihaq,* referring to the acts involved such as tribadism. Others use *musahaqa* to mean female homosexuality or lesbianism in general. Sometimes it is used to refer to rubbing of the female genitalia, whether it is between two women or between a man and a woman.

Other passages address effeminate men and masculine women that gives more conservative interpreters license to prohibit transvestitism, bisexuality, and even apparent displays of gender confounding behavior.

Because of Saudi Arabia's role as the conservator of Islam for the Muslim world, Islam's ban on homosexuality is taken very seriously in the Kingdom. Saudi Arabia's version of Sharia punishes homosexuality severely, including capital punishment. This severity stems from Saudi's conservative interpretations of all aspects of Islamic life.

VIOLENCE

The Saudi media regularly provides short reports on the government's announcements of arrests, convictions, and executions of homosexuals. Typically this information is obtained from government officials. Little is known apart from what the government itself reports to a press strapped by strict censorship guidelines.

According to Amnesty International and media reports, both Saudi and foreign, the Sharia courts regularly sentence convicted criminals to corporal punishment.[93] Beatings, floggings, and amputations are acceptable forms of punishment. Amputations are typically prescribed as punishment for theft. Floggings frequently serve as the main or as an additional punishment for most criminal offences, and are carried out on a daily basis. The highest number of lashes as recorded by Amnesty International in 2008 was 7,000 against two men convicted of sodomy in October by a court in al-Baha. Children have been among those sentenced to floggings. At least three people had their right hand amputated at the wrist after being convicted of theft.

A few examples illustrate the extent to which homosexuality is criminalized in the Kingdom, but by no means are these incidents isolated. In September 1996, Saudi Arabian authorities sentenced 24 Filipino workers to 200 lashes each following their arrest for homosexual behavior and they were ordered to be deported after the sentence was carried out. In 2000, nine Saudi men were sentenced to lashings and extensive prison terms for cross-dressing and engaging in homosexual relations.[94]

In 2005, more than 100 men were sentenced to one year's imprisonment and flogging for attending a gay wedding at which they expressed "deviant sexual behaviour," which included dancing and "behaving like women."[95] Some were sentenced with up to 2,000 lashes, a punishment that can prove fatal.[96] Ninety men were arrested for attending a gay event, only two months after the gay wedding arrests in Jeddah. Salaam, a Canadian organization for LGBT Muslims and Al-Fatiha, a U.S.-based organization for Muslim sexual and gender minorities condemned the arrests and called for their countries to pressure Saudi officials to release the arrested.[97]

Every year, scores of individuals are arrested and convicted of homosexuality, sodomy, and related crimes in Saudi Arabia. International human rights organizations have long decried the use of corporal punishment as cruel, inhuman, and degrading to individuals whose main crime is to appear sexually deviant to a conservative religious police and judicial system. Human Rights Watch Director of LGBT Rights Program, Scott Long stated that "subjecting the victims to floggings is torture, pure and simple."[98]

Death Penalty for Homosexuality

Saudi Arabia applies the death penalty for a wide range of offences, including offences with no lethal consequences such as drug trafficking, rape, and pornography. Murderers, rapists, and drug smugglers are usually executed by public beheading.[99] In 2000, a total of 123 individuals were executed for a variety of crimes; 71 of those executed were foreign workers from African and Asian countries.[100]

Saudi Arabia is one of seven countries that still employs the death penalty for homosexuality.[101] In 2000, three Yemeni men were executed for homosexuality, cross dressing, and child molestation. The Saudi Interior Ministry released a statement saying that a court had found the three men guilty of "committing the extreme obscenity of homosexuality and imitating women."[102] In the same year, three Saudi men were executed for raping children and child pornography.[103] In 2008, two men convicted of homosexuality were decapitated by sword for allegedly beating and raping a man.[104]

International organizations such as the United Nations, Amnesty International, Human Rights Watch, The International Gay and Lesbian Human Rights Commission (IGLHRC), as well as more liberal Muslim organizations such as North American-based *Salaam* and *Al-Fatiha* have tried to keep tabs on the situation from outside the country. International human rights standards disfavor the use of the death penalty for nonhomicide convictions. For years, Amnesty International has called for a moratorium on the death penalty in each report it issues on Saudi Arabia for "offences with no lethal consequences."[105] The IGLHRC has regularly protested the execution of men in the Kingdom based on their sexual orientation.[106] An additional objection to capital punishment in Saudi Arabia by international organizations is that it is imposed trials that invariably fail to meet the most basic international standards of trial fairness. In 2002, Amnesty International launched a letter writing campaign expressing concern that the three men "may have been executed primarily because of their sexual orientation and seeking urgent clarification of the exact charges and evidence brought against them, together with information on their trial proceedings."[107]

In response to protests from international human rights organizations, in 2002, the Saudi government unofficially implied that it would only carry out capital punishment in cases of pedophilia, rape, sexual attack, or murder.[108] International human rights organizations have long suspected, however, that some convicted of homosexuality and other crimes such as raping children, theft, blackmail, assault, murder, might simply be guilty of engaging in homosexual acts alone with other charges falsely added. For example, in 2002, Amnesty International and the International Gay and Lesbian Human Rights Commission (IGLHRC) released action alerts after three men were executed, "possibly solely on account of their homosexual conduct."[109] The Interior Ministry announced that the three men "were convicted of homosexual acts, adding vaguely-worded charges of 'luring children and harming others' without providing any further details. The trial proceedings of the three men remain shrouded in secrecy."[110]

There is no available information on violence perpetrated on members of the LGBT community by nonstate actors. Hate and bias crimes are not recorded. A victim of a hate crime on the basis of his or her sexuality would be extremely disinclined to report it since it is unlikely that the perpetrator would be punished and it would be undue attention on the victim for possibly being a homosexual—an illegal act in the Kingdom.

OUTLOOK FOR THE 21ST CENTURY

Despite the apparent freedom that sex segregation affords gay life in Saudi Arabia, because of the severe punishment for homosexuality in Saudi Arabia, the LGBT community is prevented from expressing their sexuality openly in public. Notwithstanding wide-spread criticism from international human rights organizations, foreign media, and the LGBT communities the world over, the Saudi government insists that its treatment of the LGBT community is not as harsh as reports make it seem and that its first priority is to uphold Sunni Islamic morality. Given the importance that Saudi Arabia places on adhering to one of the most conservative versions of Islam, cultural mores will be slow to change in the Kingdom.

The Internet and other forms of media have created a new world of possibilities for the LGBT community in the Kingdom. In cyberspace, online communities within Saudi Arabia, in the greater Muslim world, and the world at large, offer previously unheard of access to support and information. Those exploring their sexuality, whether homosexual, heterosexual or bisexual, are afforded access to information that was previously dangerous or impossible to obtain. As technology advances, and as such technologies become available to more socioeconomic groups, the Saudi government will be hard pressed to contain these forms of interactions.

In other countries, the 21st century holds the possibility of increased rights and increased visibility, better health care, and acceptance from the community at large for the LGBT community. In the Kingdom of Saudi Arabia, the best the LGBT community can aspire to is to be left alone.

The manager of www.gaymiddleeast.com, A.S. Getenio, stated Saudi Arabia was loosening some of their restrictions on access to gay web portals because of concern about the bad press it was generating in the international arena, "at the time it was involved in a multimillion dollar advertising campaign in the U.S. to improve its image."[111] Specific attention on LGBT issues, combined with general reform of the criminal justice system in Saudi Arabia, will allow more members of the LGBT community in the Kingdom to live their lives in peace. Better reporting practices and increased freedom of the press will aid in accurate reporting on the issue and give further incentive to the police and religious police to leave the LGBT community alone.

Because of the country's conservative religious code and the lack of separation between religion and politics, the fact that homosexuality is illegal and severely punished is not going to change. The areas in which change is feasible is at the arrest, trial, and sentencing phases. Changes in legal definitions could result in fewer convictions; for example, narrowing the definition of homosexuality so as to exclude activities accepted in other countries. This shift would allow the Kingdom to maintain the necessary appearance of outlawing homosexuality without unnecessarily violating human rights and raising the ire of the international community and the more liberal Muslim communities.

RESOURCE GUIDE

Suggested Reading

John R. Bradley, *Saudi Arabia Exposed: Inside a Kingdom in Crisis* (New York: Palgrave Macmillian, 2006).

John R. Bradley, "Queer Sheik: The Strange Emergence of Gay Culture in Saudi Arabia," *The New Republic,* March 5, 2004.

K. El-Rouayheb, *Before Homosexuality in the Arab-Islamic World, 1500–1800* (Chicago: University of Chicago Press, 2005).

Nadya Labi, "The Kingdom in the Closet," *The Atlantic,* May 2007, http://www.theatlantic.com/doc/200705/gay-saudi-arabia.

Michael T. Luongo, *Gay Travels in The Muslim World* (New York: Routledge, 2007).

Stephen O. Murray, *Islamic Homosexualities: Culture, History and Literature* (New York: New York University Press, 1997).

Liz Stanton, *What Happens in Saudi Arabia, Stays In Saudi Arabia (Except For This Book): A Three-Year Adventure* (Bloomington, IN: AuthorHouse, 2008).

Brian Whitaker, *Unspeakable Love; Gay and Lesbian Life in the Middle East* (Los Angeles: University of California Press, 2006).

Web Sites

Global Gays, http://www.GlobalGayz.com.

Gay Middle East, www.GayMiddleEast.com.

Towleroad, http://www.towleroad.com/saudi_arabia/.

http://cyber.law.harvard.edu/filtering/saudiarabia/SA-U.html.
     Partial list of Web sites banned in Saudi Arabia.

http://www.globalgayz.com/saudi-news.html.
     Compiled news stories on Saudi Arabia gays in the news 2000–2005.

http://www.globalgayz.com/saudi-news-06.html.
     Compiled news stories on Saudi Arabia gays in the news 2006–2009.

NOTES

1. "Saudi Arabia," Nation Master, 2009, http://www.nationmaster.com/country/sa-saudi-arabia.

2. Ibid.

3. *Ulema* is an educated class of Muslim legal scholars.

4. The Saudi Network, "Saudi Education and Human Resources," http://www.the-saudi.net/saudi-arabia/education.htm.

5. CIA, "Middle East: Saudi Arabia," *The World Factbook,* April 2009, https://www.cia.gov/library/publications/the-world-factbook/geos/sa.html.

6. UNESCO Institute for Statistics, http://stats.uis.unesco.org/unesco/Table Viewer/document.aspx?ReportId=121&IF_Language=eng&BR_Country=6820.

7. "Education Statistics," Nation Master, http://www.nationmaster.com/graph/edu_pub_spe_on_edu_tot_of_gov_exp-public-spending-total-government-expenditure, retrieved on February 25, 2009.

8. The Saudi Network, "Saudi Education and Human Resources."

9. Ibid.

10. Saudi Arabia Ministry of Education, "About Saudi Arabia," http://www.moe.gov.sa/openshare/englishcon/About-Saud/Education3.htm_cvt.html.

11. Ibid.

12. UNESCO Institute for Statistics, http://stats.uis.unesco.org/unesco/Table Viewer/document.aspx?ReportId=121&IF_Language=eng&BR_Country=6820.

13. Wahhabi is the conservative strain of Islam that Saudi Arabia follows based on the teachings of the 18th-century founder of the Wahhabiyya movement, Sheikh Muhammad Ibn Abd Al-Wahhab.

14. Abdulla Muhammad Al-Zaid, *Education in Saudi Arabia: A Model with A Difference,* trans. Omar Ali Afifi (1982), 39. See Steven Stalinsky's, "Saudi Arabia's Education System: Curriculum, Spreading Saudi Education to the World and the Official Saudi Position on Education Policy," *The Middle East Media Research Institute* 12 (December 20, 2002): http://www.memri.org/bin/articles.cgi?Area=sr&ID=SR01202.

Al-Zaid is a former member of the teaching staff at King Abd Al-Aziz University, former chairman of the department of education, and former director general of education for the western province of Saudi Arabia.

15. Hamad I. Salloom, *Education in Saudi Arabia,* 2nd ed. (Beltsville, MD: Amana, 1995).

16. Saudi Arabia Ministry of Education, http://www.moe.gov.sa/stats_trb/stud_main.html.

17. Saudi Arabia Ministry of Education, "About Saudi Arabia," http://www.moe.gov.sa/openshare/englishcon/About-Saud/Education3.htm_cvt.html.

18. UNESCO Institute for Statistics, http://stats.uis.unesco.org/unesco/Table Viewer/document.aspx?ReportId=121&IF_Language=eng&BR_Country=6820 (accessed February 16, 2009).

19. Ibid.

20. Ibid.

21. Amnesty International, "Report on Saudi Arabia 2001," http://www.unhcr.org/refworld/pdfid/3b20dc344.pdf (accessed March 29, 2009).

22. Roger Hardy, "Unemployment: the New Saudi Challenge," *BBC News,* October 4, 2006, http://news.bbc.co.uk/2/hi/business/5406328.stm.

23. The original story in the Okaz newspaper was published in Arabic. While it could not be located, the expose is extensively cited in literature on gay life in Muslim communities and in Saudi Arabia including John Bradley's "Queer Sheik: The Strange Emergence of Gay Culture in Saudi Arabia," *The New Republic,* March 5, 2004, http://www.selvesandothers.org/article6521.html and http://www.glapn.org/sodomylaws/world/saudi_arabia/saudi news025.htm.

It is also referenced in Islamic Evil Blog, "Sexual Perversion in Islam" May 5, 2007, http://www.islam-watch.org/Others/Islamic-sexual-perversion.htm, and Bill Andriette, "Arabian Nights," *The Guide,* July 2007, http://www.guidemag.com/magcontent/invokemagcontent.cfm?ID=97754AE4–4B16–4DCB-A90EA5A2B960F3B4.

24. The weekends in Saudi Arabia, as in many other Muslim countries, are observed on Friday and Saturday.

25. Sabria S. Jawhar, "Are Women Protected?" *The Saudi Gazette,* http://www.saudigazette.com.sa/index.cfm?method=home.regcon&contentID=2008102920525.

26. Name of the interviewee was changed as a condition of interview.

27. Nadya Labi, "The Kingdom in the Closet," *The Atlantic,* May 2007, http://www. theatlantic.com/doc/200705/gay-saudi-arabia.

28. Names in Labi's pieces were changed by the author.

29. Labi, "The Kingdom in the Closet."

30. Looklex Encyclopedia, "Saudi Arabia: Economy," http://looklex.com/e.o/saudi_ arabia.economy.htm.

31. *Arab News,* http://www.arabnews.com/?page=6&section=0&article=95554&d= 29&m=4&y=2007.

32. Ibid.

33. Hardy, "Unemployment, the New Saudi Challenge."

34. "Employers Skirting Saudization Quota Pledged Iron Fist: Raid Qusti," *Arab News,* December, 5, 2006, http://www.arabnews.com/?page=1&section=0&article=89550 &d=5&m=12&y=2006.

35. CIA, "Middle East: Saudi Arabia."

36. Hardy, "Unemployment, the New Saudi Challenge."

37. *Arab News,* http://www.arabnews.com/?page=1&section=0&article=114315&d =15&m=9&y=2008.

38. See http://www.shura.gov.sa/EnglishSite/EIntrd.htm.

39. At the time this chapter was written (2009), workplace harassment legislation was still being negotiated in Saudi Arabia.

40. "Hairdressing: A Trade Looked Down Upon in Saudi Society," *Arab News,* February 9, 2007, http://www.zawya.com/printstory.cfm?storyid=ZAWYA20070209061602 &l=061600070209.

41. See http://www.shura.gov.sa/EnglishSite/EIntrd.htm.

42. United Nations Development Programme, Kingdom of Saudi Arabia, "HIV/ AIDS," 2009, http://www.undp.org.sa/sa/index.php/en/our-work/practice-areas/hiv-aids.

43. Lydia Georgi, "Saudi Seeks to Break AIDS Taboo," *Middle East Online,* March 29, 2005, http://www.middle-east-online.com/english/?id=15101.

44. Manal Quota and Maryam Yamani, "AIDS? What AIDS?," *Arab News,* August 7, 2005, http://www.arabnews.com/?page=1&section=0&article=68051&d=7&m=8&y= 2005.

45. United Nations Development Program, Kingdom of Saudi Arabia, "Millennium Development Goals 2005," 2005, p. 46, http://www.undp.org.sa/sa/documents/home/ mdgrsa2005.pdf.

46. Georgi, "Saudi Seeks to Break AIDS Taboo."

47. United Nations Development Programme, Kingdom of Saudi Arabia, "HIV/ AIDS."

48. United Nations Development Program, Kingdom of Saudi Arabia, "Millennium Development Goals 2005."

49. Ibid. Saudi Arabia is not alone in this practice. Other countries that follow this practice include the United States, China, South Korea, Iraq, and Brunei.

50. This treatment of foreign nationals is not exclusive to HIV/AIDS patients. Any foreign national found to have a serious medical condition is soon deported.

51. *Encyclopedia of Islam and the Muslim World* (Woodbridge, CT: MacMillan Reference, 2004), 316.

52. The Feminist Sexual Ethics Project, Brandeis University, "Special Focus: Islam: Same-Sex Sexual Activity and Lesbian and Bisexual Women," 2002, http://www.brandeis. edu/projects/fse/Pages/femalehomosexuality.html.

53. Labi, "The Kingdom in the Closet."

54. Ibid.

55. John R. Bradley, *Saudi Arabia Exposed: Inside a Kingdom in Crisis* (New York: Palgrave Macmillan, 2005).

56. Labi, "The Kingdom in the Closet."

57. Ibid.

58. Chapter 3, Article 9, The Constitution of Saudi Arabia, Adopted March 1992 by Royal Decree of King Fahd.

59. Sarah Kershaw, "Saudi Arabia Awakes to the Perils of Inbreeding," *New York Times,* May 1, 2003, http://www.nytimes.com/2003/05/01/world/saudi-arabia-awakes-to-the-perils-of-inbreeding.html?sec=&spon=&pagewanted=2; Howard Schneider, "Saudi Intermarriages Have Genetic Costs," *Washington Post Foreign Service,* January 16, 2000, p. A01, http://www.unl.edu/rhames/courses/212/arab_inbreed/arab_inbreed.htm.

60. Jack Wheeler, "Saudi Arabia's Cousin-Marriage Epidemic: Analyst Cites Negative Health Effects of Age-Old Practice in the Kingdom," *WND,* May 11, 2005, http://www.wnd.com/news/article.asp?ARTICLE_ID=44204.

61. Labi, "The Kingdom in the Closet."

62. Ibid.

63. John Bradley, "Saudi Gays Flaunt New Freedoms: 'Straights Can't Kiss in Public or Hold Hands Like Us,'" *The Independent,* February 20, 2004, http://www.independent.co.uk/news/world/middle-east/saudi-gays-flaunt-new-freedoms-straights-cant-kiss-in-public-or-hold-hands-like-us-570584.html.

64. United Nations Development Programme, Kingdom of Saudi Arabia, "HIV/AIDS."

65. Hassan Fattah, "Saudi Arabia Begins to Face Hidden AIDS Problem," *The New York Times,* August 8, 2006, http://www.nytimes.com/2006/08/08/world/middleeast/08saudi.html. Retrieved on January 10, 2009.

66. Ibid.

67. United Nations Development Programme, Kingdom of Saudi Arabia, "HIV/AIDS."

68. Ibid.

69. Ibid.; and Fattah, "Saudi Arabia Begins to Face Hidden AIDS Problem."

70. *Encyclopedia of Islam and the Muslim World,* 727.

71. Article 1: "The Kingdom of Saudi Arabia is a sovereign Arab Islamic state with Islam as its religion; God's Book and the Sunnah of His Prophet, God's prayers and peace be upon him, are its constitution." The Constitution of Saudi Arabia, Adopted March 1992 by Royal Decree of King Fahd.

72. Article 3, The Constitution of Saudi Arabia, Adopted March 1992 by Royal Decree of King Fahd.

73. The Allegiance Institution Law, Succession in Saudi Arabia, October 20, 2006, http://www.saudi-us-relations.org/fact-book/documents/2006/061106-allegiance-law.html.

74. For Sunni Muslims, *Sunnah* refers to the teachings and practices of the prophet Muhammad during the 23 years of his spiritual leadership.

75. M. Ghazanfar Ali Khan, "15 Held on Bootlegging, Gay Prostitution Charges," *Arab News,* August 11, 2008, http://www.arabnews.com/?page=1&section=0&article=112657&d=11&m=8&y=2008.

76. "Saudi Arabia Police Break Up Gay Beauty Contest," *Global Information Gateway,* Adnkronos International, November 7, 2005, http://www.globalgayz.com/country/Saudi%20Arabia/view/SAU/gay-saudi-arabia-news-and-repo-2.

77. "Saudis Quiz 'Gay Wedding' Guests," *BBC News,* March 1, 2004, http://news.bbc.co.uk/2/hi/middle_east/3521479.stm.

78. "Saudi Arabia Police Break Up Gay Beauty Contest."

79. International Lesbian and Gay Association. The other six countries are also Muslim dominant countries: Afghanistan, Iran, Mauritania, Pakistan, Sudan, and Yemen.

80. Bradley, "Saudi Gays Flaunt New Freedoms."

81. "Saudi Arabia: Men 'Behaving Like Women' Face Flogging Sentences Imposed for Alleged Homosexual Conduct Violate Basic Rights," *Human Rights News,* April 7, 2005, http://www.hrw.org/english/docs/2005/04/07/saudia10434.htm.

82. Jane Little, "Debate Rages over Women and Sharia," *BBC News,* June 11, 2003, http://news.bbc.co.uk/1/hi/2977446.stm.

83. Lionel Beehner, "Shia Muslims in the Mideast," Council on Foreign Relations, June 16, 2006, http://www.cfr.org/publication/10903/shiite_muslims_in_the_middle_east.html.

84. The Bureau of Democracy, Human Rights and Labor, "International Religious Freedom Report 2008, Executive Summary," http://www.state.gov/g/drl/rls/irf/2008/108351.htm.

85. Quran Sura 7:80: "And Lot, when he said to his people, 'Do ye approach an abomination which no one in all the world ever anticipated you in?'"

86. These passages include Quran Sura 7:80–84, Sura 11:78–81, Sura 26: 162–168, Sura 27: 55–57, and Sura 29: 28–31.

[Lot said] "Verily, I am to you a faithful apostle; then fear God and obey me. I do not ask you for it any hire; my hire is only with the Lord of the worlds. Do ye approach males of all the world and leave what God your Lord has created for you of your wives? nay, but ye are people who transgress!" They said, "Surely, if thou dost not desist, O Lot! thou shalt be of those who are expelled!" Said he, "Verily, I am of those who hate your deed." (Quran Sura 26: 162–68)

And (remember) Lot when he said to his people, "Verily, ye approach an abomination which no one in all the world ever anticipated you in! What! do ye approach men? and stop folks on the highway? And approach in your assembly sin?" but the answer of his people was only to say, "Bring us God's torment, if thou art of those who speak the truth!" Said he, "My Lord! help me against a people who do evil!" And when our messengers came to Abraham with the glad tidings, they said, "We are about to destroy the people of this city. Verily, the people thereof are wrong-doers." (Sura 27: 55–57 and Sura 29: 28–31)

87. Quran Sura 7: 80–84.

88. In the Quran, Lot is referred to as Lut.

89. "Death Fall as Punishment for Homosexuality," *IslamOnline,* July 22, 2003, http://www.islamonline.net/.

90. Found in Hadith collection of Sahih Bukhari (72:774).

91. "Death fall as punishment for homosexuality," *IslamOnline.*

92. "Islam and Homosexuality," *Mission Islam,* http://www.missionislam.com/knowledge/homosexuality.htm.

93. Amnesty International, "Report on Saudi Arabia 2008," http://www.amnesty.org/en/region/saudi-arabia/report-2008.

94. "Nine Saudi Transvestites Jailed," *Associated Press,* April 16, 2000, http://www.sodomylaws.org/world/saudi_arabia/saudinews02.htm.

95. Patrick Letellier, "Gay Men Sentenced to be Jailed and Flogged in Saudi Arrests," *Global Gayz,* April 8, 2005, http://www.globalgayz.com/saudi-news.html.

96. International Lesbian and Gay Organization, "International Day Against Homophobia (IDAHO) Gays Protest Saudi Brutality," May 17, 2005, http://www.ilga.org/news_results.asp?LanguageID=1&FileCategory=9&FileID=589.

97. "Gay Muslims in Canada, U.S. Denounce Escalation of Arrests in Saudi Arabia," *UK Gay News,* June 7, 2005, http://www.ukgaynews.org.uk/Archive/2005june/0702.htm.

98. Letellier, "Gay Men Sentenced to be Jailed and Flogged in Saudi Arrests."

99. "Saudi Arabia Executes Men for Sexual Assault," *Reuters,* July 11, 2000, http://www.iglhrc.org/cgi-bin/iowa/article/takeaction/globalactionalerts/639.html.

100. Amnesty International, "Saudi Arabia: An Urgent Reform of the Criminal Justice System Is Needed," August 8, 2003, http://www.amnesty.ca/resource_centre/reports/view.php?load=arcview&article=701.

101. International Lesbian and Gay Association. The other six countries are also Muslim dominant countries: Afghanistan, Iran, Mauritania, Pakistan, Sudan, and Yemen.

102. "Saudi Executes Three Yemenis for Homosexuality," *Reuters,* July 14, 2000, http://www.glapn.org/sodomylaws/world/saudi_arabia/saudinews06.htm.

103. "Saudi Arabia Executes Men for Sexual Assault."

104. Blaise Gauquelin, "Arabie Saoudite (Répression) Accusés de viol, deux homosexuels ont été décapités," Tetu.Com, December 30, 2008, http://www.tetu.com/rubrique/infos/infos_detail.php?id_news=13936. English translation by Aditya Bondyopadhyay, "Saudi Arabia: Two Homosexuals Beheaded," http://www.asylumlaw.org/docs/sexual minorities/SaudiArabia123008.pdf.

105. Amnesty International, "Saudi Arabia," August 6, 2008,http://www.amnesty.no/web.nsf/pages/FF9F53DA3147BD2DC125749D00295287.

106. "Protest the Death Penalty for Homosexual Conduct in Saudi Arabia," International Gay and Lesbian Human Rights Commission, January 8, 2002, http://www.iglhrc.org./site/iglhrc/section.php?id=5&detail=88.

107. Ibid.

108. Gauquelin, "Arabie Saoudite (Répression) Accusés de viol, deux homosexuels ont été décapités."

109. International Gay and Lesbian Human Rights Commission Action Alert, "Saudi Arabia: Protest the Death Penalty for Homosexual Conduct in Saudi Arabia," January 8, 2002, http://www.iglhrc.org/cgi-bin/iowa/article/takeaction/globalaction alerts/639.html.

110. Ibid.

111. Bradley, "Saudi Gays Flaunt New Freedoms."

VOLUME INDEX

SELECTED BIBLIOGRAPHY

GENERAL/INTERNATIONAL/UNITED STATES

Adam, Barry D., Jan Willem Duyvendak, and André Krouwel, eds. *The Global Emergence of Gay and Lesbian Politics: National Imprints of a Worldwide Movement*. Philadelphia: Temple University Press. 1999.

Aldrich, Robert. *Colonialism and Homosexuality*. New York: Routledge, 2002.

Aldrich, Robert, ed. *Gay Life and Culture: A World History*. New York: Universe Publishing, 2006.

Badgett, M. V. L. *Income Inflation: The Myth of Affluence among Gay, Lesbian, and Bisexual Americans*. Washington, D.C.: National Gay and Lesbian Task Force, 1988.

Barnett, T., and Whiteside, A. *AIDS in the Twenty-First Century: Disease and Globalization*. New York: Palgrave MacMillan, 2002.

Bech, Henning. *When Men Meet—Homosexuality and Modernity*. Cambridge: Polity Press, 1997.

Beger, Nico, Kurt Krickler, Jackie Lewis, & Maren Wuch, eds. *Equality for Lesbians and Gay Men: a Relevant Issue in the Civil and Social Dialogue*. Brussels: ILGA-Europe, 1998.

Bernstein, Elizabeth, and Laurie Schaffner, eds. *Regulating Sex: The Politics of Intimacy and Identity*. New York: Routledge, 2005.

Blasius, Mark, ed. *Sexual Identities—Queer Politics*. Princeton: Princeton University Press, 2001.

Cornog, Martha, Robert T. Francoeur, and Raymond J. Noonan. *The Continuum Complete International Encyclopedia of Sexuality*. New York: Continuum, 2004.

Dawson, J. *Gay and Lesbian Online,* 4th ed. Los Angeles: Alyson Publications, 2000.

Dreger, A. D., ed. *Intersex in the Age of Ethics*. Hagerstown, MD: University Publishing Group, 2000.

Dyer, K. *Gays in Uniform: The Pentagon's Secret Reports*. Los Angeles, CA: Alyson Publications, 1990.

Dynes, Wayne, ed. *The Encyclopedia of Homosexuality*. New York: Garland Publishing, 1990.

Ekins, Richard, and Dave King. *Blending Genders: Social Aspects of Cross-Dressing and Sex—Changing*. London: Routledge, 1996.

Eskeridge, Wm. N., Jr. *The Case for Same-Sex Marriage: From Sexual Liberty to Civilized Commitment*. New York: Free Press, 1996.

Foucault, Michel. *The History of Sexuality*. New York: Viking, 1986.

Garnets, L. D., and D. C. Kimmel, eds. *Psychological Perspectives on Lesbian and Gay Male Experiences*. New York: Columbia University Press, 1993.

Gonsiorek, J. C., and J. D. Weinrich, eds. *Homosexuality: Research Implications for Public Policy.* Newbury Park, CA: Sage Publications, 1991.

Hargreaves, Tracy. *Androgyny in Modern Literature.* Basingstoke: Palgrave Macmillan, 2005.

Hausman, Bernice. *Changing Sex: Transsexualism, Technology and the Idea of Gender.* Durham, NC: Duke University Press, 1995.

Hawley, John C., ed. *Postcolonial, Queer: Theoretical Intersections.* Albany, NY: State University of New York Press, 2001.

Hendriks, Aart, R. Tielman, and E. van der Veen, eds. *The Third Pink Book: A Global View of Lesbian and Gay Liberation and Oppression.* Buffalo, NY: Prometheus Books, 1993.

Herdt, G., and B. Koff. *Something to Tell You—The Road That Families Travel When a Child Is Gay.* New York: Columbia University Press, 2000.

Herdt, Gilbert. *Same Sex, Different Cultures: Exploring Gay and Lesbian Lives.* Boulder, CO: Westview Press, 1998.

Herdt, Gilbert, ed. *Third Sex, Third Gender: Beyond Sexual Dimorphism in Culture and History.* New York: Zone Books, 1994.

Herdt, Gilbert. *Gay and Lesbian Aging: Research and Future Directions.* New York: Springer, 2004.

Herek, G. M., and K. T. Berrill, eds. *Hate Crimes: Confronting Violence against Lesbians and Gay Men.* Newbury Park, CA: Sage Publications, 1992.

Herek, G. M., ed. *Stigma and Sexual Orientation: Understanding Prejudice against Lesbians, Gay Men, and Bisexuals.* Newbury Park, CA: Sage Publications, 1997.

Hogan, Steve, and Lee Hudson. *Completely Queer: The Gay and Lesbian Encyclopedia.* New York: Henry Holt and Company, 1998.

Jennings, K., ed. *One Teacher in 10.* Los Angeles, CA: Alyson Publications, 1994.

Johnston, Lynda. *Queer Tourism: Paradoxical Performances at Gay Pride Events.* New York: Routledge, 2005.

Joseph, Sherry. *Social Work Practice and Men Who Have Sex with Men.* Thousand Oaks, CA: SAGE Publications, 2005.

Kane-DeMaios, Ari, and Vern Bullough, eds. *Crossing Sexual Boundaries: Transgender Journeys, Uncharted Paths.* New York: Prometheus Books, 2006.

Katz, J. N. *The Construction of Heterosexuality.* New York: Penguin, 1996.

Katz, J. *Gay American History: Lesbians and Gay Men in the U.S.A.* New York: Tomas Y. Crowell, 1976.

Lazar, Michelle M., ed. *Feminist Critical Discourse Analysis. Gender, Power and Ideology in Discourse.* London: Palgrave Macmillan, 2005.

Luongo, Michael. *Gay Travels in the Muslim World.* New York: Harrington Park Press, 2007.

Marcus, E. *Is It a Choice?: Answers to 300 of the Most Frequently Asked Questions about Gay and Lesbian People.* San Francisco: Harper, 1999.

Memmi, Albert. *Pillar of Salt.* Translated by Edouard Roditi. New York: Criterion Books, 1955.

Mills, K. I. *Mission Impossible: Why Reparative Therapy and Ex-gay Ministries Fail.* Human Rights Campaign, 1999. www.hrc.org/documents/missionimpossible.pdf.

Nanda, Serena. *Gender Diversity: Cross-Cultural Variations.* Long Grove, IL: Waveland Press, 2000.

Nestle, Joan, Riki Wilchins, and Clare Howell, eds. *Genderqueer: Voices Beyond the Sexual Binary.* Los Angeles: Alyson Books, 2002.

Parker, R., R. M. Barbosa, and P. Aggleton, eds. *Framing the Sexual Subject: The Politics of Gender, Sexuality, and Power.* Berkeley: University of California Press, 2000.

Parker, Richard, and John Gagnon, eds. *Conceiving Sexuality: Approaches to Sex Research in a Postmodern World.* New York: Routledge, 1995.

Plummer, Ken, ed. *Modern Homosexualities: Fragments of Lesbian and Gay Experience.* London: Routledge, 1992.

Plummer, Ken. *Telling Sexual Stories: power, change and social world*. Routledge, London, 1995.

Rayside, David. *Queer Inclusions, Continental Divisions: Public Recognition of Sexual Diversity in Canada and the United States*. Toronto: University of Toronto Press, 2004.

Reinfelder, M., ed. *From Amazon to Zami: Towards a Global Lesbian Feminism*. London: Cassell, 1996.

Richardson, Diane, and Steven Seidman, eds. *Handbook of Lesbian and Gay Studies*. Thousand Oaks, CA: Sage, 2002.

Rosenbloom, Rachel, ed. *Unspoken Rules—Sexual Orientation and Women's Human Rights*. San Francisco: International Gay and Lesbian Human Rights Commission, 1995.

Roscoe, Will, and Stephen Murray. *Islamic Homosexualities: Culture, History, and Literature*. New York: NYU Press, 1997.

Schmitt, Arno, and Jehoeda Sofer, eds. *Sexuality and Eroticism Among Males in Moslem Societies*. London: Routledge, 1992.

Seidman, Steven, ed. *Queer Theory/Sociology*. Cambridge, MA: Blackwell, 1969.

Seidman, Steven. *Difference Troubles: Queering social theory and sexual politics*. Cambridge: Cambridge University Press, 1997.

Sibalis, M. *Queer Sites. Gay Urban Histories since 1600*. New York: Routledge, 1995.

Stewart, C. *Homosexuality and the Law*. Santa Barbara, CA: ABC-CLIO, 2001.

Stewart, C. *Gay and Lesbian Issues*. Santa Barbara, CA: ABC-CLIO, 2003.

Stewart, C. *Sexually Stigmatized Communities—Reducing Heterosexism and Homophobia: An Awareness Training Manual*. Thousand Oaks, CA: Sage Publications, 1999.

Tielman, R., M. Carballo, and A. Hendriks, eds. *Bisexuality & HIV/AIDS*. Buffalo, NY: Prometheus Books, 1991.

Tully, Brian. *Accounting for Transsexualism and Transhomosexuality*. London: Whiting & Birch, 1992.

Van der Meide, W. *Legislating Equality: A Review of Laws Affecting Gay, Lesbian, Bisexual, and Transgendered People in the United States*. Washington, DC: National Gay and Lesbian Task Force, 2000.

Weeks, Jeffrey. *Invented Moralities: Sexual Values in the Age of Uncertainty*. Cambridge: Polity Press,1995.

Weeks, Jeffrey. *Making Sexual History*. Cambridge: Polity Press, 2000.

West, D. J., and R. Green, eds. *Sociolegal Control of Homosexuality: A Multi-Nation Comparison*. New York: Plenum, 1997.

White, M. *Stranger at the Gate: To Be Gay and Christian in America*. New York: Simon and Schuster, 1994.

Williams, W. *The Spirit and the Flesh: Sexual Diversity in American Indian Culture*. Boston, MA: Beacon Press, 1992.

Williams, Walter L., and Retter, Yolanda. *Gay and Lesbian Rights in the United States: A Documentary History*. Westport, CT: Greenwood Press, 2003.

Wintemute, Robert, and Mads Andenæs, eds. *Legal Recognition of Same-Sex Partnerships: A Study of National, European and International Law*. Portland: Hart Publishing, 2001.

AFRICA

Aarmo, M., Ed., E. Blackwood, and S. E. Wieringa. *How Homosexuality Became "UnAfrican": The Case of Zimbabwe, Female Desires: Same Sex Relations and Transgender Practices across Cultures*. New York: Columbia University Press, 1999.

Cameron, Edwin, and Mark Gevisser, eds. *Defiant Desire: Gay and Lesbian Lives in South Africa*. New York: Routledge, 1995.

Epprecht, M. *African Heterosexuality: The History of an Idea from the Age of Exploration to the Age of AIDS*. Athens: Ohio University Press, 2008.

Johnson, Alan Cary. *Off the Map, How HIV/AIDS Programming Is Failing Same-Sex Practicing People in Africa*. New York: International Gay and Lesbian Human Rights Commission, 2007.

Kalipeni, E., S. Craddock, and J. R. Oppong, eds. *HIV/AIDS in Africa: Beyond Epidemiology*. Cambridge, MA: Blackwell, 2004.

Long, Scott. *More Than a Name. State-Sponsored Homophobia and Its Consequences in Southern Africa*. Human Rights Watch (HRW) and the International Gay and Lesbian Human Rights Commission (IGLHC). New York: Human Rights Watch Publication, 2003.

Morrell, Robert. *Changing Men in Southern Africa*. London: Zed Books, 2001.

Murray, J. O., and W. Roscoe, eds. *Boy-Wives and Female Husbands: Studies of African Homosexualities*. New York: St. Martin's Press, 1998.

Nolen, S. *28 Stories of AIDS in Africa*. New York: Walker & Company, 2007.

Roscoe, Will, and Stephen Murray, eds. *Boy-Wives and Female-Husbands in African Homosexualities*. New York: Palgrave, 1998.

ASIA

Alexander, M. Jacqui, and Chandra Talpade Mohanty, eds. *Feminist Genealogies, Colonial Legacies, Democratic Futures*. New York: Routledge, 1997.

Berry, Chris, Fran Martin, and Audrey Yue, eds. *Mobile Cultures: New Media in Queer Asia*. Durham, NC: Duke University Press, 2003.

Chalmers, Sharon. *Emerging Lesbian Voices from Japan*. London: Routledge Curzon, 2002.

Chou, Wah-shan. *Tongzhi: Politics of Same Sex Eroticism in Chinese Societies*. New York: Haworth Press, 2000.

Hinsch, Bret. *Passions of the Cut Sleeve: The Male Homosexual Tradition in China*. Berkeley: University of California Press, 1990.

Jackson, Peter. *Male Homosexuality in Thailand: An Interpretation of Contemporary Thai Sources*. Elmhurst, NY: Global Academic Publishers, 1989.

Leupp, Gary. *Male Colors: The Construction of Homosexuality in Tokugawa Japan*. Berkeley: University of California Press, 1995.

Lim, Song Hwee. *Celluloid Comrades: Representations of Male Homosexuality in Contemporary Chinese Cinemas*. Honolulu: University of Hawaii Press, 2006.

Martin, Fran. *Backward Glances: Chinese Popular Cultures and the Female Homoerotic Imaginary*. Durham, NC: Duke University Press, 2005.

McLelland, Mark. *Queer Japan from the Pacific War to the Internet Age*. Lanham, MD: Rowman & Littlefield, 2005.

Murray, Stephen O., ed. *Oceanic Homosexualities*. New York: Garland Publishing, 1992.

Nanda, Serena. *The Hijras of India: Neither Man nor Woman*. 2nd Ed London: Wadsworth, 1999.

Pflugfelder, Gregory. *Cartographies of Desire: Male-Male Sexuality in Japanese Discourse, 1600–1950*. Berkeley: University of California Press, 1999.

Reddy, Gayatri. *With Respect to Sex: Negotiating Hijra Identity in South India*. Chicago: University of Chicago Press, 2005.

Rofel, Lisa. *Desiring China: Experiments in Neoliberalism, Sexuality, and Public Culture*. Durham, NC: Duke University Press, 2007.

Sang, Tze-Ian D. *The Emerging Lesbian: Female Same-Sex Desire in Modern China*. Chicago: The University of Chicago Press, 2003.

Sinnott, M. *Tomboys and Ladies: Transgender Identity and Same-Sex Relationships in Thailand*. Honolulu: University of Hawai'i Press, 2004.

Srivastava, Sanjay, ed. *Sexual Sites, Seminal Attitudes: Sexualities, Masculinities and Culture in South Asia*. Thousand Oaks, CA: Sage Publications, 2004

Vanita, Ruth. *Love's Rite: Same-Sex Marriage in India and the West*. New York: Palgrave Macmillan, 2005.

Wu, Cuncun. *Homoerotic Sensibilities in Late Imperial China*. New York: Routledge Curzon, 2004.

THE CARIBBEAN

Douglas, Debbie, Courtnay McFarlane, Makeda Silvera, and Douglas Stewart, eds. *Ma-Ka Diasporic Juks: Contemporary Writing by Queers of African Descent*. Ottawa, Canada: Sister Vision Press, 1998.

Elwin, Rosamund, ed. *Tongues on Fire: Caribbean Lesbian Lives and Stories*. Toronto: Women's Press of Canada, 1997.

Lewis, Linden. *The Culture of Gender and Sexuality in the Caribbean*. Gainsville, FL: University Press of Florida, 2003.

EUROPE

Baird, Vanessa. *The No-Nonsense Guide to Sexual Diversity*. Oxford: New Internationalist Publications, 2001.

Dean, Carolyn J. *The Frail Social Body: Pornography, Homosexuality, and Other Fantasies in Interwar France*. Berkeley: University of California Press, 2000.

Essig, Laurie. *Queer in Russia: a Story of Sex, Self, and the Other*. Durham, NC: Duke University Press, 1999.

Healey, Dan. *Homosexual Desire in Revolutionary Russia: The Regulation of Sexual and Gender Dissent*. Chicago: University of Chicago Press, 2001.

Hekma, G., ed. *Past and Present of Radical Sexual Politics*. Amsterdam: UvA-Mosse Foundation, 2004.

Hug, Chrystel. *The Politics of Sexual Morality in Ireland*. New York: St. Martin's Press, 1999.

Kuhar, Roman, Takács, Judit, eds. *Beyond the Pink Curtain: Everyday Life of LGBT People in Eastern Europe*. Ljubljana: Peace Institute, 2007.

Löfström, Jan. *Scandinavian Homosexualities: Essays on Gay and Lesbian Studies*. New York: Haworth Press, 1998.

Merrick, Jeffrey, and Bryant T. Ragan (dir.). *Homosexuality in Modern France*. New York: Oxford University Press, 1996.

Merrick, Jeffrey, and Michael Sibalis (dir.). *Homosexuality in French History and Culture*. New York: Harrington Park Press, 2001

O'Carroll, Íde, and Eoin Collins, eds. *Lesbian and Gay Visions of Ireland: Towards the Twenty-first Century*. London: Cassell, 1995.

Schluter, Daniel P. *Gay Life in the Former USSR: Fraternity without Community*. New York: Routledge, 2002.

Solberg, Randy. O., ed. *Let Our Voices Be Heard: Christian Lesbians in Europe Telling Their Stories*. Hamburg: Mein Buch, 2004.

Štulhofer, A., and T. Sandfort, eds. *Sexuality and Gender in Post-communist Eastern Europe and Russia*. New York: Haworth Press, 2005.

Takács, Judit. *Social Exclusion of Young Lesbian, Gay, Bisexual and Transgender (LGBT) people in Europe*. Brussels: ILGA-Europe, 2006.

Van Naerssen, Alex X., ed. *Gay Life in Dutch Society*. New York: Harrington Press, 1987.

Wintemute, R., and M. Andenaes, eds. *Legal Recognition of Same-Sex Partnerships: A Study of National, European, and International Law*. Oxford: Hart Publishing. 2001.

LATIN AMERICA

Babb, Florence E. *After Revolution: Mapping Gender and Cultural Politics in Neoliberal Nicaragua*. Austin: University of Texas Press, 2001.

Domínguez Ruvalcaba, Héctor. *Modernity and the Nation in Mexican Representations of masculinity: From Sensuality to Bloodshed*. New York: Palgrave, 2007.

Girman, Chris. *Mucho Macho: Seduction, Desire, and the Homoerotic Lives of Latin Men*. New York: Haworth Gay and Lesbian Studies, 2004.

Green, James. *Beyond Carnival: Male Homosexuality in Twentieth-century Brazil*. Chicago: University of Chicago Press, 1999.

Kulick, Don. *Travestí: Sex, Gender and Culture among Brazilian Transgendered Prostitutes*. Chicago: University of Chicago Press, 1998.

Lancaster, Roger N. *Life Is Hard: Machismo, Danger, and the Intimacy of Power in Nicaragua*. Berkeley: University of California Press, 1992.

Parker, Richard G. *Bodies and Biases: Sexual Culture in Contemporary Brazil*. Boston: Beacon Press, 1991.

Schifter Sikora, Jacobo. *Lila's House: Male Prostitution in Latin America*. New York: Haworth Press, 1998.

Schifter Sikora, Jacobo. *Public Sex in Latin Society*. New York: Haworth Press, 1999.

Whitam, Frederick. *Male Homosexuality in Four Societies: Brazil, Guatemala, The Philippines, and the United States*. New York: Praeger, 1986.

MIDDLE EAST/ISLAM

Bouhdiba, Abdelwahab. *Sexuality in Islam*. Translated by A. Sheridan. London: Routledge and Keagan, 1985.

Farah, Madelaine. *Marriage and Sexuality in Islam: A Translation of al Ghazzali's Book on the Etiquette of Marriage*. Salt Lake City: University of Utah Press, 1984.

Khalaf, Samer, and John Gagnon. *Sexuality in the Arab World*. Beirut: Saqi Books, 2006.

Maasad, Josef. *Desiring Arabs*. Chicago: University of Chicago Press, 2007.

Moghadam, Valentine M. *Modernizing Women: Gender and Social Change in the Middle East*. Boulder, CO: Lynne Rienner, 2003.

Roscoe, W., and Stephen O. Murray, eds. *Islamic Homosexualities: Culture, History, and Literature*. New York: New York University Press, 1997.

Whitaker, Brian. *Unspeakable Love: Gay and Lesbian Life in the Middle East*. Los Angeles: University of California Press, 2006.

Wright, J. W. *Homoeroticism in Classical Arabic*. New York: Columbia University Press, 1997.

WEB SITES

International/General

Amnesty International: www.amnestyusa.org
The Gay and Lesbian Arabic Society: www.glas.org
Gay/Lesbian Politics and Law: www.indiana.edu/~glbt/subject.htm
GayLawNet: www.gaylawnet.com
Gayscape: www.jwpublishing.com/gayscape
Human Rights Watch: www.hrw.org
International Day Against Homophobia: www.homophobiaday.org
International Gay and Lesbian Association: www.igla.org
International Gay and Lesbian Human Rights Commission (IGLHRC): www.iglhrc.org
Internationaal Homo/Lesbisch Informatiecentrum en Archief (IHLIA).: www.ihlia.nl

LAMBDA: www.lambda.org
UNAIDS: www.unaids.org

AFRICA

Behind The Mask: www.mask.org.za
Coalition of African Lesbians: www.cal.org.za
DATA: Debt, AIDS, Trade, Africa: www.data.org
Gay News in Africa: www.mask.org.za

ASIA AND OCEANIA

PT Foundation (Pink Triangle): www.ptfmalaysia.org
Transgender Equality and Acceptance Movement (TEAM): teamhk.org/e-index.html
TransgenderAsia: web.hku.hk/~sjwinter/TransgenderASIA/index.htm
Utopia: Asian Gay & Lesbian Resources: www.utopia-asia.com

EUROPE

Coalition on Sexual Orientation (CoSO): www.coso.org.uk
European Gay and Lesbian Sports Federation: www.eglsf.info/
European Parliament Gay and Lesbian Rights Intergroup: www.lgbt-ep.eu/news.php
European Pride Organisers Association: www.europride.info
Fundamental Rights Agency: fra.europa.eu/fra/index.php
International Gay, Lesbian, Bisexual, Transgender and Queer Youth and Student Organiza-
    tion (IGLYO): www.iglyo.com
QueerSpace: www.queerspace.org.uk

MIDDLE EAST

Bint el Nas Association for Arab Lesbians: www.bintelnas.org
The Gay and Lesbian Arabic Society: www.glas.org
Gay and Lesbian Arabs: www.al-bab.com/arab/background/gay.htm
Gay Middle East: www.gaymiddleeast.com
Gay Middle East Blog: www.gaymiddleeast.blogspot.com

UNITED STATES

ACT UP/ New York: www.actupny.org
American Civil Liberties Union (ACLU): www.aclu.org/issues/gay/hmgl.html
BiNet USA: www.binetusa.org
Dignity USA: www.dignityusa.org
Female-to-Male International (FTM): www.ftm-intl.org
Gay and Lesbian Advocates and Defenders (GLAD): www.glad.org
Gay and Lesbian Alliance Against Defamation (GLAAD): www.glaad.org
Gay and Lesbian Atheists and Humanists (GALAH): www.galah.org
Gay and Lesbian Medical Association (GLMA): www.glma.org
Gay and Lesbian Victory Fund: www.victoryfund.org
Gay, Lesbian & Bisexual Veterans of America (GLBVA): www.glbva.org
Gay, Lesbian and Straight Education Network (GLSEN): www.glsen.org
Gay/Lesbian International News Network (GLINN): www.glinn.com
Gay/Lesbian Politics and Law: www.indiana.edu/~glbt/subject.htm

GayLawNet: http://www.gaylawnet.com/

Gayscape: www.jwpublishing.com/gayscape

Human Rights Campaign (HRC): www.hrc.org

Intersex Society of North America (ISNA): www.isna.org

June L. Mazer Archives: www.lesbian.org Lambda Legal Defense and Education Fund: www.lambdalegal.org/cgi-bin/iowa/index.html

Lesbian.org: www.lesbian.org

National Center for Lesbian Rights (NCLR): www.nclrights.org

National Gay and Lesbian Task Force (NGLTF): www.ngltf.org

National Latina/o Lesbian, Gay, Bisexual, and Transgender Organization (LLEGÓ): www.llego.org

National Lesbian and Gay Law Association (NLGLA): www.nlgla.org

National Minority Aids Council (NMAC): www.nmac.org

National Organization of Gay and Lesbian Scientists and Technical Professionals: www.noglstp.org

ONE Institute and Archives: www.oneinstitute.org

Outfest: www.outfest.org

Parents, Families & Friends of Lesbians & Gays (PFLAG): www.pflag.org

Queer Resources Directory: www.qrd.org

Servicemembers Legal Defense Network (SLDN): www.sldn.org

Soulforce: www.soulforce.org

Stonewall Library and Archives (SLA): www.stonewall-library.org

Transgender Forum: www.transgender.org

Transgender Fund: www.tgfund.org

SET INDEX

Mayans, **1:**3; Belize and, **1:**13–16; depopulation of, **1:**14; family, **1:**18; homosexuals, **1:**13; marriages, **1:**13–14

MB (money boy), **1:**360, 361

McNally, Nicholas (justice), **3:**156

Me Magazine, **2:**179

Mecca, **3:**193, 213

Media, **3:**5; in Botswana, **3:**13; in Egypt, **3:**30; in Ghana, **3:**48; in Greece, **2:**210; in Jamaica, **1:**184–90; in Kenya, **3:**57; in Lebanon, **3:**179–80; in Morocco, **3:**76; in Saudi Arabia, **3:**210; treatment of homosexuality, **2:**24; in Tunisia, **3:**129; in Zimbabwe, **3:**153

Medina, **3:**194, 213

Medina, Javier, **1:**144

Medvedev, Dmitry A., **2:**360

Meem, **3:**179, 184, 185, 187

Meléndez, Eduardo Alfonso Caro, **1:**107, 125, 241, 249

Memra, **2:**76

Men: honor killings and, **3:**1, 3, 33, 82, 171, 183; Lebanese gay, **3:**184; machismo's influence on, **1:**5–6; MTF, **1:**5–6, 11; Muslim gay, **3:**76. *See also* Family

Men who have sex with men. *See* MSM

Menchú Tum, Rigoberta, **1:**131

Mendoza Ralph, Roberto, **1:**204

Mengistu Haile Mariam, **3:**41

Mental health, **2:**297; in Belgium, **2:**56–57; Netherlands and, **2:**155. *See also* Depression

Mestizos, **1:**108

Methodists, **1:**153, 276, 326, **2:**262, 315

Mette-Marit (princess), **2:**305

Mexico: Catholic Church's influence in, **1:**200, 206; community in, **1:**206–7; education in, **1:**201–3; employment and economics in, **1:**203–5; family in, **1:**206; Gay Pride festival in, **1:**207; GDP, **1:**199; health in, **1:**207–8; HIV/AIDS and, **1:**202–3, 207–8; LGBT issues in, **1:**199–212; map of, **1:**199; outlook for 21st century in, **1:**209; overview, **1:**199–201; politics and law in, **1:**208–9; population of, **1:**200; sexuality/sexual practices in, **1:**205; social/government programs in, **1:**205; textbooks and, **1:**202; violence in, **1:**209;

workplace, homosexual rights and, **1:**204–5

Micheletti, Roberto, **1:**142

Miches (homosexual prostitution), **1:**44

Middle East: antidiscrimination statutes and violence in, **3:**4–5; education in, **3:**5; HIV/AIDS in, **3:**5–6; intersexed people in, **3:**7; introduction to Africa and, **3:**1–8; Iran and, **3:**163–73; Lebanon and, **3:**175–92; LGBT issues in, **3:**4–7; marriage and adoption in, **3:**5; outlook for 21st century in, **3:**7–8; religion in, **3:**6; Saudi Arabia and, **3:**193–223; sexual and relationship arrangement in, **3:**2–3; sodomy in, **3:**4; transgender people in, **3:**6–7

Mieszko I, **2:**3, 321

Military: in Belarus, **2:**36, 41; Bolivia and homosexuals in, **1:**26–27; in Bulgaria, **2:**76; Canada and homosexuals in, **1:**54; Colombia and homosexuals in, **1:**92; coup d'état in Uruguay, **1:**290; in Croatia, **2:**79; Ecuador and homosexuals in, **1:**112; gays in, **3:**101; in Greece, **2:**207; in Norway, **2:**308; in Russia, **2:**362; spending in Belize, **1:**17–18; in Switzerland, **2:**414–15; U.S. and "don't ask, don't tell" policy with, **1:**265, 268

Minos (king), **2:**207

de Miranda, Francisco, **1:**299

Miss Gay Bolivia pageant, **1:**28

Mithuna, Jr., **1:**514

Mitterrand, François, **2:**17

Mizielinska, Joanna, **2:**321

Moawad, Nadine, **3:**175

Mogae, Festus, **3:**12

Mohamad, Mahathir, **1:**443, 444

Mohamed VI (king), **3:**75

Moi, Daniel Arap, **3:**56, 57

Moldova, 2:6; adoption in, **2:**279–80; Christian Orthodox Church's influence in, **2:**282; community in, **2:**280; education in, **2:**278–79; employment and economics in, **2:**279; Gay Pride festivals/parades in, **2:**284; GDP of, **2:**279; health in, **2:**280–81; HIV/AIDS in, **2:**280–81; languages and dialects spoken in, **2:**278; LGBT issues in, **2:**277–87; map of, **2:**277; outlook for 21st century in, **2:**285–86; overview, **2:**277–78; politics and law in,

2:281–82; population of, **2:**277; religion and spirituality in, **2:**282; sexual practices in, **2:**279–80; social and government programs in, **2:**279; violence in, **2:**282–85

Mon people, **1:**505

Money boy. *See* MB

Mongolia: community in, **1:**453–55; education in, **1:**450; employment and economics in, **1:**450–51; family in, **1:**452–53; GDP of, **1:**451; health in, **1:**455; HIV/AIDS and, **1:**450, 451–52, 454–55, 456–57; languages/dialects spoke in, **1:**448; LGBT issues in, **1:**447–58; map of, **1:**447; outlook for 21st century in, **1:**456–57; overview, **1:**447–50; politics and law in, **1:**455; population of, **1:**447; provinces in, **1:**457 n.9; religion and spirituality in, **1:**455–56; sexuality/sexual practices in, **1:**451–52; social/government programs in, **1:**451–52; violence in, **1:**456

Monsen, Nina Karin, **2:**314

de Montherlant, Henry, **2:**164

Montoya, Alba, **1:**100

Montreuil, Micheline, **1:**61

Morales, Evo, **1:**25

Morgan, Henry, **1:**242

Morínigo, Higinio, **1:**250

Mormons, **1:**73

Morocco: asylum cases in, **3:**82; bisexuals in, **3:**76–77; community in, **3:**79; education in, **3:**77; employment in, **3:**77; family in, **3:**78–79; government programs in, **3:**77; health in, **3:**80; HIV/AIDS in, **3:**80, 81; homosexuality criminalized in, **3:**81; languages and dialects spoken in, **3:**75; LGBT issues in, **3:**75–85; map of, **3:**75; media in, **3:**76; Muslims in, **3:**75; outlook for 21st century in, **3:**83; overview, **3:**75–77; politics and law in, **3:**80–81; pregnancy out of wedlock in, **3:**82; religion and spirituality in, **3:**81–82; sexual practices in, **3:**78; violence in, **3:**82

Morrissens, Elian, **2:**50

Moscati, Maria Federica, **3:**41

Moscoso, Mireya, **1:**242

Mott, Luiz, **1:**41, 44

Mouloodzadeh, Makvan, **3:**171

Mouta, Joao, **2:**341

Mouta v. Portugal, **2:**341

1:398–99; in Indonesia, 1:413–14; in Iran, 3:170–71; in Ireland, 2:244–45; in Italy, 2:262–63; in Japan, 1:431; in Kenya, 3:65–66; in Kyrgyzstan, 2:274; in Lebanon, 3:178, 189–90; against lesbians, 2:405, 3:65; against lesbians in Canada, 1:63–64; in Liberia, 3:72; in Malaysia, 1:444; in Mexico, 1:209; in Middle East with antidiscrimination statutes, 3:4–5; in Moldova, 2:282–85; in Mongolia, 1:456; in Morocco, 3:82; in Namibia, 3:90; in the Netherlands, 2:302; in New Zealand, 1:468; in Nicaragua, 1:232; in Nigeria, 3:109; in Norway, 2:315; in Panama, 1:246–47; in Paraguay, 1:254; in Poland, 2:333–34; police brutality and, 2:284, 354, 3:27; in Portugal, 2:342–43; in Romania, 2:354; in Russia, 2:369; in Saudi Arabia, 3:215–17; in schools, 2:149–50; in Singapore, 1:484; in Slovenia, 2:386–87; in South Africa, 3:120; in Spain, 2:405; in Switzerland, 2:422; in Taiwan, 1:499; in Tanzania, 3:127; in Thailand, 1:518; against transgendered people, 1:120–21; in Trinidad and Tobago, 1:260; in Tunisia, 3:132; in Turkey, 2:433–34; in Uganda, 3:143; in United Kingdom, 2:450; in Uruguay, 1:296; in U.S., 1:277; in Venezuela, 1:303; in Vietnam, 1:533; against women, 3:171; against women in Honduras, 1:147; against women in Jamaica, 1:157; in Zimbabwe, 3:158
Virgen de los Deseos (Virgin of Desires), 1:29
Virginity: abstinence and, 1:478; Guatemala and social views on, 1:128
Višeslav (duke), 2:79
Vitamine O, 2:211
Vjesnki, 2:87
Volunteers without Borders, 2:40
von Bismarck, Otto, 2:194
von Krafft-Ebing, Richard, 1:362, 2:221
von Praunheim, Rosa, 2:193
von Sinnen, Hella, 2:193
Voodoo, 1:260; as gay-friendly, 1:4, 10–11; Haiti and, 1:10, 138–39; *ounfos and,* 1:138

Vstrecha (Meeting) magazine, 2:40
Vybz Kartel, 1:187

Waldensian Church, 2:262
Wan Yanhai, 1:361
War crimes, 1:290
War of Three Alliances, 1:254
Ware, John, 1:324
Warren, Murray, 1:52
Water spirits, 3:108
Wei Wei, 1:359
Westmoreland Bouchard, Jen, 3:29, 75
Weye (homosexuals), 1:75
WHO. *See* World Health Organization
Wilets, James D., 3:69
Wilets, James Daniel, 1:115, 141
Will, Anne, 2:198
Will and Grace, 2:376
William and John, 1:324
Williams, Candice, 1:157
Williams, Walter, L., 1:13, 347, 505
Williamson, Brian, 1:157, 179
Williman, José Claudio, 1:291
Wilson, James A. Jr., 3:135
Wings (Kuzmin), 2:363
Winter, Sam, 1:375
Witchcraft, 1:75, 2:5
Wittig, Monique, 2:165
W.J. and D.P. v. the United Kingdom, 2:129
Wolfenden, John, 2:446
Women: antisodomy laws and exclusion of, 2:5; bride price and, 3:16, 61, 91, 127; Canada and lack of attention to health issues for, 1:55–56; criminalization of sexual acts between, 3:18, 92–93; genital mutilation and, 3:61; HIV/AIDS and, 1:55–56, 130; homosexual activities among married, 3:32, 78; machismo's influence on, 1:5–6; male, 1:37; marginalized in society, 3:14, 151; pregnancy and, 1:78, 92, 119, 291; in Saudi Arabia, 3:196–98; as second-class citizens in Islamic countries, 3:6; sexual/reproductive health and, 1:17; shamanism and, 1:448; social dictates constraining, 3:32; violence against, 1:147, 157, 3:171; voting rights for Uruguay's, 1:289. *See also* Family
World Economic Situation and Prospects 2006 (UN), 2:38
World Health Organization (WHO), 1:294, 2:17; "sexual

deviation" removed from illness list by, 1:27
World War I, 2:3, 4, 66, 80, 277, 359
World War II, 1:242, 2:4, 24, 55, 66, 101, 147–48, 192, 251–52, 277, 321, 359
Wowereit, Klaus, 2:198
Wu Zongjian, 1:362

X, Y, Z v. the United Kingdom, 2:128
Xing (sex), 1:360

Yahoo Group, 3:1–2, 178
Yang (masculine energy), 1:365
Yeltsin, Boris, 2:360, 367
Yin (feminine energy), 1:365
Youth Development Strategy Aotearoa, 1:461
Youth Health: A Guide to Action, 1:461
Youths. *See* Children

Zambos, 1:108
Zapatero, Rodríguez, 2:403
Zaremba, Aleksandr, 2:363
Zelaya, Manuel, 1:142
Zenawi, Meles, 3:42
Zerolo, Pedro, 2:404
Zhang Beichuan, 1:359
Zhang Jingsheng, 1:362
Zhirinovsky, Vladimir, 2:369
Zhuk, Olga, 2:368
Zhvania, Zurab, 2:179, 180
Zimbabwe: asylum cases in, 3:151; bisexuals in, 3:152; community in, 3:152; cultural views of homosexuality in, 3:149; education in, 3:150; employment and economics in, 3:150; family in, 3:151–52; health in, 3:152–53; HIV/AIDS in, 3:148–53; LGBT issues in, 3:147–60; map of, 3:147; media in, 3:153; outlook for 21st century in, 3:158–59; overview, 3:147–49; political history of, 3:147–48; politics and law in, 3:153–58; religion and spirituality in, 3:158; sexual practices in, 3:151; social and government programs in, 3:150–51; violence in, 3:158; women marginalized in, 3:151
Zinov'eva-Annibal, Lidiia, 2:363
Zoroastrianism, 3:170, 213
Zuazo, Hernán Siles, 1:26
Zuo (have sex), 1:360